A CANTICLE OF

CW00818975

A CANTICLE OF LOVE

The Story of the Franciscan Sisters
of the Immaculate Conception

JOHN WATTS

from

D & K

3/3/11

JOHN DONALD

First published in Great Britain in 2006 by
John Donald, an imprint of Birlinn Ltd

West Newington House
10 Newington Road, Edinburgh EH9 1QS

www.birlinn.co.uk

ISBN 10: 0 85976 659 4

EAN 13: 978 0 85976 659 3

Copyright © John Watts, 2006

The right of John Watts to be identified as the author
of this work has been asserted by him in accordance
with the Copyright, Designs and Patents Act, 1988

All rights reserved. No part of this publication may
be reproduced, stored, or transmitted in any form, or
by any means electronic, mechanical or photocopying,
recording or otherwise, without the express written
permission of the publisher.

British Library Cataloguing-in-Publication Data
A catalogue record for this book is available
on request from the British Library

Typeset by Antony Gray
Printed and bound by Bell & Bain Ltd, Glasgow

For
the Sisters of the Congregation,
and especially for
Sᴿ Lᴏʏᴏʟᴀ Kᴇʟʟʏ
and in memory of
Sᴿ Dᴏʟᴏʀᴇs Cᴏᴄʜʀᴀɴᴇ

Contents

PART FOUR

Water

EPILOGUE

APPENDICES

Illustrations

Acknowledgements

The author gratefully acknowledges the help of Andrew Nicol and Dr Christine Johnson the present and former keepers of the Scottish Catholic Archives, Dr Mary McHugh Archivist of the Archdiocese of Glasgow, Mrs Aileen Currie Librarian of Cardinal Newman Secondary School Bellshill, Mrs M. McCann Headteacher St Mary's Primary School Hamilton, Sr Jean Bunn Archivist of the British Province of the Sisters of Notre Dame de Namur, Richard McIntyre, Bernard Farrell and Gerald McGeady, Dalbeth Cemetery staff, Rev. Fr Gerard Nugent of St Patrick's Anderston, and the staffs of the National Library of Scotland, the Mitchell Library Glasgow and the University of Edinburgh Library.

My gratitude also to Dr Frank O'Hagan for making his draft doctoral thesis available to me, and to Archivist Ms M.A. Cosgrave for permission to use a document from the Mercy International Centre Archives Dublin.

My greatest debt by far is to those Sisters of the Congregation and others who answered my relentless questions with unfailing courtesy and patience. In particular I am indebted to the Superior General Sr Loyola Kelly for her insight, frankness and constant support, to Sr Dolores Cochrane RIP who as Archivist guided me to the sources with wisdom and great kindness, and to Sr Bernard McAtamney who along with Sr Loyola read the manuscript in draft and made valuable suggestions for its improvement. It has been a privilege and great pleasure to work with them, and to write their history. The result, such as it is, is dedicated to them all.

Foreword by Most Rev. Mario Archbishop Conti

It is a rare find indeed to come upon a book which is both an adventure story and a meticulously researched history. But that is what has been achieved in this excellent work.

John Watts has combined the narrator's pace and energy with the historian's careful eye for detail to write a worthy history of Scotland's only home-grown religious congregation.

Painting in a very attractive *chiaroscuro* the joys and sorrows, the achievements and disappointments of the Sisters whose lives have been spent in the Congregation of the Franciscans of the Immaculate Conception, the author also outlines a fascinating social history of Glasgow, its changing face and its outstanding personalities over the last century and a half.

Combined with this is the fascinating tale of the Sisters' foundations in Africa – a gripping narrative of growth rooted in the Gospel and now flourishing on the dusty streets of Nigeria and Kenya.

Those who have known the Sisters over many years, and indeed the older members of the Congregation itself, will find in this narrative a recollection of days now past; and those, especially in Africa, who have known it but shortly will rejoice in a tale which exposes the strong and generous roots of what they see today and to which they belong as a new and vibrant shoot.

Readers who have tried, and given up on, previous chronicles of religious life on the basis that they are too sanctimonious or anaemic, will be refreshed by the bold and honest way in which the dramas and natural tensions of community life are explored by the author. The reader is introduced to a fascinating array of characters whose influence has made the Congregation the force it is today.

I salute the Sisters for their determination to tell their extraordinary story and I commend the author for his scholarship and *élan* in putting together this very readable volume.

Future generations will be most grateful to the current leadership of the Congregation for their foresightedness in commissioning and co-operating with this great undertaking.

I share that gratitude and thank God for all that has been achieved amongst us. I commend the *Canticle of Love* to the widest possible audience.

✠ Mario Conti, Archbishop of Glasgow

The Lord is my strength and my song, He is my salvation.

PSALMS, 117:14

Whoever lives in love lives in God, and God in him.

I JOHN, 4: 15

I am going to lure her and lead her out into the wilderness and speak to her heart. I will betroth you to Myself forever.

HOSEA, 2: 16

PROLOGUE

By their Deeds

No-one who is at all familiar with the Franciscan Sisters of the Immaculate Conception will need to be convinced that their story is worth telling. In many ways it is unique.

Founded in 1847, theirs is the second oldest women's religious Congregation in Scotland, and it predates by some years the earliest foundations for men. But unlike all the others, which were established as branch houses of Congregations already in existence abroad, theirs was (and remains) the only Congregation in the post-Reformation Catholic Church actually founded in this country. Today it has communities on three continents.

As Christians the Sisters base their life upon the Gospel; as religious they live in community and follow the evangelical counsels of poverty, chastity and obedience; as members of the worldwide Third Order Regular[1] of St Francis they seek to imitate their founder in his humility, his care for the poor and marginalised, and his injunction to 'preach by their deeds'.[2] Like him they have never been shy to roll up their sleeves, the more thankless the task the better. Like him, too, they have been quick to read the signs of the times – and their times have in some ways been remarkably like his – and adapt to changing needs: as such they have often been pioneers, both in their Church and in society.

Their history is a human one, a story of *people*, living in community and working in the world. Though shaped by its social and religious context, it is nonetheless above all a story of communities of persons, of the individual's journey, of the impact of mind upon mind and heart upon heart. One only has to attend a golden jubilee at one of their houses, and witness the joy as the Sisters sing to the jubilarian, to know that this is so.

In telling the story, therefore, though it was important to place it within a wider historical context, I have sought to make it personal and where possible to offer glimpses of at least some of the people who have made it what it is, in so far as space permitted. The Sisters' main apostolate has been in education, and secondly in the corporate works of mercy – care of the sick and dying, the bereaved, the orphan, the prisoner and the disabled – and this I have tried to reflect, by presenting from time to time cameos of life in their schools and centres of care.

For more than a century and a half the Sisters have acted as an influence for good wherever they have lived and worked. Naturally, their role has changed over time. In the early days they were a source of support and instruction to the Catholic poor of Victorian Scotland, and they were a major reason why those poor remained so faithful to the Church. Later, their schools did much to create a Catholic professional class whose members were able to take up positions of influence within Scottish society, though for many years, since they were women, virtually the only positions open to them lay in teaching. Thus generations of alumnae, schooled in the Franciscan ideal, took that ideal back into the classrooms of the next generation and, through the very obstacles that society placed in their paths, exerted a greater and continuing influence upon it. That influence lasts to this day.

At a time when the Catholics of the west of Scotland still saw themselves as an 'immigrant' community within the larger society, their priests and bishops had developed what amounted to a separate parallel support system for them, a 'welfare state within the state', with its own schools and agencies of care. The Sisters worked within this parallel system, and indeed helped to build it. Not until after World War I did their own secondary schools and the parish schools of which they had charge come into the state system; and not until after the World War II did the welfare state begin to absorb some of their traditional areas of social care. Finally, as most of their own schools closed and lay teachers (many of whom they had educated) took over the headship of other schools previously run by the Congregation, they found ever more of their work overtaken by what they themselves had helped to create. They had, in effect, made themselves redundant in their chosen apostolate and were forced to seek out new tasks. Something not dissimilar befell them in Nigeria, where after Independence the mission of schools and hospitals that they had built since the 1950s was partly taken over by the developing state.

At precisely this time, also, the Catholic Church was itself experiencing massive change in the wake of the Second Vatican Council. The Sisters responded to the changes in Britain and Africa both, and were often in the vanguard of them.

Most recently, the reality of a membership diminishing and ageing at home but burgeoning and youthful in the Third World has posed urgent questions as to the direction the Sisters should take in the future.

In the Congregation's long history there have of course been occasions when human frailty prevailed, and there have been unsavoury incidents, even, when practice failed to match the ideal. These I have not glossed over. But the abiding impression is of good – of the difference for good that the Sisters have made, and make yet. How much the poorer would Scottish Catholicism have been and be today without them; how much richer those communities in Nigeria, Ireland, America, England and Kenya that they have touched.

Broadly speaking, their history falls into four recognisable phases, and this is reflected in the narrative, which I have divided into four parts, using the imagery of St Francis' *Canticle of the Creatures*, which seemed strikingly apt. The first phase is Fire, the bright early blaze of the new-founded Congregation; the second, Earth, when it became well established and embedded within society; the third, Wind, when the great changes in Church and society swept over it; and the last is Water, when with a limpid humility it has sought out new channels to follow.

The reader will easily recognise in this a paradigm of the typical dynamic of religious Orders and Congregations over time. More, one may discern in it a microcosm of the nineteenth- and twentieth-century Church itself, in Scotland and to some extent worldwide. The Congregation's history is of importance, therefore, both in its own right and as an exemplar, and I have tried to write it with this in mind.

Of the phases I have identified, each had its own trials and 'successes'. It might be tempting to laud one above another – to decry the ways of the past, for instance, or on the contrary to feel nostalgia for them. But in fact each has its place in the story, each was appropriate – necessary, even – for its time. Francis' *Canticle* was a praise poem, and in it he gave praise for all four elements, as gifts.

I considered extending the analogy, in fact, in the title of this book, by calling it *A Canticle of Praise*, a title that would also have alluded to the Divine Office, the daily prayer of praise around which the life of every religious community is woven. But it seemed even more important to stress the quality of *love*, which the Church sees as being at the heart of the religious life,[3] and which – practical, unassuming and undemanding – has always been the hallmark of the Sisters' apostolate.

The Second Vatican Council enjoined all religious Orders and Congregations to look again at the original vision of their founders, in order to understand better and fulfil their own particular charism, and to study their roots and past history, the better to discern their future. In response, the Sisters set about deepening their knowledge of the origins and eight-hundred-year-old tradition of Franciscanism (and especially of the Third Order Regular), and also the particular tradition begun by the founders of their own Congregation in the nineteenth century. To this end, one of their members was appointed archivist to put the Congregation's documents in order and look into its development up to the present day. Her assiduous work in both tasks has rendered the Sisters an invaluable service.

It was in this context, also, that the Superior General and Council asked me in 2002 to write a history of the Congregation, believing that such a publication would be timely.

They hoped, in the first place, that it would be useful and welcome to the Congregation itself. For its members this is a time of flux, with membership in Africa growing apace while in the mother country so few young women are coming forward that they are talking of having to recycle the old ones!

Secondly, there is in Scotland and elsewhere a whole army of women (and some men) who were taught and looked after by the Sisters at school and whose lives were indelibly touched by them. It would be hard to overstate the extent and depth of the affection in which they hold their mentors. But many feel in some way let down by the closure of the Congregation's schools, which they see as an irreplaceable loss (though no fault of the Sisters), and by the fact that no real structure now exists for channelling their loyalties and maintaining ties. Judging by the enthusiastic reception given to the Congregation's 150th anniversary commemorative booklet in 1997, which sold out in no time, this history should be welcomed by many alumnae.

Lastly, the wider public deserves to know about the Sisters' work, in view of its historic influence within society since the mid-nineteenth century in Scotland and, more recently, further afield. It is not their way to trumpet their own deeds. But their impact has been profound. Along with the other major teaching Orders they have, it could almost be said, created today's Catholic community in the west of Scotland and given it its typical, unmistakable stamp. Yet, to date, the attention given by historians to the achievements of the religious Orders in this country has done no justice to their importance,[4] and almost nothing at all has been written on the Franciscan Sisters. It is the author's hope that this book will go a small way to putting this right.

It has been written at a critical moment in the Congregation's history. It is a crucial moment in Kenya, where the new novitiate has just received its first recruits and the Sisters are developing projects of great importance and promise; in Nigeria, also, as it takes a first foothold in leadership. And it is a crucial moment at home, where contraction and ageing at a time of expansion in Africa have brought about an imbalance that poses huge questions for the future. This book has been completed in the year of a General Chapter that may well prove to be the most critical ever.

In summer 2003 one of the councillors of the Congregation, Sr Dolores Cochrane, was diagnosed as having a life-threatening tumour, admitted to hospital and afterwards sent on pilgrimage to Lourdes. Before she left the convent to which she had given more than half a century of her life, she took a look around her room, or her 'cell' as they used to call it when she first entered, and turned to the Superior General, who was there to help her pack. 'I love this Congregation,' she said to her. 'I would willingly die if it helped it to come together.' The operation seemed to have been a success, and her old sparkle returned. But there must have been complications, for at the beginning of August she relapsed quite suddenly and died.

For all its difficulties, anxieties and burdens, for all the seemingly intractable problems that it faces, how can the Congregation not thrive when it has members who love it so deeply?

ENDNOTES TO THE PROLOGUE

1 The Franciscan Sisters of the Immaculate Conception (FSIC) are a Congregation, one of about 400 within the Order. The Order as a whole shares the same Rule, each Congregation having its own specific Constitutions. The Congregation of FSIC itself has more than twenty Communities or Houses. Throughout the book I use the terms 'Order', 'Congregation' and 'Community/ Convent/ House' with these meanings.

2 St Francis, Earlier Rule, xvii, 3.

3 Cf. *Perfectae Caritatis*, Decree of the Second Vatican Council on the Religious Life. The document takes its title from the opening words of the Latin text, *perfectae caritatis* ('of perfect love'). The Decree develops in detail themes already addressed in Chapter 7 of the Council's central document, *Lumen Gentium*, Dogmatic Constitution on the Church.

4 Some information has been published in commemorative magazines, including those of the Marists (1958) and of Notre Dame (later St Andrew's) College (1945 and 1995), and in J. E. Handley's *History of St Mungo's Academy* (1958) and *History of St Mary's Boys' School, Calton* (1963). The only published works on FSIC are 'The Third Order Regular of St Francis in Glasgow', *Scottish Catholic Monthly*, May–July 1894, and 'The Franciscan Nuns in Scotland 1847–1930', a pamphlet written by 'A Franciscan Sister' and printed by the *Glasgow Observer* (1930). O'Hagan has recently completed a thesis on the contribution made to education in Glasgow by the religious Orders in the nineteenth and early twentieth centuries: O'Hagan F. G., The contribution of the Religious Orders to education in Glasgow during the period 1847–1918, PhD thesis, Glasgow University 2002. Ms S. K. Kehoe has also recently submitted a doctoral thesis to Glasgow University on the early history of four nineteenth-century women's religious Congregations in the west of Scotland: Kehoe S. K., Special Daughters of Rome: Glasgow and its Roman Catholic Sisters, 1847–1913, PhD thesis, Glasgow University, 2004; and see also Kehoe S. K., 'Nursing the mission: the Franciscan Sisters of the Immaculate Conception and the Sisters of Mercy in Glasgow, 1847–1866', *Innes Review*, vol. 56, no. 1, Spring 2005.

Setting the Scene (1847)

ARRIVAL

It had all been going so well: the short run across country in the *poste de chaise* to Ostend; the easy voyage to London in fine June weather. A second land journey of two days and nights, from which they had awoken that morning to find themselves beside the Liverpool waterfront. The sun was shining on the mile-wide river full of vessels: steamships with their black plumes of smoke caught on the sea breeze, sailing ships and ships with both funnel and sail.

There were three of them in the party. The leader, Sr Adélaide Vaast, was in her mid-thirties, tall, ascetic and serene. Sr Véronique Cordier (Plate 1) was ten years her junior, with a determination written on her features, a touch of impatience and a seriousness striking in one so young. The third was a young lady, Mlle Constantine Marchand, seemingly of some means, who, having no living relatives in France, had joined the two religious as their travelling companion.

They made their way towards the city centre. About them, the red-brick slated terraces were not so unlike those of industrial Tourcoing, the wool manufacturing town on the flatlands of the Franco-Belgian border from where they had come. But these streets were full of people, hundreds of all ages, shocking in their raggedness, who were streaming up into the town. Some of them, seeing the ladies' genteel attire, held out their hands for alms. They were the Irish, fleeing their own country and the potato famine.

Sr Adélaide had with her the address of a priest to whom they had been recommended and who was to escort them on the last stage of their journey to Glasgow. With relief they knocked at the door – but it was a woman who admitted them, and from her they learned that the priest had died quite unexpectedly just a few days before. Nor was there any word from Scotland awaiting them. They could not understand it. Surely the arrangements, which had been made a year ago, were clear enough?

In the convent that they had left, Notre Dame des Anges, Adélaide had been sub-prioress and Véronique a young professed. Both of them had long felt drawn to work in the foreign missions, and three years before, in 1844, each (unknown to the other) had written to the local archbishop seeking his permission to transfer to a missionary Order. Their abbess was reluctant to lose them, especially Adélaide who was her assistant, and she had urged the archbishop at least to delay any such move. Trying to satisfy everyone, he had granted them permission to go but imposed a three-year moratorium.[1] Over the next two years they made preliminary applications to several missionary Orders, but they were rejected in every case because they had taken vows at Tourcoing.

In the summer of 1846, Glasgow priest Fr Peter Forbes (Plate 2) travelled to Northern France on behalf of his bishop, John Murdoch, hoping to find a women's Congregation willing to send volunteers to the west of Scotland mission.[2] One of the houses he visited was the convent of Notre Dame des Anges.

His arrival there seemed like the answer to the two Sisters' prayers: he secured agreement that they could leave for Scotland in summer 1847, when the three-year moratorium imposed by the archbishop elapsed, and assured them that there would be no shortage of work for them, teaching and caring for the poor. But it was stipulated that the new foundation in Glasgow would be an independent Congregation, and that once established there could be no returning to Tourcoing.

Fr Forbes took the information back to Glasgow, and as far as the Sisters were aware all of the arrangements had been agreed. Shortly before setting out they wrote to him again, confirming routes and dates.

Now everything was thrown in doubt. Should they press on, without an escort? Perhaps Bishop Murdoch in Glasgow had not been shown their letter? They decided to write to him directly and await his reply before making any decision. Fortunately, the occupants of the house had rooms to spare, for a few days at least, but they were only too aware that the 250 francs that each had set out with were rapidly disappearing. And to complete their loneliness in a strange city, they had barely a word of English between them.

After a week the bishop's reply arrived. The news could hardly have been worse: there was no house available for them in Glasgow, he wrote, and in any case this was not an opportune time to come. It seemed doubtful whether Fr Forbes had in fact ever made any firm arrangement with the bishop after his visit the previous year, and certainly, if he had, it no longer appeared to hold. As Véronique herself later recalled, it was fairly obvious that Glasgow had forgotten about them.[3]

They sat down to discuss their options. The simplest thing might be to stay where they were and set up a community in Liverpool, where there was certainly great need and where they had heard that a local resident was keen to endow a convent.[4] On the other hand, the temptation was strong to return to Tourcoing, to the familiar security of the high-walled monastery and its lovely old chapel, while there was still time. But faith and pride alike forbade any such thought. Their hearts were set on Glasgow, and in the face of the bishop's cool letter the same faith and pride only hardened their resolve.

They left Liverpool on 16 June, and arrived in Glasgow on the evening of the 18th.[5] Their first sight of the city, grey stone under a grey sky, left them in no doubt that they were in the north, and they feared that their welcome might be equally cool.

In fact, Bishop Murdoch was happy enough to receive them, but he had no particular work for them to do and was not in a position to provide accommodation or support. They were referred to a Mrs Macdonald, who might be willing to offer them rented lodgings at her house in Monteith Row, a well-to-do street of elegant four-storey terraces just a quarter-mile east of the city centre. She kept a school at No. 25 where, as her advertisement 'respectfully intimated', she 'received young ladies to board and educate', assisted by her sister, Miss Rigg, who had 'finished her education in one of the first Establishments in France'.[6]

Terms were agreed and paid out of Mlle Marchand's private means. Their hosts could not have been kinder, and the new arrivals soon began to feel quite at home. Under Miss Rigg's tuition, they made some progress in the rudiments of English. Sooner or later they would have to find somewhere of their own, but these lodgings suited their needs in the meantime, while they considered their future.

ANTECEDENTS

The religious Congregation to which Srs Adélaide and Véronique belonged could trace its history back to the time of St Francis, and indirectly at least a hundred years further. The twelfth and thirteenth centuries had witnessed a remarkable flowering of spirituality among the laity in Europe, in which thousands of people sought to dedicate themselves more completely to God. They did so in different ways, but common to all of these *poenitentes* was a striving for conversion, a lifelong turning from sin to the Gospel, expressing itself in humility and simplicity of life, mercy, charity and service.[7]

In 1206 the young, wealthy, fun-loving Francis of Assisi himself became a penitent and gave up everything to pursue a life of poverty and preaching. The little band who joined him at first saw themselves simply as 'brothers of penance', and only later was the growing community given official recognition as an Order of the Church with its own Rule of life.[8] Inspired by his example, Clare of Assisi established a contemplative community of women under religious vows in 1215, from which numerous daughter houses sprang up in her lifetime, eventually recognised as an Order and permitted to use the Rule that she had composed for them.

Wherever Francis and his brothers went, people were moved to live a more perfect life and many wished to be more closely bound to his movement without actually joining the First Order of 'Lesser Brothers' or the Second of

'Poor Ladies'. These men and women he saw as a Third Order, and for them he wrote a *Memorial* in 1221, which was in effect its earliest Rule. The numbers continued to swell, and in 1289 Pope Nicholas IV issued a formal Rule for them, to bring coherence to the growing movement.

At an early date two distinct types emerged within this Third Order 'of Penance': those who simply followed the Rule, and others who had come together to live in community under vows.[9] These latter groups often formed under local initiative, and for more than a century they had no particular links with one another, other than that of their shared Rule. In time, however, some established federations. Among the first of them were the *Sœurs Grises*, originally a society of lay women devoted to nursing the sick, who received papal recognition as a Congregation of the Third Order in the early fifteenth century, adopted the vows of religion, and established numerous communities, particularly in north-east France and Flanders.[10] In 1455 they opened a house in Comines, some 10 km west of Tourcoing.

In the 1550s to 1560s the whole area was overrun by Calvinist forces, and Tourcoing was sacked and put to the torch. In the period of reconstruction that followed the town magistrates saw an urgent need for solid Catholic formation for a younger generation shaken by the uncertainties of the times. Believing that, for girls, this would best be accomplished by a religious Order of Sisters, they invited the *Sœurs Grises* from Comines to open a house in the town, offering them the lands and revenues of an old hospice, originally founded for the care of destitute women, on condition that they undertook to build their own convent there, provide free education for local girls and maintain the original work of the hospice. In 1632 the convent was built and ready for occupation. Thus it was that the new community of Notre Dame des Anges at Tourcoing took up teaching as their main apostolate, and secondarily the care of the old and sick.

Their work continued uninterrupted until 1792, when they were forced by the Government of the French Revolution to close the school, quit their convent, discard the habit and pursue a secular life.[11] Not until after the Concordat signed by Napoleon and the Holy See in 1801 were they able to reopen the school and convent, and only after Napoleon's fall in 1815 could they resume the habit and return to normal life.

The Church now entered a new era of prestige. Weary of enlightened rationalism, the iconoclasm of the Revolution and the horrors of war, people looked again to the spiritual and the message of the Gospel. It was a time of unprecedented flourishing of religious Orders and Congregations, with scores of new foundations springing up in Europe, and later in America; not for nothing has the nineteenth century been called 'the most vocational of centuries'.[12] But the Revolution had not been without effect, for it had deepened the social conscience, and almost all of the new foundations were established as 'active' Congregations whose purpose was to be 'useful to the people'. In the burgeoning industrial cities of the day, the most obvious scope for usefulness lay in the education and material and spiritual care of the 'new poor'.

VOCATION

It was in this climate of foundations in new places among the common people, and in the particular tradition of Tourcoing with its apostolate in education and the care of the sick–poor, that Adélaide and Véronique had received their religious formation and discerned their own vocations. It was not surprising, then, that when they had felt a call to do something 'special for God' they had been drawn to mission fields abroad, to some place where there was a crying need for teaching and bringing succour and the faith to the poor. This was the kind of apostolate they had in mind. Probably they had supposed that it might take them to a far continent, but when Fr Forbes explained the pressing need for education and parish work among the urban poor in a struggling mission in Protestant Scotland they saw that it matched all their hopes exactly.

Their training had given them a particular vision of the task of the teacher. In the first place, they shared the philosophy of the Catholic Church that education should be a fusion of the intellectual, the moral and the spiritual, and that every child is equal and precious as a child of God. Secondly, as religious they brought to teaching a particularly effective combination of commitment and detachment, a powerful sense of vocation and freely given service on the one hand, and on the other a tranquillity and perspective that came from the daily practice of their Rule. Thirdly, they had been schooled in the French system of pedagogy, whose hallmarks were thorough and systematic instruction, order and sound discipline, and high standards of expectation, in which young minds were not to be compelled by fear but won over by attractive lessons and healthy competition.[13]

Added to this, their vision was infused with the particular Franciscan spirit. At its heart was poverty. Francis himself had sent his own brothers out as Christ had sent out His disciples, in twos, 'taking nothing for the journey, neither staff, satchel, bread, money nor extra tunic', and if that original radical poverty was hardly possible for the two Sisters sent out from Tourcoing, still they carried little and owned nothing. But even more than material poverty, Francis had called for a poverty of spirit that cared nothing for fame, honour or 'safe' work but looked for God 'where He said He was to be found, among the least of His brothers and sisters'.[14] For him this had meant embracing the leper; for Adélaide and Véronique it meant seeking out the poor, unconditionally and without judgement. It was an approach totally different from that prevalent in respectable Victorian Scotland, which distinguished the 'deserving' from the 'undeserving' poor. Their aim was simply to reach out to those who suffered, and it implied a readiness (in the words of St Clare) to 'get their feet dirty'.

For Francis, poverty also meant having no home. He had enjoined his own brothers to settle nowhere and, rejecting the security of the monastic life, to 'make the world their cloister', and in that spirit Franciscans have always essentially been missionaries.[15] He had never been afraid to try the novel and the untried, to make bold commitments. As Chesterton put it, 'his life was one riot of rash vows',[16] and his followers have usually been noted for their readiness to take risks, attempt new things, and start again in faith.

But whatever the work they took up, he insisted that it be firmly and constantly grounded upon 'the spirit of prayer and holy devotion', over every other activity and concern.[17] Franciscans have always attempted to follow this injunction, and the convent at Tourcoing was no exception. Yet even within Tourcoing, Adélaïde and Véronique had stood out for their intense prayerfulness and devotion to the Eucharist.[18] Any new Congregation established by them would be sure to reflect this emphasis.

These various threads woven into the lives of the two Sisters – a practical weft across the warp of an ideal – had created a garment both comely and durable with which to face the rigours of their new life in Glasgow.

Nowhere Such Wealth and Such Misery

Though the Clyde had barely entered its great era of shipbuilding at this date, Glasgow was already a prosperous town, its wealth based particularly upon cotton and upon the coal and iron industries on its perimeter. The dozen years before the Sisters' arrival had seen a whole rash of new developments – the deepening of the river for sea-going vessels, the opening of an intercity rail network, the establishment of Scotland's first Stock Exchange and no less than six new banking companies in the town, the building of the mighty 150-metre-high chimney at the St Rollox chemical works – all of them visible symbols of the mood of expansion.[19]

But the buoyancy was deceptive, and the wealth shared only by the few in a society of huge contrasts. 'Perhaps no city,' wrote one commentator in the very year of the Sisters' arrival, 'affords more strikingly the contrast of wealth, splendour and refinement, and a degree of misery and debasement which almost seems to exhibit that lower depth which no human agency can elevate.'[20] The population had more than trebled in the first forty years of the century and now stood at more than 275,000, and this unbridled growth brought with it a downward spiral in living and working conditions.

As well as sharing in the general downturn of the national economy following the end of the Napoleonic War, Glasgow had suffered particularly from an alarming decline in the weaving industry. Some 32,000 weavers were employed in the city and its environs, but their living standards had fallen sharply and the wages now kept most families barely above starvation.[21] The invention of the power loom had left many handloom weavers redundant, and their fight for work and wages had culminated in the Calton strike of 1837. Their defeat in that action had weakened the hand of the trades unions in every branch of industry in the city and beyond.

Housing conditions had also worsened disastrously. As ever more new-comers arrived, slum ghettos developed, with massive overcrowding. Though bad housing was nothing new in Scotland, the city slum was a quite new phenomenon in its scale, its degree of deprivation, and in the social problems that it spawned.[22] To meet the demand for accommodation, once prosperous properties were 'down made' (sublet), whereby accommodation that had housed a single family might now be home for up to a dozen. Behind the properties, where once there had been gardens, new 'backlands' were built. The city chamberlain reported that in the most congested parish, the population had risen by 40 per cent in the ten years from 1831, with no increase whatever in the number of houses.[23]

Inevitably, these conditions took their toll on health. The city's population was particularly at the mercy of diseases such as typhus and cholera, spread by overcrowding and polluted air and water. Robert Cowan, a physician at the Royal Infirmary and an expert on fevers, saw the rise in these diseases as proof of the decline in living conditions. Matching it, he noted, was the alarming rise in the city's mortality rate, from 1:44 in the early 1820s to over 1:25 in the late 1830s, statistics that pointed to 'an intensity of misery and suffering unequalled in Britain'.[24]

That Glasgow topped the league table of deprivation was a view shared by Edwin Chadwick, who as secretary to the Poor Law Commission and editor of its official *Report* of 1842 was as well placed as any man to know. His work had taken him to some of the most deprived towns and cities in the kingdom, but he considered Glasgow the worst of any that he had seen.[25]

The most blighted ghetto in the city was the district adjacent to the Glasgow Cross, known generally as 'the Wynds' on account of the numerous warren-like tunnel entrances that led off its main thoroughfares (Plate 3). At the heart of it was a neighbourhood no more than ten acres in extent – just large enough to pasture ten cows, as the local Kirk minister graphically put it – where 10,000 people had their homes.[26] Chadwick and his colleagues visited some of these wynds and published vivid images of them. One they entered through a narrow close, to find themselves in a courtyard which, apart from a perimeter path, was entirely filled with a dunghill made up mainly of human excrement. A second tunnel led off this courtyard into a second court, similarly filled, and so to a third the same. There were no privies or drains, and the inhabitants were actually keeping the dung for sale to pay their rents. The visitors entered several of the houses and found them as shocking inside as out. 'We saw some half-dressed wretches crowding together to be warm,' they reported, 'and in one bed, although in the middle of the day, several women were imprisoned under a blanket, because as many others who had on their backs all the articles of dress that belonged to the party were then out of doors in the streets.'[27]

Amidst such misery, who could avoid degradation and despair? Alcohol was legally available to fourteen-year-olds at this time, and one did not have to go far to find it, for according to one contemporary estimate there was a spirit dealer for every fourteen families in the city.[28] Drink and degradation fed upon each other. Those who worked among the poor witnessed number-less tragic examples of disease, pauperism, theft, violence, prostitution and even insanity, all associated with alcohol.[29]

The missionary William Logan spent a year investigating the Glasgow brothels and what he saw was pitiable. He estimated that there were some 450 such houses, and in all perhaps 1,800 prostitutes. Some were as young as fourteen, but they had a brief career: four fifths of them were suffering from disease, and on average they could expect to die within six years.[30] According to Captain Miller of the city police, most of them had turned to the streets in desperation because they could find no other work.[31]

It was Captain Miller who had given Chadwick and his colleagues their guided tour of the wynds, and one incident from that tour, barely credible to the modern ear, aptly sums up the degradation of those who had to live there. As the party entered a backland, a crowd of curious urchins gathered round them. When asked their names, the children seemed uncertain, finally volunteering some nicknames. The captain explained that they actually had no names. He could find in the immediate neighbourhood, he added, 'a thousand children who have no names whatever, or only nicknames, like dogs'.[32]

Such was life in 'the Wynds' of the city. It was the extreme. But in several of the suburbs, notably Calton and Anderston, and increasingly in Bridgeton and the Gorbals, the position was not a great deal better.[33]

Some of Glasgow's respectable citizens, Kirk ministers and men of medicine particularly, worked tirelessly to alleviate the suffering around them. Christian charity was their prime motive, but they were prompted also by apprehension. Only twenty years before, workers' demonstrations had led to deaths in Glasgow, and violence and anarchy still simmered beneath the surface. The most celebrated philanthropist of the day, Rev. Dr Thomas Chalmers, was among those who publicly voiced their fear of the suffering populace. 'If something be not done,' he had warned at the time of the strikes, 'to bring this enormous physical strength under the control of Christian and humanized principle, the day may yet come when it may lift against the authorities of the land its brawny vigour, and discharge upon them all the turbulence of its rude and volcanic energy.'[34]

It was anxiety as well as genuine care that had prompted the appointment of the Poor Law Commission and the subsequent tabling of the Poor Law Amendment (Scotland) Act of 1845, which established the responsibility of local authorities in combating poverty.

It was with this anxiety also that the Kirk had stepped up its efforts among the labouring classes. It had established the Glasgow City Mission as early as 1826, but it was in the 1830s and 1840s that its work really took off.[35] The Church Building Society, founded in 1834, oversaw the erection of thirteen churches in new neighbourhoods in the first six years of its existence.[36] The Disruption of 1843, though it split the Church, had the effect of greatly increasing the number of places of worship in the city as the newly formed Free Church embarked upon its own building programme.

At the same time, the Kirk was making determined efforts in social and educational work. The Glasgow Young Men's Christian Association opened its doors in 1841, offering bible classes and prayer meetings, and later public lectures and library facilities, to young adults. For children there was the Glasgow Sabbath School Union, which within ten years of its foundation in 1838 had opened no less than 490 schools in the town.[37]

The Churches were also getting involved in weekday education. The traditional system of schooling in Scotland, the parish schools, had as yet gained no real foothold in industrial towns like Glasgow, and such schools as existed in the city had sprung up haphazardly, mostly by private initiative. The Kirk had recently succeeded in setting up a number of its own, but they were only reaching a tiny minority of children.[38]

For Bishop Murdoch and his priests the anxiety was that these schools and the other organisations run by the Kirk were drawing in members of his own flock. It is true that in a few of them it was the practice to excuse Catholic children from religious instruction, but in most no such privilege was given. The bishop suspected that in some cases deliberate attempts were being made to wean vulnerable children away from their religion.[39]

In 1832 an epidemic of Asiatic cholera erupted in Scotland which left 3,000 dead in Glasgow alone. Among the hundreds of orphans were a number of Catholic children. Knowing that any child taken into the city's orphanages would be brought up Protestant, Bishop Murdoch gathered them together and had them looked after at his own expense during the first winter. The Church itself was in debt and in no position to help, but his appeal for private donations met with a warm response, and in July of the following year he was able to open the Catholic Orphan Institution as a permanent home for them.[40] It was perhaps the first institute of social care set up by the Catholic Church in Glasgow as a counter or alternative to existing ('Protestant') provision, and marks the beginning of a whole parallel structure – a 'welfare state within the state'[41] – soon to be developed for the Catholic people.

THE CATHOLICS OF GLASGOW

Before the late eighteenth century there were almost no Catholics in Glasgow. It was the Highland famines of the 1770s and 1780s that first brought them to the city in any numbers. By 1786, Bishop Geddes, who used to walk from Edinburgh to say Mass for them in a tenement room off the Saltmarket, reckoned that there were close to 200 Catholics in the whole Inverclyde area, enough to warrant a resident priest of their own.[42] Five years later a number of the Glasgow manufacturers invited more Catholic Highlandmen into the town with the promise of jobs, and the Church provided them with a temporary chapel and a Gaelic-speaking priest. In 1797 a small permanent chapel was opened for them in Marshall Lane on the Gallowgate.[43]

The following year, 1798, marks the beginning of significant immigration by the Irish, as many fled their homeland after the defeat of the uprising of the United Irishmen. Some already had family ties with Scotland, or the experience of working there as harvesters or navvies. The trickle was soon to become a flood, boosted by the opening of a cross-channel steam ferry between Belfast and Glasgow in 1818, and later as competition between the ferry companies drove down fares to prices that even the poor could afford.[44]

In 1805 Andrew Scott was appointed priest for the city. He was to stay for forty years, serving the people as bishop and Vicar Apostolic from 1828. Until 1821 he was the sole priest in the town, but thereafter more were brought in to cope with the soaring numbers.

We know something about the way of life of the Glasgow Catholics, thanks to the evidence that Bishop Scott and others gave to the Commission on the Irish Poor in Great Britain in the early 1830s. There were a few who 'had raised themselves to the rank of respectable shop-keepers', he informed the commissioners – grocers, spirit dealers and pawnbrokers among them – but the 'great bulk' of the men were either handloom weavers or day labourers, while many of the women were employed on the new steam looms.[45] Most lived either in 'the Wynds' or in the weaving centres of Calton, Anderston and Gorbals, the very districts where living conditions were the worst. The bishop described them as 'belonging to the poorer or almost the lowest class of society'. On the other hand, many factory owners were apparently ready to offer them work ahead of their Scots neighbours, considering them more hardworking and reliable.[46] A small number were clearly making their way in society, and up until the mid-1840s few were actually destitute.

To what extent they were integrated into the larger community, or remained separate from it, has been warmly debated by historians. Some have recently played down the notion of a subculture held at arm's length by the host population, arguing that by mid-century their involvement in local life was already longstanding and deeply rooted.[47] But it is certain that they suffered their share of hostility and prejudice. The Orange Order had held its first walk in the town in 1821; but it was in the 1830s, following Catholic Emancipation, that hostility became more strident.[48] A new newspaper, *The Protestant*, began publication in Glasgow, and 1835 saw the founding of the Protestant Association for the express purpose of 'exposing the errors and pernicious tendency of the Popish system'. It was Bishop Scott's experience that prejudice against the Irish existed 'to a great degree, even among the respectable classes of society'.

If the press often portrayed the incomers as bringing down the tone of society, Bishop Scott took the opposite view. The more they mixed with their Scots neighbours in the slums, he believed, the greater the danger to their morals, between the degradation of slum life, the infection of Protestantism and the temptation to become involved in radical politics. A man of the rural north-east, he was by nature and upbringing conservative, and his conservatism had only been confirmed by his personal experience of revolutionary Europe as a student.[49] He did not entirely trust his congregation – the 'Paddies' as he called them – not to be led astray by irreligion or heretical religion 'against the commands and exhortations of their pastors'.[50] His great fear was a weakening of the control of the Church. To prevent it he sought, as it were, to gather his flock into a fold, to create for them a kind of moral ghetto without walls. By providing its own resources for their care and education, the Church would be helping them materially, intellectually and spiritually, and at the same time safeguarding their faith.

The key as he saw it was sound religious schooling for the coming generation, their one hope of turning out 'good men, good citizens and good subjects' in such an environment. He was behind the opening of the first Catholic schools in the Gallowgate and the Gorbals in 1818, and the others that were started in Bridgeton, Anderston, Cowcaddens and Townhead shortly afterwards.[51] The families they served were illiterate, the premises they used makeshift, the resources almost non-existent. But the teachers were dedicated, and their dedication spanned the seven days of the week. At this time St Andrew's (now the cathedral) was the only Catholic church in the city. Every Sunday as its bell rang for 9 a.m. Mass, six long lines of children could be seen converging upon it from six points of the compass, led by their teachers in black gowns, shawls and bonnets, while the few citizens abroad at that hour gazed in admiration at this powerful and orderly demonstration of faith.[52] But as the bishop warned the Commission on the Irish Poor in Great Britain, he could now barely keep these schools afloat, between lack of funds and the ever-growing poverty of the people.

Fr Forbes was twenty-eight when he came to Glasgow in 1833, and with his arrival the team of priests became five, all based at St Andrew's. Even among those diligent men his zeal and energy stood out. No corner of the town was beyond his reach, even the Poor House, where he is said to have brought one hundred of the inmates over to the Catholic faith.[53] In the same year that he arrived, John Murdoch was consecrated bishop and appointed coadjutor to Bishop Scott. Like the Vicar Apostolic they were both Banffshire men, and like him their natural conservatism had been strengthened by their experiences as students in Europe. Three years later, Alexander Smith, yet another Banffshire man, joined the team. All three were to play a vital part in establishing the Franciscan Sisters in Glasgow.

In 1839 Fr Forbes was given permission to travel to Ireland to raise funds for church building. Such were his powers of persuasion that he returned with £3,000 and three priests for the Scottish mission. In the summer of 1842 he made a second visit, this time returning with five more volunteer priests and accompanied by Fr Mathew, the leader of the temperance movement in Ireland. The famed orator had been brought over to open Glasgow's second church, St Mary's in the Calton, to which Fr Forbes had been appointed parish priest and which had been built with the funds he had collected. It was the beginning of a thirty-year career of outstanding pastoral care and leadership in the parish.

In October 1845 and in failing health, Bishop Scott resigned his post and retired to Greenock where he died the following year. Bishop Murdoch automatically succeeded him as Vicar Apostolic, and Alexander Smith was appointed coadjutor (though he was not consecrated until October 1847).

The new appointments ushered in a period of enterprise and growth for the Catholic Church in Glasgow. No less than seven new parish churches were opened in the four years between 1846 and 1850, all but one of them in deprived areas close to the city centre.[54] Bishop Murdoch was also anxious to bring education to a greater number of children, despite the lack of funds. The ideal would have been to bring some of the religious teaching Orders to Scotland, whose work in Catholic Europe was well proven. Unfortunately, following the Relief Act of 1829, men's religious Orders were prohibited from opening houses in Britain. But no such ban had been placed upon the women's Orders, and here the bishop saw his opportunity.

Sometime in 1845 he gave Fr Forbes responsibility for raising funds for the foundation of a convent in Glasgow, and for finding a Congregation who would be willing to send Sisters to the city.[55] At this date women figured little in philanthropic work among the urban poor in Scotland,[56] but they had already shown their worth in the city's Catholic schools. It is to Bishop Murdoch's credit that he recognised the value of women teachers, and the special qualities of gentleness, sensitivity and care that they could bring to their work with the young.

Fr Forbes was happy to be handed the task, for – as he said himself – education was 'the greatest object of his soul'. He turned first to Ireland, quite naturally in view of his previous successes there and the ethnic origins of the Catholics in the west of Scotland. He made contact with the recently formed Sisters of Mercy there, but they were unable to help at this time.

On his return to Glasgow a chance meeting with an Irishman, Jeremiah Joseph Buckley, pointed him in the direction of France and Tourcoing. Buckley had just arrived in the city to prepare for ordination for the Western District.[57] Part of his training had been spent at Cambrai in Northern France, the episcopal seat of Archbishop Giraud whose diocese included Tourcoing some 60 km distant, and there is some evidence that he had actually taught briefly at Tourcoing. It was almost certainly he who suggested that Fr Forbes cast his net in northern France, and in particular that he should try Cambrai. Fr Forbes took his advice. Travelling in France posed no difficulty for him, for he had himself studied at St Sulpice and was fluent in French.

On arrival at Cambrai he was introduced to the Vicar General, Abbé Bernard. Again it was a fortunate meeting. Srs Adélaide and Véronique had remained in touch with Archbishop Giraud since first contacting him in 1844. They had written again recently, Adélaide to him personally and Véronique through Abbé Bernard.[58] The Abbé was aware of their hopes, therefore, and having discussed them with his archbishop knew that he supported them. He was therefore able to advise Fr Forbes to visit Tourcoing, where he had reason to believe that there were two Sisters who might be delighted to accept his invitation, and would be free to do so in the near future.

When Adélaide and Véronique arrived in Glasgow in June 1847, they came at a time when the Church was working energetically to meet the grave material and spiritual needs of its people there. They were the first religious to respond to those needs. Others would soon follow: the Sisters of Mercy in 1849, the Good Shepherd Sisters a year later, and more in the 1860s. Not until 1858 would the first men's religious Order, the Marists, arrive to take on similar teaching work for boys.[59]

Adélaide and Véronique had the courage to plough the first furrow. They

came at a time of optimism and expansion in the Church under its new
Vicar Apostolic. But 1847 was also a year of startling new problems and
seemingly endless misery for those whom the Church sought to serve. Not
for nothing has it been called 'Black '47'.[60]

BLACK '47

The downward spiral in the living conditions of the poor that Glasgow had
been witnessing for three decades was as nothing compared with the
experience of the years 1846–9. The city suddenly found itself swamped by
a tide of utterly destitute Highlanders and Irish escaping famine in their
former homes. The Highlanders came in their thousands, the Irish in their
tens of thousands, the peak year being 1847. Between January and
November of that year officials counted 50,000 who landed at the
Broomielaw, not to mention the many others who were put off the famine
ships further down the Clyde and eventually found their way to the city.[61]
Not all settled in the area, of course. Some moved on through the country,
while others used Glasgow as a stopping-off point for an Atlantic crossing.
A number of Glasgow's existing Irish population sought the same escape,
choosing to leave a city where overcrowding, starvation and disease were
quite beyond the power of the authorities to control. These were the ones
with the wherewithal, and usually the ones with enterprise and spirit, as
Bishop Murdoch recognised. 'The best of our people continue to cross the
Atlantic, and we will be left a congregation of beggars,' he warned after a
year of such emigration.[62] But only the few were so fortunate. Thousands
wandered the streets, penniless and without food, trying to find a room in a
city that had none.

When a serious outbreak of typhus occurred at the beginning of the year,
the local press were in no doubt that its rapid spread could be traced directly
to 'the masses of diseased and famished Irish that had been thrown amongst
them'.[63] Further outbreaks of typhus and cholera were to follow, and as the
mortality rate soared, a report to the town council laid the blame squarely
on 'the masses of wandering and famishing Irish', warning that unless the
growing evil was checked Glasgow would fast become a city 'of paupers
and the plague'.[64]

The language of racism and prejudice was now current coin. It was the
language of a society bewildered and utterly unable to cope. Here was a
huge, apparently insoluble crisis engulfing the city, and it had came on top of
a wider crisis that seemed to be enveloping the country, indeed the whole
continent, threatening the old securities. The cherished traditions of religion
were already reeling from the effects of the Oxford Movement in England
and the Disruption at home; throughout Britain radical politics were in the

air, while across Europe revolution was moving like a swelling wave, a wave that would rise and break upon the barricades of Paris the following year.[65] Little wonder that officialdom was jittery and at its wits' end.

The horrors of the famine years, and the eloquent publicity given to them in the press, were to effect a sea-change in the consciousness and the conscience of the nation, and of the Glasgow city fathers. Attitudes would never be the same again. A new civic responsibility was to emerge, a new acceptance of a duty to take the city in hand, a determination to improve conditions and provide amenities that in time would bear fruit. With hindsight, Black '47 would prove to be the nadir of the town's misery, and it would be followed by a gradual upturn in its people's fortunes.[66] If any one year could be identified as the low point of the spiral, it was the year in which the Franciscan Sisters first came to Glasgow, like a candle in the dark.

ENDNOTES TO SETTING THE SCENE

1 The present account based on extracts from the Tourcoing archives; also letter abbess to archbishop 21.1.1846, copy 011, AF. Apparently the two Sisters only learned of the other's application when they were given the wrong letters of reply in error – verbal communication by Superior of Tourcoing to Sr M. Francis Campbell, relayed to the author.

2 The other purposes of his trip were to seek donations for the Western District, and to find a seminary willing to accept Scottish students – cf. Fr P. Forbes to Bishop Scott, 10.9.1846, OL 2/72/5, SCA.

3 Based on her own recollections of the event, in Tourcoing Archives: in the original, '*on ne songeait plus à elles*'.

4 Personal recollections of the original members of the Glasgow house, related to them by Sr Véronique, in *Scottish Catholic Monthly*, May 1894, p. 180. The Liverpool resident was Donald Gordon Stewart.

5 Letter Sr Véronique to Mother Vicaress, 28.12.1896, copy 040.14, AF.

6 Advertisement, *Scottish Catholic Directory (SCD)*, 1849, p. 136.

7 Pazzelli R., 1982 (transl. 1989), p. 45ff. The term used for this turning was *conversio* or *metanoia*.

8 They effectively became a religious Order when Francis and his companions received the tonsure from Innocent III in 1209. Their first Rule dates from 1221; their finalised, official Rule from 1223.

9 For a summary of the development of the Order, see Pazzelli R., 1993, pp. 1–30. There were signs of the existence of secular and religious types within the Third Order very early on – cf. the letter of Gregory IX *Nimis Patenter*, written in 1227, the year after Francis' death.

10 Their recognition as a Third Order Congregation was given in the bull *Personas Vacantes* of John XXII in 1413. By 1500 they had opened nearly 100 houses in Flanders and Burgundy alone.

11 By its *Constitution Civile du Clergé*, the Revolutionary Government effectively took control of all religious houses, giving itself, for example, authority over appointments. The Tourcoing community preferred to disband rather than accept the new provisions.

12 Short W. J., 1989, p. 99. Short gives details of a number of new Franciscan foundations for women, p. 100ff.

13 Cf. Handley J.E., 1950J, especially p. 30ff. Competition in the classroom was encouraged both between 'teams' and individuals (e.g., the *Table d'Honneur*). In Catholic schools team spirit could also be built in sodalities. The pioneering and immensely influential *Conduite des Écoles Chrétiennes*, written by Jean Baptiste de la Salle in 1724, includes many of the central ideas of the Christian, the religious and the French traditions.

14 Bodo M., 1984 (1985 edition), p. 89.

15 Cf. eg., 'Our entire fraternity is missionary', Order of Friars Minor (OFM) General Chapter, Medellin, 1971; 'Fundamentally, every Franciscan vocation is missionary,' OFM Cap Statement, Mattli, 1978. The phrase 'the world their cloister' originates from a well known story involving some of Francis' followers. When asked who they were, they explained that they were religious brothers; on then being asked where their cloister was, they pointed to the land and the horizon ahead.

16 Chesterton G. K., 1923, p. 27.

17 St. Francis, *Letter to Anthony*.

18 Tourcoing Archives, 011, AF, especially Notice on Sr Adélaide Vaast, and account of latter years of M. Véronique Cordier, of whom the authors write 'the characteristic of her soul was the spirit of prayer'.

19 Maver I., 2000, Chapter 3.

20 Pagan J., 1847, p. 105.

21 Murray N., 1978, p. 46. The figures for weavers employed in the city (18,500) and its environs (13,500) are from the *New Statistical Account*, 1841, vol. 6 Lanarkshire, p. 958.

22 Cf. Smout T.C., 1986 (1987 edition), p. 29.

23 Report of city chamberlain to Lord Provost, 1841, in Chadwick E. 1842 (ed. Flinn J., 1965), p. 189.

24 Cowan R., 1838, p. 45; p. 12 re the fever, p. 46 re the mortality statistics.

25 Chadwick E., *op. cit.*, p. 99. Among the cities he had personally visited were Manchester, Leeds, and some of the poorest parts of London. Elsewhere (p. 97) he wrote that only the wynds of Edinburgh's Old Town perhaps equalled those of Glasgow.

26 Buchanan R., 1850, p. 13.

27 Dr Neil Arnott, 'Report on the Fevers which have prevailed in Edinburgh and Glasgow', no. 1 of *Local Reports of the Sanitary Conditions of the Labouring Population of Scotland* to the Poor Law Commission, HMSO, 1842.

28 *New Statistical Account*, 1841, vol. 6 Lanarkshire, p. 195, apparently using figures proposed by William Collins to the Select Committee on Intoxication in 1832. Some scholars question their accuracy.

29 Logan W., 1849. His account has separate chapters on each of these issues.

30 Logan W., 1842 (3rd edition 1843), p. 20ff.

31 Cited by Baird C. R., Secretary of the Glasgow Relief Fund, in *Report Containing a Summary of the Material Legal Provisions Relating to the Removal of Nuisances in Glasgow*, no. 5 of *Local Reports*, 1842. Captain Miller estimated the number of prostitutes somewhat lower, at 1,475. The captain also gave the Poor Law Commission evidence on another pointer to deprivation, the pawn-shop. There were 30 licensed in the town, but he knew of another 200 unlicensed premises, or 'wee pawns' as they were called, and a further 300 'dealers in old clothes' who sold off unredeemed items and were in effect specialised pawn-brokers. Apparently, a number of the latter were Catholics of Irish origin – Levitt I. and Smout C. (eds.), 1979, p. 139: *Report of the Royal Commission on the Poor Law (Scotland)*, 1844, vol. 20, p. 323.

32 Chadwick E., *op. cit.*, p. 198ff.

33 These suburbs had only become a part of the city in 1846.

34 Dr T. Chalmers, 'Sermon on the Death of Princess Charlotte', 1828.

35 Hillis P., 1987J, p. 47.

36 *New Statistical Account*, 1841, vol. 6, p. 908ff.

37 Hillis P., *loc. cit.*, p. 48. Some 27,000 boys and girls attended the Sabbath schools.

38 There were several types of Kirk school: 'Assembly', 'Sessional' and (in the poorest districts) 'Mission' – cf. Scotland J., 1969, vol. 1, p. 242ff. Re the minority reached, cf. the estimate made in 1858 by George Anderson, president of the Glasgow branch of the Educational Institute of Scotland (EIS), that c. 1:14 children of school age attended school city-wide, with a far lower proportion in the poorest districts.

39 According to Hillis, historian of the nineteenth-century Kirk missions, much effort went into attempts to draw Catholics away from their faith at this time – Hillis P., *loc. cit.*, p. 51. It was in Glasgow's four 'Assembly' schools that Catholic children were excused from religious instruction.

40 Anon, *Catholicism in Glasgow Thirty Years Ago, or Reminiscences on the Last Years of the Life of Mrs Kelly*, 1863, p. 12ff. The orphanage was in Marshall's Lane off the Gallowgate. Mrs Kelly was appointed its first matron/governess.

41 The phrase is from Aspinwall B., 1992J, p. 128.

42 Bishop Geddes to Bishop Hay, 30.11.1786, BL, SCA.

43 The temporary chapel (1791–7) was in the tennis court in Mitchell St. The permanent chapel was in premises in Marshall's Lane off the Gallowgate, the same building later used by Bishop Murdoch for his orphanage.

44 Cf. Handley J. 1943 (1945 edition), pp. 38ff. and 24ff. The cheapest fare on the first ferry was 14/– single, but at one stage fares of 3d. were on offer. By 1836 there were services running directly from Belfast, Derry and Dublin, with some thirty sailings in all every week.

45 Bishop Scott, evidence in *Report on the State of the Irish Poor in Great Britain*, Appendix G of *Report of the Inquiry into the Condition of the Poorer Classes in Ireland*, British Sessional Papers, House of Commons, 1836, vol. xxxiv, p. 427ff. Most of Bishop Scott's evidence appears on pp. xvi and xix of the main text, and in the appendix on Glasgow, p. 103ff. Further references to his evidence below are from the same source.

46 Cf. e.g. paper presented by Dr Cowan in 1840, cited in Chadwick E., *op. cit.*, p. 199.

47 Cf. McCaffrey J.F., 1988J, p. 58, also p. 52ff.

48 Muirhead I. A., 1973J (a) and (b). Many Protestants felt vulnerable, and believed that Emancipation had given Catholics a dangerous influence in society. Feeling ran highest in the west, and particularly among tradesmen and other workers.

49 Cf. McCaffrey J., *loc. cit.*, p. 50.

50 Bishop Scott to Bishop Paterson, 26.10.1825, BL. For a detailed account of the attempts of Bishops Scott and Murdoch to keep control over their people, see Mitchell M. J., 1998, *passim* but especially pp. 129ff and 236ff.

51 Re the Gallowgate and Gorbals schools, *Glasgow Herald*, 24.8.1818. For an account of the early schools in Glasgow, cf. Sr Martha Skinnider, section I, Chapter 1 of Bone T.R. (ed.) 1967.

52 Anon, *Catholicism Thirty Years Ago*, 1863, p. 11.

53 Aspinwall B. 1984J, p. 33. All other details of Fr Forbes are based on his obituary notice in *SCD*, 1873, pp. 152–7.

54 They were St. Alphonsus' (a former Seceders church bought in 1846), St John's in the Gorbals (1846), St Mary's Pollokshaws (1849), St Mungo's Townhead, St Patrick's Anderston, St Paul's Shettleston and St Joseph's Cowcaddens (all 1850).

55 Bishop Smith later recalled that Fr Forbes was already making appeals among the Catholics of Glasgow for funds for a convent of teaching Sisters in 1845 – Bishop Alexander Smith, *Statement re Convent of Mercy Glasgow*, n.d. (*c.*1850), 30–2.5, MIA.

56 Cf. Checkland O., 1980, *passim*.

57 For details of Fr Buckley, see Johnson C., 1989J (a).

58 Sr Adélaide to Bishop Giraud, 20.1.1846, and Sr Véronique to Abbé Bernard, 14.1.1846, copies 011, AF.

59 For details of all the subsequent female and male religious working in Scotland, with dates, see Dilworth M., 1978J, Appendix.

60 Neal F., *Black '47, Britain and the Famine Irish*, 1998.

61 *Ibid.*, p. 63, citing the precise figure of 49,993 given at the Glasgow Parochial Board meeting of 30.11.1847.

62 Bishop Murdoch to Bishop Smith, 18.10.1848, BL, SCA.

63 *Glasgow Herald*, 22.3.1847.

64 Report to the city council, 28.3.1849.

65 This religious and political background to the famine years is very well described in Ross A., 1978J, p. 34ff.

66 Cf. p. 69ff. of this volume.

PART ONE

FIRE

Be praised, my Lord, through Brother Fire,
By whom the night is illumined for us;
He is beautiful and cheerful, full of vigour and strength.

St Francis, *Canticle of the Creatures*

CHAPTER ONE

A Candle in the Dark (1847–1855)

Adélaide and Véronique spent the summer house-hunting, and in September secured a rented property at No. 11 Monteith Row (Plate 4), just a few doors down the road from their current residence. It was their first convent. It was small by Monteith Row standards, but sufficient. There were separate rooms for each of them, a communal drawing room, and a second public room that would serve as an oratory. It was this room that they furnished first and with most care, having received Bishop Murdoch's permission for the Blessed Sacrament to be reserved there. Their intense devotion to the Eucharist set a precedent for the future, for in every new house that the Congregation has opened since, it has always been the practice to prepare the chapel first and bring in the Blessed Sacrament as soon as possible; its arrival, indeed, has always been considered to mark the real opening of the house.

Often that autumn they discussed the way forward. Now that the excitement of arrival was over, the differences in their outlook began to emerge. Adélaide envisaged them joining one of the Orders already established in Britain and opening a daughter house in Glasgow devoted primarily to the religious life. For Véronique there could be no abandoning of her Franciscan commitment, and her hope was for them to found a new Third Order Congregation on the model of Tourcoing. She had seen the needs of Glasgow's poor for education and, ever impatient to begin, was for recruiting young women postulants and opening schools at once.[1] In the age-old dichotomy of the active and the contemplative lives, she was drawn towards the first, Adélaide more to the second.

On 3 October Alexander Smith was consecrated bishop in St Andrew's church. For the Sisters his appointment as coadjutor to Bishop Murdoch could not have been more opportune. It was only after years of silence, and in obedience to an instruction from her Superior, that Véronique later told the real story of their first months in Glasgow and revealed the truth of Bishop Murdoch's failure to help them and Fr Forbes' almost total neglect of them at that time.[2] Had it not been for Alexander Smith, whom she called their angel of consolation, they would certainly not have survived. It may well have been he who secured the house at No. 11 for them. Certainly he was the one cleric taking any interest in them. Unfortunately, in the spring of

1848 he left on a fundraising tour of America that kept him out of the country for most of the year.[3]

At about this time Sr Adélaide opened a private day school at the convent. It may seem an irony that after being invited to Scotland to serve the poor, her first act should be to the benefit of the few well-to-do Catholic families in Glasgow. But we know from Véronique's diaries that the two Sisters had always seen their work as being among all social classes. Like St Francis himself, though their preferential option was for the poor, they saw all of humanity as equal, and equally deserving of their service. Like the community at Tourcoing, which had always run a fee-paying school alongside a free school in order to pay its way, they viewed this private school as the means by which they could exist, and so serve the poor. Their intention was to move into the parish schools as soon as the convent was firmly established. It was a familiar strategy among religious teaching orders, and it set a lasting pattern for their successors.

A Mrs Gordon was employed to assist Adélaide and teach languages. Mlle Marchand, who had no aptitude for languages herself and to the end of her life never really mastered English, offered optional lessons in needle-work, plain and ornamental. Two sisters, Mary and Margaret Gatherer, were also added to the teaching staff. They were in their mid-thirties, from a well-to-do Banffshire Catholic family, and lived in the house as 'parlour boarders'.

There were clear regulations for parlour boarding, following the practice at Tourcoing. Only committed Catholic women of some education and proven moral character were accepted. They were expected to keep regular hours for rising, retiring and sitting to table. As paying guests they were provided with a room, basic furniture and plain meals, all other requisites being at their own expense. They had use of a common parlour – hence the name – but were excluded from the convent proper. They were permitted to attend Mass, Benediction and Exposition with the Sisters, but not the daily Office; nor could they converse with the Sisters unless on necessary business. They might assist in the community's pastoral work, such as teaching or visiting the sick, but without payment. In effect, they formed their own separate community in the house.[4]

To live in as a parlour boarder involved some sacrifice, in short, and little of the freedom or comfort that a paying guest might normally expect. On the other hand, it offered an opportunity for giving practical support to the convent, and because it provided an environment of tranquillity, spirituality and Christian living, it was an attractive option for a certain type of woman, and in particular for one who might be considering her own religious vocation.

In January 1848 Bishop Murdoch moved his Marshall Lane orphanage to new premises in Abercromby Street. The gaunt stone buildings, large enough to house 100 girls, with similar space for boys next door, were close to Fr Forbes' new St Mary's church, separated from it only by a small graveyard. Caring for orphan girls was closer to the kind of work that Véronique had in mind, and her offer to teach there was readily accepted. She continued to live at the convent, and walked the half-mile twice daily along the greasy pavements and labyrinthine alleys of the Calton.

Her constitution was less robust than her will. Seven years before, in the safety of the Tourcoing convent, she had contracted typhoid fever and been close to death with it. Now, in the breathless summer of the Glasgow back courts, fever was in the air again. In the tenement warrens, where close contact was unavoidable and hygiene impossible, the typhus virus – carried by body lice – spread easily. Of those who worked among the poor it was the most dedicated, those who ventured without concern for self into the most penurious neighbourhoods, who were at greatest risk. Four priests had died of the disease in the west of Scotland in the previous eighteen months.[5]

When Véronique arrived back at the convent one evening that summer complaining of a severe chill that soon turned into a burning fever and dizziness, Adélaide suspected the worst, put her straight to bed and kept everyone well away. In the darkness of her room her eyes deceived her with flashing lights, and in its silence her ears were full of noise. Hallucination turned into delirium. Her pulse was racing, her body hot to the touch. The whisper went round the house that she was dying.

But after two days the fever passed as quickly as it had come. And in a few days more – far too soon – she was back teaching at the orphanage. But her weakened body was unfit to cope with the rigours of the work, or with any chance infection. That autumn she succumbed again, this time to cholera, probably contracting it from infected drinking water while visiting the sick. Mercifully, it was a mild attack, and she had her own remedy – regular doses of brandy and water – to stave off dehydration.

Thousands were less lucky that autumn, and by December it was becoming clear that the whole country was in the grip of another cholera epidemic. Before it ran its course, 3,700 were to die of it in Glasgow alone.[6] Every day Bishops Murdoch and Smith and their priests visited the wynds and the tenements to administer the sacraments to those beyond hope. Death followed upon death so fast that the cemeteries were utterly unable to cope. In the graveyard that lay between the orphanage and St Mary's, trenches were dug as makeshift mass graves. But the digging only uncovered other bodies so recently buried that they had had no time to decompose. Corpses lay one upon another, in various stages of decay. The rain that fell upon them washed them partly away, only spreading the pollution further.[7]

Adélaide had joined Véronique at the orphanage in the new year of 1849, at the height of the epidemic, and every morning they would look out from the upstairs windows at the tragic scene. Normally they attended daily Mass at St Mary's, which was less than two minutes from their door if they took the short cut through the cemetery. But because of Véronique's recent illnesses, Adélaide instructed her not to venture out of the orphanage for any purpose. She herself continued to pay her daily visit to the church, and as she picked her way among the open trenches of the graveyard she would cover her face with her handkerchief against the rising miasma.

It was after she returned for lunch on Sunday 12 February that Adélaide began vomiting. Diarrhoea followed, continuing through the day and the following night. The next morning, those tending her noticed the tell-tale contraction of her pupils, the spasms of her stomach and legs, the skin that was cold to the touch and the duck-egg-blue tinge to her face. Fr Forbes was called, and without a second look he gave her Extreme Unction. The diarrhoea stage had now passed, but it had left her exhausted and severely dehydrated. Over the next two days she suffered agonies of thirst, and repeatedly called for water in a voice strangely husky and not her own. By Thursday the muscles of her face were shrunk to the bone, and the skin on her fingers had become corrugated as if her hands had been in soapy water. As her pulse grew more feeble, a drowsiness fell upon her. Uraemia was poisoning the body and damaging the kidneys beyond repair. Drowsiness was turning into coma.

That Friday, Véronique sat for most of the day at the sick-bed. In one of Adélaide's waking moments she asked, 'Do you know who I am?' and saw her nod feebly in reply. Cheered by the recognition, she asked for her blessing. With painful effort the patient stretched out her hand and laid it upon the bowed head. Then she fell into a sleep, and Véronique gently returned her arm under the cover. She never woke again. On Saturday 17th she died.[8]

She had died, one might say, through her reckless love for Christ in the Eucharist. She was buried without delay at the edge of the cemetery close against the church wall. Véronique's last act of respect was to arrange the habit about the body.

Since the Thursday of her illness, Adélaide's mother in France had been troubled by a recurring image in her mind, that of a vine branch laden with fruit, which came to her with such vividness each time she prayed the rosary that it seemed to be real. For some reason it had brought her daughter into her thoughts, and recounting it to her confessor she asked him if any news had arrived of Adélaide. He told her that he had heard nothing, but promised to let her know should any news be brought to him. On the Friday she had the same vision, and again on the Saturday, but this time a beautiful child appeared in her mind's eye, who came forward and gently plucked the grapes. When a few days later she sought out her confessor again, he had the sad news to give her, and when he pressed her as to the time of her last vision he found that it matched exactly the hour of Adélaide's death.⁹

The loss of the convent's leader – indeed, of half of the fledgling community – was a blow that should have finished it off almost before it started. But such was not in Véronique's nature. From her deep faith, and from a character so dogged as to appear at times perverse, she found an inner strength that fed upon adversity. To others the position was clear: she was now a 'community' of one, young, with little experience of the religious life and none of taking authority, quite lacking in Adélaide's administrative skill. She was hardly the person to build a new Congregation. Understandably and very reasonably, Bishop Smith urged her to do the wise thing: either return to France or enter an existing Order.

But to her the position was equally clear. 'Return to France, my Lord, not at all! Enter another Community, even less! I am a Franciscan and I have no wish to change,' was the answer she gave him. She still believed that providence had work for her in Glasgow. The first task was to keep open the school that Adélaide had started. She returned at once to Monteith Row. Now that she was the decision maker, and as if to announce that she was in the city to stay, she took to calling herself 'Veronica' and expected others to address her thus. It was as if she was publicly scuppering any chance of a return to France. From now on we too will call her 'Veronica'.

In April Fr Forbes paid a return visit to the Sisters of Mercy in Limerick to make another attempt at recruiting volunteers to work in Glasgow. This time he met with more success, and the Superior agreed to send five Sisters over. Bishop Smith acquired the three-year lease of a house for them at 76 Charlotte Street, just off London Road and a short step from Monteith Row. No. 76 was a particularly desirable residence in a street of desirable residences (Plate 5), a corner house looking onto the Glasgow Green that had been built for David Dale, the cotton magnate, in the late eighteenth century.

The Sisters had not long arrived when Bishop Murdoch approached them, apparently prompted by Fr Forbes and certainly without consulting Veronica, proposing that Veronica be accepted into their community. It was a suggestion that both parties turned down. Shortly afterwards, again without speaking to Veronica, he arranged for the Sisters to take over the school at No. 11. Veronica's own account leaves no doubt that her hand was forced; Bishop Smith's states bluntly that she was 'turned out'.¹⁰

Without work, home or income, she returned to teaching at the orphanage. She was offered a flat in one of the workers' tenements nearby, but turned it down. Her reasons for doing so tell us something about her personality, and how she saw her work. 'I did not wish to take it,' she explained. 'I was not disdaining to be poorly lodged, but, being in a Protestant country, I was anxious to present the dignity of my vocation.'[11] Instead she and Constantine Marchand took rooms in Bellgrove Street, a neighbourhood that she felt was more in tune with that dignity. There they had the sevices of a maid, Margaret Campbell. Surprisingly perhaps, Bishop Murdoch allowed them to reserve the Blessed Sacrament in the house. Hitherto Veronica had had Fr Forbes as her confessor, but in view of his treatment of her she felt she could no longer confide in him and asked to be transferred to Bishop Smith.[12]

That summer Bishop Murdoch also handed the orphanage over to the Sisters of Mercy, and after a matter of weeks they moved their convent there. We can understand why he preferred them to Veronica for the work. They were a community of five, and part of a recognised Order of the Church with a Rule approved by Rome. One of the modern-day Congregations, in existence less than twenty years, their Rule was adapted to the new age and gave them a freedom to move among the urban poor denied to the long-established Orders.[13] They were used to caring for the sick–poor, and indeed had worked in the cholera hospital in Limerick during the epidemic of 1848–9. Most importantly, they were Irish, at a time when virtually all the Catholics of Glasgow and more than half of the Church's priests were Irish.[14] Veronica had none of these things to recommend her. One cannot blame the bishop for choosing as he did, but for her it was yet another rejection, one more option lost.

So low were her spirits that she now seriously thought of joining an Order elsewhere in Britain. According to Mlle Marchand, she actually wrote letters of application to several houses to accept her as a subject.[15] It was at this darkest moment that Bishop Smith again rallied to her support. As her confessor he had come to know her well. He must have been impressed by her integrity, conviction and remarkable persistence, and recognised in her a strength that only needed the chance to express itself. No. 76 Charlotte Street had remained in the possession of the Sisters of Mercy, but since their move to the orphanage it had been lying unused. It was he who persuaded his Vicar Apostolic to offer the house to her.

It was the turning point in her fortunes, and perhaps in her life. All thoughts of joining another Order vanished. She moved in at once, with Constantine Marchand, and at the same time contacted Tourcoing to request that two young Sisters be sent over to strengthen the community.[16] (The fact that she felt able to do so indicates that leaving Tourcoing had in no way soured relations with her former Abbess and colleagues there). Meantime Bishop Smith wrote to a number of religious houses in Ireland on her behalf, asking them to help her find postulants. On 4 October, the Feast of St Francis, he celebrated their first Mass, and just eleven days later she opened the school. She arranged for Margaret Gatherer to return as an assistant teacher, and engaged several other young women part-time. She apparently also opened a night school for working girls at No. 76, taking charge of the running of it herself.[17]

It was a spacious building, with more than enough room for both convent and school, and she could now take in a few boarding pupils, as well as parlour boarders again.[18] Miss Gatherer moved in, as did Eliza Russell, who was also in her late thirties and unmarried. At Bishop Murdoch's suggestion, a young convert, Miss Mary Margaret Brewster, who had been virtually put out of the house by her father for joining the Catholic Church, was offered accommodation and part-time employment teaching English and music.[19] In November, two younger ladies from Cork, Julia Condon and Joanna Fitzgerald, joined them, the first fruits of Bishop Smith's enquiries in Ireland. All four were women of means; all had thoughts of a religious vocation and wished to observe community life at close hand.

On 8 December Constantine Marchand was accepted as the first postulant of the embryo community, along with the two Irish women. The following April (1850) the three of them were received as novices in a formal ceremony in St Andrew's church, with Bishop Murdoch officiating.[20] It was the first such ceremony to be held in the west of Scotland since the Reformation. For security's sake, admission was by ticket only. The three applicants, attired in white as brides of Christ, approached the altar, each accompanied by her palm bearer and followed by girls, some carrying their habits, others flowers and tapers. At the most solemn part of the liturgy they lay prostrate before the tabernacle as a sign of submission of will to God. Behind them knelt a bevy of some thirty young schoolgirls, robed in the white of innocence, with blue sashes and floral crowns. Then they were given their religious names – Mlle Marchand: Mary Francis; Julia Condon: Mary Hyacintha; Joanna Fitzgerald: Mary Joseph – and dressed in the black habit and white veil of the novice.

Three months later five more postulants were admitted as novices by Bishop Smith. Among them were two sisters, Hannah and Mary McSwiney, who as Sisters M. Angela and M. Catherine were to become the community's first leaders after Veronica.[21] Another was Jamaica-born Basilia Mackintosh, the daughter of a Scottish planter, who with her younger sister Mary had been living in Glasgow as wards of Bishop Smith. Learning of their interest in the religious life, the bishop had recommended them to the convent at Charlotte Street, where they had been accepted as parlour boarders. On joining the novitiate Basilia took the religious name M. Aloysius (Plate 6). She had showed much promise during her brief postulancy, but her close association with the bishop was soon to prove an embarrassment, and she herself a divisive force in the community.

The Rule and Constitutions in use in Glasgow up to this date were those that had been inherited from Tourcoing – the Rule of the Third Order of St Francis as revised by Leo X in 1521, with Constitutions drawn up by an archbishop of Cambrai in the seventeenth century. But certain articles had been changed over time, especially during the troubled days of the French Revolution, and Veronica was now anxious to have a new Rule and Constitutions drawn up and approved by the Vatican. Through Bishop Murdoch, permission was granted by Rome for this to be done.[22]

Veronica and Bishop Smith worked together on the document in the winter of 1850–1. He would write the draft, a section at a time, and read it over to her. Their ideas often clashed. According to her, when she expressed disagreement with a particular proposal he effectively excluded her from the exercise and never discussed the text with her again. She was sure that he was being influenced by Sr M. Aloysius, who wanted to make wholesale changes to the practice of Tourcoing.[23]

It is impossible here to summarise the finished document, which ran to thirty-eight chapters. It dealt comprehensively with the structure and work of the Congregation, its office-bearers, religious vows and regulations on specific matters such as monastic silence, recreation and correspondence with outsiders. It also included a section on Lay Sisters, distinguishing and segregating them from Choir Sisters, and providing separate arrangements for them regarding the daily Office, meditation, recreation and even name (they were not given the normal prefix 'Mary'). Though equal in the sight of God, they were clearly not so in the community, for even the most senior Lay Sister was bound to obey the youngest novice Choir Sister.

This kind of hierarchical view in fact characterised the whole document. The authority of the prioress was that of a 'mother for her children'. She was 'in loco Dei' to them, and they were bound to show 'every mark of respect and submission' to her, rising in her presence and bowing as she passed. Great store was set upon the letter of the law, for (it was asserted) 'contempt for even the smallest observance would soon lead to the total subversion of the Rule'. These and similar strictures were intended as a way to perfection, but their effect was perhaps to overstress an external compliance, and to leave too little room for freely chosen action, adult responsibility and trust. Thus, for example, the prioress controlled the Sisters' correspondence even with their own families, giving permission for outgoing letters and pre-reading and even withholding incoming mail. Permission was required even for the use of trifles such as pens, twine or scissors. In all of this there was an implicit assumption as to the nature of authority, responsibility and obedience, perhaps best exemplified in the rule regarding illness: 'A Sister who has once informed the Prioress of the state of her health may remain perfectly indifferent as to her decision, whether the Doctor is to be called or not. The responsibility is entirely removed from herself and rests entirely with her superior.'

The Rule also made provision for a Chapter of Faults, in which each member must publicly accuse herself of any infraction in front of all her seniors. Penances for such faults might include kissing the feet of a Sister to whom one had been uncharitable, marking a cross with the tongue on the floor for breaking silence, or (*in extremis*) eating a meal in refectory upon one's knees. Humiliation was practised for humility's sake, and 'obedience was preferable to prayer'. The Rule also stipulated that while internal authority was vested in the prioress, ultimate control resided with the bishop of the Western District.

Though some of the articles would be unacceptable today, the overall impression is still that of a document based on counsels of perfection and yet which is compassionate and practical. Bishop Smith's wisdom and prudence come through at every turn: in his reminder of the need for understanding between old and young religious, for example, or his urging that the Sisters preserve their health by a sensible lifestyle, avoiding excessive mortification. It is an impressive work; it might easily have been written for a house of one of the monastic Orders. And this perhaps identifies both its strength and its shortcoming for the purpose. It feels more Benedictine than Franciscan. If we set it alongside the earliest Rules of the Third Order, we can see how 'monastic' it is, and how far removed from the original spirit of Francis.

Bishop Smith completed his manuscript version in February 1851 and posted it to *Propaganda* in March.[24] To have it published and approved was in everyone's interests. For the community itself, it was a prerequisite to its becoming an independent Congregation, it defined the way forward, and by doing so it also acted as a defence against unfair imposition by outsiders. For the Church authorities in Scotland (and thus for Rome), it provided an explicit mandate for control. The Vatican was glad of the proliferation of new and active women's Congregations at this time, which greatly enhanced the work of the Church, but it was wary of nuns on the loose.

With numbers growing, the community was able to begin the pastoral work among the poor that Veronica had always planned. Quite unexpectedly that year, they found themselves in charge of three of the city's parish schools. St Andrew's, St Alphonsus' and St John's had originally been offered to the Sisters of Mercy, who had accepted them and actually moved into the last-named. But when no agreement could be reached regarding evening classes, their Superior withdrew them from all three.[25] The priests of St Andrew's and St John's, and also of St Joseph's in the Cowcaddens, then turned to the Franciscans. Each of these parishes ran both weekday and Sunday schools, with great numbers to be supervised in the one- or two-roomed buildings: some 250 in St John's day school, for instance, and 600 on Sundays in St Andrew's.[26] In addition to their teaching duties, the Sisters accompanied and supervised the children at Sunday Mass, and took responsibility for preparing them for the sacraments. They also worked with the adult parishioners, visiting the sick and instructing would-be converts. At the same time the work at their own Convent school was becoming more demanding, with over seventy pupils now on the roll, including seven boarders.[27]

It might have been wiser to break into the work more gradually, but the community was in the first flush of young growth, the needs were great and the clergy persuasive. The priest of St Joseph's was still deep in debt from his recently completed church, but he had not been deterred from building and equipping a large schoolroom which he was ready to hand over to them. 'All was ready. I could say nothing,' Veronica recalled.[28]

For several years, Scottish schools had been eligible for government grant funding, depending on their passing an inspection for efficiency. The Protestant schools were already being inspected by a team of Her Majesty's Inspectors (HMIs) based in Edinburgh, and could therefore receive grants. But to date no Catholic inspector had been appointed in Scotland, and it was not until 1849 that arrangements were made for the inspection of Catholic schools by an HMI based in England.[29] His arrival was timely for the Sisters. Comparing the girls' schools run by the religious Orders in Scotland with those under lay leadership, he found the contrast striking. He was in no doubt that the former were 'immeasurably superior.'[30]

When travelling to school or visiting the sick the Sisters always went in twos, and the sight of them walking across town from Charlotte Street soon became a familiar one. Since it was illegal to appear in public in a religious habit in Scotland at this date, and it would in any case have been dangerous, they adopted a black habit rather than the Franciscan grey or brown, and when going out they wore it under a special street costume of black widow's cloak and matching straw bonnet. For the same reason they took to tucking their crucifixes and rosaries out of sight under their Franciscan cord. The bonnet was abandoned in 1896 and the cloak adapted soon afterwards,[31] but the tucked-up crucifix and rosary became permanent features of the Congregation's habit, and remained so long after their original purpose was forgotten.

For all their precautions, the fact that they went in twos as well as something about their bearing often gave them away. Youngsters especially were quick to spot them and would run after them shouting 'Nuns! Nuns!'

It was harmless mischief, but some of the adults were less innocent, and it was not uncommon for the Sisters to receive verbal abuse and even physical threats. But they had friends, too, local Catholic residents such as Michael Jeffrey, who knew the routes they travelled and would follow behind at a discreet distance to see them safely home.[32]

In spring 1851 the three-year lease for No. 76 expired and the landlord declined to renew it, having arranged to rent the premises to the city for use as an eye infirmary. Fortunately a property was available for sale at No. 58, which offered them the promise of security for the first time if they could find the means to buy it. Since they knew they would be turned down if they approached the owner openly, they made their offer in the name of their friend Michael Jeffrey. The deal was duly signed, and in May they moved in. But when the owner discovered that the house was being used as a convent he at once sought to cancel. The matter was referred to the court, and 16 July was fixed for the case to be heard.

By chance this was also the date on which the community's eight novices were due to make their first profession and when a further nine postulants were to receive the white veil of the novitiate.[33] The eight had only been novices for about a year, a far shorter term than was normally allowed under Canon Law. But it was desirable and in everyone's interests for the community to have professed Sisters in place as quickly as possible, to enable them to hold a formal Chapter for the purpose of electing leaders and ratifying the recently compiled Rule and Constitutions. Only then would they become an independent Congregation. For this reason, and in view of the particular circumstances of the Catholic Church in Scotland, a special dispensation had been granted to curtail the normal terms of postulancy and novitiate to three months and one year respectively.[34]

On the morning of 16 July the whole community gathered before the two bishops in a packed St Andrew's church. Among the guests were many of high rank, including a number of leading Protestant citizens. It was a historic day. These were the first professions to be made in Scotland for nearly three centuries: no longer would Veronica stand out as the sole black veil among the white. Who could have envisaged such numbers in just two years? The atmosphere was charged. All eyes were on the figures kneeling with lighted candles at the sanctuary steps. Yet now and again some thoughts must have wandered towards events in the courtroom across town. Bishop Smith asked the novices to say a special prayer for a successful outcome at the hearing as they lay prostrate before the altar and at the moment of taking their vows.[35]

Walking home after the ceremony, they had not got as far as Clyde Street when word came that the judge had ruled in their favour. No. 58 was theirs. It was to be theirs for 138 years.

With the security they now enjoyed, and with their fast growing numbers, the decision was taken to extend the house at the rear, despite the debt they had already incurred. Ambitious plans were drawn up for a refectory and common room, cells, cloister, chapel and classrooms. The extensions required the demolition of part of the existing building, and for six months the Sisters lived as best they could, setting down beds in the parlour, the kitchen, the corridors, anywhere they could find a spare corner. As usual they made the chapel their priority and had it ready for the formal opening and blessing in February (1852). The date chosen was the 2nd of the month, the feast of the Purification, since it had become an established practice of the community to hold important events on one of the feasts of Our Lady. The rest of the building was still bare and the plaster damp, but they were keen to move in at once. Charcoal and coke fires were lit in every room and kept alight day and night through the winter and spring until the walls dried out. More than once, untended fires threatened to set the house ablaze as the Sisters slept; what the damp did to their health we can only imagine.[36]

In June the draft Rule was formally approved by Pius IX in an audience with Cardinal Barnabo, prefect of the Congregation *de Propaganda Fide*.[37] During the autumn the Congregation for Religious scrutinised the draft Constitutions and made a number of emendments to them. In November the cardinal wrote to Bishop Murdoch confirming the papal approval of the Rule and listing the required emendments to the Constitutions.[38] Bishop Smith spent the first few weeks of 1853 rewriting the emended sections, and returned them to Rome that spring. The pope gave them his final approval later in the year.[39]

At this time Pius IX was preparing his encyclical *Ineffabilis Deus*, to be published the following year, in which he was to declare the immaculate conception of Mary a doctrine of the Church. In approving the Glasgow community's Rule and Constitutions, he expressed his desire that they should recognise and honour Mary's special place by taking as their name 'the Franciscan Sisters of the Immaculate Conception'. It was a happy choice. As we saw, they already had a special devotion to the Blessed Virgin, using her name as a prefix to their own religious names and choosing her feast days (along with that of St Francis) for important events in their calendar. And who was more apt as a patron than Mary, the medium of the incarnation and the perfect model of that poverty, chastity and obedience upon which their lives were founded?

How should we picture the daily life of these first Sisters? In Tourcoing the people had come to the monastery; here the Sisters went out to the people. It was a new way of doing, to meet a new need, and yet it was as old as the earliest Franciscans. Travelling out to the parishes each morning and returning to their convent in the evening for prayer and meditation, the Sisters were doing just what St Francis' own first Brothers had done. The words of a thirteenth-century witness describe it exactly: 'During the day they go out into the cities and neighbourhoods, giving themselves over to the active life of the apostolate; at night they return to their hermitage or withdraw into solitude to live the contemplative life.'[40]

Their active apostolate, teaching upwards of seventy children in a class and visiting the sick and the dying in the most wretched parts of the city seven days a week, taxed them to the extreme. Their lives in the convent were hardly any easier. Veronica saw to it that they practised the Franciscan poverty of their Rule to the letter. She was herself 'a living Rule', and hers was an austere virtue. She practised poverty relentlessly throughout her long life, and (it is said) would patch and repatch her clothes until nothing remained of the original material. At No. 58 she slept in a box bed in one of the classrooms. While she was in charge, the poverty of the convent was jealously safeguarded.[41] The community lived in solidarity with the poor. More than once their house was broken into, but each time the burglars went away empty-handed, finding nothing to steal.

Thus the evenings brought little comfort or respite from the labours of the day. Indeed, it became increasingly difficult to honour both the daytime work and the requirements of community life. The problem touched on an inherent dilemma: an incompatibility between the apostolic and the monastic life embedded in the Rule itself. It was a monastic Rule for workers in the world. In the years to come, frequent adjustments would be made to the horarium (the set hours for rising and retiring, the Office, meals and recreation) in an attempt to reconcile the two that would never be wholly successful.

Inevitably, the life told on the Sisters' health. In March 1853 the community suffered its first loss with the death of M. Magdalen Mackintosh, the younger sister of M. Aloysius. She was just nineteen and in the first year of her profession. In the 1850s six Sisters were to die, burned out, their average age 22½ years. All bore their lingering illnesses with great patience. The youngest of them was Colette Burnett, who was eighteen, but hers was in fact a special case. She was diagnosed with TB before she ever entered the convent, but was accepted so that she might have her wish of dying in religion. She lived for only a few days after taking her vows.

It was especially at such times that Bishop Smith showed his friendship to the community. He never failed to be present at the Sisters' deathbeds to offer consolation and administer the last rites, and when he purchased land at Dalbeth for a Catholic cemetery in 1853 he gave a plot within it to them. Sister M. Magdalen Mackintosh was the first to be buried in it. Nor was this the only time that he helped the community financially. He also celebrated

Mass in the chapel once or twice a week, as he had done since the day of its opening, and thrice weekly he gave instruction to the novices and postulants.

The steady stream of new recruits continued, and although entries in the *Ledger of Profession Register* show that a number dropped out,[42] others persevered. Nine postulants graduated to the novitiate during the year, and eight who had been novices for the previous year took their vows as professed religious. Despite the hard life, or perhaps because of it, more were seeking to be admitted than the convent was prepared to take. It would have been tempting to accept them all, for the work was growing daily. The school rolls were rising every year,[43] and the numbers of children to be prepared for First Communion and Confirmation – some 500 annually – were really too great to cope with. But Veronica was determined to move forward slowly, and to set the highest standards for admission. She wanted to avoid more dropouts. Perhaps, also, she foresaw the potential for disharmony where all were so young, inexperienced and culturally diverse, hailing as they did from Ireland, France and Belgium, the Western Highlands, the north-east, Gibraltar and the Caribbean. Above all, as she herself explained, she was determined to 'safeguard the true religious spirit' as she and Adélaide had always envisaged it.[44]

The Sisters were a new phenomenon in Glasgow, and they made a deep impression. As Veronica recalled, it was not only the Catholics who were attracted by them. 'The community made a great bruit,' she wrote. 'Even Protestants came to see us, and though on arrival they had strange ideas as to our way of life, they departed changed and quite happy.'[45] They arrived curious, and went away impressed. People could not but see the Sisters' transparent and winning goodness, and many hearts warmed to it.

Early in 1854 Veronica received a request from Fr William Dawson, the priest of St Mary's Inverness, for Sisters to work in his parish. There was only a small congregation in the town, with little money and a large debt, and Fr Dawson had nothing to offer them but a house in Huntly Street for use as their convent. Four Sisters agreed to go. Veronica travelled with them and helped them to move in, staying on to see them properly settled. She appointed as Superior Sister M. Angela McSwiney, and arranged for the Blessed Sacrament to be reserved in the house. Judging that this, as it were, sealed their permanent arrival, she felt she could safely return to Glasgow.

Following the example of the mother house, the new community opened a fee-paying school in the convent in order to pay their way. Two of the Sisters were engaged as teachers in the parish school, which had opened twelve years before and served, in addition to the native children, the many permanent settlers from the Highlands and Islands and the large numbers of Highland families who wintered in the town.[46] The building was cramped and uncomfortable, 'a regular patch-up affair', as Fr Dawson himself admitted.[47] The community also took on the now familiar parish duties, visiting the sick, giving instruction in the faith, and preparing the children for the sacraments. It was an apostolate that was to continue for over eighty years in the town and provide a blueprint for every future branch house.

That July the Congregation held their first General Chapter. According to the Rule, Chapters were to be held every three years, and only Choir Sisters professed for three years or more were entitled to participate in them. Had it been strictly applied, therefore, only the eight who had taken their vows in July 1851 should have been eligible for this first Chapter. But on Bishop Murdoch's authority this section of the Rule was waived, allowing the five professed in 1852 and even the seven from 1853 to be included. It was important that the Chapter be seen to represent the Congregation as a whole, and with twenty Sisters entitled to speak and vote it could fairly be said to do so.

The first item on the agenda was the election of office bearers. The Rule required the election of a prioress, sub-prioress and three discreets for a term of three years, the five to comprise the Council, the decision-making body of the Congregation between Chapters. Its recommendation that all be five years or more professed could obviously not be applied in this case.[48] The votes were cast in the presence of the bishop. Sr Veronica was unanimously elected prioress, Sr M. Aloysius Mackintosh sub-prioress, and Srs M. Hyanintha Condon, M. Catherine McSwiney and M. Francis Marchand councillors.[49]

The second item was the adoption of the Rule and Constitutions as emended by Rome. This was in fact a formality, since the Congregation had been following them since their final approval the previous year. The last item concerned a revision of the 'Customs' (day-to-day activities) of the community. This was necessary since those in use hitherto had been inherited from Tourcoing, and some were clearly unsuited to the situation in Scotland. The Chapter drew up a revised list and gave a copy to Bishop Smith along with the Rule and Constitutions, for printing.

The bishop first had the Rule printed on the Church's own press. He then used a copy of it to make a 'scissors and paste' working copy of the full document, by cutting out each separate rule, sticking it into a blank notebook, and hand-writing beneath it those articles of the Constitutions that applied to it.[50] Early in 1855 he had the whole document printed, for distribution to the communities in Glasgow and Inverness.[51] Finally, he himself made a manuscript copy and appended to it the list of Customs drawn up at the Chapter, with additional mini-Rules for particular activities such as work in the parish schools and recitation of the Office.[52] All were written in his elegant hand, all showed his good sense, care and pastoral experience, and all broadened the scope of his control.

In every way, the Congregation could now feel itself well established – properly constituted, approved by Rome, supported and firmly guided by the Church authorities at home. The candle had remained alight. The pattern of its work in Glasgow had been set, and a first branch house had been successfully opened elsewhere. It was time to spread the flame further.

ENDNOTES TO CHAPTER ONE

1 This according to Véronique's own written account, Tourcoing Archives, copy extract in translation, 011, AF.

2 *Ibid.*

3 He left at the end of March – cf. Bishop Smith to Bishop Murdoch, 30.3.1848, OL 2/75/6, SCA.

4 Cf. 'Rule for Parlour Boarders in the Convent of the Immaculate Conception Glasgow', 012.2, AF, n.d. Though the Rules were not codified until a later date they were applied *de facto* from the outset.

5 The priests were Frs Daniel Kenny in Houston, William Welsh in Coatbridge, John Bremner in Paisley and Richard Sinnott in Greenock (deaths between 13.1.1847 and 19.8.1847); see *SCD*, 1848, Obit list p. 91, and details of priests' careers, p. 106ff. They were all described as dying of 'typhoid fever', but it is not clear that the two diseases were distinguished at this date, and in any case both are spread by insanitary conditions. Fr Peter Keenan had also died of typhus in Greenock in the summer of 1843. A further fourteen priests were to die of typhus in Scotland before the end of the century, in addition to one who died of cholera and another of typhoid fever; cf. clergy lists in Johnson C., 1989J (a) and (b).

6 Maver I, 2000, p. 85. Re Bishop Murdoch visiting the dying, *Glasgow Herald*, 1.1.1849.

7 Description based upon an account of the graveyard at the foot of Abercromby Street in *Glasgow Herald*, 6.1.1849.

8 Based on Véronique's own written account, *loc. cit.*

9 Recounted by her confessor the Dean of Merville to the Superior at Tourcoing – Tourcoing Archives.

10 Her diary states that the school was 'taken from us' – written account, *loc. cit.*; and Bishop Alexander Smith, *Statement*, n.d. (c. 1850), 300–2.5, MIA.

11 Veronica, written account, *loc. cit.*

12 Bishop Alexander Smith, *loc. cit.*

13 The Order had been founded by Catherine McCauley in 1831 and its Rule approved by Pope Gregory XVI in 1835, with final confirmation in June 1841. Because of the freedom to mix in secular society allowed by their Rule they became known as 'the walking nuns'. Cf. King M.I., n.d., and Anon, *The Sisters*

of Mercy in Glasgow 1849–1976, 1976. Ms S. K. Kehoe's PhD thesis, Glasgow
University (2002), covers the early years of the Order in the West of Scotland.
See also Kehoe S. K., 2005 J.

14 In 1849 six of the eleven priests working in Glasgow were Irish-born. Of the
rest, two hailed from the north-east, one from Glasgow, and one from the
Western Highlands – Johnson C., *loc. cit.*

15 Congregation of the Franciscan Sisters of the Immaculate Conception, *Annals*,
anno 1849, 011, AF; the account of the early years based largely on the
personal memories of Mlle Marchand.

16 Miss Mary Margaret Brewster to Mrs Kyle, 13.10.1849, quoting verbatim
from Bishop Murdoch's letter to her (12.10.1849) that 'other two French nuns
have been sent for so that the commencement of community may be formed' –
copy of letter in possession of Hannah McCarthy, Saint John, New Brunswick.
In fact it was more than 2½ years before the first two, Julie Dalle and Damacine
Dulette, arrived. They were received in autumn 1852 and took the religious
names M. Philomena and M. Helen. Two years later, three more arrived:
Catherine Douelle, Laurente Charlet and Victoire Noël, *Register, Professions
and Receptions*, vol 1, AF.

17 *Ibid.*

18 Terms per quarter: boarders £4/10/- plus 10/- for washing; day scholars 10/6
for the full curriculum; French, Italian, drawing and music were extras; special
terms for two or more from the same family – Advertisements, *SCD*, 1850, p.
122.

19 Miss Mary Margaret Brewster to Mrs Kyle, 29.12.1849.

20 *Register, Professions and Receptions*, vol. 1, nos. 2, 3, 4. Details of the ceremony
based on *Glasgow Herald*, 12.4.1850.

21 *Register, Professions and Receptions*, vol. 1, nos. 5–9. The other two received
into the novitiate were Mary Robertson and Ellen Barry. The dates of the two
ceremonies were 8.5.1850 and 9.7.1850. Customarily in the Congregation,
religious names were always preceded by 'Mary' and normally written 'M.
Francis', etc. This style is frequently used in this book from now on. In recent
years the prefix 'M.' has been dropped.

22 Rule and Constitutions, 1867, *Decretum*, Cardinal Barnabo, p. 164ff., copy
RO8/25, AGA.

23 Veronica's notes in *A Tribute of Affection*, 1947 (Tourcoing), (based on written
notes and personal reminiscences, correspondence and eye-witness accounts),
011, AF, p. 24.

24 Rule (no title), countersigned by Bishop Murdoch, 7.3.1851, with Letter of
Application (in Italian), 19.3.1851, 031.30, AF. The Sacred Congregation *de
Propaganda Fide*, commonly referred to as '*Propaganda*', had been founded in
1622 as the Catholic Church's official Congregation for the regulation of its
ecclesiastical affairs in 'mission countries', i.e., those parts of the world that
were either non-Christian or predominantly Protestant. In such places the
Church was not organised through local hierarchies, but through local vicars
apostolic under *Propaganda*'s direct control.

25 Bishop Alexander Smith, *loc. cit.*

26 *SCD*, 1851, p. 88, table of Catholic schools in the city; re numbers also *SCD*, 1852, p. 95ff. The Sisters also took over St Alphonsus' Girls' school in 1852.

27 Account of the first years of the Congregation, *SCD*, 1851, p. 119.

28 Veronica's notes, in *Tribute*, 011, AF, p. 16.

29 The Catholic Church had formed a Catholic Poor Schools Committee in 1847 to negotiate with the government for its share of available funding. The first grant paid to a Catholic school in Scotland was in 1851. Cf. Skinnider, Sr M. in Bone T.R. (ed.), 1967, p. 16; and Bone T.R., 1968, pp. 20ff. and 41.

30 Parliamentary Papers – *General Report for the Year 1850 by HMIS T.W.M. Marshall on the RC Schools in Great Britain*, in *Accounts and Papers*, vol. 14 *Education – Committee of Council*, session Feb to Aug 1851, vol. xliv, London 1851, p. 673ff.

31 Notes of 1896 Chapter, Register of Elections, 16.7.1896, 028.2, AF. The cloak was replaced with a long circular one sometime between the 1902 and 1908 Chapters.

32 Veronica's memories, in 'Tourcoing Archives'; re Michael Jeffrey – *Obituary Register*, Benefactors, AF.

33 The nine received into the novitiate were M. Clare Cattanach, M. Stanislaus McAuliffe, M. Magdalen Mackintosh, M. Margaret Gatherer, M. Bonaventure O'Callaghan and Srs Agatha and Anne Sullivan. The surname of Srs Angela and Catherine is spelled variously in the Congregation's records, but according to Sr Angela's own signature the correct spelling, which I use, is 'McSwiney'. I similarly follow Sr Aloysius' signature for the spelling of 'Mackintosh'.

34 Rev. A. Grant to Bishop Murdoch, Rome 31.7.1851, OL 2/80/13, SCA.

35 Account based on *Annals*, 1851, 011, AF; and Council Minutes, 034.10, AF, p. 1.

36 *Annals 1846–61*, 011, AF.

37 Cardinal Barnabo, *Rescript*, 1852 (original in Latin, English translation), 031.30, AF. The delay was caused by the fact that neither Rome nor Glasgow could find documentary evidence to substantiate the claim that the existing Tourcoing Constitutions had been drawn up by an archbishop of Cambrai.

38 Copy of letter Cardinal Barnabo to Bishop Murdoch, 24.11.1852, appended to *Rules and Constitutions*, 1855, 031.2, AF, p. 129ff.

39 *Rule of the Community . . . as revised and modified by the Sacred Congregation of Bishops and Regulars at Rome, and approved by his Holiness Pius IX, AD 1853*, 031.30, AF.

40 Bishop Jacques de Vitry, 1216.

41 Based on 'Tourcoing Archives', memories of Veronica by members of the community, and her own notes, in *Tribute*, p. 16ff.

42 *Ledger of Profession Register*, vol. 1, 1850–1866, AF, lists seventeen Sisters who left without making their final profession or were excluded *re infecta*.

43 There were, for instance, 156 girls in the day school at St Alphonsus', and 500 in the Sunday school; 180 girls (day) and no less than 900 (Sunday) attending St Andrew's; cf. *SCD*, 1853–4.

44 Veronica's notes in 'Tourcoing Archives'.

45 *Ibid.*

46 Council Minutes, 1854–1872, 034.10, AF, no. 1, p. 2; Letter Rev. Angus McKenzie to Bishop Scott, 31.1.1842, OL, SCA.

47 Reports on the Missions of the Northern District, vol. iii, Inverness, Rev. W. Dawson, 1868, SM 9/2/3, SCA.

48 *Rule and Constitutions*, 1853, Rules 2 and 3.

49 Election of the prioress and sub-prioress required a percentage majority, that of councillors a simple majority. Councillors were elected 1st, 2nd and 3rd according to the number of votes cast for them on a first or subsequent ballots. Some sources refer to Sr Mackintosh as 'Aloysia', but according to *Register, Receptions and Professions*, vol. 1, p. 6 she was professed as 'Aloysius'.

50 'Rule and Constitutions written by our Dear Departed Father the Rt Revd Dr Smith, Glasgow 1855', 031.2, AF.

51 *Rule of the Community, etc.*, printed 1855 at the Episcopal Press, 031.30, AF.

52 *Rule of the Community, etc.*, MS, 1855, 031.30, AF.

CHAPTER TWO

The Flame Spreads (1856–1878)

Several of the parishes that had opened in Glasgow since the arrival of the Sisters[1] were now erecting new schools to replace the cramped old buildings that had been in use for decades. Most were built on tight budgets, and were utilitarian in design and workmanship. But not so the new school opened for St Andrew's parish in Greendyke Street in May 1856. Serving the poorest area of the city, it had been built with money collected by Fr John Gray on a fundraising tour in America and was quite the finest school building belonging to the Church anywhere in Scotland. Designed in the Early Tudor style, it stood two stories high and could accommodate 1,000 children. The girls' school was upstairs and mainly comprised a single large room, which doubled as a hall said to be the largest in Glasgow outside the City Hall itself. On the front wall was a striking oriel window and a sculpture of globe, books and ship symbolising the world, learning and commerce, with an inscription in gold Gothic letters: '*Religioni ac Bonis Artibus*'. The property stood as a statement that the Catholic community could compete with the best. A separate building next door accommodated 300 infants. The Sisters were invited to assume charge of the new girls' and infants' schools,[2] giving them a responsibility for 400 in the daytime, 200 in the evenings, and no less than 1,000 at Sunday catechism.

Officially there was no free education in Scotland at this date, though fees were often covered in cases of need through trusts, endowments and parish levies. The Catholic schools of Glasgow had little such income, but made every effort to keep fees to a minimum since the families they served were among the poorest in the community. Official figures show that they were in fact noticeably cheaper than other city schools,[3] and there is no doubt that the Franciscan schools in the inner city kept fees as low as anywhere. But they still contrived to maintain respectable standards, notably higher according to the inspectors' reports than the corresponding boys' schools which were taught by lay staff.[4] St John's Girls' school in the Gorbals was judged to have made more progress than any other school in the city, while even St Joseph's in the Cowcaddens, in probably the worst premises of all, made the very best of itself 'under the active superintendence of its devoted mistress'.[5]

Their 'night' schools served the needs of girls from twelve and upwards who were in daytime employment. The dedication of these young people, their perseverance and commitment to education in the midst of poverty and indifference, merit huge respect. They certainly left a lasting impression on one government inspector up from England at this time. He would never forget, he reported, leaving the muddy city street and entering a room crowded with mill-girls, heads down at their books. They had just finished a long day-shift, and instead of spending their few free hours at leisure they had gone home, washed and dressed, and come straight out again to night school. And when the lesson ended, every one of them made her way to the church next door for night prayers and devotions.[6]

These devout and dedicated girls were tough and well able to look after themselves, and at the end of the evening a small group of them would wait to escort the Sisters back to Charlotte Street. They looked out for them because they looked up to them. They respected them for what they were doing, and recognised their dedication and courage. They knew that they were willing to do things and go to places almost unheard of for 'respectable' women at this time.

In spring 1856 Fr John Sutherland appealed to the Congregation to open a branch house in his parish of St Joseph's Aberdeen and to provide schooling for local girls. He was prepared to offer them a building in Constitution Street and every other necessity for their convent, and to pay their maintenance at a rate of £20 annually per Choir Sister and half that sum for Lay Sisters. The Council agreed to his terms and arranged to transfer Sr M. Angela McSwiney from Inverness to be superioress of the house. The community of five moved in in July, and that year opened a parish middle school for girls in the convent building and an infants' school in Chapel Court nearby,[7] and also took over an existing private school in the town.

Although Veronica had been unanimously elected prioress, there were now signs of a faction within the community that was critical of her régime. The clique centred around Sr M.Aloysius Mackintosh, who was apparently trying to use her friendship with Bishop Smith to turn him against Veronica. The problem seems to have started shortly after the General Chapter of 1854. The bishop had not forgotten Veronica's disagreement with him over certain items of the Constitutions. Determined to ensure that his own vision of the Congregation would prevail, he instructed that the formation of new recruits should be taken out of her hands and given to a separate novice mistress. She proposed Sr Angela McSwiney for the post, but he overruled her and insisted on appointing Sr Aloysius.[8]

Once in post, it was not long before she clashed with her prioress, accusing her of reprimanding her charges unnecessarily over some minor acts of negligence. She then took the matter to the bishop. The following day Veronica received a letter from him instructing her to apologise to the novices. He informed her that he could no longer give her absolution, and that he would be visiting the convent to hear the Sisters' grievances against her. Before she had the opportunity to carry out his order, a number of the community came to assure her that she had acted properly and that it would be wrong and harmful to the Congregation for her to go on her knees to the novices. They then met Bishop Smith and managed to persuade him in her favour, to the extent that he offered to resign as the community's guardian and confessor.

Sr Aloysius' personal ambition undoubtedly played a part in the dispute. A woman of strong personality and persuasive eloquence, she also had a tendency to intrigue and was not above using her talents to that end.[9] She very possibly had her eye on Veronica's post. On the other hand, there may well have been some substance in her accusation. Veronica's greatest admirers concede a certain inflexibility in her make-up, 'following the Rule to the letter with even a kind of rigidity in the observance, wishing others to have a similar exactness, and not easily forgiving small weaknesses of nature'.[10] There was sometimes as much of Cornelius Jansen as of St Francis in her spirituality, and there was perhaps not an abundance of laughter at the convent in her time. As she told one of the Sisters: 'The religious life is something serious; it is no laughing matter to be a Religious.' For the novices there may have been a certain rueful truth in the well-known definition of a martyr as someone who has to live with a saint. She could be inflexible in non-spiritual matters too: so for example, when Sr Paula Charlet joined the convent as a seventeen-year-old novice from Tourcoing, she forbade her from ever speaking French even to her fellow countrywomen, though it was easy to see that the girl was desperately homesick.[11]

Whatever the case, Veronica very understandably felt that her position had been undermined by Bishop Smith's intervention, and on the advice of her new confessor she tendered her resignation at the next Council meeting. Sr Aloysius also resigned as sub-prioress, as did the councillors and even the headmistress of the school.[12] According to the Constitutions, elections had now to be held to replace them, pending permanent appointments at the next Chapter. In view of the delicacy of the situation it was decided that voting for the office of prioress should take place confidentially by individual letter to Bishop Smith, and that he would appoint to the other positions himself. The outcome was that the community bypassed Sr M. Aloysius, electing Sr M. Angela McSwiney as their new prioress. At thirty-seven she was the oldest in the community, two years older than Veronica herself, and was obviously chosen to steady the ship. Her younger sister, M. Catherine, was appointed sub-prioress, with Hyacintha Condon, Francis Marchand and Clare Cattanach appointed as councillors.

The new positions were ratified at the Chapter the following summer.[13] In overlooking Sr Aloysius the members perhaps already saw in her the early signs of the imbalance of mind that within a year would force her to leave Glasgow and seek recovery in a convent in Viterbo that treated mental illness. The damage that she had already done among the impressionable young community we can only guess at.

Veronica now held no post of authority in the Congregation. It was a delicate situation, for she still carried a moral authority among most of the Sisters, while others were still bearing complaints against her to the bishop. She kept silent about it, but in her heart she knew that there was no longer a future for her in Glasgow and that she must look elsewhere. She loved the city where she had fought so hard to stay. But leaving was necessary for her and, even more important, for the Congregation: only thus could its wounds heal. Her own hopes seemed to have been dashed once again, and her vocation thwarted. But before the year was out she would be able to see the whole unsavoury episode as providential.

Christianity had first come to Jamaica with the Franciscan missionaries in the early sixteenth century, and the Church had flourished there for a hundred and fifty years. But following the annexation of the island by the British in 1655, Catholicism was outlawed. Not until 1792 was a Catholic priest permitted to enter the country; and only in 1837 was its first Vicar Apostolic appointed. By now there was a sizeable Catholic community in Kingston and elsewhere, mainly of Hispanic or French origin.

In 1855 James Dupeyron SJ succeeded as Vicar Apostolic. One of his first acts was to engage an English Jesuit, Fr Joseph Howell, as parish priest in Kingston. This was a time of new religious foundations in the Americas, and the two men recognised the benefits for the Church if they could attract a women's teaching Order to the island where there was as yet no Catholic school for girls.

Before coming to Jamaica, Fr Howell had been on the teaching staff at Stonyhurst, where one of his colleagues was Thomas Meyrick. The two men had been ordained in the same year and were close friends. The Society of Jesus had recently opened a house in Glasgow, just across the road from No. 58 Charlotte Street. In the winter of 1851–2 Fr Meyrick had spent his school holiday at the Glasgow house, and while there he was asked to stand witness at the clothing ceremony of three novices of the Franciscan convent on New Year's Day. On his return to Lancashire he would certainly have told his friend about the Glasgow Sisters and their fast-growing community.

In July 1854 Fr Howell himself visited Glasgow to act as a witness at the inaugural Council of the Jesuit house.[14] His stay coincided with the Sisters' own first Chapter, at which he was appointed second witness.[15] He spent two full days with the Congregation and discussed their work with both Mother Veronica and the bishop.

When he arrived in Jamaica the following year and the question of a teaching Congregation for the island was being aired, he no doubt recommended the Sisters to the Vicar Apostolic. He wrote to Veronica several times between 1855–7 begging for recruits,[16] and probably also contacted his Jesuit colleagues in Glasgow and asked them to sound her out. Now his letters offered her a lifeline. She did not take long to decide that if she could persuade enough Sisters to accompany her, she would go.

She found three willing to try the adventure: Sr M. Paula Charlet, the girl who had come to Glasgow from Tourcoing in 1851; Sr M. de Sales O'Neill, just one year professed; and twenty-six year old Philomena Dalle, a Lay Sister.[17] They were in truth a young and wide-eyed party to be starting a new Congregation. Veronica herself, though about to be a foundress twice over, was still only thirty-six.

That summer they made their preparations. Several Glasgow shop-keepers donated provisions, and one who ran a bookshop close to Charlotte Street and had previously gifted schoolbooks to the convent presented Veronica with a case of useful items for their new life.[18] The prioress gave them a small travelling allowance from the community funds.

Veronica left Glasgow knowing that the Congregation she had founded was firmly established and, with some forty Sisters now professed, would certainly survive. With her young companions she took the chaise to Liverpool from where their ship was to sail, in her last-ever journey on British soil retracing in reverse the first journey that she had made ten years before.

We know nothing of the month-long voyage, or of the weather in the Atlantic that autumn. But it is recorded that when the travellers at last set foot on Jamaican soil on 5 November they had just 2/6 (12½p) left between them.[19]

The Catholic community had been informed of their imminent arrival, and one of its most prominent members, Henri Vendreyes, offered them his house in Kingston's East Queen Street for as long as they wished to use it. There was accommodation for themselves and room to spare, and having it enabled them to start their work at once. In January 1858 they opened a day and boarding school in the building, and soon afterwards a Sunday club for local girls.

For the Catholic community their coming was like a vacuum that had been waiting to be filled, and within weeks a number of women sought to be admitted to the convent as postulants. All were of French background. Caroline and Josephine d'Aquin were daughters of one of the wealthiest traders in Kingston, Henri d'Aquin, who could trace his ancestry to the family of Thomas Aquinas. Élise Branday stood out from the others, for she was already sixty. Though attracted to the religious life as a young woman, she had been tied to Jamaica nursing her sick mother, but she had made a promise that if an Order ever came to the island in her later life she would apply to join it. Young Henriette Duverger was a victim of polio, deformed in her limbs, and at first Veronica turned her down, fearing that she would not cope with the rigorous life. It was customary for aspirants to donate whatever they could afford to the Congregation upon their reception as postulants, by way of a 'dowry' (so named because they were to become brides of Christ). The sum that Mlle Duverger offered was impossible to refuse. Apparently it was large enough to pay for the house in Duke Street that the community purchased that summer as their permanent home.[20]

The new house was just as one imagines a Victorian convent in the Caribbean. It was an elegant detached villa of red brick in a street of similar residences, with lawns at the rear, across which the black-clad Sisters moved silently amidst the heady fragrance of shrubs – crepe-myrtle, oleander, Martinique rose, frangipanni and japonica. At the foot of the garden, beside the high weathered wall topped with bottle glass, a great mango tree stood tall against the Jamaican sky and cast a welcome shade.[21]

As soon as they were able, the Sisters had several more buildings erected in the grounds as an extension to the school, and one of them they used as a single-room free school for the children of the poor. Their hope eventually was to acquire a country house within striking distance of the capital, for use by the community and their boarding pupils during school holidays. And in 1859, quite unexpectedly, the opportunity to do so presented itself. Marengo Park, a property with twenty-five acres of land in the country yet only two miles from Duke Street, came on the market for £600. It was of course quite beyond their means and not to be given a second thought. But Henri d'Aquin knew of their long-term plans from his daughters Caroline and Josephine, who were now novices in the community. It is said that he sold two wharves on the Kingston waterfront to raise the cash, and once he had secured the estate he approached Veronica and asked her if she could make use of it. It was a wonderful act of generosity and affection. She accepted the gift, and changed the name on the gate to 'Mount Alvernia'. It was a name that meant a great deal to Franciscans but nothing to the people of Kingston, who preferred to call it simply 'the Nuns' Pen'.

Elizabeth Lockhart was born in Oxford in 1811, the daughter of an Anglican vicar. Educated by a private tutor, she later qualified as a teacher. In her early twenties she befriended Archdeacon Henry Manning, and with

A Canticle of Love

his encouragement opened a Church of England school in Chichester. From a young age she had been drawn to the religious life, and in 1848 she was invited to become Superior of an Anglican teaching institute, the Sisters of St Mary the Virgin. It was the height of the Oxford Movement in England. Her younger brother William had already converted to Catholicism under Newman at Littlemore, and in 1850 she followed him into the Church. Two years later she joined the Sisters of Charity of the Precious Blood, a new Congregation being established in Greenwich, where because of her talents and experience she was at once appointed Superior.

Manning had himself converted the previous year and was subsequently ordained into the Catholic priesthood and given charge of St Mary of the Angels in Bayswater, London. There he saw a great need for a women's teaching Congregation to educate the poor of the parish. In 1857, at his invitation, the Sisters of Charity of the Precious Blood moved to Bayswater and took over the girls' school. They were as yet following no approved Rule. Being himself an admirer of St Francis and a member of the Secular Third Order he advised Sr M. Elizabeth to seek affiliation with a Congregation of the Third Order Regular.[22]

That year he visited Inverness, where he called in at the convent, saw the work of the Sisters and heard from them in detail about the mother house in Glasgow. This seemed like the ideal solution for his Sisters, and on his return to London they agreed that he should make a formal request to the Scottish Congregation on their behalf. The Council in Charlotte Street accepted his request in principle[23] and invited Sr Elizabeth and her assistant Sr Francis Burton to spend some time living as novices in the community, so that both parties could be certain of their desire for affiliation.

The two Sisters travelled north in September 1858, stayed seven weeks, and received the habit from Bishop Smith on 26 October.[24] They then returned to London in the company of one of the Charlotte Street Sisters, M. Gertrude Foley, whom Council had appointed Superior of the Bayswater convent. The choice was not a happy one. The community at Bayswater were mature, well-educated women, most of them members of the English upper-middle class, and this was a second novitiate for them. The person appointed over them was a twenty-two year old Irish girl, younger and of less learning than they. It was a delicate situation that demanded tact. But Sr Gertrude's rule was strict and at times petty, and her frequent unfavourable comparisons between the Bayswater and the Glasgow communities upset everyone. It seems that she had already been something of a disruptive influence in Charlotte Street,[25] and it is possible that she was chosen for Bayswater to relieve Glasgow of her: if so, it was a most irresponsible choice.

Fortunately, her reign was brief. When in mid-November eight more of the Bayswater community took the novice's habit, three of them (along with two postulants) opted to pursue their novitiate in Glasgow, and Sr Gertrude returned with them. She was replaced as Superior by Sr M. Margaret Gatherer, the Glasgow community's first ever parlour boarder.[26]

One of the postulants at Bayswater at this time was Elizabeth Hayes. Her background was strikingly similar to that of Sr Elizabeth Lockhart. Like her, she was the daughter of an Anglican clergyman, privately educated and trained as a teacher; like her she had been drawn to the religious life by a leading member of the Oxford Movement. The two women had met at Wantage, and Elizabeth Hayes had taken over the Anglican school there in 1850 when Sr Elizabeth converted to Catholicism. Soon afterwards she joined the Sisterhood there, and was consecrated abbess in 1855. When the following year she herself decided to convert she went to live as a paying guest in the convent of Sr Elizabeth's Sisters of Charity of the Precious Blood at Greenwich. And when the community removed to Bayswater in 1857, she followed them there and entered the convent as a postulant.[27]

She received the habit in November 1858 in the presence of Fr Manning, taking the religious name M. Ignatius. The following day she set out for Glasgow.

She chose the Scottish community because of her long-held desire to serve the poor in the foreign missions. She knew of the Congregation's recent foundation in Jamaica, and saw Glasgow as her way in. Immediately upon arrival she wrote to Bishop Smith telling him of her hopes, and was encouraged by his reply. He was able to tell her that he had written to the Jamaica community and 'half promised' her to them, though he had not identified her by name.

The new novice found the life in Glasgow very taxing. She took her share in the schools by day and in the evenings, often not returning until 9.30 p.m.. Somehow the Office had then to be fitted in, as well as domestic duties – mending vestments, or scouring cutlery in the kitchen. She found the régime restricting, and Sr M. Catherine McSwiney, her novice mistress, often petty. When her health threatened to break, the doctor instructed that she must not be allowed out in the night air, but that very evening (a particularly foggy one) Sr Catherine ordered her to attend night school as usual, as a test of her obedience.[28]

Bishop Smith wrote to her again in July, advising her not to reveal her plans to the Sisters at Charlotte Street; the life in the convent in Jamaica was more comfortable, he explained, with better food, easier pupils, and little teaching or charity work among the poor, and if the Glasgow community heard that she was using them as a stepping stone they might well vote against her final profession. He had also learned that Sr M. Catherine had ordered her to destroy his letters, and he was furious, assuring her that she was under no obligation whatever to obey.[29]

By now the novices who had remained in Bayswater had completed their novitiate and taken their final profession. Her task over, Sr M. Margaret Gatherer returned to Glasgow, and by mutual consent the Bayswater community was made an 'independent house'.[30]

Sr Ignatius' novitiate was also close to completion and her final profession due in November. Despite Bishop Smith's advice she decided to inform the prioress of her plans, so that she could go into the ceremony without false pretences. Sr M. Angela naturally discussed the matter with Council at their monthly meeting in October, and explained that the novice had the bishop's support. Council unanimously voted their approval of her profession.

The ceremony took place on 26 November in the presence of Bishop Murdoch.[31] With his permission, Sr Ignatius added to her three vows of poverty, chastity and obedience a fourth, that she would devote her life to work in the foreign missions.[32] The bishop then transferred her vows to the Vicar Apostolic of Jamaica, and the prioress delegated authority over her to Mother Veronica as Superior of the Jamaican community. In December she crossed the Atlantic on board the *Atrah*, carrying their letters with her.

That same month Sr M. Annunciata Roberts, one of the Sisters who had come to Glasgow from Bayswater, left the community in the company of a novice and a postulant to establish a convent in Exeter. The following February Sr Gertrude Foley joined them. According to the Council she had been showing 'evident signs of discontent' for some time. Returning her vows to her, they decided that 'neither she nor any other Sister who would voluntarily separate herself from the parent community should ever be allowed to return to it'. Bishop Smith, as the Congregation's ecclesiastical director, sanctioned the decision,[33] which would have far-reaching implications, immediately and in the years to come.

On 15 June 1861 Bishop Smith died at the age of forty-eight. His passing was widely mourned by people of every class and denomination, for he was loved for his humility, compassion and loving concern for all. For the Sisters it was a shattering blow. As the death notice in their *Obituary Book* stated, it left a void in their community that would be hard indeed to fill; the lengthy encomium appended to the notice was a mixture of deep gratitude and sadness. Council instructed that the *De Profundis* be recited for their 'beloved and revered Father and Founder' thrice daily for a year and daily thereafter in perpetuity. It was a promise that the Glasgow community has kept to this day.

Fr John Gray succeeded him as coadjutor bishop. He was already well known to the Congregation, having acted as secretary at their first Chapter in 1854. Inheriting his predecessor's mantle as their ecclesiastical director, he inherited also his dedication to them, and for the next ten years he would fill as well as anyone could the void Bishop Smith's death had left.[34]

In May of the same year a much-loved young Sister, M. Magdaline

Maguire, who had been Adélaide's first ever school pupil, left to join the Exeter convent. Almost at soon as she arrived, her health broke. Sick, unhappy and far from home, she asked to be readmitted to Charlotte Street. But fearing that to accede would set a dangerous precedent, Council voted to uphold their recent decision as binding on all.[35]

By now disharmony reigned in the Exeter community. Much of it centred on Sr Gertrude Foley, and that autumn the superioress (whose considerable personal wealth was at the convent's disposal) incredibly offered Charlotte Street £1,000 to take her back. Council unanimously rejected the offer, resolving that 'on no account' would they ever readmit her. By now it was clear that Sr M. Magdaline was dying, and again she pled, as her last wish, to be allowed to die in the Glasgow house. The matter was put to the full Chapter, who voted to take her back as an act of mercy.[36] She was readmitted on Christmas Eve, and died three weeks later. In 1862 the Exeter community was disbanded on the orders of the local bishop, and Srs Gertrude and Annunciata entered the Franciscan convent in Taunton.

In June 1863 Sr Aloysius Mackintosh returned from Italy, her health apparently restored, and sought readmittance into Charlotte Street. Council were opposed to accepting her, but were forced to do so on the express order of Bishop Gray. For the Congregation it was like a test case, and demonstrated all too clearly that the decisions of Council counted for little when they clashed with the wishes of bishops. Sr Aloysius obviously still had supporters in the community, for later that same month, quite incredibly, she was elected prioress by a huge majority on the first ballot, ahead of two longstanding councillors.[37]

In summer 1863, the Jamaican capital was full of disease, and in July Mother Veronica fell prey to a severe case of blood poisoning. She tried to throw it off by leaving the heat of the city, but after two months in the mountains it had only worsened. Her doctor warned her that she would never make a lasting recovery in Jamaica and that her only hope was to return to Europe.

She therefore wrote to the abbess at Tourcoing requesting a refuge there, stressing that it would only be for the duration of her illness and that she intended to return to Jamaica as soon as her health permitted.[38] In view of the doctor's diagnosis, we do not know if this was in fact her firm intention: perhaps she really was determined to return to Kingston, whatever the risk; but it is possible that she thought a request for temporary refuge at Tourcoing would stand more chance of success than asking at once to be readmitted permanently. She must have remembered the condition under which she and Adélaide had left in 1847, that once their new Congregation was founded there would be no going back.

She may also have been aware of Glasgow's ruling on readmissions, and the recent Sr Gertrude test case. There is no evidence in the Glasgow archives that she applied for readmission there and was refused, as has sometimes been asserted,[39] and certainly had she done so the request would have been raised in Council and recorded. It seems in fact that Tourcoing, her first house, was her preferred choice to be her last.

Armed with a letter of recommendation from the Jamaican Vicar Apostolic,[40] she set sail in late September and arrived at Tourcoing a month later in a state of utter exhaustion. She was received into the convent, though not with unanimous approval, and ordered to bed at once. She remained convalescing and more or less confined to her room for a full year.

When the Congregation had taken over the orphanage in Abercromby Street from the Sisters of Mercy in 1860, the institution was still fulfilling its original function. But with the passing of the Industrial Schools Act the following year, its circumstances changed. In 1862 it was officially registered as an industrial school[41] and began to take in vagrant children as well as orphans, receiving an annual grant of 5/– for each one referred by a magistrate.[42] Under the Act the Sisters were required to provide the girls with vocational training for domestic service. Children could now be referred to them from anywhere in Scotland. The immediate effect of these changes was to double the number of girls on the roll to sixty.[43]

For a year the Sisters continued to run a hybrid school. Then in 1863 the Church acquired Smyllum Park, an estate in the Clyde Valley near Lanark, as a far more suitable home for orphan children than the grey, hemmed-in building in Calton. It was put in the charge of the Sisters of Charity and opened its doors that spring.[44] Thenceforth Abercromby Street functioned as an industrial school only. In a sense, though, it still played a double role, for such schools were expected to take in homeless children as well as those actually convicted of crimes. Further legislation in 1866 only confirmed this duality, by including among those liable to be committed any child found begging, destitute or out of control as well as those actually charged with criminal offences.[45] Abercromby Street thus remained at once a refuge and a reformatory, in uneasy coexistence, the latter role gradually replacing the former with the passing of successive legislation.

Since the death of Bishop Smith, the Sisters had not had the benefit of a priest to celebrate daily Mass at Charlotte Street. Several priests had acted briefly as their confessor,[46] and when in 1864 Fr William Caven was appointed to the post he was also given the remit of convent chaplain, enabling them to return to the practice of daily Mass. A member of the Franciscan Secular Third Order himself, this 'saintly priest and devoted friend' (as the Sisters called him) was to give them sixteen years of unstinting service, devotion and support both spiritual and financial.[47]

After the departure of Mother Veronica, Sr Paula Charlet had been appointed as acting superioress of the Jamaica convent. If we are to believe the *Diary* of Sr M. Ignatius Hayes, it was not a happy community at this time. It was not known how long Veronica would be away, or indeed if she would ever return, and the uncertainty affected everyone, including Sr Paula, who was unwilling to take any binding decisions. The councillors failed to give her loyal support and seemed to despise her authority. Sr Ignatius found the régime oppressive, arbitrary and conspiratorial. Furthermore, the Glasgow Rule had been modified – flouted, in her view – to meet the conditions of the climate, by relaxing the regulations regarding abstinence, enclosure and penances.[48] The schools were being neglected: there were now only eight pupils in the private school, no school had been opened for indigenous children, and Sr Paula was only awaiting Veronica's return to close the parish school whose roll had fallen to fifteen.[49]

Not surprisingly, the early flood of vocations had all but dried up. Nor was there any prospect of recruits from Europe. The archbishop of Cambrai, indeed, had from the beginning strongly advised Tourcoing against permitting Sisters to join what he considered a risky enterprise.[50]

Sr Ignatius was disenchanted, and wanted to leave. 'I do not regard this mission as my home,' her *Diary* records. But where should she go? Not to Glasgow or Bayswater, for they were not the foreign missions she had vowed to serve, and in any case she had 'neither attraction for nor faith in them'; why, she did not record. In the end she sailed for England accompanied by Sr M. de Sales O'Neill, hoping to find recruits there for a new foundation on St Thomas' Island. But she and her companion proved incompatible, and in London they parted company.[51] She was forced to abandon her plans.

While convalescing in Tourcoing, Veronica was contemplating a new foundation. The thought of joining her former prioress in such an enterprise had attractions for Sr Ignatius, for to her she exemplified the original wisdom and purity of the Congregation's Rule.[52] But the plan never materialised. Veronica had been warned by her doctor in Tourcoing against ever returning to the Caribbean, and she seems to have decided that her health would not stand further adventure. In autumn 1863 she formally resigned as prioress of the Jamaican community and the following February requested to be permanently readmitted to Tourcoing. The Council sought the view of Abbé Bernard, who had known Veronica since her days as a novice, and accepted his advice when he backed the request, on condition that she made a commitment to remain there for life. On 10 May she renewed her vows and after all her years of authority humbly took the lowest rank in the convent, as of one newly professed. Ironically, because there was already a Sr Véronique in the community, she herself retained the title 'Mother'.[53]

Sr M. Ignatius now turned her thoughts again to establishing a new foundation. In March she wrote to Bishop Murdoch of her hopes to found a community in France for the support of British and Irish expatriates. He replied warmly, recommending that she contact the bishop of Orléans. The French bishop, however, questioned the validity of the Glasgow Rule and Constitutions for such a foundation. Disappointed, she moved on to Rome. There the Charlotte Street prioress contacted her, requesting that while she was in the city she should seek rulings on certain contentious issues within the Rule that in the past had been given varying interpretations by different spiritual directors. Points requiring clarification concerned the vows (were they simple or solemn?) and questions of enclosure, recital of the Office, and the apostolate (in particular, were Sisters permitted to teach outside the convent in the evenings?).[54] They were all issues that inevitably arose in an active Congregation living by a monastic Rule.

Propaganda's response was to require a full account of the Congregation's origins and history before definitive rulings could be given. When the prioress learned of this she wrote to Sr Ignatius suggesting that, if Rome agreed, she should undertake the task. She also penned a petition to Pius IX, explaining the changes that had been made to the Rule in the difficult years after the French Revolution, and begging permission to return to the Rule of Leo X.[55] It was posted with a covering letter of support from Bishop Murdoch, in which he expressed his debt to the Sisters at this time: 'I can scarcely measure the great benefit they are to Religion in this unhappy kingdom,' he wrote.[56] No doubt the two letters helped persuade the Prefect of *Propaganda* to approve the appointment of Sr Ignatius, and the General of the Franciscan Order to sanction it on his recommendation. Anselm Knapen, Franciscan Consultor at *Propaganda*, was appointed to act as her director in the work.

The whole task – the history of the Congregation and the revision of its Rule and Constitutions – took Sr Ignatius eighteen months. Fr Anselm gave her willing and learned assistance, but he had little understanding of her own needs. Apparently he could not see that he was pushing this delicate, highly strung perfectionist beyond her strength; it did not register with him even when, as happened often, he observed her sitting for hours on end among her books, her head bandaged tightly with damp cloths.[57] More than once she fainted at her desk.

Her revised Rule and Constitutions were accepted by *Propaganda* in July 1866, for a trial period of six years in the first instance, and formally approved by the pope. Word of the decision reached Glasgow just in time for the Congregation's General Chapter at the beginning of August.[58] The following month the Bayswater community also received a Rescript entitling them to live according to it.

One face missing from the Chapter was that of Sr Francis Marchand, who had died that spring. Because of her poor command of English she had never been on the teaching staff, and for years had cared for the pupil boarders at Charlotte Street. She had never acclimatised to the cold and damp of Glasgow, and latterly had suffered from crippling arthritis which she bore with edifying patience. Though always a background figure, the Congregation owed her a great debt: it is probably true to say that without her financial aid it would not have survived the first year of its foundation.

The Chapter also heard details of the hugely successful lottery masterminded by their chaplain, Fr Caven, and organised with the help of local laymen during the spring. It had made a profit of £4,000 and completely wiped out their debts.[59] It was the first fundraising project ever undertaken on behalf of the Sisters in the Catholic community, and the forerunner of many more until the present day: whenever the Congregation has been in urgent need for its works of mercy the laity have never failed to rally to its aid.

Mother Aloysius took the opportunity of the Chapter to stand down as prioress. She wished to move to France where, perhaps following Sr Ignatius Hayes' example, she planned to found a new house of the Congregation. She travelled that July, accompanied by a novice, Maria Simmons. For whatever reason – and I have found no record or explanation in the Congregation's archives – no house was in fact established. But the move severed Sr Aloysius' contact with Scotland. She never returned, living out her days in convents in Italy, latterly in unsound mental health, until her death in Rome in 1902.[60] She was succeeded as prioress by Sr Angela McSwiney, who thus took office for a second, non-consecutive, term, the only Superior in the Congregation's history to do so.

That summer, Council voted to accept a request from Fr Forbes to take over St Mary's Girls' school from the Sisters of Mercy. It was agreed that he would pay the Congregation £100 annually and that they would provide a certificated teacher and an assistant for the day school, three sisters for the night classes and staff for the Sunday school, as well as undertaking parish work among the sick.

They inherited a school in a sad state of disrepair, with barely any furniture, but one with an excellent reputation nevertheless. The Sisters of Mercy were perhaps as noted as the Franciscans for setting high standards in the midst of deprivation. In their *Report on the State of Education in Glasgow*, the government's commissioners had been fulsome in their praise for all of the schools run by nuns, which they judged strikingly superior to comparable schools:

Apart from the education we were struck, in the girls' schools especially, with the harmony existing between the Nuns or Sisters and their charges. The good manners and respectful tone of the children contrasted favourably with any other school for the same class in Glasgow. There is indeed something attractive and pleasing in the Sisters' schools. There is an air of tranquillity and refinement about the Sisters themselves. There is generally also considerable taste and neatness displayed in school arrangement. These seem sensibly to have affected the children, who are orderly and affectionate in their bearing. Probably the knowledge that the Sisters have devoted themselves in a purely unselfish spirit to the task of educating the young without fee or reward begets on the part of parents and children a corresponding gratitude and respect.[61]

Here the writers touched on a cause, and an effect, that have continued to ring true and with which generations of families could identify.

Sr Ignatius Hayes had returned to France, where in autumn 1866 she finally fulfilled her ambition of founding a new religious house. The community at Sèvres was established under the Rule and Constitutions revised by herself, and as such was technically a branch house of the 'Charlotte Street' Franciscans. Knowing of her plans, Bishop Murdoch had before his death given permission for several of the Charlotte Street community to join her once the convent was founded. But his successor Bishop Gray now refused to sanction the move, on the grounds that the undertaking was uncertain of success, making an exception only in the case of the late prioress Mother Aloysius Mackintosh.[62]

She joined Sr Ignatius in December, but the two found it impossible to work together. Both were women of strong will, and each saw herself as having a rightful authority: Sr Ignatius as the founder and Sr Aloysius as the senior professed. They parted, and Sr Aloysius returned to Italy and entered her previous convent there. The new foundation at Sèvres maintained a precarious existence for three years, when it was forced to close on the outbreak of the Franco-Prussian War. The several members who had joined it from England now returned home, and Sr Ignatius herself made her way to the war front to tend the wounded of both sides.[63]

The following spring, the Congregation in Scotland undertook a Renovation of Vows according to the new Rule and Constitutions, while Council addressed the main change required, that of emending the horarium (and in particular the recitation of the Daily Office) to bring it into line with the traditional practice of the Third Order Regular. It was a case of squaring the circle. The horarium had been emended at least four times since 1847 in an attempt to make it compatible with the Sisters' working lives. The new arrangements were more 'monastic' than before, but they still had to be built around the daily apostolate of the community. For the Choir Sisters, this meant working around the demands of the day, evening and Sunday schools. In the case of the Lay Sisters, whose daily work comprised domestic duties within the convent, no such strictures were necessary and a quite different horarium could be devised. As a result, the two groups now only met for Mass and meditation, and never ate together or came together at recreation.[64] They became, more than ever, two separate communities living parallel lives who saw one another at a distance but rarely or never spoke. The new arrangements were intended to be permanent, but in fact they would frequently need to be adjusted in matters of detail in future years as circumstances continued to change, and the circle would never be squared.

In July 1867 Fr Bonnyman of St Vincent's Duke Street approached the Congregation and asked it to take charge of his parish schools. He was not in a position to provide any salary but hoped that this would change in the new year, depending on the pupils' penny-a-week fees coming in! His 'terms' were accepted, and the school opened in August.[65] This strange arrangement highlighted the great problem for both the Sisters and the parish priests at this time – how to serve the poor on the one hand and pay their way on the other. It was an issue that Bishop Gray was aware of. In summer 1868 he intervened on behalf of the Congregation, instructing the parish priest of St Patrick's to pay them a fixed annual sum of £100 rather than *ad hoc* payments which gave them no security.[66]

Three months before the Congregation's 1869 Chapter, Charles Eyre succeeded Bishop Gray as Vicar Apostolic of the Western District. Rome had chosen him and brought him from England to restore discipline and unity to a Church badly damaged by ethnic factions,[67] at the same time 'accepting' the retirement on grounds of ill health of Bishop Gray, who had been an innocent participant in and victim of the quarrels. The bishop moved to the quiet of Rothesay, his going felt keenly by the Congregation, who esteemed him as a friend and guide second only to Bishop Smith. As his letter of farewell to the Sisters shows, he remembered them with affection and gratitude for their loyalty and frequent kindnesses.[68] He continued to offer them what support he could for the remaining three years of his life, and on his death he bequeathed to them his library and all his possessions. These were few enough, for he had spent a lifetime giving to the poor.[69]

The Chapter was presided over by Fr Anselm Knapen, who was in Glasgow to assess how the Sisters were faring under the new Rule and Constitutions. One of the required changes involved replacing the title 'prioress' with that of 'abbess', a small enough change in wording but a milestone for the Congregation, for it showed that they had come of age. Voting for the office ran to six ballots and was so close that the president had to seek the advice of Archbishop Eyre as to how to reach a verdict.[70] Sr

Gonzaga Sim (Plate 8) was finally elected by a single vote over Mother Angela McSwiney. She would hold office for a record three terms, a total of fifteen years,[71] and she is remembered as one of the outstanding leaders in the Congregation's history.

The arrival of Eyre signalled a tightening of control at all levels. This made more work for the Sisters, for he insisted on personally examining and signing their annual accounts. But overall it benefited them, since he effected what his predecessor had never fully managed to achieve: a contractual arrangement for their employment in the parish schools, with a standard salary of £100 per annum irrespective of the income from pupils' fees. He also had a contract drawn up for their chaplain, Fr Caven, fixing his annual salary at £40 with free board and lodging, and spelling out his duties.[72]

The title deeds of the Charlotte Street property had until now been held by the bishops of the Western District as a guarantee for the Congregation's debt. Now that this had been cleared through the profit on the lottery, Council were anxious to have them signed over to themselves. Fr Knapen agreed to raise the matter on their behalf with Archbishop Eyre while he was in Glasgow. As a newcomer to the district, the archbishop consulted with his senior clergy, who advised him that the Sisters had 'no right whatever' to the deeds and that the property belonged to the Glasgow mission. When Fr Knapen reported back to Council, they drew up an exact statement of all financial transactions since the original purchase of No. 58, clearly proving the property to be theirs, which he presented to Eyre in September.[73] But the archbishop sat on the matter for some months, apparently still inclined to believe his senior clergy.

Finally, Fr Caven stepped in on the Sisters' behalf with a pointed letter of concern to his archbishop, signed by himself and ten others who had been involved with the lottery. Since the lottery had been organised solely to clear the Congregation's debts, he wrote, the profits were theirs 'without reserve'. 'If we had ever imagined,' he added, 'that the Mission or District was to be mixed up with it, or was to exercise any control or claim over the moneys realised by the lottery, we should never have engaged in it.'[74] At the same time the abbess alerted Fr Knapen, now back in Rome, as to the lack of progress.

The result was a letter from Cardinal Barnabo to Eyre judging in favour of the Sisters' petition and recommending that their names be added to the deeds. The matter, however, was complicated by their plans to extend the property, and by regulations for government grants. They refused to surrender their right to be trustees nonetheless, preferring if need be to build without a grant.[75] The dispute was to rumble on for a further fourteen years, before the deeds were finally transferred into their hands.[76]

In autumn 1871, Mother Gonzaga proposed that rather than build on the cramped site at Charlotte Street the Congregation should purchase a property in the country, move the boarding school there, and so create more space for the community and the day school in Glasgow. The house she had in mind was in Innellan, six miles south of Dunoon on the Cowal peninsula. Council approved the plan and called a meeting of alumnae and friends to form a fundraising committee. The following May they held a bazaar which raised more than the purchase price of the property, and the school opened that summer. Fr Caven volunteered to act as chaplain there as well as in Charlotte Street, regularly making the lengthy journey from Glasgow by train, boat and trap to celebrate Mass for the boarders, each time arriving weighed down with messages from the city shops.[77]

In 1870 the Elementary Education Act was passed for England and Wales. It caused something little short of panic in Catholic circles south of the Border, for by making schooling compulsory for all five- to thirteen-year-olds, it gave the Church the prospect of a massive building programme yet excluded it from building grants. A Catholic Poor Schools Committee was at once set up in London to gauge the financial implications, for which the Scottish bishops were also requested to provide local data since it was recognised that the English Act was likely to be the forerunner of something similar in Scotland. In June a Catholic Education Crisis Fund Committee was appointed to raise and disburse monies according to local need. In a letter to Archbishop Eyre, its chairman warned of the dangers of delay in getting Glasgow's returns to him. 'It is of the utmost importance,' he wrote, 'that we should commence operations without loss of time. If we do not hasten to provide school accommodation for our children they will, in a short time, be beyond our reach.'[78]

In response Eyre appointed a District Poor Schools Committee under his own presidency, whose members included Mother Gonzaga and other religious, clergy and laity, to determine existing accommodation and predicted need, parish by parish. They calculated that twelve thousand more school places would be required in Glasgow, and nine thousand in the rest of the Western District.[79]

In January 1872 they learned that they had been allocated £6,000 as their share of the crisis fund. It was a mere fraction of their needs, and the grants they were able to allocate – £450 to the Sacred Heart, and £300 to Our Lady & St Margaret's Kinning Park, among others – were really little more than a token gesture: the new schools in these parishes were likely to cost up to ten times as much.[80]

The Scottish Act was duly passed that spring.[81] Under it, education was made compulsory for all five- to thirteen-year-olds. The state took over the existing parish schools and many of the Kirk's schools in the towns, creating a national system of elementary education to be run by local school boards; the latter were given rights to levy rates in order to generate income for school building and maintenance and for teachers' salaries. Schools choosing to retain their denominational status remained eligible for government grants as before, but they were not entitled to funding from the rates.

With the help of the crisis fund several parishes now embarked on building programmes to cope with the expected influx of pupils. In Sacred Heart, Fr Noonan engaged architects to draw up plans for boys', girls' and infant schools. The girls and infants were to be housed in one building, for which he was quoted an estimate of £3,000. On its completion in autumn 1873 he approached the Franciscans to take charge of both girls and infants. Council agreed to begin work in the day school in the new year, and in the evening school the following summer.[82]

In the same year, Fr Michael Condon broached the possibility of the Sisters opening a branch house and taking over the girls' school in his parish of St Lawrence's in Greenock. The town lies in a narrow hinterland between the Clyde estuary and the Renfrewshire hills and was already at this date spreading up the slopes. St Lawrence's church and school were in Stanners Street, Cartsdyke, a district close to the waterfront known as 'wee Dublin' because of its concentration of Catholics.[83]

Fr Condon offered them the now standard £100 per annum for teaching the day and night schools, and also a rent-free property, Bank House, suitable for a convent and private school, which he had bought two years before with a teaching Congregation in mind. It was an imposing red sandstone residence of four storeys, set into the hill, with a stylish façade and 'horseshoe' entrance steps, in an elevated position beside the Wellpark, looking across the estuary to Ben Lomond by day, and by night to the far-off lights of Helensburgh low upon the river.

The classrooms the Sisters inherited in Stanners Street had originally been a flat above the boys' school into which the girls had moved in 1869 when the tenant's lease expired, since when they had been taught by lay mistresses. They was desperately cramped, and Fr Condon was already planning to move into new premises up the hill in Belville Street. Sr Annunciata Murdoch took over the headship in January 1874, but it would be eight years before the new building was completed.[84]

Innellan had now been open for eighteen months, but it was already clear that it had been ill conceived from the start. It was too distant to attract the number of boarders needed to make it viable, and the hard decision was taken to give it up. The house was sold in May, but the concept of a boarding school in the country was not abandoned, and the income from the sale was invested and earmarked for a purchase nearer home.[85]

After ten months on the war front, Sr Ignatius Hayes had returned to St Thomas' Island in spring 1872 in the hope of starting a community there.[86] But almost at once she contracted yellow fever and was quarantined. That summer she moved on to the United States, where she purchased a plot of land in Little Falls, Minnesota. It lay close to the Mississippi, looking out onto endless fields and pinewoods, and glorious sunsets. There in 1873 she built a house and a small school with two dormitories, all in wood in the mid-west style. The date is taken as marking the founding of her new Congregation, which she named 'the Missionary Franciscan Sisters of the Immaculate Conception', a title that alludes both to its origins in the parent institute and the fourth vow of 'mission' that she had taken. The new foundation now went its own way, and its subsequent history strictly forms no part of the present narrative.[87]

By the mid-1870s the implications of the 1872 Education (Scotland) Act were becoming apparent and the Catholic Church could see clearly the predicament it faced. By choosing to retain its own schools it had excluded itself from the financial support enjoyed by the state schools, yet it was legally bound to match them in provision and morally bound to match them in quality. As demand continued to rise, it faced the prospect of making ever greater efforts, and ever greater calls on the laity, merely to stand still.[88]

The Act brought new work for the Sisters. School rolls were rising and new schools opening. With demand always outstripping supply, they now had an even more important role to play, both in teaching the present generation themselves and in educating the next generation's teachers. They had never been more in demand.

In fact the Scottish Catholic schools were coping more successfully than could possibly have been expected. As one government inspector remarked of those in the Western District, 'my surprise is, not that [they] are not what they should be, but that they are what they are'. They served the most deprived section of the community, he added: the parents were 'poor and migratory' and the children 'lawless, restless and very difficult to catch or keep'. Yet the schools themselves 'deserved an honourable place', especially for their standards of behaviour and the 'intelligent, energetic and fair' management of the parish priests. His one criticism was of their academic attainment, which was restricted by the generally low ability of the children and the mediocre level of teaching.[89] Recruiting well-educated Catholic teachers of calibre remained the Church's greatest problem and made the Sisters' presence even more vital. Yet there was probably little truth in the commonly held view that the Catholic schools were academically inferior. As another inspector pointed out, they used the same books and examinations as other schools, and thanks to the 'enormous' fundraising efforts of the faithful their buildings were often excellent. He praised the parish priests also, whom he found 'as anxious as any managers ever could be, or ever would be, to give their children a good education'.[90]

From the log book of St Joseph's Aberdeen we can gain a detailed picture of what these schools were like.[91] As in the rest of Scotland, Aberdeen parents were only beginning to come to terms with compulsory education. Many were still not education-minded and resented the effects of compulsory schooling upon their own working lives. Scottish fishermen's children were notoriously bad school attenders,[92] and many of the St Joseph's families actually moved house for the summer herring season, so that the school lost them entirely between late May and the end of August. Others who found work in local mills transferred to the schools attached to them. As the schoolmistress Sr M. Seraphina Kerigan noted ruefully, the tailing off of attendance every summer 'rendered all exertions to advance the pupils hopeless'. Not surprisingly, since government grants were based on pupils' attainment, she was somewhat obsessed with attendance figures. Whereas the parish priest encouraged good attendance by means of treats and prizes, the mistress kept standards as high as possible by setting regular 'home lessons' and frequently detaining children for an hour at the end of the day for unsatisfactory work. She could do this since all the girls walked to school, and she gave parents no prior warning of such detentions.

The curriculum comprised the '3 Rs', plus singing and catechism, to which a fourth – a standard Britain-wide Catholic RE syllabus – was added in 1876.[93] Domestic Economy was introduced two years later, but there was no physical education.

The school underwent its annual government inspection in October. The pupils were examined in all subjects, on the basis of which the grant was awarded and they were judged ready for promotion or occasional demotion (since classes or 'standards' were based on attainment, not age). Those pupils of Standard 5 who passed the examination were entitled to leave school: most would be aged about thirteen, but a bright child might be much younger, and by a loophole in the Act she could legally leave on reaching her tenth birthday.[94]

The mistress, Sr Seraphina, was the only qualified and certificated teacher, and had four 'pupil–teachers' working under her. These were girls of thirteen and upwards who were learning the profession and who remained for five years in the school before sitting the entrance examination for training college. For nearly all Catholic girls aspiring to the teaching profession at this date, this was the normal way in. They taught by day and studied the theory and practice of education under Sr Seraphina in the evenings and on Saturdays. Since they were only entitled to five hours' tuition per week but were required to teach for up to twenty, they were in fact far more 'teachers' than 'pupils', yet they had none of the status of teachers and were referred to in the log as 'apprentices'. With too much work and too little study, the course equipped them well enough for the practice of teaching but hardly educated them to be educators. For their labours the state paid them £10 per annum, rising to £20 in their final year. Their progress was examined annually.[95] If they failed, as happened more than once at St Joseph's, they were permitted to continue as 'stipendary mistresses' and might be reinstated as pupil–teachers after a successful resit.

Among their tasks, Sr Seraphina expected them to scour the neighbourhood for absentees, and one girl was noted in the log for refusing this duty. They frequently displeased Sister, in fact, and were regularly logged for being 'indolent and disobedient', or 'idle and inattentive at their studies', and for neglecting their charges and allowing them far too much freedom. The inspector also found the classes under their care too lax, and called for a firmer approach in checking whispering. More than once he threatened to withhold the annual grant because of the poor standards achieved. Such threats, it should be said, were commonplace at this date, almost incumbent upon the inspector and in fact his only leverage upon a school, and they did not prevent St Joseph's winning consistently favourable reports. 'The condition of this school is in every aspect very satisfactory,' read the report for 1874. 'This is the result not only of much assiduity on the part of the Mistress, but also of the great interest taken in the school by the Manager. The intelligence of the children and general tone of the school are very good.'[96]

The manager referred to was the parish priest of St Joseph's, Fr John Sutherland. He was, as the report noted, an excellent support to Sister and a conscientious visitor. He frequently brought the children gifts – every Hallowe'en it was apples and nuts – and regularly donated prizes of beautifully bound story books. In November 1874 he was transferred to Huntly and was succeeded as parish priest by his curate, Fr Stopani. The new manager was equally caring. For nearly twenty years, until a month before his death, he visited the school at least weekly. He regularly accompanied the children on their outings to the seaside, and in winter donated clothing to the needy.

The school was still housed in its original building at this date, which was quite inadequate for the purpose. The classrooms had no fixed lighting and relied on roof-windows for illumination. Whenever snow covered them, the teachers had recourse to candles. With no building grant to assist him, it would be into the 1880s before Fr Stopani was able to provide the girls with a more fitting school.

Since the closure of Innellan, the Congregation had been seeking a new home for their boarding school. Not only had the roll of the day school risen to breaking point, the once highly respectable Charlotte Street was now in fast decline as the merchant class had moved out and the neighbourhood became engulfed in the poverty of the East End. It was no longer thought a suitable location for boarding girls. In February 1878 the Sisters found what they were looking for: a property in three acres of ground belonging to the North British Railway Company in Bothwell, which the owners were willing to sell at well below its true value. Even so, after adaptation the final cost was expected to approach £10,000. Even counting the money invested from Innellan and subsequent benefactions, they would incur a debt of over £8,000, but they decided to go ahead, confident of making up the difference through donations from the Catholic community.[97]

On 27 April, Mother M. Vincent Dolan escorted the boarders to their new home, accompanied by four teaching Sisters and two Lay Sisters.[98] Its very name, 'Elmwood', evoked pictures in their imagination, and when they alighted at the station right beside it, it was like a magic new world (Plate 9). If there had been doubts and tears as they left the city, they were forgotten now, as they entered by the iron gates and surveyed the striking red sandstone mansion and the evening spring sunshine upon the lawns and terraces, the pond with its fountain, the banks of daffodils and the orchard in bud. It was a haven of peace, with not a sound but the rustling of a breeze among the cedars, limes, yews, sycamores and chestnut trees that hid it from the world beyond. The house was set back 200 feet from the lane outside. The girls were enchanted by its turrets and crenelations, its Tudor-style stone chimneys and great oriel window. It even had its own motto engraved in stone above the door.

They entered to find themselves in the hallway with its fine fireplace in the Adam style, and facing them a carved staircase on which the sun threw splashes of colour from the stained glass window on the landing. The first owner must have been an admirer of John Knox, for more than one bust of the stern reformer peered down at them from the wall in reproof, as if they were trespassers. Upstairs they found the library, with cornicing depicting rural fruitfulness, wall-high mirrors, carved heads of Calvin and Huss, and a magnificent chandelier. Then someone discovered the little doorway and concealed spiral stair that led to the maids' quarters in the attic. Finally they explored the cellars and found to their delight that they led to old tunnels of uncertain origin and history, which none dared venture into.[99]

This was their new home, then. It would be their home – haven, nursery for young minds, place of fond memories – for ninety-nine years. The next morning Fr Caven arrived promptly to celebrate Mass at 7 a.m., as he was to do every day. He continued to live at Charlotte Street as chaplain to the day school. To say Mass at Elmwood he would often stay overnight, but sometimes he would walk the ten miles from Glasgow, setting out at 4 a.m.[100]

When the parishioners of St Mary's Greenock had opened their new church in Patrick Street in 1872 they had their old church in East Shaw Street converted for use as the parish school. It had just two main classrooms and one smaller room into which were squeezed the 555 children on the roll, with no playground in which to stretch their legs. Work had finally begun on a new school on the same site in 1877. The foundation stone was laid by Archbishop Eyre in a very public ceremony, with flute and brass bands and a procession two thousand strong met by a crowd of 10,000 at the site.

It was a fine two-storey building with twin Gothic spires, and to mark the 'new start' the Franciscan Sisters were engaged to take charge of the girls' and infants' departments. The work was completed in summer 1878 and the premises officially opened by the archbishop in October in another colourful ceremony attended by a thousand pupils, ex-pupils and pupils-to-be, who marched from Mass to their new school led by the boys' head-master and the girls' headmistress, Sr M. Angela Farnon.[101]

Eyre had attended the first event as Vicar Apostolic of the Western District, but by the time of the opening he was Ordinary of the newly created archdiocese of Glasgow, following the Restoration of the Hierarchy the previous March. The Restoration was a crucial step on the Catholic Church's road to recovery in Scotland, and it gave the archbishop greater authority to continue the work of consolidation and stabilisation that he had been brought in to undertake. Under his guidance and that of his predecessors the Church had already grown, both in size and in its acceptance by society. He could now build more effectively upon this work, continuing its journey, as one historian has aptly put it, 'towards respectability – from hired halls to massive Pugin churches'.[102]

If the Church had changed in the thirty years since the Sisters first began their work in Glasgow, so too had society. Great strides had been made in education, with the founding of the EIS in the very year of their arrival, the establishment of the pupil–teacher system (a 'turning point in British education'),[103] the Argyll Commission of the 1860s, and the subsequent Act of 1872.[104] Behaviour patterns were changing too, and the worst excesses of urban degradation were being gradually eliminated. The combined effects of legislation, the moral persuasion of the Temperance movement and rising prices had reduced alcohol consumption by a third in twenty years from its high point in the 1840s.[105] Armed with new powers, the police had also had some success in combating prostitution.[106]

Above all, progress had been made in improving the living conditions of the urban poor. Glasgow Corporation had established a sanitary department in 1862 and for the first time set regulations for the building of houses. Later in the decade, a city improvement trust had been formed to buy up and clear congested areas, as a result of which eighty-eight acres of the worst slums had been demolished in those very parts of the town – the Wynds, Calton and the Gorbals – where the Sisters worked. In 1867 the Public Health (Scotland) Act was belatedly passed in parliament, implementing some of the recommendations made by Edwin Chadwick's commission a quarter of a century before. The 1870s had seen slum clearance stepped up and the worst of the old haphazard warrens replaced by broad streets laid out in imitation of the regeneration of Paris. The removal of the university from the stinking High Street to the leafy west end in 1872 exemplified the new concept of creating 'breathing space' and letting fresh air into the claustrophobic city.[107] Finally, in 1878 the drive for hygiene took a major step forward with the opening of the corporation's first public baths and wash-houses.

We should not exaggerate the improvements: in housing, for example, two thirds of the city were still living in one- or two-roomed apartments and would continue to do so well into the twentieth century. But much had been achieved in taking the edge off the worst deprivation, and calming some of the old anomie and lurking threat.

The Congregation were themselves enjoying a period of stability, as that summer Mother M. Gonzaga Sim was elected by General Chapter to her third term of office. Their boarding school was now opened, and space had been created for the day school to develop. They had extended their work into new parishes, and the schools in their charge were settling down now that the effects of the 1872 Act were understood and the direction forward was clear. With the new stability in education, the Church and society as a whole, the ground was now ready for the Sisters to enter an era of consolidation.

ENDNOTES TO CHAPTER TWO

1 The city was formally divided into seven parishes in 1849, though three of these had no church at the time – *SCD*, 1850, p. 79.

2 *SCD*, 1857, p. 100.

3 Comparison of weekly fees in schools in the west of Scotland in 1856: in RC schools, 62.3% 1–2d., 90% 3d. or less; in Church of Scotland schools, 11% 1–2d., 46.2% 3d. or less – Committee of the Privy Council for Education in Scotland, *Minutes and Reports*, 1856–7, cited in Scotland J., 1969, p. 258.

4 Government inspectors' reports, *SCD*, 1856, p. 89ff.

5 Re St John's – inspector's report in *SCD*, 1857, p. 100; re St Joseph's – report of inspection of May 1857 in *SCD*, 1858. St Joseph's was at this time awaiting a new building.

6 *Parliamentary Papers – General Report for the Year 1859 by HMIS J. Reynell Morell on RC Schools in North England and Scotland*, in *Accounts and Papers*, vol. 11, *Education: Minutes of Council*, session Jan–Aug 1860, vol. liv, London 1860, p. 222.

7 Council Meeting Minutes, 1854–72, 034.10 no. 1, AF, meetings of April and July 1856; and *SCD*, 1857, p. 117.

8 Written account of Mother Veronica, Tourcoing Archives, upon which the present account of the whole episode is based.

9 Years afterwards she acted similarly towards another Superior: at the convent of Ischia di Castro in 1879, she apparently interfered in the election of the abbess, incurring criticisms of intrigue from Bishop Fornacelli – cf. de Breffny B., 1980, p. 67.

10 Account of her at the convent of Tourcoing, 'Tourcoing Archives', copy 011, AF.

11 Told by Sr Paula's mother to the Tourcoing community, 'Tourcoing Archives', copy 011, AF.

12 Council Meeting Minutes, December 1856, 034.10, no. 1, AF. According to Veronica's own account 'my charge was too heavy and above all my conscience was too obstructed [*trop gênée*] to be Superior in these conditions' – Mother Veronica, written account, Tourcoing Archives.

13 Council Meeting Minutes, July 1857. Unfortunately, no Chapter reports are extant for the early years of the Congregation.

14 Details of Frs Howell and Meyrick from the archives of the English Province of the Society of Jesus, 114 Mount St London, Records of Priests, pp. 179 and 285, copy (courtesy of Rev. Francis Edwards SJ), 014.1, AF.

15 Chapter notes, 23.7.1854, Register of Elections, 028.2, AF.

16 Delany F.X., 1930. For an account of the Catholic Church in Jamaica to this date, see also Osborne F.J., 1988.

17 There was a fifth member of the party, the teenager Isabella Grant, who was not a member of the community but travelled with them in order to visit her brother Charles, a merchant in Kingston.

18 Veronica's notes in *Tribute*, p. 21.

19 The date of their departure was 3 October – letter Mother Paula Charlet to Mother Veronica's secretary, 5.10.1913, Tourcoing Archives.

20 Rodrigues V.I., 1976MS (Allegany), p. 76.

21 Based on a description by Ewan MacPherson, quoted in Rodrigues V.I., *op. cit.*, p. 82.

22 Based on 'M.A.' (Sr M. Agatha McEvoy), 1969, pp. 1–17. Fr (later Cardinal) Manning was a member of the Secular Third Order, open to lay people and secular clergy, which from the fourteenth century had a distinct existence and Rule from that of the Third Order Regular (see p. 10 above). Over the centuries the Secular Third Order attracted thousands of devout Christians and included among its membership persons as diverse as St Louis King of France, Dante, Giotto, Galileo, Catherine of Aragon, SS Elizabeth of Hungary, Francis de Sales, John Vianney, Bernadette and Pius X. Today the two Orders are known as SFO (Secular Franciscan Order) and TOR (Third Order Regular) respectively. Elizabeth's brother William (1819–92) is best known as the founder of the

72

A Canticle of Love

Institute of Charity – cf. *Father Lockhart of the Institute of Charity* (London, 1932), based largely on the biography written by Fr Hirst, a member of the institute, the year after his death.

23 Council Meeting Minutes, 1858 (no month), 034.10, AF.

24 Dates from the Braintree (previously Bayswater) Congregation Archives, in letter Sr M. Cuthbert to Sr M. Dolores Cochrane (Archivist, FSIC), 13.10.1985.

25 Cf. letter abbess (signed also by the members of the Council) to Cardinal Simeoni, 5.11.1888, copy 025.1, AF, in which it is stated that 'for some years' before 1860 Sr M. Gertrude had 'caused much dispeace and annoyance between the Ecclesiastical and Religious superiors and the members of the community'.

26 Council Meeting Minutes, (n.d., but probably November or December 1858). Sr M. Margaret was accompanied by Srs M. Sacred Hearts O'Neill and M. Sylvester Rodgers.

27 Details of Elizabeth Hayes' life up to 1857 in de Breffny B., 1980, pp. 11–56. The 'leading member' of the Oxford Movement was Dr Edward Pusey.

28 *Memories of the Life and Works of Mother Ignatius of Jesus, Founder of the Institute of the Missionary Franciscan Sisters of the Immaculate Conception*, n.d.; the anonymous author was a Sister of her institute who knew her personally and based much of the book on her verbal reminiscences.

29 Bishop Smith to Sr M. Ignatius Hayes, 25.7.1859, in de Breffny B., *op. cit.*, p. 74ff.

30 Council Meeting Minutes, p. 16.

31 Act of Profession of Sr M. Ignatius Hayes, 26.11.1859, copy 011, AF.

32 Note written by her secretary, Sr M. of the Angels, appended at the end of her *Diary* – Shaw, Sr M.F., OSF, (ed.) *Diary of Sr M. Ignatius of Jesus*, 1994.

33 Council Meeting Minutes, meetings of December 1859 and February 1860.

34 *Obituary Book – Benefactors*, AF, describes him as the Congregation's second great support.

35 Council Meeting Minutes, July 1861.

36 *Ibid.*, p. 34; the Chapter voted 15:7 to readmit her.

37 Register of Elections, 4.7.1863, 028.2, AF. The voting was: Sr Aloysius 28, Mother Vincent Dolan 4, Mother Angela McSwiney 3.

38 This and the previous paragraph based on a letter (in English) found among her papers at Tourcoing, quoted in Rodrigues Sr V.I., 1976MS, p. 76.

39 Eg., by de Breffny B., 1980, p. 92.

40 Letter of Recommendation, J.E. Dupeyron SJ, Vicar-Apostolic of Jamaica and British Hobduras, 8.9.1862 (in French), original in Tourcoing Archives, copy in *Tribute*, Tourcoing 1947, 0.11, AF. The letter requested that she 'be received with kindness as a true servant of God'.

41 *Glasgow Roman Catholic Industrial Schools Official Inspection*, 1896, copy 012.2, AF.

42 Cf. Scotland J., 1969, p. 269. This act was a follow-up to the Dunlop's Act of 1855, by which courts were authorised to commit young offenders to the existing refuges, which were henceforth to be registered as industrial schools (for under-fourteens) or reformatories (for over-fourteens).

43 Figures for 1860–1 – *SCD*, 1861, p. 88; for 1862 – *SCD*, 1862, p. 92. Re girls received from throughout Scotland – *SCD*, 1864, p. 98.

44 It opened on Good Friday 1863 – *SCD*, 1868, p. 129.

45 Industrial Schools Act, 1866, 29 and 30 Vic, C. 118.

46 These had included Fr McIntosh of St Andrew's parish, the Benedictine Fr Anselm Robertson and, from 1863, Fr Walter Sidegreave.

47 *Obituary Book – Benefactors*, AF.

48 *Diary*, p. 35ff. (D 31) and p. 36ff. (D 32), (D numbers refer to pagination in the original MS diary). As a caveat, we should perhaps treat Sr Ignatius' views with a certain caution, particularly in view of Fr William Caven's expressed opinion of her as a religious – see note *infra*.

49 Draft of a letter to Fr Dupeyron SJ, *Ibid.*, p. 41 (D 38).

50 Letter Canon Philippe on behalf of the archbishop, June 1858, Tourcoing Archives.

51 Sr M. de Sales apparently sought re-entry into Charlotte Street, and when this was refused she joined the Poor Clares in Baddesley, Warwicks, and later in York. She afterwards left the York convent and established an irregular foundation in the USA.

52 *Diary*, p. 46 (D 47).

53 Details from Tourcoing Archives. Council unanimously voted to readmit her, after which they sought permission from the archdiocese and clarification as to the terms under which she could be received – Mother Alfonse Liefquint to Archbishop, 24.4.1864, and Abbé Bernard to Mother Alfonse, 2.5.1864.

54 *Diary*, p. 54 (D 53).

55 Petition, quoted in Council Meeting Minutes, meeting of September 1866.

56 Bishop Murdoch to Pope Pius IX, 30.3.1865, quoted in Council Meeting Minutes, meeting of September 1866.

57 This and the previous paragraph based on *Memories*, p. 18ff.

58 Approbation of the Rule and Constitutions by Raphaele di Ponticulo Minister General OFM, acceptance by *Propaganda*, 30.7.1866; formal approval by pope, 5.8.1866; Decretum, Cardinal Barnabo, 17.8.1866; Rescript to Bayswater community, 20.9.1866. All in Rule, MS. 031.30, AF: and in printed version, *Rule of the Regular Third Order of St Francis of Assisi and Constitutions for the Religious of the Same Order of the Convents of the Immaculate Conception*, 1867, copy RO8/25, AGA.

59 Statement, W. Caven and J. Maguire, 23.4.1870, copy 071. 01, AF.

60 *Profession Register*, entries for Srs Aloysius Mackintosh and Maria Simmons.

61 Greig G. and Harvey T. *Report on the State of Education in Glasgow*, Edinburgh 1866, p. 81; published in Argyll Commission, *Reports from the Commissioners*, vol. xxv *Education Scotland*, London 1867. pp. 345–507, ref. on p. 429.

62 Annals, 1847–93, 012.1, AF.

63 Cf. de Breffny B., *op. cit.*, p. 104ff.

64 Council Meeting Minutes, meeting of 26.4.1867 gives full details of both horaria.

65 Council Meeting Minutes, July 1867 meeting; *SCD*, 1868, p. 91.

66 Council Meeting Minutes, meeting of August 1868. The bishop also

recommended that they give up St Peter's Partick, because of the small sum received from the children in fees. Council heeded his advice in regard to the night school, since journeys of such distance after dark were in any case undesirable, but voted to continue the day school despite the lack of income.

67 Cf. eg., McRoberts D., 1978J. The Church in the west of Scotland had been split through rivalry between Scottish and Irish clergy: some of the latter wished to create in effect an Irish Church in Scotland, to serve what was still very largely an 'Irish' Catholic community.

68 Bishop Gray to Mother Angela McSwiney, n.d. but summer 1969, OL 2/117/7, SCA.

69 *Obituary Book – Benefactors*, AF.

70 After the fifth ballot, Archbishop Eyre instructed that, according to Article XX of the Constitutions, neither of the two chief candidates should vote in the sixth ballot. The resulting vote was: Sr Gonzaga 17, Mother Angela 16. Letter Archbishop Eyre to Fr Knapen, 10.8.1869, copy in Register of Elections, 11.8.1869, 828.2, AF.

71 Up until 1872, the term of office was three years. That year, at the instigation of Archbishop Eyre, it was increased to six years in line with the 'new' Constitutions – Register of Elections, 17.7.1872, 028.2, AF. It has remained thus to the present day. Mother Gonzaga's first term was therefore of three years, her second and third of six years each. At the election of 1884 she only missed being elected for a fourth term by a single vote on the sixth ballot.

72 Council Meeting Minutes, meeting of August 1869.

73 Finance Committee Minutes, 13 December 1869, FR 1/1, p. 21, AGA. The records show, however, that Nos. 62–64 Charlotte Street were at least originally the property of the Western District and rented by the Congregation: Contract of Lease of Property, signed Bishop Smith on behalf of Proprietors and countersigned by Mother Veronica, 10 and 12.12.1855, lease to commence 28.5.1856, OL 2/85/12, SCA.

74 Fr William Caven (and ten other signatories) to Archbishop Eyre, 23.4.1870, copy 071.01, AF.

75 Eyre to H. Allies (Hon. Sec. Catholic Poor Schools Committee), 14.10.1871; F.R. Sandford (Education Dept.) to Eyre, 3.11.1871; Eyre to Sr Emmanuel, 11.1.1872; Sr Emmanuel to Eyre, 12.1.1872, all RO8/2, AGA. Council Meeting Minutes, meetings of November and December 1871.

76 Council Meeting Minutes (1873–1974), 034.10 no. 2, AF, meeting of July 1887 stating that the deeds had been transferred 'within the past year'.

77 Council Meeting Minutes, meetings of November 1871 and January and June 1872. Innellan cost £1,050 to purchase, and the bazaar raised £1,100. Re Fr Caven – *Obituary Book – Benefactors*, AF.

78 Duke of Norfolk to Archbishop Eyre, 13.10.1870, GC 2/22, AGA. Fearing that any similar legislation extended to Scotland might threaten the Church's control over its schools, Archbishop Eyre had convened a meeting of his clergy in March to press the government to exempt denominational schools from any forthcoming bill – Notes of meeting of 10.3.1870, GC 2/22, AGA. That month also, the bishops of England, Scotland and Ireland presented a petition to

parliament, calling for no change to the existing law – petition of 12.3.1870 (printed), copy GC 2/22, AGA.

79 Diocesan Education Board Minute Book, first meeting 4.10.1870 and subsequent meetings, ED I/I, AGA.

80 *Ibid.*, meetings of 9.1.1872 and 14.3.1872.

81 Education (Scotland) Act, 35 and 36 Vict. Ch. 62, 1872.

82 Re plans and estimate, Dunn and Hanson, architects (Newcastle) to Archbishop Eyre, 2.5.1872, 4.5.1872 and 15.5.1872, GC 4/27/1, 2 and 5, AGA; re acceptance, Council Meeting Minutes, meeting of November 1873. The final cost of the three schools was £7,300 – LB – 1/2/320, AGA. The rolls of the girls' school were 350 (day) and 130 (evening) – *SCD*, 1876, p. 89.

83 St Lawrence's was the second parish to be founded in Greenock, having opened in 1855, and it served the eastern half of the town. Until recently it was always spelt thus.

84 Fr Michael Condon to Archbishop Eyre, 20.8.1873, RO8/21, AGA; Council Meeting Minutes, meeting of December 1873; Minute of Agreement (1874), RO8/2.1, AGA. They based the fees for their private school on those at the Greenock Academy. Re the new school in Belville Street, see *Greenock Telegraph* 6–11.8.1880: the land was bought in 1875, the foundation stone laid by Archbishop Eyre in 1880, and the school opened the following year.

85 Council Meeting Minutes, meetings of December 1873 and May 1874.

86 The intention was that she would replace the Sisters of St Joseph of Cluny, who had left the island in 1871, and continue their work of assisting the Redemptorist Fr Louis de Buggenoms, who ran a hospital there. The present account based on de Breffny B., 1980, p. 111ff.; Rodrigues V.I., 1976 MS, p. 80ff.; and Anon, *Memories of the Life and Works of Mother Mary Ignatius of Jesus*, n.d., p. 21ff.

87 For an account of its subsequent history, see *The Institute of the Missionary Franciscan Sisters of the Immaculate Conception*, Rome 1939; *Missionary Franciscan Sisters of the Immaculate Conception, 1873–1973*, place of publication unspecified, 1973; and *Love Counts Nothing Hard*, Lincoln Massachusetts, n.d. but 1994.

88 The Church's only regular source of income was the annual education collection taken in parishes around the country on the feast of the Sacred Heart.

89 Donald Ross, HMIS (Her Majesty's Inspector for Scotland), in *Education (Scotland) Report*, Scotch Education Department, 1875–6, p. 155ff.

90 Statement by Dr David Middleton on the occasion of his being promoted to HMSIS (Her Majesty's Senior Inspector for Scotland), 27.1.1877, reported in the *Glasgow Herald*, 29.1.1877.

91 Except where otherwise stated, this section is based on the log book, AF, entries between 1874 and 1889. The parish schools had been built in 1833 and the girls' school taken over by the Sisters in 1856. The Congregation had also opened their present convent school in 1864, and in 1866 they had been given charge of the newly built Poor School for girls. In addition they continued to run the girls' night school – Reports on the Missions of the Northern District, vol. I, Aberdeen, Rev. J. Sutherland, 1868, SM 9/2/1, SCA.

92 Cf. Scotland J., 1969, p. 186.

93 Education Papers – Religious Inspection, Reports of meetings of Diocesan Inspectors held in May 1875 and February 1876, copy ED 7, AGA. The first RE inspections were made in 1878.

94 Cf. Treble J.H., 1978J, p. 120. The loophole was not plugged until 1901.

95 For good summaries of the pupil–teacher system, cf. Wilson J.D. in Bone T.R. (ed.), 1967, p. 192ff., and Bone T.R., 1968, p. 35ff.

96 James Smith, HMIS, report of inspection of April 1874, as reported verbatim in the *Log*. (It was a statutory duty to log such reports in their entirety.)

97 The prediction of the final cost was accurate – £6,150 purchase price plus £3,342 for adaptation = £9,492 – RO8/13, AGA. The Congregation was also justified in believing that the money could be recouped afterwards: within three years it had reduced the mortgage to £3,000 – Council Meeting Minutes, meeting of July 1881.

98 Council Meeting Minutes, meeting of April 1878.

99 Tradition had it that the tunnels led from the local Bothwell pit and emerged at the square in Fallside Road, and that they had been dug because, in the days before pit baths, the respectable citizens of Bothwell refused to allow the miners to walk home unwashed through the town.

100 In 1880 the Coach House at Elmwood was converted into a chaplain's home and renamed The Hermitage, allowing Fr Caven and his successors to stay overnight.

101 Description of the foundation ceremony in *SCD*, 1878, Appendix pp. 172f, and of the opening in *SCD*, 1879, p. 102. The building cost £6,000–7,000. The boys' school headmaster was Mr Fagan. At the opening ceremony, the pupils presented Archbishop Eyre with a silver ink stand and Fr Alexander Taylor (who had led the fundraising for the new school) with a writing desk. See also Dunlop F.M., 2001, p. 78ff.

102 Aspinwall B., 1982J, pp. 45ff. and 53.

103 The phrase is from Bone T.R., 1968, p. 35. The system was established in 1846, the first pupil–teachers entering training college in 1851 and graduating as certificated teachers in 1853.

104 The Argyll Commission report (*Education Commission Scotland, Second Report by Her Majesty's Commissioners appointed to inquire into the Schools in Scotland, Elementary Schools*, Edinburgh, HMSO, 1867) included criticisms of existing accommodation, teaching standards, the certification of teachers and attendance of children, and made radical recommendations – including that of creating a national education system – that led to the Act of 1872.

105 Cf. Smout T.C., 1986, p. 142ff. The most important legislation was the Forbes-Mackenzie Act of 1853.

106 In particular, the Glasgow Police Act of 1856, and the General Police and Improvement (Scotland) Act of 1862.

107 Cf. Maver I., 2000, p. 172ff.

PART TWO

Earth

Be praised, my Lord, through Sister our mother Earth,
Who sustains and governs us,
And produces diverse fruits and coloured flowers . . .

St Francis, Canticle of the Creatures

CHAPTER THREE

New Planting (1878–1900)

The community in Jamaica was ailing. It had never numbered more than twelve and by now was down to seven. The prioress invited recruits from the Glasgow house, but because of the growing demands in Scotland none could be spared. There was talk of amalgamation with Bayswater, or possibly with a Franciscan Congregation in Calais, but on further consideration it was recognised that this would be impossible at such a distance.

In spring 1878 the Vicar Apostolic for Jamaica, Fr Thomas Porter SJ, was in Rome where he chanced to meet Fr Leo da Saracena, the Franciscan Custos Provincial for Allegany, New York. Their conversation turned to the work of the Franciscan Sisters in Kingston, and to the fear that the community might not survive. Fr Leo at once suggested the possibility of their affiliating with St Elizabeth's Convent in Allegany, the mother house of a Congregation of the Third Order Regular who, like them, were mainly dedicated to teaching.

Letters were exchanged between the two communities, and that October the vicaress of St Elizabeth's visited Kingston to discuss the proposal in person. Following her favourable report, three Sisters volunteered to transfer from Allegany to the Jamaican convent, to prepare the ground for its affiliation with the American house. They sailed in January 1879 and at once found themselves in the teeth of a storm. To save the ship, the captain ordered every item of cargo to be jettisoned. The Sisters arrived at Duke Street with nothing but what they stood up in.

The following November, Fr da Saracena travelled to Kingston, where he delivered the new Rule and Constitutions to the community and witnessed the renewal of their vows into the Allegany Congregation.[1] The year 1879 should thus have marked the end of the Jamaican convent as a community of the Franciscan Sisters of the Immaculate Conception, but it did not quite. At the time of the affiliation there was one young novice, Sr M. Immaculate Conception Filippi, already receiving formation in the house.[2] Since she had chosen to pursue her vocation in the 'old' Congregation, she was permitted to take her final vows under the Rule and Constitutions of her original choice. Technically speaking, therefore, the Congregation kept a foothold in

Jamaica, a foothold that was to last until Sr Filippi's death in 1940 at the age of eighty-one.

The Ursulines were the first women's Order to establish a house in Scotland in the post-Reformation era, having opened St Margaret's Convent in Edinburgh in 1834. For years they ran St John's schools in York Lane, attached to the parish of St Mary's. When they gave up that charge in 1880, Bishop Strain invited the Franciscan Sisters to take their place. A Minute of Agreement was signed that summer, by which the Congregation pledged to provide three certificated teachers for the girls' and infants' schools, and to take responsibility for catechesis and the children's Mass on Sundays. For this they received a house at 37 Albany Street rent-free and an annual salary of £200, and retained all monies from their 'select' school and from private tuition. Income from pupils' fees and government grants was to be retained by the parish priest.

The community of four Choir Sisters and one Lay Sister took up residence under Mother M. Baptist McLaughlan ready for the autumn term. By the time her office as superioress ended in 1884, the house was well established and self-supporting.[3]

Glasgow's Duke Street prison lay on the edge of St Mary's parish, about a kilometre's walk from the Charlotte Street convent. Within its twelve-acre site, great stone wings radiated from the central building, one housing men, another some 200 women, a third 250 children aged between nine and fifteen.[4] The male prisoners had the benefit of a visiting Catholic chaplain, Fr Michael Berger, but nothing was available for the women. In 1885, with the governor's permission, Fr Berger suggested that the Congregation should undertake regular visitation of the women in the jail. The new abbess, Mother M. of the Cross Black (Plate 10), voted her agreement, Archbishop Eyre gave his blessing, and the work began that autumn.

The Sisters made their visits in twos – usually an older, experienced leader with a young 'learner' – but once inside the prison they often split up in order to get round as many cells as possible. They very soon won the trust of the staff and were allowed to converse freely with the prisoners without any escort. The inmates spent much of their day employed in weaving, spinning, tambouring, sewing and making clothes. Most of them were poor wretches, serving time for drunkenness, prostitution and petty thieving, but some had a reputation for violence. Yet the Sisters had no fear of them, and in turn were trusted by them. In time they established a routine of visitations every Wednesday, with a return visit for Mass on Sundays. They also often helped the women after their release by offering friendship and providing support with funds donated by friends of the community.[5] This twice-weekly apostolate was to continue for eighty years, until the mid-1950s, when Duke Street's dwindling number of female prisoners were transferred to the Greenock women's prison.[6]

The girls' industrial school was now thriving under the Sisters' care. A new and far more suitable building had been completed in 1878,[7] and the roll now stood at two hundred. Every year Fr McIntosh visited on behalf of the archdiocese to inspect the girls' religious knowledge, and every year he gave them an excellent report.[8] In 1885 Kenneth McLeod of the city's Sanitary Department made a formal inspection of the school and pronounced himself 'highly satisfied'. 'All the arrangements and general appearance of your well appointed and well managed Institution gave me great satisfaction,' he wrote. 'The citizens of Glasgow have great reason to be thankful that the children under your charge are so comfortably lodged and kindly attended to.'[9]

It was an apt description of the care the girls were given by Sr M. Ursula McNally and her team of Lay Sisters at this time. The staff included Sr Winifride, who for twenty years tirelessly taught the children their prayers; the kindly and patient Sr Scholastica; and Sr Martha McLaughlin, who for close to forty years tended to their medical needs.[10] This last was no easy task, for many of them arrived at the school in chronic ill-health, and despite all the care of staff and visiting doctors two died on average in the school every year, most commonly from respiratory disease in the smoggy atmosphere of the East End.[11]

The controlled and caring environment offered a safeguard to their health, but once an infection took hold the close confines of the school made control almost impossible.[12] In November 1885 typhus found its way inside the building and more than half of the girls fell ill with the disease. Sr Martha was run off her feet trying to cope, even with the rest lending a hand. Sr Ambrose Stalker left her kitchen whenever she could to nurse the invalids, seemingly oblivious to the danger, but eventually she succumbed. The priest was sent for and she was given the Last Rites, more as a precaution than from any apparent emergency. But the following day she failed suddenly, and on 7 December she died.

In 1887 the Congregation took on another apostolate when they began visiting the women and children in the city's Barnhill Poor House at Townhead. First opened after the Poor Law Act of 1845 as a compassionate refuge for 'the friendless and impotent poor', it was by now indistinguishable from the notorious workhouses of England. It was a place of unrelieved monotony where the changeless regimen – oatmeal pottage morning and evening, broth at noon – marked out each unchanging day; an awful, soul-numbing place of misery, full of the sounds of cursing from dawn to dusk and the moans of troubled sleepers by night.[13] The vicaress, Sr Clare Cattenach, visited weekly, accompanied by a younger Sister, and she also attended Sunday Mass there. They usually brought with them whatever supplies of tea and sugar they could gather through the week, with sweets for the children, to add a little solace to those sad lives.

With every year the workload of the Sisters in the parish schools was mounting. The rolls had risen by 50 per cent in the previous decade.[14] The combined roll of St Andrew's girls' and infants' schools now stood at 646, while that of St John's was 820 and St Mary's, St Patrick's and St Mary's Greenock averaged over 750. But the rise in the numbers actually attending had been even greater – 68 per cent – as the people had gradually come to accept compulsory schooling. Moreover, the Catholic schools were particularly ill-provided with qualified teachers. There were no less than 172 pupil–teachers in charge of classes in the archdiocese at this time, and a heavy onus fell upon the certificated teachers – the Sisters among them – to uphold standards, instruct the pupil–teachers and compensate for their limitations. It was becoming quite impossible to fit in their school work along with their religious duties, and Council were yet again forced to emend the horarium to find them more time for administration work and rest.[15]

When Sr M. Gertrude Foley entered the Franciscan convent in Taunton in 1862, it was not long before she fell foul of the community. Eventually she was invited to leave, and when she declined she was awarded a pension of £25 per annum for life and dismissed. For the next twenty-five years she moved from one religious house to another on the Continent.[16] She was now staying at the monastery of S. Lucia Selvi, from where she wrote to Archbishop Eyre, explaining that she was seriously ill and begging him to have her readmitted to the Glasgow community to die among her friends. She also made a similar request to Cardinal-Vicar Parocchi in Rome;[17] indeed, she must have written several times to him, for he soon came to view her as a nuisance and an embarrassment, and wanted her out of Italy.[18] It was probably for this reason that he brought her request to Leo XIII and persuaded him that it deserved support. He then wrote to Charlotte Street and to Archbishop Eyre informing them of the pope's view and requesting that it be followed.[19] After consulting with Council, the abbess wrote to Sr Gertrude inviting her to return 'as a penitent'.[20]

The archbishop met the Council to discuss the conditions for her readmission. It was agreed that she would be given a room in the infirmary until her health improved; thereafter she would reside in the convent, but have no place in the choir or voice in Chapter. She would say her Office at the back of the chapel, receive communion last among the Choir Sisters and take her meals in the lowest place at table. The abbess at once wrote to her spelling out the conditions.[21]

Sr Gertrude was meantime making her way slowly across Europe, in the

1. Mother Veronica Cordier.
Photo: Archive of the Franciscan Sisters of the Immaculate Conception, Possilpark, Glasgow (AF)

2. Fr Peter Forbes *Photo: AF*

3. A close in 'The Wynds' – No. 80 High Street. *Photo: Thomas Annan*

4. No. 11 Monteith Row. *Photo: AF*

5. Charlotte Street, c. 1850. *Photo: AF*

6. Mother M. Aloysius
Mackintosh, Prioress
1863–66. *Photo: AF*

7. Sr M. Anastasia Martin,
one of the Bayswater Sisters,
d. 1886 *Photo: AF*

8. Mother M. Gonzaga Sim, Abbess
1869–84. *Photo: AF*

9. Elmwood school. *Photo: AF*

10. Mother M. of the Cross Black, Abbess 1884–96. *Photo: AF*

11. Charlotte Street chapel – sanctuary and choir. *Photo: AF*

12. The improvised chapel at Mt Alvernia, Kingston Jamaica, 1907.
Photo: AF

13. Sr Adélaide's unmarked grave, Dalbeth cemetery, 1911. *Photo:
Ciorsdaidh Watts*

14. Mother Veronica's grave, Néchin, Belgium, 1913. *Photo: AF*

15. Our Lady and St Francis Secondary School, new building 1922. *Photo: AF*

general direction of Scotland. By January 1888 she had reached Lyons. The viatic gifted to her by the Cardinal-Vicar was already gone, spent on less than frugal lodgings and expensive medicines, and she wrote to the Glasgow community for money to pay off her debts and cover the rest of her journey. With debts enough of their own, they refused. She contrived to borrow money locally and moved on. In April she was in Nîmes, whence she wrote again to Archbishop Eyre, rejecting the abbess' conditions for readmission as unreasonable and advising him that she was on her way to Scotland. She sent no news of her plans to the Congregation.[22]

She arrived at the door of Charlotte Street on 11 July and was readmitted into the community. Almost at once there was friction. She insisted on having her own confessor and receiving her mail direct from the post office. She seemed to expect the standards she had enjoyed as a guest in the European houses, demanding wine at every sitting and despising the plain fare. She even threatened to take her case to the newspapers and to court.[23] Meantime she appealed to the archbishop, accusing the community of punishing her out of spite because they had been forced to back down by Rome. She claimed that the Sisters had been instructed not to talk to her and that she was being ostracised like a criminal. All she asked was a little kindness, to help her recover her health.[24] By autumn her presence was becoming almost unbearable, and forty-six members of the community signed a petition to *Propaganda* requesting her removal.[25]

In the Congregation's long history some Sisters have inevitably been unhappy in their vocation, and some unable to live in harmony with those around them. Inevitably, therefore, similar disputes have occasionally arisen, involving requests for exclaustration or readmission. One or two have been long-running and acrimonious. Considering the demands made on those living in close religious communities, the Congregation's disputes have in fact been surprisingly few, and it would be entirely misleading to exaggerate their importance by including others in this history. But since they have played a part in community life from time to time – a human though hardly an inspiring part – I felt it important to include this one early example to give a rounded picture.

In January 1888 an epidemic again struck the industrial school. The exact nature of the disease was not entirely clear, but it appeared suddenly and spread rapidly through the boys' building. Sixty-six cases were diagnosed in all, and four of them ended in death. Two girls also died at this time, but apparently of other causes.

Because of the outbreak no inspection was made of the boys' school that spring, but the girls were inspected as usual. HMIS Henry Rodgers found them all in good health and spirits. As ever, he was able to give a first-class report of the school, which was 'carefully and thoughtfully managed, and doing very good work in all points of view'. The girls were thoroughly instructed and well behaved, and rarely needed correction. He particularly noticed the caring relationship that existed between them and the staff: it was quite obvious, he reported, that they received 'the utmost consideration' from the Sisters to whom they were entrusted.[26]

Rodgers' published *Report* provides much useful information on the school. It shows that the age of admission varied greatly, and though most of the girls were at least ten years old on entry, some were as young as six. Theirs was a long, full day, beginning at 6.30 a.m. with prayers and daily Mass, followed by seven-and-a-half hours of work divided equally between school lessons and vocational training (i.e., sewing), and two hours' recreation. On Sundays they attended Religious Instruction, Catechism, Rosary and Benediction, and also enjoyed an hour's walk in Alexandra Park. The older girls retired to bed at 8.30 p.m., the youngest ones an hour earlier.

Under the care of the Sisters for twenty-four hours a day in a purposeful yet loving environment, the girls made notable progress. Two thirds of them arrived totally illiterate, but almost nine out of ten were said to be able to read and write 'fairly', and over half 'well', when tested by the inspector. Although many had been referred to the school by the courts, less than one in fifty were convicted again within three years of leaving, and 95 per cent were known to be 'doing well'. This was in no small measure due to the follow-up care that the Sisters saw as an essential part of their work, helping to place the girls in domestic service with good families and keeping contact with them wherever possible.

The school was a success story, in fact, and even the epidemic in a sense confirmed this. The city's medical officer of health strongly criticised the school in a published report, asserting that the outbreak had been a febrile disease attributable to the insanitary conditions, but his claims were strenuously refuted, and compelling evidence was advanced that the disease was in fact a form of influenza to which the children had succumbed because they came from the very poorest backgrounds and were in many cases 'constitutionally feeble' on admission. In particular, many suffered from poor circulation and as such were especially at risk if exposed to cold and damp. Whereas other industrial schools routinely discharged pupils who fell prey to disease, St Mary's pursued a policy of holding on to them wherever possible and seeing them through.[27] If anything, therefore, the epidemic pointed to a strength rather than a weakness.

Nevertheless, the deaths and the heated debate that followed them focused attention on the hazards and problems of the system, and brought some benefit to the children and staff. The board of directors promised immediate improvements – warmer clothing and enhanced heating – and, in the longer term, new premises in a more suitable location for the younger boys and delicate girls.[28] For the first time the principle was recognised that the countryside, not the Calton, was the place for such a school. But it would be eleven years before thought was translated into action.

In 1888 the Scotch Education Department introduced a national leaving certificate as a qualification for pupils completing a standard course of secondary education.[29] Awarded at lower, higher and honours levels, it covered the traditional secondary curriculum of English, Latin, Greek, mathematics, science and languages. Since it was recognised by the professions and the universities, its introduction immediately raised the standing and popularity of schools offering secondary courses. Within three years the number of candidates presenting for the certificate more than tripled.[30]

Major changes were also taking place in the elementary schools. Though the 1872 Act had made education compulsory for all children aged 5–13, it had not made it free, and the requirement to pay had proved a major obstacle to the law's wholesale implementation. In 1889 the Department introduced free schooling for younger children, extending it over the following five years to apply to all 3–15-year-olds.[31] Again, the changes were very soon reflected in increased attendance figures.

Both initiatives promised to have immediate implications for the Sisters. If the Catholic community was not to be left behind, it was essential that they introduce the leaving certificate at Charlotte Street and Elmwood and gain recognition for them as Higher Grade schools. To achieve this, a broader curriculum would be needed, which in turn would require larger premises and more qualified staff, something not easy to sell to the 'old brigade' in the Congregation, who still saw their real apostolate in primary and private education. As to the Catholic elementary schools, which were not rate-supported, fees were still being charged. But they too experienced some increase in numbers through a 'halo effect' of the changing practice in society as a whole. Here again, the larger numbers were putting a strain on accommodation and staffing.

This was a time of large-scale housing development on the edge of Glasgow. On the south side, new middle-class suburbs were rising in Shaw-lands, Langside and Crosshill, an expansion both reflected in and accelerated by their absorption within the extended city boundaries in 1891. In 1886 the new parish of Holy Cross was created in Crosshill to serve the Catholics of the area, but to date no parish or 'select' school had been established in the neighbourhood, and many of the children were attending the local Protestant schools.[32] Archbishop Eyre was anxious to rectify this situation and in summer 1889 invited the Congregation to open a branch house in the area. Since the Sisters had themselves been considering precisely the same thing for some time, they readily agreed to his request.[33]

It was not a good time to be purchasing property, when major extensions were also needed at Charlotte Street and Elmwood, or to be committing more teaching Sisters when their workforce was already under severe strain. In summer 1891, the abbess convened an extraordinary Chapter in order to argue the necessity of extending the two existing schools, for which initial estimates suggested a total outlay of £5,000. Winning the Sisters' unanimous support she at once sought Archbishop Eyre's permission to go ahead with the plan for Charlotte Street, involving the demolition of No. 64 and a rebuild from scratch on the site.[34] She then followed up this request with a second for a day school at Elmwood, for which there was a proven demand, pointing out that the mortgage on the boarding school was now paid off, and that conditions were so cramped that the Sisters had given up part of their own living space to make room for the girls.[35] After some hesitation His Grace finally gave his consent.[36] She hastily made arrangements for building work to begin immediately at both sites, so that the projects would already be in progress and unlikely to be halted when the question of the new purchase on the south side came to be considered.

As to the problem of finding more teaching Sisters, it was Archbishop Eyre's view that the Congregation should make his archdiocese their priority – it was to Glasgow that they had come in the first place, after all – and that with the greater demands 'at home' they should now close their branch houses elsewhere.[37] This was hardly likely to be acceptable to the Church authorities in Aberdeen, Inverness and Edinburgh, or indeed to the Sisters in those communities. Closing Inverness had been tried more than once before, and successfully resisted. Nor would Edinburgh, where the redoubtable Canon Donlevy was parish priest, be any easier.

It would in fact have suited the abbess well to pull out of Edinburgh. The work was thriving there, but according to the new superioress, Mother Stanislaus MacDonald, the canon was inclined to take advantage of the Sisters' goodwill, expecting them to undertake duties not included in the contract while failing to honour his own obligations. As a result, several had already been withdrawn from the house on grounds of health, and Mother Stanislaus herself had incurred his displeasure by standing up to him.[38]

One of the factors that had kept them in the city was the support and friendship of Archbishop William Smith, who was also their Extraordinary Confessor. When he died in March 1892, the abbess seized the opportunity of the interregnum to serve the canon the statutory six months' notice of her intention to withdraw the Sisters from the school and convent.[39] He immediately contacted the Vicar General of the Glasgow Archdiocese, Provost John Maguire, protesting with some animus against her decision.

She had never taken an interest in Edinburgh, he wrote, and had 'invariably succeeded in giving trouble'; she had saddled him with several useless teachers, and seemed to have a personal dislike of him. He disbelieved her claim that she was closing the convent on the instruction of Archbishop Eyre.[40]

Estimates for the building at Charlotte Street and Elmwood had now risen to over £6,000.[41] Faced with a massive outlay if these and the south-side project all went ahead, the Vicar General contacted the whole Congregation in May to gauge each person's views as to which project(s) should take priority and which would be the best location for the mother house. He received fifty-eight replies in all, expressing a range of opinion.[42] Some feared the crippling cost of proceeding with all three projects; others noted that Charlotte Street was hopelessly cramped for a mother house. Given the chance to air their grievances, several seized it with both hands: the Elmwood dormitories were 'simply dreadful', with the beds so close-packed that in the mornings the air was 'sickening'; Charlotte Street was 'plagued with rats, clocks, cats and bad air' and the condition of its 'select' school 'far behind even any of [their] poor schools'; in both houses the Sisters were expected after a hard day's work 'to try to sleep in close, unhealthy, low-roofed holes and corners'. A good number recommended making either Elmwood or the proposed south-side convent the mother house, and there seemed a real possibility that Charlotte Street could be relegated to a branch house.

Though most Sisters favoured the proposed new house in Crosshill they could not accept the archbishop's condition of closing Aberdeen and Inverness. Their dilemma was well expressed in the response of Mother Gonzaga, the former abbess. She believed in the new house and did not wish to jeopardise it, but asked to be excused from supporting any of the options. 'I think I would regret to the latest day of my life,' she wrote, 'if I had any part, no matter how small, in closing the Northern houses.' Many must have shared her dilemma, for when the issue was raised at the Chapter in July the members could not face making a decision but voted to leave the matter to Council. The latter decided unanimously to open the school and convent on the south side and accept the archbishop's condition of closing the branch houses.

They also took a definite decision to develop Charlotte Street and Elmwood as Higher Grade schools.[43] If the 'old brigade' had any doubts on the matter, recent events had clinched the decision for them: earlier that year Ordinance No.18 of the Universities (Scotland) Act had given women access to the universities for the first time. It promised to open up a whole new world of opportunity in the professions to them, and if the Catholic community were to have a share in it, they would need Catholic Higher

Grade schools. The Congregation's decision was soon to prove timely for another reason, too, as we shall see.

At its August meeting, Council confirmed the decision to withdraw the Sisters from Edinburgh, but at Canon Donlevy's request the abbess agreed that they would remain until summer 1893, since the school was due to have its annual inspection in May of that year and she did not wish to jeopardise its government grant. In their correspondence both parties were at pains to heal old wounds: the canon asked that there be 'no more disagreeables', and she expressed her regret for all the trouble he had had. The convent finally closed on 8 July.[44]

As we saw, the Congregation had been suffering for some years from a growing shortage of qualified teaching Sisters.[45] Their difficulty was part of a more general problem in Scottish Catholic education: there were simply not enough certificated Catholic teachers to be had. The numbers were rising slowly, certainly, but there were still close to two hundred pupil–teachers making up the shortfall in the west–central belt alone. Without them the schools would not have run at all, yet their presence, along with other poorly educated staff, only served to lower standards. It was a problem not lost on the inspectorate. 'There is a point beyond which the work, especially in the senior classes, will not rise,' they had warned in a recent report, 'a point considerably lower than that attained in Board [i.e., state] schools. . . . It is a deficiency which no industry of the teachers, no skill of the managers, no stimulus of inspection can remedy; for it arises solely from the intellectual defects of a staff who have not received a regular and thorough training.' To solve the problem, they 'earnestly recommended' that a training college be opened for Catholic teachers in Glasgow.[46]

This was not the first time that the proposal had been made, and everyone accepted its logic. As things stood, female Catholic students had nowhere to train but Liverpool or London, and the men nowhere but London or Dublin. Not all families could afford the costs, though; nor, in the case of women, did they relish their daughters living so far from home.

In the face of growing pressure from officialdom to make provision nearer home, the hierarchy could put the matter off no longer. There were two options open to them. They could either establish a day college for women, whose students would be drawn mainly from Glasgow and its immediate neighbourhood, or open a residential college to cater for women from throughout Scotland. Each proposal had its supporters among the senior clergy.

Archbishop Eyre was aware of the work of the Sisters of Notre Dame de Namur, who had been running the residential women's college at Mount Pleasant Liverpool for nearly thirty years, and in 1892 he deputed Canon Chisholm of Paisley to sound them out regarding the possibility of their setting up something similar on Clydeside.[47] When the archdiocese acquired a property, Glen Huntly near Port Glasgow, that autumn, the proponents of the 'residential' option saw their case as strengthened, for it seemed ideal for the purpose. The archdiocesan Chapter appointed a committee to look into the costs of adapting it, and to that end detailed one of their number, Canon James Cameron, to visit the college at Mount Pleasant. The Chapter hoped to offer the Notre Dame Sisters a firm invitation to come to Scotland and set up the new college, should the scheme prove feasible.[48]

The canon travelled down in February 1893, saw the college for himself and held lengthy discussions with the principal, Sr Mary of St Philip Lescher, and other senior staff. On his return he presented a detailed and very favourable report to Archbishop Eyre, who appeared 'perfectly satisfied' with the proposal but felt unable to act upon it until he had gauged the views of the Church's Poor Schools Committee, the education department, and his own Vicar General, Provost John Maguire.[49] Now seventy-five, he was coming to depend ever more on Provost Maguire, who would be consecrated his coadjutor bishop the following year.

The Vicar General, however, was a firm supporter of the 'day college' option, and furthermore favoured the Charlotte Street Franciscans to run it. He no doubt preferred them as being a home-grown Congregation (a consideration that would have counted less with the English-born archbishop), and because he had first-hand knowledge of their record in education. But he must also have been influenced by the fact that two of his own sisters, M. Magdalen and M. Lucy, were members of the Congregation, and a third, M. Francesca, had been so until her death ten years before. According to Canon Cameron, he had already in fact earmarked Sr Lucy as the college's first principal.[50] It may indeed have been his support for the Franciscans that caused him to favour the day college option in the first place, for he knew that they lacked the experience, and probably the inclination, to run a residential college for adult women.[51]

In the course of their own enquiries, the Chapter members learned that most of the senior parish priests of the archdiocese were opposed to a day college, because they feared that much of the teaching would have to be undertaken by non-Catholic outsiders. In addition, the principals of the existing Protestant normal colleges, and other education professionals in Scotland, were also advising them of the benefits of a residential college. In the light of this, the Chapter's support for the residential option had now hardened.[52] But Archbishop Eyre, who now rarely attended Chapter meetings, apparently remained unaware of their views – he believed, on the contrary, that they favoured the day college model.[53] Influenced as he was by his Vicar General, his own judgment of the issue was now veering in that direction too.

Alarmed to have heard no word of progress and warned by Canon Cameron of a likely *volte face* by the archbishop, Sr Mary of St Philip wrote to His Grace in April, asking him to clarify the position. In his reply he assured her that the archdiocese was as yet uncommitted either way.[54]

The Church's Poor Schools Committee included the issue on the agenda of its meeting in London later that month, during which the Glasgow representatives tabled a motion for a residential college to be established in the city. The motion was passed by a large majority. By now, also, Archbishop Eyre had discovered the real views of his Chapter. He at once wrote to Sr Mary of St Philip, acknowledging that he had been 'under a mistake' and promising immediate action.[55] He made a point of attending the next meeting of the Chapter on 12 May in person, where the issue was debated under his chairmanship and voted upon. The decision was almost unanimous: to establish a residential college, and to invite the Notre Dame sisters to take charge of it. No location was decided upon, though it would certainly not be Glen Huntly, since it was stipulated that the site must be within five miles of the city centre.[56]

The way was now clear to move forward, pending government approval and the purchase of a suitable property. The first was granted before the end of the year; the second finally clinched in June 1894 with the acquisition of premises at Dowanhill in the west end of the city that were to serve for three-quarters of a century. The Sisters took possession that August, began scholarship classes the following month, held examinations in December and welcomed their first students in the new year.[57]

I have passed swiftly over these latter stages of the founding of the college, since they did not involve the Franciscan Congregation and have in any case been well documented in the histories published by the Notre Dame Sisters. But the earlier events – the dispute concerning the type and function of the college, and who should run it – have never been published, and indeed are not generally known even by members of the two Congregations themselves.[58] Yet they are crucial. For if Provost Maguire's wishes had prevailed – as seemed for a while very possible, given his powerful influence with the archbishop; if the day college model had been adopted and the Franciscan Sisters had been chosen to run it, the whole history of Catholic teacher training in Scotland, and of both Congregations, would have been altogether different.

In anticipation of the opening of Notre Dame, Mother M. of the Cross and her Council had been pressing ahead with the upgrading of Charlotte Street, Elmwood and St Mary's Greenock to secondary status. The work was timely, for it was from such schools that the college could expect to recruit most of its students.

In 1894 everything came together: the building work in Glasgow and at Elmwood was completed, the application to have Charlotte Street recognised as a secondary school was accepted by the education department,[59] and Council started negotiations to have Elmwood similarly recognised and to create the new secondary centre at Greenock.[60] At the same time, the other religious Orders in Glasgow were making similar moves: the Mercy Sisters' Garnethill Convent school was raised to secondary status, as was the Marists' St Mungo's Academy for boys, joining the Jesuit-run St Aloysius' College, which already offered a secondary education. By a happy coincidence, also, the opening of the council-run Tramway Company that year promised to make travel across town to the secondary schools and the college far easier.

1894 was a milestone for Catholic education in the west of Scotland, in fact, an *annus mirabilis* as one historian has been moved to call it.[61] The Church now had a women's training college, and four Catholic schools offering a secondary curriculum, with two more soon to follow. For many years to come they would be the only such in Scotland. All were run by religious, half of them by the Franciscan Sisters. The schools were equipped to prepare young men and women for university and for the training colleges, whence many would return to teach the next generation in a Catholic school system which had chosen to remain outside the state. The whole enterprise depended upon the existence of the secondary schools, and they in turn upon the presence of the religious. As the same historian has remarked, 'had the Religious Orders not borne the burden of secondary education at this time, it is difficult to see how the Catholic system could have survived'.

The Congregation certainly understood the significance of their schools' new status and their crucial role in the future of Catholic education, and when the headship of Charlotte Street fell vacant that spring, they were determined to make the best possible appointment to the post. Their choice was Sr M. Jerome Gordon, a native of Aberdeen who had been educated by the Sisters in that city and had been a governess in France before joining the Congregation. Though she could not be released from St Patrick's Anderston until August they were prepared to wait if it meant getting the right person.

Sr Jerome was to remain in office for twenty-four years. Standing six feet tall, with massive hands and a presence in proportion, yet gentle to children and colleagues alike, she was a natural teacher and a dedicated religious. She would become one of Charlotte Street's greatest headmistresses, under whose guidance the school would grow from a small private institution to one of the leading secondary schools in the west of Scotland. Among the qualities that profoundly influenced her pupils and for which they especially remembered her were her talent for music, her enthusiasm for beautiful things and delight in experiment, her capacity for bringing languages alive for them, and her scorn for anything underhand or mean, which made them prefer to own up to a misdemeanour rather than risk losing her trust and affection.[62] She had in abundance that special quality, the ability to inspire.

Under her stewardship the school's secondary department officially opened in January 1895, almost on the very day that Notre Dame received its first students, many of them Charlotte Street alumnae. The following month the Congregation finally settled on the property for their new convent and school on the south side of the city. The purchase of Orchard Villa, 86 Albert Road in Crosshill was completed that April, giving the Sisters a footing in the parish of Holy Cross that they have maintained until today.

At the Chapter of July 1896, Sr M. Athanasius MacLean succeeded to the office of abbess. One of her first acts was to send a gift to Mother Veronica in Tourcoing, to mark the half-century since that first meeting with Fr Forbes that had brought her to Glasgow. From her letter of thanks, in which she signed herself 'Your fond Mother Véronique', it was clear that after all her years away she still retained a loving parental interest in the Congregation that she had founded.[63]

If she could have returned she would have found it in the most fundamental respects much as she had left it. There was the same defining vision; the same daily activity; the same silence in corridors, refectory and cloister (which applied even to the silent closing of doors). But she might have noticed also a certain tightening of the Rules and customs, which had begun before she left but had accelerated under the influence of successive bishops, and in particular Archbishop Eyre. There had been a Canonical visitation that very summer, and the Visitor's report had dwelt almost entirely on regulations and the letter of the law. He had insisted on strict adherence to the horarium; on sisters visiting their parents only in case of grievous illness, and even then not taking meals with them; on Lay Sisters being clearly distinguished by dress; on Choir Sisters not normally going shopping, and certainly never alone; on making special arrangements with the new Tramway Company to transport the Sisters privately to the schools. These and the whole corpus of Constitutions, read out to the community every week, must have created a communal mindset of admirable order and efficiency but in which the institution itself perhaps sometimes over-shadowed the spirit of the work.

The Visitor had also warned against overwork and insisted that Sisters teaching during the day should not work in the evening schools or take responsibility for pupil–teachers on Saturdays.[64] It was a sound instruction, for although conditions in the city were improving, the work and the working environment were still injurious to the Sisters' health. Council meetings at this time had to deal with a rash of physical and mental break-downs, and two young Sisters, still in their twenties, had recently died of consumption.[65] Following the Visitor's recommendation, Archbishop Eyre urged that all those working in the public schools should be able to take their summer vacation at the coast. Council responded by acquiring a house in Girvan; in its first summer twenty Sisters spent a month's holiday there.[66]

From the earliest days, when M. Angela and M. Catherine McSwiney had been received, the Congregation had been notable for attracting 'multiple vocations' from the same families, and this tradition continued. We have already come across the three Maguire sisters – Francesca, Magdalen and Lucy – two of whom were still living at this date. But there were also three MacLeans from Glenuig: Srs M. Paula, M. Elizabeth and Athanasius, the newly appointed abbess. There were also three Farnons, Innocent and Imelda Doherty, and Gabriel and Felicitas Egan. Lastly, there were three Kerigans: M. Perpetua, M. Patricia, who taught the infant class at the Sacred Heart for well over thirty years, and M. Seraphina, whom we met at St Joseph's Aberdeen and who was now the mistress at St Patrick's, devoted to the children of Anderston and fondly loved in that community.[67]

Long and dedicated service was in fact a quality of the Congregation, and of the age in which they lived. M. Aquinas Kelly was now well into her thirty-seven years as mistress at Kinning Park, and the gentle and pious Lay Sister Sheila Forsyth was beginning what was to become her forty years as infirmarian in the mother house. Others enriched the community with particular talents. Sr M. Hildegarde Stromeye was noted for her exquisite embroidery, and Mother Stanislaus MacDonald, now back at Charlotte Street from Edinburgh,[68] was the Congregation's creative writer – in a good Franciscan tradition – and her collected poems, *Cloister Chimes*, were well received in their day.

The cook in the mother house at this time was the Lay Sister Zita Biggins. During her childhood in Galston there was no parish in the town, which was served by a missioner from Kilmarnock. Her house was used as an oratory and had the Blessed Sacrament reserved there, and the deep impression that this made upon her had sown the seed of her religious vocation.

Also seen about the house was Miss Jane Robertson George. Now in her seventies, she had been accepted as a parlour boarder as long ago as 1856. She was devoted to the community and its interests and personified the striking loyalty that the Sisters have always commanded among the Catholic laity. Charlotte Street was her life, and her last act after half a century in the parlour would be to bequeath her estate to the Congregation.[69]

Teachers in the Catholic schools enjoyed none of the security of their colleagues in the board schools at this time.[70] Hiring and firing them remained within the power of the managers, with little or no redress. To employ a religious teaching Sister was an attractive proposition for many parish priests, since they felt they would be getting a special dedication, idealism and commitment to the faith, and that on a lower salary than they would have to pay to a lay mistress. Indeed, the beneficial influence of the teaching Orders upon the Catholic community was undeniable, but for the wider profession, and for the advancement of good Catholic lay teachers, the effect was anything but beneficial. The preference for religious, and their guarantee of the right of succession in certain parish schools over many generations, acted as a bar to the ambitions of lay staff that is hard to justify today.

Such a case occurred in 1896 in St Mary's Hamilton. For the previous nine years Frances Fagan had been mistress of the school, receiving consistently good reports from Her Majesty's Inspectors.[71] In the autumn of 1896, Fr Peter Donnelly decided to replace her with a Sister of the Congregation. For £90 per annum, plus £60 for an assistant, he could thus cover the teaching and management of the school, the children's Sunday Mass and the supervision of the pupil–teachers. His offer was accepted by Council, and Sr M. Philippa Boyle took up her post in November. The outgoing mistress' laconic entry in the log, 'Frances G. Fagan resigns her charge today', masks a whole welter of emotion, a human story and an issue of natural justice. From the parish community's point of view, it was no doubt a good move. The school was to enjoy a continuity of leadership and care under the Sisters into the 1930s, and to earn excellent reports from the inspectorate.

In spring 1898, the Catholic Education Committee of Lanarkshire requested the Congregation to create a pupil–teacher centre at Elmwood, to serve the industrial area of the county south of Glasgow. Two Sisters were appointed to run the centre, which opened that August. The following year a similar request was made for a centre at Charlotte Street to cover the east side of the city. Once it was up and running, all female pupil–teachers took their training there.[72] To bring them together in this way was clearly a far more effective arrangement than having them scattered in a large number of schools as was the case previously, where tuition and examination were uneven and where they had little chance to learn from one another. The new centres thus represented a major step forward in the preliminary training of a Catholic teaching workforce, and they gave the Sisters an even more vital role in the building of the Church's education system in the west of Scotland.

The new facilities in both schools, added to the outlay on Crosshill, left the Congregation with a debt that had now risen to £7,500. In spring 1899 a group of former pupils and friends approached the abbess with a proposal to establish a Franciscan Association, to commemorate the fiftieth anniversary of the opening of Charlotte Street and help erase the debt. A large and enthusiastic crowd gathered for the inaugural meeting in the new luncheon hall, at which a committee was appointed and plans were laid for a number of fundraising events. The first, a summer garden party at Elmwood, was judged a great success, and more followed, the most ambitious a three-day bazaar at Charlotte Street which realised a clear profit of over £2,300.[73]

Minor miracles had been achieved at the industrial school, and as the most recent inspection had shown, the girls were receiving excellent training for future domestic service.[74] They had the constant example of the Sisters, and they 'learned by doing', actually running the house, working in the kitchen, cleaning, laundering for the staff and the boys' school, machine-sewing and knitting their own clothes as well as saleable articles, and waiting on visitors. Discipline was good, with an emphasis on prizes and privileges rather than punishment. A library containing 400 volumes, lantern slide shows, and visits to the circus and the pantomime helped fill their leisure time. In short, they enjoyed an effective grounding in both practical and personal–social education, and as a result the staff found no difficulty in placing them with good families when they left. Their health was given attention, too, with picnics in the country, an annual outing to the coast, and holidays at a house near Rothesay made available by the generosity of the Marquis of Bute.

There were still deaths, though, from phthisis, opthalmia and other diseases; scrofula and eczema were rife, too, and this state of affairs could only continue while living conditions remained as they were. The toilet facilities belonged to a previous age, and the girls still used the old graveyard as their playground. The doctor had drawn attention to their unhealthy appearance and the high incidence of delicate and strumous cases among them; it was only by the great care and attention of the Sisters, he added, that they remained in such good spirits, but the real solution was to move to where the air was purer.

This was not the first such warning that the archdiocesan authorities had received, and now at last they were heeding it. In spring 1899 they purchased Kenmure House near the village of Bishopbriggs, in bracing open country between the city and the Campsie Hills, to house a new industrial school. On 4 June over a hundred girls moved into their new home, in the charge of four Sisters.[75] At least a third of the pupils had to remain in Abercromby Street, however, due to restrictions on space, an arrangement that was supposed to be temporary, although staff and pupils were in fact to live with the frustration of a split site for thirty-four years. Kenmure was not entirely the end of the old era, therefore, but it was certainly the beginning of a new.

In October 1900 the Congregation took charge of the new St John the Baptist parish school in Uddingston at the request of Fr Beyart, serving it from the convent at Elmwood, whence two Sisters travelled daily by train.[76] This was the last invitation that they accepted. The new century, as it turned out, marked the end of the 'new planting', for the Congregation was now devoting its energies to building on what it already had, bringing to greater maturity plants already growing, and there were to be virtually no fresh undertakings for the next fifty years.[77]

ENDNOTES TO CHAPTER THREE

1 From the Jamaica Congregation, Community Record Book (1857–1907), entry by Mother M. Teresa O'Neil, superioress, in Rodrigues V.I., *op. cit.*, p. 88.

2 She was twenty-one and a native of Panama. She was sent to the Convent School at twelve and joined the community in 1876.

3 *Scottish Catholic Monthly*, 1894, p. 228; Minute of Agreement, August 1880, 030.1, AF; Minute of Agreement, Bishop Smith, 1881, ED 4/115/3, AGA; Edinburgh House Reports (1881–93), 030.1, AF.

4 Details from *Old Glasgow Club Transactions*, vol. II, 1908–12 (Glasgow, 1912), p. 101; House J., 'Behind Prison Gates', *Evening News*, 11 and 13.6.1955. For a detailed account of the buildings from the eighteenth century to the late nineteenth, see Markus T.A. (ed.), 1982, p. 47ff.

5 *Scottish Catholic Monthly*, 1894, p. 229.

6 See p. 155ff. *infra*. The work of visitation was then taken on by the Congregation's Greenock community.

7 Fr William Caven to Archbishop Eyre, 14.4.1878, GC 11/34, AGA, giving details of the cost (c. £1,700) and funding.

8 Religious Education Inspections, 1880–1, ED 7/1/2; and 1886–7, ED 7/1/4, AGA.

9 Kenneth M. McLeod to Lewis McKenzie, 12.3.1885, in *Report on the Industrial School for Girls Abercromby Street*, 1888. From the year that Abercromby Street became an industrial school under the Franciscan Sisters it had gained consistently good reports – cf., Sydney Turner, Office of Reformatories and Certified Industrial Schools, London, to Bishop Murdoch, 14.11.1863, OL 2/108/11, SCA; Report by Henry Rogers HMAI, 1874–5, copy SM 13/3/2, SCA; Ditto, 1880, copy SM 13/3/4, SCA.

10 *Obituary Register*, AF. The account of Sr Ambrose Stalker is also from this source.

11 According to *Scottish Catholic Monthly*, 1894, sixty-one girls died in the school in the first thirty-two years under the Sisters (1862–94); this represents 1/20th of the 1,204 girls admitted. Some seventy are buried in a single plot in Dalbeth Cemetery.

12 There had been an outbreak of typhoid in the school in 1873, infecting several of the staff and killing one pupil. So many children were infected that the charge for accommodating them at the city's fever hospital amounted to £52 – Kenneth Macleod to Rev. Ramsey, priest of St Mary's, 17.8.1873, SM 8/6/12, SCA.

13 There is a letter extant in the Glasgow Archdiocesan Archives, written to Archbishop Eyre by a blind orphan who had spent some years under the Sisters at the orphanage, and who ended up in the Poor House. In it she describes the moral degradation of the place and begs his help to get her moved –Mary Ann Coxhead to Archbishop Eyre, n.d. (c. 1880?), GC 10/29/1, AGA. See also Motion J.R., 'Poor Law in Olden Times', *Old Glasgow Club Transactions*, vol. II, 1908–12, Paper no. 16.

14 This and the rest of the statistics in the present paragraph are from *Reports of the Religious Examination of Schools*, 1887, ED 7/1/4, AGA.

15 Council Meeting Minutes, 1873–1974, 034.10, no. 2; AF, meeting of August 1887.

16 Mother Mary of the Cross Black to Cardinal Simeoni, 5.11.1888, 025.1, AF.

17 Sr Gertrude Foley to Cardinal-Vicar Parocchi, 11. 6. 1887, RO8/10, AGA.

18 Mgr J. Campbell, Rector Scots College Rome, to Mother M. of the Cross, 17.10.1888, 025.1, AF.

19 Cardinal-Vicar Parocchi to Mother M. of the Cross, 6.7.1887 (in Italian), and same to Archbishop Eyre, 27.7.1887 (in Italian) copy, both 025.I, AF.

20 Mother M. of the Cross to Archbishop Eyre, 12.7.1887, RO8/10, AGA, in which she refers to her letter to Sr Gertrude.

21 Council Meeting Minutes, meeting of 5 August 1887.

22 Sr Gertrude Foley to Archbishop Eyre, 16.4.1888, RO8/11, AGA; and Council Meeting Minutes, meeting of 16 May 1888.

23 Mother M. of the Cross and Council to Cardinal Simeoni, Prefect of *Propaganda Fide*, 5.11.1888, 025.1, AF.

24 Sr Gertrude Foley to Archbishop Eyre, n.d., RO8/22, AGA.

25 Mgr J. Campbell to Mother M. of the Cross, 26.9.1888, 025.1, AF.

26 *Report on the Industrial School*, 1888, p. 7. The rest of the present account is from the same source.

27 *Statement of the Case for St Mary's Industrial Schools*, printed 1888, copy 012.2, AF, especially pp. 3–8.

28 *Ibid.*, p. 10ff. The board was chaired by the archbishop himself.

29 This and the other initiatives mentioned below were largely the work of the energetic and forward-thinking Henry Craik, who had been appointed secretary of the newly autonomous department in 1885.

30 See Dobie T.B., 'The Scottish Leaving Certificate 1888–1908', Section 3 of Bone T.R. (ed.), 1967.

31 Wade N.A., 1939, p. 68.

32 Mother M. of the Cross to Provost John Maguire, 24.10.1889, RO8/12, AGA. The nearest parish schools were St. John's Gorbals or Our Lady & St Margaret's Kinning Park, the nearest 'select' schools Charlotte Street or Garnethill Convent.

33 Mother M. of the Cross to Provost Maguire, 12.8.1889, RO8/12, AGA; and same to same, 1.9.1890 and 7.9.1890, RO8/13, AGA. Council agreed in principle in 1889, but elected to await the decision of the full Chapter, to be held in the summer of 1890. Chapter voted unanimously in favour.

34 Council Meeting Minutes, meeting of 15 July 1891; Mother M. of the Cross to Provost John Maguire, 10.9.1891, RO8/14, AGA. The two plans for Charlotte Street had been drawn up by Canon Caven (less ambitious) and Canon Cameron (more ambitious and expensive). The finance committee approved the cheaper plan – the one dissenting voice being that of Canon Cameron himself – and minuted the members' hope that the cost should not exceed £3,000 – FR 1/1, AGA, meeting of 19.2.1891. The following year they approved the architect's revised plan, at a cost of £4,250 – FR 1/2, meeting of 19.2.1892.

35 Mother M. of the Cross and Council to Archbishop Eyre, 19.10.1891, and same to same, 30.10.1891, RO8/14, AGA.

36 Mother M. of the Cross to Provost John Maguire, 28.1.1892, 9.2.1892 and 22.2.1892 (in which she thanked him for his help towards the successful outcome).

37 Mother M. of the Cross to Provost John Maguire, 17.2.1892, RO8/15, AGA, in which she made it clear that this was the position of the Church authorities in the archdiocese. (Exactly thirty years before, the Congregation had almost pulled out of Inverness for the same reason – that the Sisters were needed in Glasgow. Bishop Murdoch had supported the move, but was persuaded to change his mind by Bishop Kyle, his opposite number in the Northern District – Bishop Kyle to Bishop Murdoch, 26.2.1862, 7.3.1862 and 23.4.1862, OL.)

38 Mother Stanislaus MacDonald to Provost John Maguire, 11.11.1890, RO8/13, AGA.

39 Mother M. of the Cross to Provost John Maguire, 15.4.1892, RO8/15, AGA. Archbishop Smith's successor, Angus MacDonald, was appointed in July of the same year.

40 Canon Donlevy to Provost John Maguire, 26.4.1892, RO8/15, AGA.

41 Joseph Cowan, architect, to Provost John Maguire, 23.5.1892, RO8/15, AGA. The estimate for Charlotte Street was £4,004/0/41/2), that for Elmwood £2,035/5/6.

42 The fifty-eight letters extant in RO8/15, AGA are bundled and probably represent the complete set of responses.

43 Mother M. of the Cross to Provost John Maguire, 17.7.1892, RO8/15, AGA. The Chapter had voted 33:2 to leave the decision to Council.

44 Canon Donlevy to Mother M. of the Cross, 8.9.1892, and Mother M. of the Cross to Canon Donlevy, 10.9.1892 and 17.9.1892, RO8/15, AGA; re closure date – Council Meeting Minutes, meeting of 27 July 1893.

45 In order to ease the problem, Archbishop Eyre had recommended the Congregation only to accept as postulants women who already held a teaching certificate –Archbishop Eyre to Provost John Maguire, 15.4.1887, RO8/10, AGA – but his suggestion had proved unworkable, its only effect being to cause recruitment to dry up entirely, and Council were finally forced to abandon it – Mother M. of the Cross to Archbishop Eyre, 28.8.1895, RO8/18, AGA.

46 William Bathgate HMIS, in *Education (Scotland) Report*, 1891, vol. 13 of Parliamentary Papers – *Reports from Commissioners, Inspectors and Others*, vol. xxxi, London 1892, p. 257.

47 'History of the College of Notre Dame Dowanhill Glasgow', Ms, p. 1, based closely on the 1892 entry in the 'Annals' of the Congregation, NDA, Liverpool.

48 Canon James Cameron to Sr Mary of St Philip Lescher, Superior and Principal Mount Pleasant, 3.2.1893, NDA.

49 Same to same, 14.2.1893, NDA.

50 Same to same, 8.4.1893, copy NDA.

51 This cannot be firmly substantiated, but see the tradition regarding the views of the abbess, note 58 below.

52 Canon James Cameron to Sr Mary of St Philip Lescher, 8.4.1893, copy NDA.

53 Archbishop Eyre to Sr Mary of St Philip Lescher, 14.4.1893, NDA.

54 *Ibid*; and Canon James Cameron to Sr Mary of St Philip Lescher, 8.4.1893, NDA, in which he explained 'to understand properly the turn matters have taken, you must know that the Archbishop is completely under the influence of Provost Maguire'.

55 Same to same, 19.4.1893, NDA: 'We are going to move in the matter at once, & you will hear more about it very shortly'.

56 Canon James Cameron to Sr Mary of St Philip Lescher, 12.5.1893, NDA.

57 Notre Dame College was officially opened by Archbishop Eyre on 14 January 1895. For published sources re the founding of the college, see especially Gillies Sr D., 1978, pp. 13–29; also 'A Sister of Notre Dame', 1922, espec. p. 280ff.; and Donnelly B., 1997, chapter 1.

58 There is a tradition among a few members of the Franciscan Congregation merely that they were 'asked first', but that the abbess Mother M. of the Cross turned the invitation down on the grounds that they had been founded to teach children, not women students – Sr Felicitas Bradley interview. The author relayed this possibility to the archivist of the Notre Dame British Province in Liverpool, Sr Jean Bunn, and asked whether any documentary evidence concerning it was to be found in her archives. Unaware of any, she undertook a search and unearthed the correspondence referred to in notes 47–56 above, as well as furnishing me with a copy of the Congregation's *Annals* for these years. I am most grateful to her for making these documents available to me, and for her permission to make use of them.

59 Council Meeting Minutes, meeting of 11 December 1893; and OLSF log book, D ED. 7.160.1, ML.

60 A purpose-built higher grade school, St Mary's, was completed in Patrick Street Greenock in 1907 and opened to pupils in 1910, with William Horgan in overall charge. A Sister was appointed as girls' mistress. In 1914 the school was put in the charge of the Marists. Cf., Dunlop F.M., 2001, p. 99ff.

61 Fitzpatrick T.A., 1986, p. 32.

62 Recollections of former pupils in *OLSF Magazine*, 1948, p. 41.

63 Mother Véronique to Mother M. of the Cross, vicaress, 28.12.1896, 012.1, AF.

64 Canonical visitation Report, 31.7.1896, 071.03, AF.

65 Srs M. Bonaventure Lochnane (27), d. 1.4.1892, and M. Emmanuel McLaughlan (23), d. 18.11.1893. An example of mental breakdown was M. Paulina McCaig, who became such a danger to herself and the other Sisters that she was confined to Gartnavel Asylum in June 1897. She later transferred to St Vincent's Asylum in Dublin, where she recovered sufficiently to be able to return to Charlotte Street in 1899.

66 Council Meeting Minutes, meeting of July 1897.

67 Details from the Congregation's *Obituary Register*, AF, on which the following two paragraphs are also based.

68 Mother Stanislaus was of humble birth and had entered teaching via the pupil–teacher system. She was one of the many Scots girls to receive her training at Mount Pleasant College in Liverpool – cf. the list in Aspinwall B., 1994J.

69 *Obituary Book* – Benefactors.

70 The 1872 Act had actually reduced the job security of staff in the board schools, and their full statutory rights would not be recovered until the passing of the new Act in 1908 – cf. Bone T.R. 'Teachers and Security of Tenure, 1872–1908', Section 2 of Bone T.R. (ed.), 1967. They nevertheless enjoyed considerably greater security than the teachers in the Catholic schools.

71 Inspectors' Reports, annually 1888–96, verbatim in St Mary's log book, in possession of St Mary's School. The assessment of 1888 that the school was 'conducted with much ability, method and fidelity . . . and [was] generally in a very good condition indeed' was substantially repeated in every succeeding report.

72 Council Meeting Minutes, meeting of August 1899; and ED 7/1/12, AGA. For the first year after its opening, half of the female pupil–teachers continued to use St John's Portugal Street as their centre. Thereafter all were trained on a 'half-time' basis, Monday–Friday. The men continued to use St Alphonsus'.

73 Council Meeting Minutes, meetings of March and July 1899 and February 1900.

74 *Glasgow Roman Catholic Industrial Schools Official Inspection*, 1896, copy 012.2, AF, upon which the present account is based.

75 Council Meeting Minutes, meeting of July 1899.

76 Council Meeting Minutes, meeting of October 1900.

77 The sole exception, apart from a very brief term in St Ninian's Gourock (1916–19), was their taking charge of St Bride's parish school, Bothwell, close to Elmwood convent, in 1910.

CHAPTER FOUR

Fruits of the Earth (1902–1923)

On 3 May 1902 Sr M. Clare Cattanach and the Lay Sister Agatha Kennedy celebrated their golden jubilees. It was a day of very special significance for the Congregation, for they were its first ever jubilarians and seemed to symbolise its 'coming of age'. The anniversary was marked with full ritual. High Mass was celebrated by the community's confessor, Fr John Ritchie, while Bishop Maguire gave the homily and afterwards presented the two Sisters with the crown and staff.[1] Joining the Charlotte Street community in the Congregation and at the jubilee tea were representatives of the Bothwell, Greenock and Crosshill convents, and the large and diverse gathering again brought home the growth and strength of the Congregation, whose numbers now stood at just over one hundred.[2]

There were to be nine more golden jubilees over the next five years, but this was also a time when the older generation of Sisters, some of whom had been professed under Mother Veronica, were dying out. In autumn 1903 the community lost Mother M. Gonzaga, for fifteen years their abbess and much loved for her calm and gentle courtesy. The following year saw the passing of M. Magdalen Maguire and the first two jubilarians. Sr Agatha had been the portress at Charlotte Street for years and still held that office almost to the day of her death. Sr M. Clare Cattanach was the convent sacristan, and she died following an accident in the sacristy. She was found unconscious with the tabernacle key in her hand and was brought to the infirmary where, in intense pain, she hung on patiently to life for a fortnight.[3]

The HMIs were now being far more rigorous in their annual inspections of Charlotte Street school and much more critical in their reports, and this was not by chance. The year 1899 had seen the creation of a new species, the higher grade school, to which schools with secondary departments might aspire if they could show that their standards and curriculum merited the award.[4] Charlotte Street was seeking such recognition and so had to be more closely scrutinised. Where before the annual inspection had been carried out by a lone HMI, now the school found four or five descending on it.

The inspectors' main criticism was the narrowness of the curriculum. Sr Jerome responded by introducing courses in biology and botany, for which the older pupils clubbed together and purchased a 'museum' of stuffed animals in glass cases. An aquarium was also acquired for observing the life cycle of the frog, and plots of ground were set aside at the front of the school for class gardens. Further subjects were introduced – Spanish and dynamics among them – a typewriter was bought for the Pitman Phonographic commercial course, and the school changed from slates to jotters.[5]

Though the inspectors noted the improvements, they remained critical of the unevenness of the teaching and the fact that some of the staff were uncertificated. Sr Jerome tried to solve these shortcomings by engaging specialist masters from local Protestant schools, introducing a Latin teacher in 1901 and two scientists three years later, but the solution was not altogether successful since the subjects could only be offered after school hours, by teachers who had no opportunity to meet their colleagues, and to pupils jaded after a full day's work. By 1905 she had four such masters on the staff, and only two full-time certificated teachers apart from herself. Staff shortages forced her to timetable composite classes and even to withdraw core subjects temporarily (there was no mathematics in 1904), making any real continuity almost impossible.[6]

Not surprisingly, the HMI Report for 1905 was damning of the poor and 'mechanical' work in mathematics, and it also found fault with the teaching of science and English. The inspectors nonetheless recommended the school's recognition as a higher grade institution, and this had an immediate effect upon its standing in the Catholic community. The numbers admitted into the secondary department more than doubled in the first year, increasing the roll to 120.[7] Most of the girls followed a standard three-year syllabus leading to the intermediate certificate, but more advanced courses were also being developed where staffing permitted. Theirs was a privileged education, open to less than one in fifty of the children of the archdiocese.[8]

In June 1905 the Congregation bought a house on the coast at Saltcoats as a summer vacation retreat for its teaching Sisters. Part of the purchase price and nearly all the furniture were donated by friends of the community.[9] It was a timely acquisition. Life in the parish schools was extremely wearing, and in the secondary schools the burden was growing by the year. Elmwood had been raised to higher grade status at the same time as Charlotte Street, and for the teachers in these schools and in the secondary centre at St Mary's Greenock there was to be little respite over the next few years. Not only were their rolls rising rapidly,[10] they were also required to expand their curricula in response to developments in the national system of teacher training. When the state took over the Protestant training colleges in 1906, new arrangements for preparation and admission were introduced which were to apply equally to Notre Dame. After passing the intermediate certificate at fifteen, prospective teachers were now to remain at school for a further three years as 'junior students' in order to sit for the full leaving certificate, which henceforth would serve as the standard entry qualification for training college.[11] For Sr Jerome and her colleagues it was now essential to develop a full six-year curriculum if they were to meet the need for the training of Catholic teachers.

The new arrangements had a further and more serious effect on Catholic education. The junior studentship was to replace the old pupil–teacher system, which was now formally abolished. This promised to hit the Catholic schools particularly hard, since they had traditionally relied heavily on the system. Unlike the board schools, they had to cover their teachers' salaries, and pupil–teachers, whose wages were paid by the state, were an essential means of saving on staffing costs. Abolition came just at a time when the Church seemed to have mastered the system and had invested in large pupil–teacher training centres, including those at Charlotte Street and Elmwood.[12] There were 370 pupil–teachers in the schools of the archdiocese[13] and it was quite impracticable for them all to be replaced by qualified teachers at a stroke: supply did not begin to match demand, nor could the parishes afford the salaries involved. Pupil–teachers continued to be used in some parish schools until the Great War, though from 1906 they no longer counted as part of the teaching staff; they became in fact a tolerated anachronism.

The government inspectors had been putting pressure on the Charlotte Street higher grade school in successive reports since 1900, and their report for 1906 was the most critical yet. They called attention to 'the very uneven character of the instruction' and logged their 'considerable hesitation' in awarding the full government grant, warning that they would be looking for a marked improvement at the next inspection. They again highlighted the poor qualifications of some staff and threatened that unless they were replaced at once the school would lose its higher grade status. The threat was heeded, and the following year they were able to point to real improvements, especially in English, maths and languages. All subjects passed muster except science, which was still being taught after school hours by part-time visiting staff.[14]

The plans for developing a strong six-year curriculum that Sr Jerome had been working on for over a decade were bearing fruit at last. That summer they came to final fruition when eighteen-year-old Annie Conway was accepted to read classics at Glasgow University. She was the first Catholic woman to be admitted to a degree course there, and her achievement was hugely important to the Congregation, who rightly saw it as the climax of sixty years' patient and devoted progress in education. Her success would be crowned four years later when she graduated with first class honours, and her name now has a place not only in the story of Charlotte Street but in the history of Catholic and women's education in Scotland and in the democratisation of the university.[15]

For the people of Kingston, Jamaica the winter of 1906–7 was the coldest in memory. The Franciscan community had left their convent in Duke Street, as they always did, to spend the Christmas vacation at 'Mt Alvernia', accompanied by those boarders who lived abroad and could not get home.

After the severity of the previous weeks, Monday 14 January dawned a lovely day, cloudless and wafted by a gentle breeze. It was mid-afternoon; the children were relaxing in their common room, and the Sisters had just left chapel after second Vespers. Sr M. of the Immaculate Conception Filippi, who still followed the old Glasgow Constitutions, later recalled how they had barely reached their cells when they heard a deep rumbling and were at once thrown off their feet as the whole building rocked.[16] The sensation was indescribable: from indoors it seemed that the earth was like a rat taken up and shaken by a cat, while to those outside the whole island seemed to be spinning like a top. The Sisters knew at once that a major earthquake had hit the city.

The children dashed out onto the lawn, turning to watch the building they had just left implode behind them. The Sisters had no chance to get out of the convent building, but scrambled under tables. Only Mother Paula and Sr Isabel were not in their cells. The room they were in seemed about to fall: bricks were hurtling past them, débris rained upon them. Several times they tried to leave the room, but each time some force seemed to prevent them. When they were eventually found, completely buried, neither had a scratch on her, but the corridor they had been trying to reach was piled high with huge lumps of masonry that would certainly have killed them.

When everyone was gathered and the roll called, it was discovered that all were safe and uninjured, apart from one Sister slightly grazed by a flying brick. But there was no returning indoors. They spent the evening and night upon the lawn, watching the burning city as after-shocks continued sporadically and more fires broke out here and there. As the night wore on, stragglers arrived from the downtown area, and the Sisters shared their garden with them. From one of them they learned that in the military camp next door many of the invalid soldiers had been burned alive, unable to move from their beds.

That morning Mass was said under the trees. The chapel was in ruins and the tabernacle buried deep under rubble. It was some days before the priest could clear his way through to retrieve the Blessed Sacrament. In the meantime he erected a temporary chapel on the lawn, with an improvised tabernacle – a sewing-machine cover wrapped in a white silk Benediction veil (Plate 12). Later that day word came up from Duke Street that nothing remained of the convent there. The chapel, beautifully renovated just weeks before, had fallen; the boarders' classrooms and study lay in ruins; and the school museum, considered the finest in Jamaica and famed for its collection of minerals, was nothing but dust and débris. The evening brought more ill news: not one of the Congregation's twelve schools on the island remained habitable. The work of half a century had been erased in thirty seconds.

For the next twelve nights everyone slept on the lawn. Here and there they could see bonfires, where bodies were being burned for fear of an epidemic. Rumours were rife that men had escaped from the jail and the lunatic asylum in the confusion, and were heading their way. Certainly, knots of wild-eyed people were now passing the gate, and by the second night thousands seemed to be on the move. The Sisters tried asking a passer-by who they were, but he hurried on, shouting over his shoulder that a great tsunami was rolling into the bay and that the governor had ordered the whole city to make for the mountains. Mother Paula felt it would be safer to stay where they were since 'Mt Alvernia' was on high ground, but shortly afterwards a messenger dashed up on horseback, warning them to flee for their lives, for the tidal wave had already engulfed the harbour area. On Paula's orders, each Sister took charge of two children. Leaving everything, they had just started out of the gates when official word came from the police that the sea was normal.

Once order was restored, Admiral Davies of the American fleet stationed in Kingston harbour set up an emergency hospital in the Jesuit College, and the Sisters were put in charge of it. Several also volunteered their services in the public hospital, whose staff was overrun. Their presence helped save lives, and through their help many of those who died were able to receive comfort and the Last Rites.

After twelve days tents were delivered to 'Mt Alvernia'. The Prefect Apostolic, Fr Collins SJ, visited the community and urged them to resume their normal work as soon as possible, to help restore confidence to the population. Theirs were the first schools in the whole area to reopen, but many of the children had already gone home, some as far as Haiti and South America, while others had seen their families reduced to penury. Of the 3,000 on roll before Christmas, only 1,200 were able to return. Classes were resumed nonetheless, in tents and under trees. Sr Filippi watched one lesson in progress in the pouring rain, the girls crowded under a large table while the Sister taught them from beneath a quake-battered umbrella.

The community applied to the government's relief committee for assistance towards the restoration of their schools, but this was refused following objections from several of Kingston's Protestant clergy. They were deter-mined to rebuild, however. Work was begun on the public schools and on reroofing 'Mt Alvernia' before Easter, but the costlier tasks of rebuilding the private school, the Duke Street convent and the academy were postponed while they sought funding from abroad. In April Fr Collins made an appeal to the Catholic people of Britain through a fellow Jesuit of the English

Province. Every building on the mission had been destroyed, he told them, including the schools of the Sisters, 'the best taught in the island'.[17]

Charlotte Street at once sent a donation of £25, little enough but more than they could afford considering their own debts. In her letter of thanks, Mother Paula asked the community to publicise their plight to any friends of means in Scotland. It was now mid-June and she was being pressed by the Prefect Apostolic to restore the mother house. She was seventy-four and almost penniless. It seemed impossible, but she went ahead, armed only with her parish priest's words of encouragement, 'a building whose corner stone is faith and obedience is sure to rise again'.[18] She was indeed beginning again from nothing in faith, like Veronica before her. Within eighteen months the house was ready.

The main ambition of the Catholic parish schools of Scotland at this time was to keep pace with developments in the state sector, but without the benefit of rate-funding they were finding the struggle ever more difficult. With the raising of the school leaving age to fourteen in 1901,[19] their rolls had increased overnight. By 1910 the Franciscan Sisters had some 9,500 children under their care in the archdiocese, including 933 in St Patrick's Girls' and Infants', over 1,000 in St Mary's Greenock, close to 1,200 in the Sacred Heart, and 1,255 in St Mary's Calton.[20]

The schools had not been built to handle such numbers, and the Sisters were forced into diverse stratagems in order to cope at all. Thus in Our Lady & St Margaret's Kinning Park the juniors were promoted into the senior department early in the year, well before they were really ready and simply in order to ease the congestion, but this could only be done by persuading the senior girls to leave as soon as they reached their fourteenth birthday, before they had completed their courses, in order to create desk space.[21] A new building was opened in 1910, but the parish could not afford to furnish it. Classrooms lay empty for nearly two years, and dozens of infants were transferred to the junior school, though everyone knew they were not ready, simply because there were no seats for them in their own department.[22]

This was only one of several schools in the Sisters' charge to be extended or rebuilt at this time. New premises were completed at St Mary's Hamilton and St Mary's Greenock in 1910, a new building was in the course of construction for St Patrick's, and work was about to begin at the Sacred Heart.[23] June 1911 saw the beginning of a major project at St Mary's Calton involving the demolition of the old schools and their replacement by a single school to accommodate boys, girls and infants. The plan was ambitious: a three-storey block large and square as a fort, with high airy classrooms, wide corridors and stairs, and a playground on the roof. It would take two years to complete, at a final cost of nearly £22,000,[24] by far the most expensive Catholic school building in Scotland to date.

The new, larger site encroached onto the parish graveyard. Planning permission included provision for removing the graves immediately beneath the building and for several yards beyond it.[25] That autumn workmen were sent in to start clearing the ground.

Mother M. Lucy Maguire, the new abbess, was anxious to seize the opportunity if possible to recover and remove the coffin of Sr Adélaide, for which the Congregation had sought the city council's permission more than once in the past without success (they had always refused hitherto because Adélaide had been a cholera victim). Mother Veronica's description of where she was buried had been passed down to them, so that they were pretty certain of the exact location. Following the abbess' instructions, the workmen searched close to the church door, where on 11 October they came upon a coffin somewhat away from the rest and set deep in the earth. The abbess and two councillors arrived from Charlotte Street and joined the Sisters of the industrial school who were gathered round the hole, watching every stroke of the spades. At last the men got ropes under the coffin and hauled it up. At a nod from Mother Lucy they prized off the lid. Inside lay a skeleton, the jaws open to reveal the teeth, clothed in the black Franciscan habit, with scapula and veil decayed but still visible. The rosary, much rusted, lay at her right side, but there was no sign of the crucifix: perhaps Veronica had kept it as a relic of her friend. The men stood bare-headed as the Sisters took it in turn to touch the habit (they particularly noted its wide six-inch hem), after which Mother Lucy placed a crucifix and a new rosary upon the recumbent form, then ordered the lid to be fastened down and the crumbling coffin to be placed inside a new, larger one.

The next day the remains were borne along the London Road and left in the mortuary chapel at Dalbeth cemetery. On Saturday 14th they were laid in a new grave in the Congregation's plot beside the wall. Because of the circumstances of Sr Adélaide's death, the whole episode was kept low-key. The ceremony was witnessed only by a small knot of Sisters, and – in the tradition of the Congregation – no headstone or individual nameplate marked the grave (Plate 13).[26]

It was not only the lack of space in the schools under the Sisters' care but also the poor quality of the accommodation that caught the eye of the inspectors. Managers who had to find most of the money for buildings and furniture from parish funds could usually only afford second best. The inspectors found the premises at St John's dirty, cold and in general 'most unsatisfactory'. They recommended that thermometers be placed in every classroom, and after several warnings threatened to reduce the government

grant unless the standards of cleanliness improved.[27] The St Alphonsus'
building they found 'quite inadequate . . . dingy and depressing', while in St
Andrew's girls' school they noted the poor lighting and recommended that
the downstairs windows, which were fitted with opaque panes to prevent
the pupils from being distracted from their lessons, be replaced with clear
glass. The suggestion made sense since the school had no gas lamps and
relied entirely on natural light: on particularly dark or foggy days the
children were simply dismissed.[28]

Classes were still known as 'standards' at this date, and as the name
implies pupils were assigned to them not according to age but level of
attainment. Despite the fact that children were regularly promoted before
they were ready, the log books of all the schools under the Sisters' care refer
to the large numbers of overage girls in most standards and the small
proportion who actually reached the top standard and completed the
elementary course, which in theory all children were capable of doing by
school-leaving age.

There were evident reasons for this. The teachers were having to cope
with huge numbers in each class. St Alphonsus', for instance, had over
seventy girls in two of its junior classes, and sixty-seven in another where
there was space for only fifty, while in Our Lady & St Margaret's nearly all
the classes were still of sixty or more. In such conditions genuine individual
attention was out of the question.

Secondly, the poverty and home conditions of the pupils stifled academic
achievement or even the desire for it. For many parents, getting their children
to school was perhaps the extent of their ambition, and for some even this
would have been almost impossible without help towards equipment,
clothing and meals. The school boards provided books and arranged free
dinners at local centres in cases of need, for meals were not available at the
schools themselves at this date. Their criteria were apparently more stringent
than today's, though, for (to cite one example) only about fifty girls at Our
Lady & St Margaret's were judged eligible. On the other hand, perhaps as
many as eighty were granted free boots at the same school every winter.[29]

We can readily picture those classes of sixty or more children, all raised
by struggling parents in a hard neighbourhood, labouring at their drills or
bent over their slates, covering them with words or sums and erasing them
with spittle. Attendance was poor, particularly in the afternoons when many
pupils failed to return from lunch at home, and this made serious progress
impossible. One school log recorded the 'good number' who had still not
returned from the summer holiday in October.

The school managers tried to encourage good attendance with rewards.
Most donated prizes or put on a tea party at Christmas for perfect attenders.
At St Andrew's, Canon Ritchie used to arrange an excursion in summer and

a party in winter for the best attenders. Like the other managers he also distributed an apple or orange to every pupil on special occasions such as Hallowe'en or the last day of the Christmas term. At St John's it was customary to start the new year with 'a tea party and magic', and to end the summer term with an excursion to the grounds of the industrial school at Kenmure.

The Sisters sought to keep standards high by personally examining the children in every subject, testing the seniors every month. They also introduced new practical courses in cookery and dressmaking to make the curriculum more relevant and enjoyable, bringing in peripatetic specialists employed by the local school boards, and generally tried to keep abreast of modern methods. Thus 'inventive composition' was introduced at Our Lady & St Margaret's in 1913, which the children – who were 'encouraged to write whatever they liked' – found far more interesting than more formal, humdrum work. The following year, Sister gave them a practical nature study lesson in Bellahouston Park and introduced the older girls to writing with pen and ink.

Though many of the girls were 'backward' for their age, there were some who made rapid progress up the standards and completed the elementary course well before they were old enough to leave. For such pupils many of the schools created a special supplementary class with a more advanced syllabus.[30] But it was in some ways a frustrating arrangement. In Our Lady & St Margaret's, for example, only one teacher could be spared for the work, and she had to cope with more girls than were strictly permitted under the code. The children's attendance was always erratic – it was apparently only the cookery and dressmaking that held them – and they usually left as soon as they were able.[31]

St Alphonsus' was the least enterprising of the Congregation's schools at this time. The brief, untidy entries in its log book give the impression of a mediocre and rather disorderly place, and this was exactly how the HMIs found it. Among their complaints were its outmoded methods (the girls endlessly practising stitching on small squares of material, for instance, and never being allowed to create real garments), the premature promotion of pupils, grimy classrooms, widespread copying during tests, and inaccurate (and probably falsified) pupil assessments. They were critical too of the indiscipline of the children during the inspections, and their habit of shouting out during oral examinations. More than once they reduced the government grant because of the school's failure to address its shortcomings.

This was the exception, however. All the other schools under the Franciscans' care were being run admirably in the face of difficulties that we cannot easily contemplate today, and consistently succeeded in winning the approval of the government inspectors. 'Thoroughly creditable', 'of good quality', 'making a most satisfactory appearance' were typical phrases used in their reports, and while they recognised the children's academic limitations they were quick to laud their discipline and good attendance. Equally praiseworthy was the religious grounding they received. The Sisters' schools nearly always attained marks above 90 per cent in the annual RE examination, even better than the high scores achieved by the boys' schools in the same parishes.[32]

In summer 1912 the Congregation decided to discontinue night classes at its schools, due to the 'trouble and irregularity' that they involved.[33] When it had first introduced them in 1851 for girls working in the mills, it had been an inspired initiative, offering a new chance for those who had missed out on schooling through the need to feed their families, and ahead of its time when hardly anything of the kind existed in Glasgow. But the classes had always posed problems, taxing the energies of the Sisters and disrupting community life. Attempts had been made to accommodate them – changes in the horarium, and rulings confining evening teaching to those who did not teach by day – but none had been wholly successful.

Now the need for them seemed less urgent. Changes had taken place in society's thinking, changes that the Sisters' pioneering work had itself helped to create, prompting a more widespread acceptance of the value of such classes. The government had belatedly given its imprimatur to them in the Evening Continuation School Code of 1893, provision had expanded massively, and the numbers enrolling had leapt from a mere 3,000 in the 1870s to over 100,000.[34] The Sisters could justly argue that the needs were now being well met elsewhere – for unlike the day schools the evening institutes were not denominational – and that they could withdraw without loss to the Catholic community. So the work of sixty years was ended.

Mother Veronica was now in her mellow old age. It was fifty years since her return to Tourcoing. Some of those years she had spent as infirmarian, and for over thirty she had been responsible for preparing the *pastilles* for which the monastery was famed and from which it gained much of its income. In the face of anti-clericalism in France, the convent had moved to Néchin in Belgium, where latterly her only Obedience had been to pray for the community. Her spirituality was as marked as ever, and she was now often to be seen caught up in ecstatic contemplation. Her devotion to the Rule was undiminished, but it had softened and become more understanding of others' failings. In the words of those who remembered her last years, 'the old rigidity had gradually disappeared, and she was now only the kind and saintly Mother Véronique'.[35] The humility that had allowed her to accept happily the lowest place in the community had also kept her silent concerning her own past achievements in founding two new Congregations of the Church, and it was only as her end neared that she was persuaded by the convent chaplain to answer the questions of her fellow Sisters. It was as if, after the long years of perseverance, the human dross had melted and fallen away and only the refined and tempered Godly metal remained.

Early in November 1913 her health began to fail rapidly, following a fall in her cell. On the 11th she received the Last Rites. Two days later, on the 13th, she died, in her ninety-second year and the seventy-third of her profession, and was buried in the Néchin monastery graveyard (Plate 14).

Shortly before Veronica's death, Mother Paula Charlet had written to Tourcoing from Kingston, paying warm tribute to her one-time mentor. By now she was herself eighty. Six months after Veronica's passing, she too died, with the community she had led so long around her bed. This diminutive woman, the 'little mother' as she was affectionately known, had been much loved for her humility and patience. With her passing, Jamaica's last direct link with Glasgow was ended.[36]

The once-affluent Charlotte Street had been in decline for years and was now a slum. The old convent buildings were also falling into disrepair. When Chapter met in July 1914 the members were asked to consider transferring the mother house to a better building in a more salubrious neighbourhood. Their response was unanimous: they would move as soon as possible.[37] But all such plans had to be put on hold, for within three weeks war was declared.

Germany's invasion of Belgium had driven thousands into exile, and many of them had arrived in the west of Scotland. A special Belgian Committee was set up to organise welfare for these refugees, and in response to its appeals the Sisters offered their rest home at Saltcoats as accommodation for thirty persons. The first of them took up residence in November, but they had hardly settled in when the government decided that they would have to leave, since the Ayrshire coast had now been designated a restricted area. The house remained unused for the next two years, for wartime prices had risen so steeply that the Congregation, like everyone else, was forced to make strict economies, including cancelling the Sisters' holidays at the seaside. They were obliged to look for other sources of income too, selling off their war loans and organising extra sales of work. Even so, Council remained seriously concerned at the state of their finances. In September 1918 they voted to let the Saltcoats house, which the Sisters were still unable to use while the country remained at war: only the armistice in November overtook their plans.

The war had brought some unforeseen difficulties. It had delayed the reception of postulants from Ireland, whose arrival had been held up by the threat from submarines. It had also put at risk the welfare of the girls of the industrial school, many of whom had found employment in the munitions factories. Some had been placed in undesirable lodgings, and Council feared that all their own work might be undone unless the authorities provided a special, safe home for these vulnerable young people.[38]

For years the Catholic Church had been fighting a losing battle trying to run its schools outside the state system. By every touchstone – accommodation, class size, attainment, staying-on rate, teachers' salaries – they were falling ever further behind the board schools. Their pupil–teacher ratio was now 1:61, compared with 1:41 in the state sector, and a mere 7.4 per cent of Catholic children were receiving post-elementary education, half the national average.[39] The salaries of their male teachers were only 60 per cent of those of their board school counterparts, their headteachers' barely half. In the schools run by the Franciscan Sisters, there were tales of classes far above the statutory maximum of sixty pupils, of mornings spent doing physical exercises merely to keep warm, and of children sitting on window ledges for want of desks: one teaching Sister told of an emaciated little boy approaching her and shyly asking, 'My ma says can I be on a bench today?'[40] The system was near breaking point.

As early as 1911, the Secretary of State for Scotland had proposed bringing the denominational schools within the aegis of the state, but although his suggestions had found wide support in Catholic circles they did not reach parliament until the last year of the war. Provision was then made in the draft bill for their purchase or lease by the state, with guarantees regarding any new provision that might be required in the future, and safeguards for preserving religious ethos and Church control over the appointment of staff. The Catholic Standing Committee urged its prompt acceptance, but it met stern opposition from Archbishop Maguire and the Glasgow clergy. The subsequent negotiations, the pressure for acceptance exerted by Rome through the Apostolic Visitor Mgr Brown, and the latter's bypassing of the hierarchy in informing the government of the Church's support, have all been well documented.[41]

In 1918 the bill became law.[42] At a stroke it reversed the fortunes of Catholic education in Scotland. There were benefits for all concerned: for pupils, the promise of equal opportunities and of competing on an even playing field at last; for teachers, equal pay and the prospect of a rewarding and satisfying career; for the Catholic community, release from the burden of paying twice over for education; for the Church, reasonable guarantees and the chance to come closer into the mainstream of society.[43]

For the Sisters, new experiences were coming one upon the heels of another. On 11 November, the war ended. On 14 December they used their newly won women's right to vote for the first time in the parliamentary elections. Later that month, Council discussed the implications of the Act for the Congregation but were unable to lay plans since so little was known of what would be demanded. The following May all of their parish schools, as well as Charlotte Street and Elmwood, were formally transferred to the newly created education authorities (EAs).[44]

According to the Act, the latter could either purchase or lease the schools, depending upon the wishes of the local diocese. Still opposed to the legislation, the Glasgow archdiocesan authorities elected to hold onto their properties and rent them to the EAs, though allowing them to purchase the furniture. For the purpose of negotiation, the existing diocesan education board was reconstituted as a 'transfer board', while for their part the education authorities each appointed a transfer committee to liaise with the Church in questions of valuation.

Separate arrangements were necessary for Charlotte Street and Elmwood schools since they were the property not of the archdiocese but of the trustees of the Congregation. Again it was agreed that the buildings should remain in their hands and be rented out, but that the furniture would be sold off to the two EAs concerned.[45] According to the terms of the lease, responsibility would lie with the Congregation for making such structural alterations and additions as might be required in the future, but the EAs were to be responsible for internal alterations and maintenance. It was also acknowledged that the Sisters could continue to use the buildings for parish activities.[46]

Charlotte Street seemed well placed to meet the requirements of the new era. Sr Jerome had added to the staff progressively, and the new head-mistress, Sr M. Clare Paterson, who had succeeded her in 1918, now had sixteen full-time teachers and four part-time visiting mistresses and was able to offer the full range of subjects.

Most of the girls left at fifteen on completion of the 'intermediate' course, but perhaps one in five stayed on for a further three years to gain the full leaving certificate. Nearly all of them were 'junior students' seeking entry into Notre Dame College. (Scottish Catholic girls still saw teaching as the one profession open to them, and in the early 1920s their normal path into it remained the training college rather than the university.[47]) They were placed in a special junior students' class, to gain admission to which they had to pass the intermediate certificate examination and also show some evidence of their suitability for teaching by giving one or two dummy lessons. The syllabus comprised two and a half years of academic courses and half a year's instruction in pedagogy. The latter was overseen by Sister M. Clare in her capacity as mistress of method, a paid post that involved not only lessons in theory but observation of the girls on teaching practice.[48]

The school was now earning consistently good HMI reports and building a particularly strong reputation in classics, languages and experimental science. The one obstacle to real progress was the building itself, a perennial problem for decades and now heavily criticised in the report of 1919–20. Plans were in hand to improve the situation, however,[49] and discussions were held between the headmistress and the director of education on the subject in January 1920. When stopgap solutions using hired annexes failed to get the necessary permission from the Scottish Education Department (SED),[50] the Congregation had no choice but to commit itself to a major building programme. The issue brought to the fore again the question of moving the convent out of Charlotte Street, a possibility that had been long debated as desirable in itself and as a means of freeing space on the site for new school buildings.

Throughout the war, Mother Lucy Maguire had been collecting funds, as far as she was able in those stringent times, for the new mother house recommended at the 1914 Chapter. The war had prevented any action on the matter, but at the 1920 Chapter it was now raised again by Council as 'an urgent necessity'.[51]

The Chapter was presided over by Fr Alex Murphy OFM, who also took the opportunity to make a formal visitation to the mother house. His report to Archbishop Maguire echoed Council's concerns regarding the building but was warm in its praise of the community. Religious discipline was being faithfully observed, he told the archbishop, a spirit of unity and charity prevailed, and he was especially impressed by the care given to sick Sisters. Much of the credit, he believed, was due to the outgoing abbess, Mother Lucy, whose 'long administration had been most fruitful of good results'. '*All* whom I have met in the Visitation,' he added, 'concur in admiring her as a Religious and Superior.'[52] Her term of office had partly coincided with that of Sr Jerome as headmistress of Charlotte Street. It had been an era when both school and Congregation had been steered forward by outstanding leaders at the helm.

To date, the archdiocese and the EAs had totally failed to find common ground regarding the valuation of school buildings. In Glasgow the city valuator was proposing a figure 40 per cent below the Church's valuation; no agreement had been possible with Renfrewshire; Ayrshire's proposal was 'not to be taken seriously'; and Lanarkshire's offer of £600 annual rental for Elmwood was rejected out of hand. So dissatisfied were the diocesan education board that they refused to allow the Catholic schools to be used as polling stations in the autumn municipal elections. Both sides accepted the need for arbitration,[53] but although arbitrators were appointed for each EA the wrangling continued for another two years.

The transfer of Elmwood in 1919 had posed a particular problem in that the school had a boarding as well as a day department, to which girls had traditionally come from throughout west-central Scotland, and indeed from England and the mainland of Europe. Lanarkshire EA agreed to continue supporting the boarding school, though it was an anomaly within the system, but only for girls from within the county. From spring 1920 it was officially recognised as the sole Catholic girls' secondary school for Lanarkshire, and Our Lady's High Motherwell – its counterpart for boys – ceased enrolling girl pupils. As a result, Elmwood's roll doubled to 280 over the next three years. At the same time, where in the past boarders had accounted for some two fifths of the roll, the new restrictions reduced them to a mere one tenth in 1926.[54] Thus in the space of half a dozen years the character of the school was utterly transformed.

In spring 1920 representatives of the Lanarkshire EA and the Elmwood headmistress together drew up plans for major extensions, which were submitted to Council and accepted at its June meeting. The estimated cost of £14,000 was a crippling figure for the Congregation to find unaided, and Mother Abbess appealed to the diocesan board for a grant from its central reserve fund. The members were inclined to support her, but Bishop Toner vetoed the request on the grounds that Elmwood was not a diocesan site but the property, and therefore the responsibility, of the trustees of the Congregation.[55]

The decision was a setback for the Sisters, but it brought some benefit to the Catholic community, for Elmwood's needs had focused the minds of the board on the fact that secondary provision was a special problem that had to be addressed. With the implications of the 1918 Act still not worked out for the secondary sector at a national level and no uniform provision yet in place, there was a danger that the Catholic secondary schools would also be allowed simply to grow *ad hoc*. Yet they were the Church's flagship schools and a key part of its hopes, in particular as nurseries for the next generation of Catholic teachers. The Elmwood debate had convinced the board of the need for a coherent strategy of provision and funding, and for the appointment of a sub-committee to plan it.

The new body held its first meeting in October 1920. Concerning those secondary schools run by the religious orders, it proposed that they be entitled to loans from the central reserve fund on 'favourable terms', and that in the case of a deficit on any future building project, two thirds of the shortfall should be borne by the feeder parishes and one third by the Order or Congregation.[56] This was welcome news for the Sisters, since it specified the responsibility of the parishes and permitted borrowing from the Church rather than the bank, so keeping their debts 'in house' and at an easier rate of interest. Nonetheless, the outlay that faced them was daunting. When Council met the local parish priests the following spring, they estimated that

the cost of Elmwood might now lie between £15,000 and £18,000. But with
the county council demanding action they had no choice but to sanction it,
along with extensions at Charlotte Street estimated at over £20,000. The
EAs had set minimum requirements for their recognition as secondary
schools. Visiting the Chapter in summer 1920, the diocesan secretary for
education stated the position starkly – 'their choice lay between building or
closing the schools'.[57]

In May 1921 the headmistress of Charlotte Street, Sr M. Clare Paterson,
died suddenly at the age of thirty-nine, after only three years in post. The
obvious candidate to succeed her, Sr Bernardine Simpson, would not be
free until the new year, and since no-one else of the required calibre was
available, Sr Jerome Gordon was recalled from retirement to bridge the gap.
Her experience proved invaluable in the negotiations that had already begun
for major building on the site. The secondary department was growing
by the year, and another large intake was expected that August.[58] Until the
new school was completed there was no way of accommodating everyone.
Council held an emergency debate in July, at which it was agreed to hire a
church and hall in St Mungo Street to take the overflow.[59]

Sr Bernardine took up her post in January 1922. Like Jerome she was a
six-footer from Aberdeen and had been educated by the Sisters in that city,
though she had completed her schooling as a boarder in Charlotte Street.
Like her, too, she had the natural gravitas of a leader. She was a talented
artist and musician, and made an immediate impression on pupils and
teachers alike.

She arrived to the chaos of builders and annexes, but by August six rooms
of the new school were habitable, and before the end of September the entire
building was ready (Plate 15). On the feast of the Immaculate Conception
it was officially opened by the recently consecrated archbishop, Donald
Macintosh. With its new facilities, the secondary department could only
grow in popularity, and the following spring 250 girls from around the city
sat the 'classification examination' for the hundred places available.[60]

Though the numbers presented for public examinations were rising, the
results were only moderate. The government report of that year praised
'the fine atmosphere of ordered industry', but noted that 'the material
from which the school was recruited was somewhat mixed in point of
intellectual ability, and that this fact was reflected in some of the Certificate
examinations'. There was no lack of ambition among the pupils, though,
even if some of it was unrealistic: indeed, the numbers of post-intermediate
students were now becoming 'unwieldy'.[61]

It would be Sr Bernardine's great achievement over the following two
decades to raise standards of attainment to a high point of excellence. She
would do so by a determined and meticulous attention to every aspect of the

school, and by her personal involvement. Girls would arrive every morning to be greeted by 'Barnie' herself at the gate, and taken aside if their work, behaviour or uniform, or indeed their religious practice, was less than satisfactory. She it was who really built the school's name between the wars. Charlotte Street school has been blessed with several outstanding leaders in its long history, and none more outstanding than she.

In 1923, a young Sister who would herself one day succeed her as headmistress was given the task of visiting the Duke Street prison. Sr Philippa Gilhooley was only twenty-eight, and as was customary she made her twice-weekly visits in the company of an older member of the community. One of the prisoners was Susan Newell, a married woman exactly the same age as herself, who had been sent there in September after trial at the High Court of Justiciary. Her case had been, in the words of Lord Alness, the Lord Justice Clerk, 'stranger than the most sensational fiction'.

On 10 June that year, her husband had walked out of their single-end in the Whifflet after a quarrel. That evening, thirteen-year-old John Johnstone delivered a newspaper to the apartment and was invited in. Shortly afterwards a neighbour heard bumping noises inside, and she later saw Susan Newell go to the public house with her six-year-old daughter, Janet, and return with a jug of beer. When the little girl was questioned, she remembered watching her mother drinking the beer, with 'a little wee boy dead on the couch' beside her. Mrs Newell then sought to hide the body, first by trying to borrow a box and then by attempting to lift the floorboards with a poker, but without success.

Early the next morning she wrapped the body in a red cloth, and loading it onto a go-cart set off up the Glasgow Road with Janet trotting at her heels. When the little girl grew tired her mother set her upon the bundle, telling her that if anyone saw the body she was to say that her father had killed him. Somewhere on the road the go-cart broke down, but a passing hawker took them and their load on his lorry as far as the east end of the city. By now it was mid-morning. He dropped them off near the end of Duke Street, Mrs Newell insisting on lifting the go-cart down herself. As she struggled with it, a woman at a nearby window saw a foot sticking out from under the cloth, and when this was hastily stuffed back a head toppled forward. The woman sent her husband in search of the police, and alerted two neighbours, who followed the go-cart up Duke Street. Mrs Newell must have realised she was being watched, for as she reached No. 650 she suddenly turned into the close, and telling Janet to push the cart, she herself took the bundle on her back. As her pursuers approached, she managed to clamber with her burden over a six-foot wall into the next court. There the high railings of a play-ground prevented her from going any further.

Within minutes, a constable arrived and met her coming out of the close, wiping her hands. He brought her back into the court, where he found the body under a wooden outside stair, 'trussed up like a fowl'. There were strangulation marks upon the neck, signs of burning on the head and ear, and the neck appeared broken. Her first words were, 'my husband did it.'

Originally, both Mr and Mrs Newell were charged with the murder, but he was discharged when he was able to establish that he had left the house some hours before the event. With the evidence so strong against her, Mrs Newell's counsel advised her that her one hope lay in pleading insanity. He argued the case persuasively, but was contradicted by all the medical experts called to the witness box. With nothing further to fall back on, the case was over within two days. The all-male jury took only half an hour to reach a guilty verdict, adding, however, a unanimous 'strong recommendation' for mercy. Undeterred, Lord Alness pronounced a sentence of death upon her. Neither when the verdict was read nor the sentence pronounced did she betray the least emotion. Her eyes remained lacklustre, as they had throughout the trial.

She was taken to Duke Street, where for seven weeks she lay in the condemned cell, visited only by the two Sisters. Shortly before 8 a.m. on 10 October she was led to the prison yard, where the scaffold stood high and ready. She walked with steady legs, the Sisters in front of her and the Catholic chaplain, Fr Culley, behind. Round her neck was the rosary that Sr Philippa had given her. A little knot of officials stood around. As the executioner made to place the cap upon her, she waved him aside. 'Don't put that thing over my head,' she said. She spoke no other words. The job was done almost before anyone was ready for it.

She was disengaged from the noose and her death confirmed. The certificate was signed and countersigned. As they prayed for her soul and for little Janet's wellbeing, the Sisters could not help but reflect that in death, with the bruising and rope burns on her broken neck, she bore a strange resemblance to her victim. If she had a motive for the apparently purposeless killing she took it with her to the grave. She was the first woman to be hanged in Scotland for seventy years, and the last ever to be hanged in this country.[62]

ENDNOTES TO CHAPTER FOUR

1 Council Meeting Minutes, May 1902. The Sisters had been professed on 3 May 1852 – *Register of Professions and Receptions*, Vol. 1.

2 The precise number was 101, including 93 in the archdiocese and 7 in Inver-ness – cf. abbess to Rev. John Ritchie, 23.11.1903, GC 35/100, AGA.

3 *Obituary Register*, nos. 70, 71, 68, AF.

4 The higher grade school was introduced in the *Code of Regulations for Day Schools in Scotland*, 1899, Article 138: cf. Wade N.A., 1939, p. 105ff.

5 Charlotte Street school log, 1902–4, D ED 7 160.1, ML.

6 HMI Reports 1904–5, in Charlotte Street log. Mathematics was resumed in October 1904, but only as an after-school course.

7 Council Meeting Minutes, July and August 1905; Charlotte Street log, 1905–6. Admissions rose from 30–40 per year to c. 80.

8 Pupils numbering 1,022, out of 56,204 in all schools of the archdiocese in 1904 – DE 7/1/16, 1904, AGA.

9 Council Meeting Minutes, July 1905. The purchase price was £1,550.

10 The roll at Elmwood rose to 80 in 1906, three-quarters of whom were day pupils – Sr M. Francis to Fr John Ritchie, 6.4.1906, GC 35/100, AGA.

11 Cf. Cruickshank M., 1970, p. 138ff.

12 In 1906 there were 99 girls enrolled at the Charlotte Street pupil–teacher centre – M. Stanislaus MacDonald to Fr. John Ritchie, 13.4.1906, GC 35/100, AGA. The Sisters had been running the Elmwood Centre as a private concern for the previous six years, since Lanarkshire Council had withdrawn its support on grounds of cost.

13 ED 7/1/19, 1906–7, AGA.

14 HMI reports of spring 1906, autumn 1906 and 1907, in Charlotte Street log.

15 In the 1990s, her graduation medal was released to the university by the Congregation on permanent loan, and was displayed in an exhibition entitled 'Women in the University'.

16 The present account is based on her very full letter – Sr I. C. Filippi to Mother M. Athanasius MacLean, 19.6.1907, with additional material from Mother Paula Charlet to same, 17.6.1907, both 014.1, AF.

17 Fr P. Hassan to Rev. Mothers of convents, 3.4.1907, and same to Catholic papers of Britain, April 1907, both on behalf of Fr. Collins SJ – 014.1, AF.

18 Mother M. Paula Charlet to Mother M. Athanasius MacLean, 17.6.1907; *Catholic Opinion* (Kingston, Jamaica), June 1914, Tribute to Sr Paula.

19 Education (Scotland) Act, 1 Edw VII, ch. 9, 1901.

20 ED 7/1/22, 1909–10, AGA.

21 Charlotte Street log, 27.4.1909, D ED 7 161 2/2, ML.

22 *Ibid.*, 2.6.1911.

23 ED 7/1/22 and ED 8/1/1, AGA.

24 The original estimate was £18,000. The final cost, including heating, furnishing and fees, was £21,742 – FR 1/6, 118, AGA. See also Handley J.E., 1963, p. 35.

25 The decision to clear well beyond the actual foundations was taken on the recommendation of A.K. Chalmers, the city's medical officer for health, who had personally witnessed the fatal results of not clearing sufficient graves during the building of the Glasgow Royal Infirmary – A.K. Chalmers to John McLachlan, Writer, 14.10.1913, and John McLachlan to Canon John Ritchie, 16.10.1911, both GC 43/118, AGA.

26 Account based on Extract, Tourcoing Archives, English version, 012.2, AF. Also, eyewitness account by a Lay Sister at the graveside, relayed to St Aloysius MacDonald, and by her to Sr Bernard McAtamney – Sr Bernard McAtamney interview. Since the exhumation it has been the tradition of the Congregation to have a six-inch hem on the habit.

27 HMI reports in St John's log, 1911–15, D ED 7 222 2.2, ML. All references to St John's in the following account are from this source.

28 HMI report 1912 in St Alphonsus' Girls' log, D ED 7 190 3, ML; and St Andrew's log, 25.10.1912 and HMI report 1915, D ED 7 192.2, ML. All references to the two schools in the following account are from their logs, 1911–15.

29 Decisions regarding free clothing and footwear were made not according to financial criteria by a clerk in the education office, as today, but by the school's own medical officer on grounds of health.

30 Not all of the Congregation's schools had the space or staff to put on such courses. St John's and St Alphonsus' did not: any of their pupils who completed the elementary syllabus and wished to take their education higher transferred to Charlotte Street.

31 The headmistress also allocated one teacher to give individual help to the 'weak end' of Standard Senior III, an enlightened use of staff well ahead of its time. None of the other schools run by the Sisters was able to make such special provision for what today would be called 'learning support'.

32 ED 8/1/2, 1911–12, AGA. The mean for the Sisters' schools was 92.34 per cent, that for the boys' schools from the same parishes 86.78 per cent.

33 Council Meeting Minutes, 21.8.1912.

34 O'Hagan F.G., *The Contribution of the Religious Orders to Education in Glasgow during the Period 1847–1918*, PhD thesis, Glasgow University 2002. At the time of writing, the thesis was not yet available for general consultation. In the draft version, which Dr O'Hagan kindly made available to me, the reference is on p. 157.

35 Tribute, in Tourcoing Archives, p. 32ff, copy 011, AF.

36 Date of death 24.5.1914. Details of Mother Paula from obituary article in *Catholic Opinion* (Kingston, Jamaica), June 1914. Of the three who had travelled to Jamaica with Veronica in 1857, Sr M. de Sales left to join the Poor Clares and Sr Philomena died in 1906.

37 Chapter notes, Register of Elections, 12.7.1914, 028.2, AF.

38 Council Meeting Minutes, 3.3.1917; and Reports to Chapter, Industrial School, 1917, 030.1, AF.

39 Cf. Treble J.H., 1978J, p. 120ff., and 1980J, p. 40ff.

40 Sr Benedicta Collins interview: told by an old Sister to the interviewee shortly after she entered in 1943.

41 Cf. especially, Darrach J., 1990J, text and Appendices V, IX and XI.

42 Education (Scotland) Act, 8 and 9 Geo V, chapter 48, 1918.

43 Fitzpatrick T.A., 1986, espec. p. 48.

44 Council Meeting Minutes, 27.12.1918 and 15.5.1919.

45 The Congregation employed a licensed appraiser to value the items to be sold.

Charlotte Street's furniture, including the museum of stuffed animals, Sister's antique writing desk, its sole Yost No. 4 typewriter, Singer Drop Head sewing machine and two pianofortes, was valued at precisely £1,906/1/10½ –Inventory, 24.5.1919, 041.10, AF.

46 Elmwood School, Minute of Lease, 22.5.1940, copy 044.11, AF, continuing the conditions of the original lease.

47 Cf. Fitzpatrick T.A., *op. cit.*, espec. p. 71ff., quoting students' reminiscences from the Notre Dame sound archive. According to the Charlotte Street log of 1918–20, some 40 girls sat the intermediate, and about 12 stayed on for the full leaving certificate.

48 For details of the working of the junior student system, see Wilson J.D., Section 4 of Bone T.R. (ed.), 1967; and Cruickshank M., 1970, p. 140ff. The girls took their teaching practice in the city parish schools run by the Sisters. As recognised junior student centres, Charlotte Street and Elmwood received an enhanced grant for every junior student on their rolls.

49 Charlotte Street log, Report of Inspection 1919–20 (received Nov. 1920).

50 Council Meeting Minutes, 30.1.1920, 6.2.1920 and 5.3.1920.

51 Chapter notes, Register of Elections, 11–13.7.1920, 028.2, AF.

52 Fr Alex Murphy OFM to Archbishop Maguire, 16.7.1920, RO8/48, AGA. Fr Murphy was a member of the Friary at Gorton, Manchester.

53 Diocesan Education Board Minutes, 21.6.1920 to 4.10.1920; also John McLachlan to Clerk Lanarkshire EA, 12.1.1921, Diocese of Motherwell papers, DM 31/1, SCA.

54 Reports to Chapter, Bothwell convent, 1920–26, 030.1, AF. In 1926 the number of boarders stood at 26.

55 Diocesan Education Board Minutes, 13.9.1920 and 1.10.1920; and Council Meeting Minutes, 2.10.1920. The final cost was in fact £18,500.

56 Diocesan Education Board Minutes, Secondary Schools Committee meeting, 11.10.1920, ED 1/3, AGA.

57 Chapter notes, 11–13.7.1920, Register of Elections, 028.2, AF. Council sanctioned the building programmes at its meeting of 23.10.1921.

58 The roll had risen from 268 to 420 between 1919 and 1921: Annual Reports, Religious Inspector, ED 8/1/9 and 8/1/11, AGA.

59 Council Meeting Minutes, 14.7.1921. The rental was £100 per annum. So urgent was the problem that Council took the vote despite two of their five members being absent.

60 Charlotte Street log, 14.8.1923. With the numbers enrolling for the 1923–4 session too large for the staff to cover, it was necessary to borrow a teacher from the junior school.

61 SED Report, 1924, in Charlotte Street log. In 1922, 28 girls were awarded the intermediate certificate, and 13 the leaving certificate; the numbers for 1923 were 38 and 10 respectively: school log, 30.6.1922 and 29.6.1923.

62 Account based on *Glasgow Herald*, 22.6.1923 (report of murder), 19.9.1923 and 20.9.1923 (trial), and 11.10.1923 (hanging).

CHAPTER FIVE

Digging in (1923–1947)

In spring 1920, when rebuilding the secondary school at Charlotte Street became a matter of urgency, Council had taken the decision to move the convent to the south side of the city in order to make space on the site.[1] For a year they watched the market for a suitable property. When Merrylee House became available in January 1921, it seemed to meet their needs exactly. A fine stone mansion set in ten acres of land in the Briar Road area of Newlands, it stood among detached turn-of-the-century villas in a suburb that was still semi-rural. The asking price was £8,700. It took a further eighteen months to secure and renovate the property, by which time the debt on the purchase was completely cleared.[2]

Council did not originally plan to move the entire community to Merrylee. They intended to use it as the Congregation's novitiate house, seeing the area as far more suitable for young and impressionable Sisters than the noisy and run-down Charlotte Street.[3] This was the proposal they put to the specially convened Chapter. To their surprise, however, Chapter rejected the plan by a large majority, voting that the novitiate remain in Charlotte Street, and that a new convent be built at Merrylee as soon as possible, which would then become the permanent mother house, with Charlotte Street reduced to an annexe. This was a far cry from the original intention.

In April 1923 four Sisters moved into their new home. After Charlotte Street they found it eerily quiet, too quiet indeed for them to be entirely at their ease. The neighbourhood was secluded, the houses hidden behind tall hedges, the deserted roads ill-lit and full of shadows at night, so that they were wary of venturing out after dark. They were happy to see a high perimeter wall already in the course of construction around the whole property, and relieved to see it completed that summer.

At one end of the grounds stood a cottage known as The Stables which had been occupied under the previous owner by a Mr and Mrs Welsh and their son. After the Sisters moved in, Mr Welsh acted for a time as gardener and general factotum for the community, doing odd jobs in lieu of rent. But with the new development planned at Merrylee, the Congregation needed The Stables, and in spring 1924 the abbess instructed their solicitors to serve notice on the family to vacate by Whitsun. The Welshes resisted any move, even when alternative accommodation was offered, on the grounds that their son was ill and required to be cared for at home. The solicitors recommended immediate legal action, but the abbess Mother Wallburga Broe preferred to seek the help of the local parish priest first, in the hope that he might be able to influence the family. Only when he failed to budge them did she agree to take the matter to court. It proved an ill-judged decision that brought neither the desired outcome nor did good to the Congregation's name.

The case dragged on for three months. During the hearing it was alleged that after Welsh declined to vacate, the abbess had instructed the community not to speak to him or have any dealings with him. The judge finally dismissed the action in favour of the tenants, and ruled that the Congregation bear the costs.

In December the abbess had the gas disconnected at Merrylee and the meter removed from The Stables. She even brought Archbishop Macintosh into the affair, but all attempts to persuade the family to move proved fruitless. In March 1925 she contacted the solicitors to inform them that Mr Welsh had been seen scaling the perimeter wall as a short cut to the road, and recommended that they threaten more legal proceedings. The whole business was becoming thoroughly petty.[4]

By now Council had decided to press ahead with the new convent, and an architect had been engaged to produce drawings for an imposing brick building with a frontage of stone. As soon as she was in receipt of the plans Mother Wallburga wrote to the archbishop to seek his permission for a project which, at an estimated cost of over £35,000, would be quite the most expensive ever undertaken by the Congregation. He was happy to give it his blessing, but advised her that since it would involve borrowing some £7,000 it would be necessary to have the Vatican's agreement also before incurring such a debt. In October the required permission arrived from Rome and she was able to proceed.[5]

In January 1926 word came to her in confidence that all was not well in the mother house. There was a feeling of disharmony that could not be identified. She made discreet enquiries to discover the seat of the problem, but at first met silence and secrecy. Probing further she finally narrowed it down to the novice mistress, Sr M. of Dolours Black, who believed that the Congregation had become too lax in following the Rule and wished to establish a new foundation of strict observance. It emerged that she had been the centre of secret negotiations among a small group of Sisters for several years, about which their superiors had known nothing.

Mother Wallburga had no choice but to ask her to resign her office, which she did that February. Soon afterwards she applied to the archbishop for permission to establish a new community. When he refused she left the Congregation. But the damage was already done. Five professed Sisters were induced to follow her, and she left the novitiate in a state of confusion. The new novice mistress did her best to reassure her charges and hold on to them, but they had been warned to tell her nothing of their real intentions and she was unable to win their confidence. Between March and August five of them left, along with one postulant. Of the twelve lost to the Congregation, ten joined enclosed Orders, and two (both novices) returned to their families.[6]

The triennial Chapter was held that July, at the height of the disruption. Mother Wallburga's term of office had now expired and M. Camilla Hamilton was elected to succeed her. Mother Camilla was at the time superior of the Glenlea convent in Greenock and had previously been headmistress of the St Mary's and Sacred Heart schools in the east end of Glasgow. She was noted for her energy, exactness and efficiency, and for a warm nature that revealed itself especially in her devotion to the children in her care. Taking over the reins at a painful and delicate time for the Congregation, it was likely that she would need all these resources of character and experience to restore its shaken confidence.

The mother house incident had given vivid proof of the power and influence of novice mistresses within communities, particularly over young minds, and of the need for the utmost prudence in their appointment. It had also brought to the fore again the old dilemma inherent in the Rule and Constitutions of the Congregation: of striking the balance between the active and the contemplative life, of the problem of authentic poverty for those necessarily involved in the world, and of reconciling the needs of community and liturgy inside the convent with those of the apostolate outside.[7] It was a dilemma that would continue to perplex the Congregation into and beyond the war years, figure large in the radical changes of the 1970s, and not be finally resolved until the 1990s.

In 1928 Elmwood celebrated its golden jubilee. It had changed immensely in the decade following the 1918 Act, turning from an international private school into a local state secondary. Where once it had offered a 'finishing school' curriculum for young ladies, it now prepared girls for the full national leaving certificate. Its roll had more than doubled, but its boarders had been reduced to a handful. To house the expansion, a new wing had been built in 1923, which had forced the Bothwell convent to take out loans totalling over £14,000, of which only half had been repaid to date.[8]

The school had been steered through these changes by Sr M. Anthony MacNeil (Plate 16) who had been headmistress for half of the school's life, having been appointed in 1904 when it had first been granted higher grade status. She was now sixty-one and would remain at the helm for a further four years. Like Jerome and Bernardine at Charlotte Street, whose terms as head she straddled, she was a north-easterner, and like them one of the outstanding educators produced by the Congregation. Esteemed for her gentleness and humility, her kindness and concern for the individual, and her grasp of the real priorities, after her retirement from Elmwood she would bring these same qualities to her work as novice mistress and later as abbess. All who came under her, child and adult, saw her as an inspirational guide and mentor.

Over the years she had built up a vibrant school community and gathered together staff who gave generously of their time and talents to enrich the girls' education. She had hand-picked them for their dedication and love of learning, but even more for the people they were: women who exemplified Christian living. A high proportion were unmarried, and for them Elmwood was the great part of their life and creativity; many, once appointed, remained there until they retired or died. Among them were Miss MacDonell, tall and lean, who strode into class like a Caesar, a qualified mathematician whom Sr Anthony had brought in to introduce Latin and who influenced every girl's life in a myriad ways; short, stout Miss Oliphant, principal of modern languages; the historian Miss Candy from Dublin, who had 'everything under control'; Miss Leonard, who taught elocution in the forlorn hope of ridding the girls of their Lanarkshire accents; and Miss O'Neill, who had entered the school in 1900 as a four-year-old and would remain until 1956, a lover of plainchant whose choirs were ethereal. Like her, many of the staff were themselves alumnae, and together they formed a remarkably close-bonded team.

Epitomising them all, perhaps, was Miss Eunice Rea. Raised on South Uist, where her father was a headteacher, and educated at Notre Dame High School in Glasgow, she had graduated in English from the university at the end of the Great War, and after some years teaching in England had joined the staff at Elmwood in 1925. In her first year she had started a highly successful literary society which the girls ran themselves under her guidance. In the jubilee year they organised debates, held an election for school poet laureate and produced two dramatic entertainments. The society was to continue in existence into the 1950s, but it was by no means the sum of Miss Rea's involvement. In her thirty-seven years on the staff she took a lively interest in every facet of school life, and was described as 'an originator or participator in nearly every school activity'.[9] To them all she brought a generosity of heart, a graciousness and a gentle humour that made her an institution and endeared her to generations of girls and colleagues. With her there was no forcing of learning, but an individual prompting and a beautiful reading voice that encouraged each pupil to explore literature for herself. There was substance to her lessons: her classes covered a wide corpus of authors (they had read several novels of Scott by the age of thirteen), with a breadth and depth that one can only envy today. She exemplified, exactly, the quality that the school aimed for and so strikingly achieved, the ideal expressed in its motto: *Suaviter in modo, fortiter in re*.

Over the fifty years of its existence, Elmwood had consciously developed an ethos of family and freedom. The girls were respected, and could express their opinions without discouragement. From the beginning there had been a school council to air and voice their views – well ahead of its time in 1878 – and it had always been more than a mere token body. In 1926 it was extended, and now comprised a captain with nine councillors forming the executive body, assisted by a pupils' representative council elected from every class down to the youngest.

In 1929 Sr Anthony introduced a prize-giving ceremony for the sixth form, with awards for excellence in each subject and a special prize for conduct – a silver cross presented by Archbishop Macintosh to the winner chosen by her peers. The following year the event was extended to cover the whole school, and further awards were added: the Sr Anthony Medal for school Dux, and other prizes for general excellence and for the most promising 'junior student' in teaching practice.

Nor was the girls' out-of-class education neglected. The school had a ramblers' club, a savings certificate association, a netball group which ran an open tournament every term, and a gymnastics club which put on an annual display in the gardens. The school racing club held private athletics events every summer, and from 1930 organised an annual public sports day at the Hamilton Academicals football park.

The Elmwood Magazine first appeared in 1927 and was another brain-child of Miss Rea. Published annually at Christmas and professionally printed, its planning and production were entirely the work of a committee of pupils working in their free time, and its contents a mixture of news and children's prose, poetry and artwork. It sold at 6d. a copy and paid its way by carrying local trade advertisements. Among those who took out advertising space were the Bell's Shipping Agency, who offered sea travel to Canada for £2 with situations guaranteed on arrival, as well as free travel to Australia for boys and domestics; Burns Oates and Washbourne Ltd, advertising Christmas cards at 1d. each or teachers' packs at 2/6 (12½p) for 100; the Scottish Co-operative Wholesale Society, serving 690,000 households to whom it paid nearly £5½ million annually in dividends; and Tunnocks, Bakers and Purveyors, who at this time owned just two small restaurants in Uddingston and Bothwell where luncheons, dinners and teas were tastefully served at moderate charges.

In addition to the normal spiritual activities of a Catholic school, a special Guild of St Francis was formed by Sr Anthony for senior pupils in 1929, following a highly successful retreat. The members, not unlike young Franciscan tertiaries, committed themselves to weekly meetings and monthly Benediction, conference and Mass at which (a rare privilege at this date) they were allowed to make the responses.

All of these initiatives were fruits of a conscious enterprise to build the school and with it the young person according to a single coherent vision embracing mind, body and spirit.

The annual prize for best 'junior student' reflects the fact that these pupils preparing for teacher training college still made up a large proportion of the upper school at this date. The junior student system had been abolished altogether for boys in 1924, when new legislation made a university degree a requisite for male teachers. But the traditional path into teaching – three years as a junior student at school followed by two years at training college – remained open to women and would do so through the 1930s and 1940s,[10] and it was a far more frequented path at this time than that leading to university. According to the records, there were forty-five Elmwood alumnae at Notre Dame Training College in 1928, and fifty-one the following year, twice as many as were attending 'the University'.[11] The use of this latter phrase is also revealing: it was not necessary to specify which university was intended, because at this date and for many years after, Glasgow was the only option offered to Elmwood or Charlotte Street girls by their teachers, since studying at any of the other three would have required them to live away from home, a risk to their welfare not to be considered.

The Notre Dame teacher training course included a compulsory unit in religious education, for entry to which candidates sat a prospective teachers' religious examination in their last term at school. The record of Elmwood in this examination was outstanding. In their jubilee year, forty-five girls gained passes, with seven in the first class, while Mary Jackson, one of only three students in Scotland to be awarded honours, was placed first in the whole country. The following year no less than twenty-four of the thirty-eight candidates gained first class, seven achieved honours, and one – Annie Vallely – scored perfect marks in doctrine. Such results reflect the pride of place that RE lessons held in the curriculum and the absolute priority given to the spiritual in the life of the school.

Though elementary schooling had been free for forty years in Scotland, the secondary schools were still fee-paying in 1928. The day pupils at Elmwood paid £10 per term for their education, the same fees as were charged at Charlotte Street, though funds existed in both schools to allow low-income families to pay nothing. National legislation the following year abolished all such fees, making secondary education dependent solely on academic ability and (in theory at least) within the reach of every pocket. With the passing of these laws the transformation of Elmwood was complete.

On 19 March 1928 Archbishop Mackintosh visited Merrylee to lay the foundation stone for the new convent (Plate 17). Over the following eighteen months the abbess and vicaress resided there alternately, in order to be on hand to oversee the building work. As it neared completion, they sought the views of the Congregation as to whether they should sell the Charlotte Street convent and move the entire Glasgow community to Merrylee, or retain it as an annexe in the city centre. The decision was to vacate entirely, but to retain the chapel and several other rooms for the school.[12]

On 24 June 1930 the old convent was closed and the new occupied. The community took possession with no debt, for despite a massive final expenditure of almost £49,000 they had paid all their bills before moving in and could show a healthy balance in the bank.[13] The whole building was habitable apart from the chapel, which awaited final furnishing and for which items were arriving daily. Many, including the striking Romanesque high altar in Carrara marble complete with angels and pedestals, the side altars dedicated to Mary and Joseph,[14] and the sanctuary lamps, organ, carpets, Stations of the Cross and statues, were gifts from friends and alumnae.

All was in place by 15 November when the chapel was consecrated by the archbishop with a Mass concelebrated by forty priests, followed by luncheon, Benediction and the singing of the *Te Deum*. The community could now feel that they were finally and fully in their new home. We can catch their excitement and sense of the moment in the normally staid minutes of Council: 'Today marks a great epoch in the history of the Franciscan nuns in Scotland . . . at last [we have] a convent worthy of the Franciscan Order . . . today will complete the happiness of the Sisters.'[15] The project conceived in 1920 had come to birth at last. It had been a long gestation.

When the convent had been in Charlotte Street, the teaching Sisters had been on hand for the secondary school and within walking distance of most of their parish schools in the city. Now there were far longer journeys to be made, and since they all left and returned at the same hour it was decided to purchase a motor charabanc to ferry them to their destinations. A sixteen-seater was acquired and painted in a brown Franciscan livery, and twice daily it made a circuit of the city, the community's new handyman at the wheel.[16]

An early visitor to the new house was the abbess of the Bayswater Franciscan Congregation founded by Elizabeth Lockhart from Charlotte Street in 1859. Never a large community, it had been badly depleted by a killer influenza epidemic in the 1890s. Three years later the Sisters had removed to Braintree, Essex, where they opened a poor school and orphanage. They had continued to follow the 'Glasgow' Rule and Constitutions and keep in touch with Scotland. In October 1931, with numbers

low, the abbess travelled to Merrylee to broach the possibility of amalgamation.[17] After some discussion, both sides agreed not to pursue
the matter. (Twenty-three years later, however, the English Congregation
amalgamated with the Missionary Franciscan Sisters of the Immaculate Conception,[18] the Congregation founded by Elizabeth Hayes, who had begun her
religious life with them in Bayswater and been professed in Charlotte Street,
and whose 1866 emendments to the Glasgow Constitutions had been adopted
by all three Congregations. Thus a circle was completed.)

On 8 December 1932, the Feast of the Immaculate Conception, a
children's retreat was held at Merrylee, during which a white marble statue
of the Blessed Virgin was unveiled in the quadrangle, a gift from the pupils
of Charlotte Street and the convent private school to mark the golden
jubilee of Mother Camilla Hamilton. It made a worthy centrepiece to the
elegant buildings grouped around it amid the lawns and rhododendrons.

The Sisters' new home was a place of spirituality and peace, a con-
summation of all their hopes. The old mansion and adjacent new convent
seemed to symbolise the rise of the Congregation, matching the
'respectability' and station to which some at least of the wider Scottish
Catholic community were now aspiring. The extensive grounds, and in
particular the six-foot perimeter wall, spoke of seclusion, permanence and
security. It was all an unimaginable distance from their origins in 1847.

Yet perhaps this gave some pause for thought. The determined attempts
to eject the Welshes in order to build at Merrylee had been far from the spirit
of Francis, and the great expense of the property was no close imitation of
the way of life of the Poverello. Now, as the community were – so to say –
digging in behind their high barricade, some may have reflected that for him
real solidarity with the poor could only be found *outside* the walls of
respectable Assisi.

The mid-1930s were a time of restructuring of the system of state education
in Scotland, aimed at a clear separation of primary and secondary provision.
Though it was the secondary schools that provided the full six-year secondary
curriculum, the more enterprising elementary schools, including a number of
Catholic parish schools, had for some years been running 'supplementary
classes' offering a limited post-elementary education to their abler children. In
some parts of the country these classes had recently been separated from the
elementary schools and moved into 'advanced division centres'. In St Mary's
Calton, for example, such a centre had been opened in West Street in the late
1920s. Now, with the restructuring, this separation was to become standard,
creating from the advanced division centres a new type of school, the 'junior
secondary', for pupils of twelve to fourteen years of age. Henceforth the
elementary schools would provide a primary education only and be limited to

children aged between five and twelve years. To distinguish the new junior secondaries from the 'full' secondary schools, the latter were now to be known as 'senior secondaries'. The new structure was not brought in overnight but as the education authorities were able to afford the costs involved.[19] It would survive virtually unchanged, save only for the raising of the leaving age, until the introduction of comprehensive education in the 1970s.

Traditionally, nearly all the Catholic elementary schools had run separate departments for boys and girls under separate headteachers and often in separate buildings. With their rolls now reduced through the loss of the advanced classes, many were able to amalgamate. Of the schools in the charge of the Franciscan Sisters, St Patrick's Anderston and the two Greenock schools remained as girls' and infants' since their rolls were too large and their buildings too antiquated to admit of amalgamation. But St Alphonsus', St Andrew's (whose roll had reduced greatly with depopulation), St Mary's Hamilton and St John the Baptist in Uddingston all became mixed schools in 1932–3.

By coincidence, the headmistresses of the last three all resigned their posts at about the time of amalgamation: in 1932 the head of St Andrew's left to fill a vacancy at Charlotte Street, while Sr Philippa Gilhooley was withdrawn from St Mary's Hamilton to replace Sr Anthony MacNeil as headmistress at Elmwood, and the following year Sr Margaret Kelly resigned from the headship of St John the Baptist.

Since the 1918 Act there had been an unwritten agreement with the education authorities that any religious resigning the headship of a parish school would automatically be replaced by another member of his/her Order. It was a convenient arrangement that made for continuity and had never been challenged. But the Act had created a genuine profession for lay Catholic teachers, and with it professional expectations: no longer were they necessarily content to dedicate their whole teaching lives to working as assistants. At the same time, the very success of the religious Orders in producing an educated Catholic laity and a growing corpus of able lay teachers also threatened the old assumptions. Under pressure from the teachers' union, the EAs were now quite understandably looking to appoint by open competition rather than reserved right.

When Sr Philippa left St Mary's Hamilton and its departments were amalgamated, the headship of the new mixed school was advertised and a layman, Charles McGregor, appointed, despite lobbying by local parents to keep the Franciscans. In the case of St Andrew's, where the boys' school had long been run by the Marist Brothers, the new mixed school was given to Br Gordian. When Sr Cecilia resigned from St John the Baptist Uddingston the following year, she too was succeeded by a lay head.[20] Thus in the space of a year the Congregation lost three of its longstanding parish schools. The only mixed school still in their hands was St Alphonsus'. It was a sign of things to come, and the lesson was clear: for all their great record and unquestioned dedication, they could no longer count on a continuing dynasty in a parish school, unless they had a Sister available at the right time who was demonstrably the best candidate. There was a second lesson, also: in a mixed school, a man would usually win out.

The Catholic schools in Greenock were restructured in 1933. The well-established higher grade department became St Columba's senior secondary, and the advanced classes of St Mary's and St Lawrence's were separated from their elementary schools and joined to form St Mary's junior secondary, housed in the old Patrick Street building. St Mary's junior girls' continued in the gaunt old premises in Captain Street, with the infants' in the 1870s-vintage East Shaw Street.

In the year before giving up their post-elementary classes St Mary's girls' and infants' had been struggling to fit over 1,000 pupils into the Captain Street building,[21] and for them and St Lawrence's the changes brought a welcome reduction to more manageable numbers without the upheaval of moving premises or major changes of staff. Both schools indeed were enjoying a welcome continuity at this time, under renowned and long-serving headmistresses. The indefatigable Sr M. Bernard Cronin had already been at St Lawrence's for over twenty years and would remain there until the outbreak of war. In charge of St Mary's was Sr M. Teresa O'Connor, who had come into education via the old pupil–teacher path. She had been six years in post, and was to remain until her retirement in 1950. A much-loved figure in the town and known for her visitation of the poor almost as much as for her care of children, she was an inspirational leader. The school choirs and bands that won countless trophies under her baton were famed throughout Renfrewshire, and she was never seen better than when caught up in the excitement of their public performances.[22] Together these two women exerted a profound influence upon generations of children during the war and interwar years, and on the entire Catholic community in Greenock.

Perhaps as influential and quite as much a household name in the city of Inverness was Mother M. Imelda Doherty, the recently retired headmistress of St Mary's parish school who still worked tirelessly in the parish. The school dated from the mid-nineteenth century and was badly in need of improvement. One possibility discussed by the abbess and the county director of education was to amalgamate it with the small convent private school, but the convent building was itself old and suffering from damp, and both the director and Canon Shaw preferred that the community should vacate and the whole site be cleared to make way for a new school. The canon raised the question of vacating with the Sisters several times in the summer and autumn of 1934, to their alarm. Council considered the possibility of purchasing a new property but found it not feasible, and in January 1935, when it had become clear that the ambitions of parish priest and convent were incompatible and relations between them beyond repair, they voted to close the house at the end of the school session in August.[23]

Mother Camilla wrote to Bishop Bennett of Aberdeen informing him of the decision and her deep regret at having to make it. In his reply he did not try to dissuade her, and his letter, though a model of discretion, seemed to side with the Congregation rather than his parish priest. 'I am not surprised at your decision,' he wrote, 'which for a long time I have felt to be inevitable . . . I think it is wise under the circumstances.' The Sisters, he added, would be greatly missed by the Catholics of Inverness. The feeling was mutual. Leaving after eighty years was a wrench for them all. For Mother Imelda, facing a new start at the age of nearly seventy, abandoning her beloved home was one of the great sorrows of her life.[24]

Nowhere was the depression of the mid-1930s felt more keenly than in the mining communities of Lanarkshire, and its impact touched all of the schools, including those in the charge of the Franciscan Sisters. St Bride's Bothwell, where attendance had been hit by the miners' strikes of the 1920s, was now damaged again by the distress of unemployment. In 1933 a high proportion of pupils applied for boots for the winter and were inspected by the school's medical officer to assess their need. Many were kept at home for lack of footwear and only returned in the new year when the consignment finally arrived. The pattern was repeated for three successive years, with the children's schooling further disrupted by outbreaks of impetigo and by the holiday camps organised in term time by the Unemployment Bureau.[25]

In marked contrast was the holiday enjoyed by forty pupils of Charlotte Street in the summer vacation of 1935, when Sr Bernardine accompanied them on the National Pilgrimage to Lourdes. They stood out in their uniforms on the quayside at the Broomielaw, on the boat journey to Le Verdon aboard the *Athenia*, and leading the daily procession at the grotto, the more because they were the first Scottish school group ever to take part in the pilgrimage.[26]

When they returned to school in August the roll stood at 867 and plans were being drawn up for yet another extension. Council received the drawings in November and forwarded them to the education authority for approval, but there they encountered a problem similar to that in 1920: the EA rejected them, pressing for a more ambitious extension than the Congregation could afford. It was a conflict of interests always likely to arise in state schools belonging to religious Orders, where the authority determined accommodation needs but the Order had to bear the costs. The

Catholic parish schools of Glasgow had been purchased by the EA in the late 1920s, and having this privately owned school in their midst was an irritant to them. When the convenor of their property committee met Sr Bernardine the following April (1936), he proposed that she sell the land and building to the city, a proposal firmly rejected by Council, who also turned down his plans for a larger extension.[27]

For the first time in its history the school's roll had been falling for the previous four years, and it was likely to decline further, partly through depopulation of the inner city, but also by the opening that year of Holyrood School and the imminent opening of St Gerard's Govan, the first two mixed Catholic senior secondaries in the city. On these grounds, Sr Bernardine again appealed to the authority in autumn 1937 to reconsider the original plans. Again the convenor persuaded his property committee to turn them down and suggest instead that Charlotte Street revert to fee-paying status. The proposal was flatly rejected by Council as contradicting the very essence of the school's mission in the inner city.

To resolve the impasse, Council agreed to sanction a major emendment of the original plans and eventually produced what was virtually a new design, involving the demolition of the existing buildings. Still the authority found fault. The main point of dispute was their insistence on suitable rooms for domestic science, a subject Sr Bernardine thought barely worthy of a place on a senior secondary timetable. It was June 1938 before the two sides finally reached agreement, but when it seemed that the work could at last begin, it was turned down by the SED.[28] A year later, with war now a certainty, it was shelved indefinitely.

Attendance at St Bride's Bothwell had been further damaged in 1937 when many of the Viewpark parents decided to keep their children at home in expectation of a new school being opened in their own village.[29] If the headmistress imagined it would be a brief gesture she was badly mistaken, for the families held out through the following spring, their determination all the greater when word went round that St Bride's was in danger of collapse through old mine workings beneath the foundations. In May the janitor noticed cracks in the walls: his report brought hurried visits from officers of the authority and the SED who were at pains to reassure the parents that the school was perfectly safe, but their words counted for little when the wall of the girls' playground fell down the very next day. The damage was made good over the summer holidays and the building itself was strengthened with steel braces, but the damage to attendance and public confidence was less easily repaired.

That autumn the school received visits almost weekly from diverse officials, including a government mineral engineer who was of the opinion that there was 'no danger just now', a choice of phrase hardly guaranteed to convince the Viewpark parents. In the last week of November a hard core of them announced that their children were now 'on strike'. Over 160 pupils stayed away, the Christmas tests were cancelled and – far worse for the school's image – the triennial government inspection had to be postponed because of the high absence rate and the 'unsettled state' of those still attending.

The Viewpark families finally got their own junior school in the spring of 1939, while the older children were transferred to the advanced division classes at nearby St John's Uddingston. For St Bride's, the changes involved the loss of four staff and a sharp fall in the roll to eighty-eight, a figure that put the school's very future in doubt.

The government had now been preparing for war for at least a year and had drawn up plans for evacuation as early as July 1938.[30] This involved the voluntary removal of schoolchildren and teachers, pre-school children and mothers, and certain other vulnerable groups from those parts of the country, including Glasgow and the shipbuilding and dockyard towns, thought to be under greatest threat of air attack. In spring 1939 a census indicated that perhaps two thirds of the Glasgow families involved would agree to take part. In June, many of the schools held practice evacuation days. The summer holidays came and went with the country still on the brink of war.

Like the other city schools, Charlotte Street reopened on Friday 25 August, only to close at midday to allow staff to prepare for the evacuation, which was expected any day. The following week the girls were given lessons but no timetable, since many had already made private arrangements and left the city. On the Friday evening, a meeting was held for the parents at which Sr Bernardine announced that she was under instructions to put the evacuation into effect the following morning. The girls should arrive at 8 a.m., she told them. They should bring a warm coat, a change of underclothes and socks, night clothes and toiletries, and on arrival each would be given a gas mask, a tin cup and enough food for the journey.[31]

The next day, Saturday 2 September, the register of nearly two hundred names was called and recorded in triplicate. The girls were divided into groups, keeping family members together. Belongings were checked, and a few pupils sent hurriedly home to fetch forgotten items. Identity labels were hung round necks. Brown carrier bags were handed out and peered into – inside were spam pieces, corned beef and chocolate bars. The waiting and checking seemed endless.

Suddenly they were on the move. Parents at the gate watched as the crocodile made towards Greenhead Street station, young Sr M. Francis Campbell leading them, with Sr Bernardine in the rear. Senior girls held the hands of the youngest. The orderlies in armbands provided by the city to help shepherd the moving mass, and the police escort fore and aft, were quite superfluous. At the station they found boy scouts waiting to offer a hand with the luggage.

The journey along the Clyde coast was snail-paced and, for all the exhilaration of the day and the drama and freedom of the hills and sea, it grew wearisome at last. The day was nearly over when the girls were finally let out, a few at Inverkip and the rest at Wemyss Bay. They were taken to the community hall where their hosts awaited them, and their new parents took them home. To girls from the tenements, the detached houses were wondrous. One, Redholm, took in twenty of them. Some had four-poster beds; a few were homely cottages. Nearly all of the hosts were Protestants, but all were welcoming and gave the girls every support in the practice of their faith. That first week, those of secondary age were enrolled in the nearest Catholic schools in Greenock – St Columba's senior secondary and St Mary's JS – but they could only be accommodated by being put on half-timetables, along with the local children.

On 30 September, Sr Bernardine returned to Glasgow: it was her sixtieth birthday, and she was retiring from teaching. Appointed in her place was Sr Philippa Gilhooley, who was released from the headship of Elmwood in order to take up her post in the new year. Charlotte Street remained closed, but temporary arrangements were made from October onwards for those girls still living in the city. The fourth- to sixth-year pupils were offered lessons every morning at Merrylee and had to make their own way there. Second and third years were briefly taught in St Alphonsus' parish hall, but this private initiative of the acting head was withdrawn after three weeks at the bidding of the authority because it did not comply with safety regulations. The main school was partially reopened in November, with a maximum of sixty pupils at any one time. By operating a rota, the primary children and first- to third-year secondary girls each received three hours of schooling per week. The upper school continued to travel out to Merrylee.[32]

By now the evacuees were drifting home. Not because of bad experiences, for there had been remarkably few, given the huge numbers involved. Most of the girls had been fed well, but it was wholesome food such as porridge, and they wanted chips. The long autumn evenings were pitch black in the country villages: even the warships off the coast were unlit and only recognisable by their lonely muffled sound as they passed by. Many of the children were fretting for home, and in the 'phoney war' of autumn 1939 it seemed safe enough to let them have their way. By the end of October almost half were back in the city.[33]

When Sr Philippa took up her post at Charlotte Street in January, all but one of the Wemyss Bay girls had returned and only a dozen remained with one teacher at Inverkip. The senior students were still at Merrylee, but with the school now permitted to take 300 it was possible to return to something like normality for the rest. Sister had air raid shelters erected in the yard, and she attended headteachers' meetings to ensure that there were normal arrangements for the public examinations and to press for the reopening of the feeder schools. From 22 April, schooling was again made compulsory in the city for children of seven years and upwards. At the end of May registers were drawn up for a second phase of evacuation. A much disrupted school year was about to end, but Sister kept the school open through the summer vacation to enable the certificate pupils to make up lost time. No less than 239 girls attended in the first week, and although the numbers dipped afterwards, about 100 persevered throughout the holiday.

The parish schools returned in August to weekly rounds of air raid drills. The St Mary's Greenock school log records that it took just 2½ minutes for the whole school to reach the assembly point during the emergency drill, and that with practice this was reduced to two minutes. The school's solitary stirrup pump was tested every week without fail and found to be in good order. At St Lawrence's, the teachers covered all the windows with anti-blast netting just days before the town suffered two air raids in one night. As Christmas approached, the school day was progressively reduced so that the children could reach home before the blackout.

In February 1941, with more raids anticipated, the Renfrewshire EA ordered firewatching teams to be appointed at its Greenock schools. The Church assumed that the authority itself would make the arrangements in the Catholic schools since the buildings were its property, but their lawyers advised them that responsibility fell not on the owner but the occupier and that arrangements should be made by the headteachers and the parish priests. Thus at St Lawrence's Sr Anastasia Bogan drew up a rota of volunteers to mount a round-the-clock watch: men of the parish through the night, teachers in the evenings and on Saturdays, and teachers and the janitor on Sundays. Three weeks later the town suffered another all-night raid.

It was the first of many on Clydeside that spring. On 7–8 April, bombs were dropped in the centre of Glasgow, wrecking the eye infirmary on the corner of Charlotte Street, the original home of the Congregation under Mother Veronica. The school suffered some damage in the blast: windows were shattered, plaster was blown away and the roof partly stripped of slates. Interior repairs were begun at once to make it habitable, though the war damage commission refused to sanction work on the exterior – judging it 'non essential' – until the end of the war.[34]

Whenever the air raids lasted beyond midnight, pupils were excused school the following morning. This occurred regularly in the first fortnight of May, when the raids on Glasgow reached a peak, and for a full week Sr Philippa kept three teachers on all-night duty.

On the night of 5–6 May, Greenock took its worst pounding to date, and in the morning many families fled to the countryside. It was the saving of them, for the next night no less than 250 enemy planes attacked the town, leaving 280 dead and some 1,200 injured. Many houses in the Strome Farm area and the neighbourhood of St Lawrence's were flattened. Cartsburn School was annihilated and Belville so badly damaged that it remained closed until the autumn. St Lawrence's school was not hit, but a number of its children were killed in their homes. The church itself was destroyed, and while it burned the priests and housekeeper found themselves trapped underground, unable to escape because of rubble blocking the door. Only a parishioner breaking a hole in it saved them, but they emerged to find the presbytery uninhabitable. Sr Anastasia gave them a part of 'Belltrees', the Congregation's boarding house and private school adjoining the Glenlea convent, for use as a home and Mass centre for the duration of the war.[35] In the days that followed she spent every spare moment visiting the injured and the bereaved, winning the gratitude of many in the town for her support and care amid the tragedy.

On 10 May she received a visit from Colonel Craig Barr of the admiralty, who informed her that his organisation was commandeering St Lawrence's for the duration of the war and would be taking the building over that week. They intended to convert it into drawing offices for Scott & Co., shipbuilders and engineers, who had been contracted to undertake work for the government.

This was totally unexpected news. The children were dismissed at once, the furniture was removed to a nearby motor garage and the stationery stored in a local special school. For a week the girls were given lessons in the church hall while arrangements were discussed for sharing the boys' school. It was agreed that the boys would attend the morning sessions and the girls afternoons, an arrangement that was made slightly easier by the large number absent in the weeks following the blitz. Two groups of girls were evacuated with their teachers in June, and with many other families making private arrangements to leave the town the roll had fallen to 500. Less than half of these pupils were actually attending. Some had not been traced since the bombing. Had they moved house? Were they with relatives? Were they absent because their parents were destitute? Were they dead? With the neighbourhood in ruins it was impossible to be sure.

The children remained on half-time schooling throughout the autumn. Many were living in temporary lodgings and it was an especially hard time for the youngest ones, but the teachers tried to make the school day as happy as possible. In the last week of term they put on a Christmas party, with a tree, presents and a special surprise of parcels gifted by children from USA for those who had lost their homes.

By March 1942 there was still no sign of the girls' school being returned to its proper use and it was now urgent that some arrangement be made to resume full-time education. At the request of the parents, the two head-teachers decided not to amalgamate into a mixed-sex school but to run the two schools separately in the one building. This was achieved by combining the streamed classes into large mixed-ability groups, thus saving on classroom space. For the girls it involved classes of close to sixty, but the parents found this preferable to having boys in the same class, and the staff willingly took on the extra workload. The younger pupils remained on half-timetables. Any hopes of a swift return to normality were dashed that summer when the admiralty requested that the requisitioning of the school should continue for two years after the end of the war, or that they purchase the building outright. Both requests were refused, but the message was clear.[36]

By 1943, Charlotte Street was running almost normally again. The pupils were active in the war effort, collecting nearly £600 in the nationwide 'wings for victory' week in June, amassing an incredible 6½tons of books in a book drive, and 'adopting' a Royal Navy destroyer for whose crew they knitted numerous woollen scarves. To make up for their lost education, the summer holiday was reduced by three weeks and new teaching staff were appointed in order to restore the full curriculum. Spanish was added to the timetable, and PE was reintroduced after a gap of two years and strengthened by the appointment for the first time of a principal teacher. Another 'non academic' subject, domestic science, was similarly strengthened, though the school had as yet no purpose-built cookery facilities and lessons were held in St Alphonsus' primary. For a school of Charlotte Street's traditions, these were bold departures: one could hardly have imagined the concept of principal teachers of such lowly subjects in Sr Bernardine's day.

Even more radical was the decision taken in 1944 to cease admitting new pupils to the primary department and progressively to phase it out. Henceforth the staff would focus solely on secondary education and on restoring and developing even further the standards of excellence of the pre-war era.

Meantime, the war effort continued. Since 1943 many Scottish schools had been helping with the harvest, Charlotte Street among them. In the first year Sr Philippa had signed the school up for berry-picking at Forfar and lifting potatoes in Blairgowrie. In 1944 it was tattie-howking again, in Kincardineshire. A large party of girls and ten teachers volunteered to spend a fortnight at the camp, and in order not to disrupt their education further the school had two separate month-long 'summer' holidays that year, the second of them during the potato harvest in September–October. The camps were repeated every year until 1948: they were always hard work and great fun, the evenings filled with impromptu talent shows, with the last night invariably involving a huge sing-song and party to which the St Mungo's boys camping nearby were invited, unknown to the girls' headmistress 'Pip' in faraway Glasgow.

It was now almost two years since the admiralty had taken over St Lawrence's, and 600 of the 1,000 children were still on half-time schooling. The frustrated parents had formed an action committee and in March 1944 took their case to the diocesan education board.[37] As a result, within a fortnight the EA erected three huts on the site of the bombed Cartsburn school to house the girls, a measure that was no more than a sop and totally inadequate. Three weeks after the classes moved in, the huts were flooded by rain. The parish priest declared the whole affair an insult.

The Church contacted the EA through their lawyer twice that summer requesting the authority to persuade the admiralty to vacate. Meeting with no success, they then contacted the Scottish Education Department and the admiralty direct. In its reply, the SED informed them that the admiralty had now produced a list of 'priority' schools for decommissioning and that St Lawrence's was on it.[38]

By the autumn all but four infant classes were back to full-time education. The teachers and children of the girls' school were performing admirably in their scattered classrooms. They were following a close-to-normal timetable and enjoying the usual out-of-school activities and treats, including the eagerly awaited annual visit from the 'bird man', who told them stories of birds and mimicked their calls. When Sister personally tested the qualifying class of 1944 she found the standards excellent in the difficult circumstances, and her judgment was vindicated when all but one passed the final examination. And when HMI Deans made his inspection the following year, he praised the pupils' attainment and pronounced himself 'very satisfied' with the whole school.

The talk of 'priority' was proving meaningless, though. By spring 1945 the admiralty was going so far as to claim that St Lawrence's was now on its '*first category* of priority', yet a letter from its senior surveyor of lands stated that decommissioning would be impossible in the foreseeable future since no alternative accommodation could be found for Scott's draughts-men. Since £20,000 had been spent on adapting the building, his letter added, and a similar sum might be required to restore it, the admiralty again wished to pursue the possibility of purchasing it. The diocesan board referred his proposal to the archbishop, with a strong recommendation for refusal.[39] A delegation of parents and board members met the EA in May, but though vocal in their resolve to fight on, they came away frustrated at an inconclusive meeting.

The ending of the war that summer appeared to effect no change in the admiralty's position, for they made no attempt to contact either the Church or the county authority. Having heard nothing for six months, the EA pressed for a meeting in February 1946, at which, for the first time, there seemed to be some room for manoeuvre. Officials of the Church who met the Secretary of State in April were also received favourably. Within a fortnight, a representative of the admiralty appeared in Greenock to inspect the Cartsburn huts as a possible location for the drawing-office staff, and declared them suitable.[40] Scott's vacated the girls' school in the summer, and work began on restoring the building to its former use.

Since 1932–3, when the Congregation had lost St Mary's Hamilton and St John the Baptist Uddingston to lay headteachers, it had been clear that the religious Orders could expect no automatic right of succession in state schools. There was no such guarantee in law or contract, nor could there be. There had indeed traditionally been a tacit agreement between Church and EA in such cases, but this had come increasingly under threat over the years through pressure from the union, but not least through the irritation of the education authorities at the failure of some religious Orders to follow the correct procedures. Many Superiors still appeared to think that it was they who made the appointments, putting forward unsuitable candidates or even replacing staff without notifying anyone. The worst offenders were those based in mother houses in England, who had little grasp of the Scottish education system and assumed that the schools enjoyed a similar degree of independence from the state as obtained south of the border. The Franciscan Sisters themselves had always been faultless in their dealings with the authorities, but as a religious Congregation they suffered under the general disenchantment. Several EAs were now no longer willing to recognise the existence of a 'gentlemen's agreement' at all; some were only willing to appoint religious already in their employ; nearly all insisted on a leet of three candidates.[41]

The diocesan education board had been aware of the growing problem for a decade, and by the end of the war were seriously concerned that more headships would inevitably be lost. Their fears were soon to be confirmed. When the headship of St Columba's Viewpark fell vacant in December 1946, Mother Abbess requested that it should automatically be filled by her nominee, as in the past. Lanarkshire EA refused her request and advertised the post. Council put forward the one suitable candidate they had available at the time, Sr M. Sebastian McEleny, but she failed to secure the position, which went to a lay teacher.[42] So another school was lost to the Congregation. It was a disappointment that would become a pattern of the post-war era.

It took the tradesmen six months to restore St Lawrence's for school use, but in January 1947 they finally moved out, and on the last day of the month the children and teachers returned. They found the classrooms, corridors and toilets all bright with new fittings and paint. But it was only the oldest qualifying class that had ever been in the place before, and they could barely remember a school they had left as infants. It had been a wait of five years and eight months. A generation of children had been the pawns of war, procrastination and bureaucracy, and for them there could be no rerun of their education.

ENDNOTES FOR CHAPTER FIVE

1　Council Meeting, 27.2.1920, in Chapter Reports, Mother House, 1920–23, 030.1, AF.

2　Council Meeting Minutes, 21.1.1921, 17.2.1921 and 13.10.1921, 034.10, AF. The final cost, including interest, solicitors' fees, etc., was £8,999 – Statement, Hill & Hoggan, Solicitors, 14.10.1921, 040.12, AF.

3　Mother Wallburga Broe, Abbess to Archbishop Maguire, 10.12.1922, RO8/15, AGA.

4　Based on Business Account, Hill & Hoggan, Solicitors, entries from 19.3.1924 to 30.3.1925, 041.11, AF; and defences by Welsh's lawyer, n.d., RO8/51, AGA.

5　Mgr John Ritchie to Mother Wallburga Broe, 13.6.1925 and 28.10.1925, 071.01, AF.

6　Account based on Council Meeting Minutes, entries between 10.3.1926 and 26.8.1926. Of the ten who continued in religion, five joined the Benedictine convent in Dumfries, three the Franciscans in Woodchester, one the Poor Clares in Darlington, and one the Good Shepherd Order in Finchley.

7　The problem was not unique to the Scottish Congregation. Similar issues were a concern of the Third Order Regular worldwide at this time, and the subject of special attention in Rome. Pius XI was himself preparing a Constitution on the Order's Rule, in which he gave notice that because of changed conditions in society and the Church, it was now imperative to emend the four-centuries-old Rule of Leo X, and that he was giving the Sacred Congregation for Religious Affairs the task of doing so – Pius XI, *Rerum Conditio*, 4.10.1927.

8　Chapter Reports, Bothwell House, 030.1, AF; details of loans, 044.11, AF. The loans included £9,000 from the diocesan education board in nine £1,000 payments between Sept 1922 and Sept 1923, as well as £1,000 from the mother house.

9　From the obituary article on her in *The Elmwood Magazine*, 1960 issue, CNS. Most of the details concerning Miss Rea are from this source, and from Sr Benedicta Collins and Miss Susan McCormick interviews.

10　There were still junior students in 26 schools in Scotland, many of them in the Glasgow area, when the system was finally discontinued in 1950. Cf., Wilson J.D., Section 4 of Bone T.R. (ed.), 1967, p. 233ff.

11　*The Elmwood Magazine*, vol. 1 no. 2 Dec 1928, and vol. 1 no. 3 Dec. 1929. Even more telling was the fact that only two FPs graduated from the university in 1928–9, showing how recent was the tradition of aspiring to a degree course.

12 Chapter Reports, Mother House, 1926–32, 030.1, AF; and Council Meeting Minutes, 3.7.1928 and Sept. 1929.

13 Council Meeting Minutes, 8.7.1929. Total expenditure £48,938/2/8; balance in bank as at 30.6.1929 £10,090/19/4. Also, detailed breakdown of expenditure in Abstract of Final Accounts, n.d., 040.12, AF.

14 Receipt of Payment, E. Quadrelli, sculptor's agent, 6.6.1930, 040.12, AF. The cost of the main altar was £575, the side altars £175 each.

15 Council Meeting Minutes, 15.11.1930.

16 Merrylee was also less convenient for those priests of the Franciscan Friary in Cumberland Street who acted as the community's chaplains, and Mass and Benediction became more sporadic. The problem was solved by increasing their annual salary to £100 and purchasing a small car to take them in and out of town.

17 Council Meeting Minutes, 18.10.1931.

18 'A.M.' (Sr Agatha McEvoy), 1959, p. 23f.

19 Thus, for example, West Street RC Centre was not upgraded to become St Mary's Junior Secondary Calton until 1937.

20 Chapter Reports, Mother House, 1926–32, 030.1, AF; St Mary's Hamilton *150th Year Commemorative Brochure 1846–1996*, p. 13; Education Papers, ED 8/1/18, 1933–4, AGA.

21 Account based mainly on *St Patrick's Primary School Greenock Centenary 1878–1978*, especially p. 22. In 1932 the school admitted no less than 210 into the first year infants'.

22 *Obituary Register*, nos. 168 and 188, AF.

23 Council Meeting Minutes, 6.5.1934 (regarding possible amalgamation); 1.7.1934 and 27.1.1935 (decision to close).

24 *Obituary Register*, no.143, AF.

25 St Bride's Log, AF, 18/22.10.1926 (re attendance during miners' strike), 13.10.1933, 29.1.1934, 8.8.1936 and October 1936.

26 Account in *Our Lady and St Francis Magazine*, Centenary number, 1948.

27 Council Meeting Minutes, 10.1.1935 and 19.1.1936; and Business Account, B. Caulfield and McGowan, Solicitors, 1935–40, 040.12, AF, entries between Sept 1935 and Sept 1936. The author of the Congregation's plans was the Glasgow architect Alexander McAnally. The convenor of the EA's property committee was Bailie Biggar. The following paragraph is also based on the same sources. (The parish schools of the archdiocese, which at first had also been leased to the EAs after the 1918 Act – cf. p. 113 *supra* – had been sold to them in the late 1920s).

28 Council Meeting Minutes, 16.1.1938 and 27.6.1938; and Business Account, Caulfield and McGowan, entries between 22 Sept 1937 and 6 June 1938.

29 Account based on St Bride's Log, entries 1937–9.

30 Report of the Committee on Evacuation (the 'Anderson Report'), Cmd 5837, July 1938, published 27.10.1938.

31 Account based on Sr M. Francis Campbell and Mrs Anna Keegan interviews

(the former a teacher who accompanied the evacuees, the latter a young evacuee), OLSF Log, and generally applicable details from Belford A.J. and Third J.R. in Boyd W. (ed), 1944.

32 OLSF Log, 5.10.1939, 12.10.1939 and 3.11.1939. It was necessary to hold some third-year classes in a private house in Monteith Place.

33 Forty-three per cent, according to Boyd W. (ed), *op cit*, p. 95.

34 B. Caulfield & McGowan, solicitors, to abbess 17.4.1941, and same to same 7.10.1941, 041.11, AF. The estimated cost of interior repairs was £500, the final cost over £1500, of which the Congregation eventually received £850 in compensation – War Damage Commission, Edinburgh, 7.1.1943, 041.11, AF.

35 Though its address was 13 Newark Street, Belltrees was actually next door to the Glenlea House convent in Madeira Street, whence the community had moved from their original Bank House in 1913. Located in the affluent west end of the town, the two houses were almost identical, both stone-built bay-windowed villas built for shipping magnates at the turn of the century.

36 Diocesan Education Board Minutes, 6.7.1942, ED 1/7, AGA.

37 Diocesan Education Board Minutes, 4.2.1944, 6.3.1944; St Lawrence's Log, March 1944, 17.4.1944, 28.4.1944.

38 Diocesan Education Board Minutes, 1.5.1944, 3.7.1944, 2.10.1944 and 4.12.1944.

39 Diocesan Education Board Minutes, 5.3.1945.

40 Diocesan Education Board Minutes, 4.2.1946, 1.4.1946 and 2.5.1946.

41 Diocesan Education Board Minutes, 5.2.1945, which include a lengthy account of discussion of the issues.

42 Council Meeting Minutes, 30.11.1946; and Diocesan Education Board Minutes, 2.12.1946.

CHAPTER SIX

Fresh Fields, Full Harvests (1947–1962)

In Charlotte Street and Elmwood schools, where demand for places always outstripped supply, 1947 opened to the familiar problem of overcrowding. In Elmwood's case there was at least the prospect of a solution. The roll stood at over 650, more than should strictly have been admitted according to national regulations, and plans for an extension had first been postponed during the war and finally abandoned after it.[1] Instead the Congregation had purchased a new property in the neighbourhood in which to house the convent so that the Elmwood buildings could be devoted entirely to the school.[2] 'The Lindens' (Plate 18), a detached red sandstone house of character set back from the tree-lined road in a wedge of gardens, was a worthy complement to Elmwood. The renovations were now well ahead, and removal to their new home was expected within a year or two.

The future at Charlotte Street was less clear. Its inner city site had long been recognised as unsuitable, and its whole history had been one of 'add and patch'. At the end of the war, Council had minuted its intention to remove the school to Merrylee 'at some future date' and had discussed the matter with the city education authority, who expressed its support for a new school 'when circumstances permitted of its being built'. The principle of closing Charlotte Street was thus agreed, though the time and the means were left unspecified.

That summer the school leaving age was raised to fifteen.[3] The effect on Charlotte Street and Elmwood was minimal, but it was felt immediately in the elementary schools, including those run by the Sisters, which now faced something akin to a rerun of the post-World War I years. More pupils required more teachers, and if, in the case of men, the need was partly met by those lately returned from military service (who were given priority in training and placements), there was no such ready source from which to recruit women. Yet again, therefore, as in 1872 and 1918, this was a time when the task of the religious Orders in preparing a supply of good female lay teachers took on a new urgency.

The abbess and Council spent much of the spring of 1947 holding a series of meetings with friends and alumnae. On 18 June, it would be one hundred years to the day since Adélaide, Veronica and Mlle Marchand had first arrived in Glasgow, and it seemed everyone wanted to play a part in the celebrations. *Ad hoc* committees of former pupils from Charlotte Street, Elmwood, Greenock and Inverness were set up to plan events to complement the Congregation's own programme and raise funds. The Charlotte Street committee assembled a centenary choir of former pupils for a planned autumn concert.[4]

The heart of the celebrations took place in the centenary week, with a civic reception hosted by the lord provost in the City Chambers on 18 June itself, followed by three High Masses on successive days, the first for the community concelebrated by Archbishop Campbell and forty priests at Merrylee, the second for Charlotte Street pupils in the cathedral, the last for all former pupils of schools run by the Congregation.

On 23 June the pupils of Charlotte Street put on a public concert in the St Andrew's Halls, at which Miss McCann's choir figured large. The FPs' concert took place in October in the same venue and was based on the theme 'the foundation of the convent in Scotland'. The organisers took the opportunity to announce to the large gathering of alumnae their intention to continue their fundraising drive, with a view to building a memorial hall at Merrylee. The enthusiasm kindled by their work for the centenary led to the formation of a Franciscan former pupils' association at the end of the year, open to ex-pupils of all of the Congregation's schools.[5]

While Sr Philippa awaited the half-promised new school she continued to wrestle with the accommodation at Charlotte Street. The school was spilling out beyond its own walls. Domestic Science classes were being taught a mile away at Sacred Heart Junior Secondary,[6] a prison-like place whose small exercise yard was encircled by a six-metre-high factory wall. Over 100 pupils had to take their lessons in St Andrew's primary, hardly ever seeing their friends in the main school. During the 1948 Easter holiday, four prefabricated classrooms were erected in the convent garden.[7] These makeshift arrangements were to last seven years, but they did not eliminate the problem.

Cramped it may have been, but the school continued to build on its reputation for excellence. It remained much in demand. Pupils enrolled from no less than seventeen primary schools from every quarter of the city, though the great majority lived in the east end and its own primary department (not yet fully phased out[8]) still provided the largest single group. Close to a fifth of its upper school students won university places and a further 30 per cent entry to the teacher training college.

From its own magazine, re-established in 1946 and run entirely by the pupils, we get the impression of a buoyant, enterprising school community and of a rounded education in and out of the classroom. We read of schooltime visits to the Cosmo Cinema, the Citizens' Theatre and a debate on the future of religion between the Catholic author Arnold Lunn and the agnostic Dr Joad; of tennis in the public courts on the Glasgow Green; of interschool netball matches at which the girls were under orders to applaud their opponents as heartily as their own team – an injunction put under some strain in the biannual 'Old Firm' game against arch rivals Elmwood. There were trips to the Highlands, the annual concert in St Andrew's Halls with the archbishop as guest of honour, and a Christmas party and upper school dance to which, however, the only invited male guests were the local clergy. A few weeks after performing at their own centenary celebrations, Miss McCann's choir sang at a concert in the Bridgeton Halls organised by the EIS, whose own centenary fell in the same year. Every month at this time they led the singing at a *Missa Cantata* in St Alphonsus' church. On such occasions the crocodile of hundreds of brown-clad girls crossing busy London Road with near perfect decorum was one of the familiar sights of East End life.

The spiritual was quite naturally at the heart of all their activities. Many events took place out at Merrylee, among them the annual retreat held over a weekend in May, the floral Corpus Christi processions on the lawn, and the monthly meetings of the Franciscan Third Order group established by the school chaplain Fr John.[9]

The school day was orderly and conducted to order. The girls entered the building and moved to their classes to the sound of a marching tune – 'When the Guards were on Parade' was a favourite – played on the piano by one of their number. But if the pupils took school discipline 'in their stride', visitors found it deeply impressive. It was not harsh. In the main it was self-discipline, into which new pupils fell easily, unconsciously embracing the prevailing ethos in an environment of mutual respect. Above all, perhaps, it sprang from the desire of inner city girls (and their parents) for an excellent education, and their pride in knowing that they were getting it.

Like Elmwood the school was built upon the existence of a stable and dedicated staff. Of the thirty-nine teachers in the secondary department in 1948, thirty-one, including every principal teacher, were unmarried women, and for most of them the school was their vocation. They gave prodigally of their time. Sixteen were themselves former pupils; four were religious. Thus the Franciscan tradition of education pervaded every classroom, and many of the staff had known no other. Miss O'Neill, whose presence as pupil and teacher spanned almost six decades, was one such. Another was Annie Conway, also an alumna and the first ever to graduate from Glasgow University, who had returned to Charlotte Street in 1913 and taught classics continuously until her retirement in the centenary year. In her loyalty and dedication, her understanding of the principles of Christian education, and her own high standards as a scholar, she epitomised those qualities that were the foundations of the school's excellence.

16. Sr M. Anthony MacNeil, right, with her cousin Sr Gertrude Collins. *Photo: AF*

17. Group at laying of foundation stone of Merrylee chapel by Archbishop Donald Mackintosh, March 1928. *Photo: AF*

18. The Lindens, Bothwell. *Photo: AF*

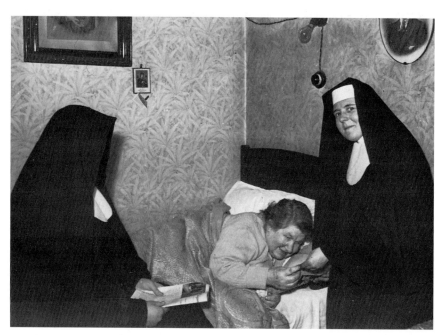

19. Sisters visiting the sick, 1940s. *Photo:AF*

20. The convent at Falcarragh, December 1947. *Photo: AF*

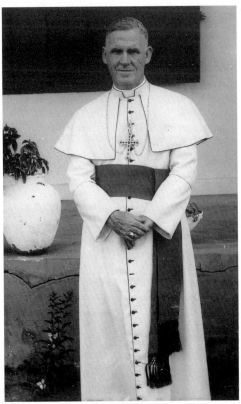

21. Bishop Owen McCoy WF. *Photo:AF*

22. The convent at Osogbo, 1950. *Photo: AF*

23. Sisters with Bishop McCoy and Olotan. *Photo: AF*

24. St Anthony's Cinderford, the first intake, autumn 1960. *Photo: AF*

25. Sr Felicitas with OLSF pupils, 1960s. *Photo AF*

26. Srs Gertrude, Angela and Gerard with Mother Gabriel, Renovo, August 1971. *Photo: AF*

27. Mother Gabriel with Archbishop Winning, OLSF Prize-giving, City Halls, 1973. *Photo: AF*

28. Mitre House, Househillwood. *Photo: AF*

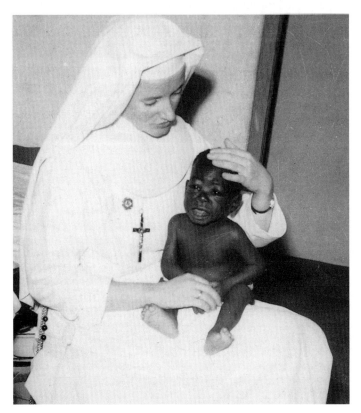

29. Sr Emmanuel with one of the abandoned babies. *Photo: AF*

30. Taju and Ayo. *Photo: AF*

The four religious formed something of a separate group from the rest of the staff. They were still bound by the spirit of the monastery while at work, and normally took their lunch in a different room and refrained from conversing with colleagues unless on school business. They arrived together in the brown bus driven by the Merrylee handyman and departed together shortly after 4 p.m. Their social contacts with the lay teachers were almost nil.

Like everyone else in the convent they rose at 5.10 a.m. and began their daily Office at 5.40. Matins, followed by prayers for friends and benefactors recited with arms held in cruciform and a half-hour meditation, took them to Mass at 7.00. A light and hurried breakfast just left them time to board the bus before it set off on its circuit of the city, dropping the teaching Sisters at their various schools and others at the university and Notre Dame.

It was 4.45 p.m. before the bus completed its afternoon pick-up run, and the Sisters had no time to spare if they were to make 5 o'clock dinner in the refectory. After the meal they snatched ten minutes to themselves before evening Office, after which they had to catch up on the rest of the Office, as well as Rosary, a visit to the Blessed Sacrament and the spiritual reading they had missed during the day. Between supper and night prayers they had twenty minutes for recreation, after which the Great Silence took them to 'lights out' at 10 p.m. Any lesson preparation or marking not completed during their school lunch break could be finished at this time, but only with the special permission of the abbess.

Such was a teaching Sister's day from Monday to Friday. On Saturdays she made home visits in her pupils' parishes. On Sunday mornings she supervised the children's Masses. Hers was a 6½-day week, in fact, and relentless, with hardly time to draw breath let alone improve the mind or indulge in reflection. Her only chances to take stock were the monthly day of recollection and the annual retreat.

Thus was the community's day mapped out; a monastic day, apportioned and marked by bells, purged of needless distraction, requiring no forethought. Monastic, too, the architecture of the house, with its cells, cloister, community room and visitors' parlour. Within it every Sister had her allotted place, based on seniority of profession – a set place in the refectory, even a particular hook in the laundry numbered according to the day she took her vows. The community entered the chapel in set order: the postulants first in their lay clothes, light veil and lace cap; then the novices, their habit distinguished by its white veil; next the 'young professed' who had taken first vows; and finally the 'ancients', those who had made their final profession, who themselves lined up in order, the newest to the longest-serving. Each took her own allotted stall in the choir. The Lay Sisters, who entered separately, sat in stalls away from the rest.

The main stages towards final profession were thus clearly distinguished, and progression from one to the next was marked by *rites de passage*, each with its own ceremonial. When a young woman first took the habit of the novice, she was dressed as a bride in white, with a train; a female relative acted as her palm bearer and children in white attended her, one carrying the scapula, another the scissors, others scattering fresh flowers; her hair was sheared and she was presented with cord, crucifix and the Rule and Constitutions. When at the end of her novitiate she took the first vows of the 'young professed' and put on the black veil, the ceremony took place during a special Mass and was followed by a celebratory community breakfast. Strangely, her final profession was a quiet event marked by the least ceremonial, almost like a normal day – no special Mass, and just the usual breakfast, after which the newly installed young 'ancient' went off to do a normal day's work.[10]

The habit of the professed Sister was a heavy affair of thick black material, hardly designed for an active apostolate. Its long sleeves copied the habit of St Francis, who wore them thus out of humility to cover his hands and so hide the stigmata, but they were quite impracticable and had to be turned up for everyday use. No less than seven separate items were worn upon the head and had to be assembled daily – the white cap or *sur tête*; the white *chaperon* pinned under the chin; the starched white *bandeau* covering the forehead; the white neckerchief crossed over at the front; the black under-veil; the top veil, also black; and the heavy starched white *gampe* – the names betraying their Tourcoing origin. The habit was girded by a Franciscan cord of three knots representing the three vows of the religious, over which hung a black scapula. Tucked under the cord on the left side was a crucifix and on the right a rosary, the tradition of tucking them away dating from the early Glasgow days when it would have been dangerous to leave them visible.

The Sisters also wore a black ceremonial cloak for morning Office and Mass. Before approaching the altar for Communion they were required to unpin the top veil and let it fall over the face, lifting it briefly to receive the Host upon the tongue, then lowering it again before returning to their stalls. As well as showing reverence for the Blessed Sacrament, the purpose of the custom was modesty or 'custody of the eyes', a symbolic monastic enclosure as if they were 'carrying their cloister with them'. But this too was highly impracticable, if not risky, for each Sister moving forward could barely see enough to avoid treading on the cloak of the one in front.

At this date the Constitutions made no provision for visits home unless *in extremis*, and set very tight limits even on close relatives entering the convent. The Sisters were allowed out strictly for 'business' only – when visiting the sick, for example (Plate 19) – and had to spend their annual holiday at the

Saltcoats house or in another convent. For a young woman to take the vows was in fact to enter into a lifelong commitment not only rigorous and exacting, but one that separated her for ever from family and friends and from which there was no remission. The sacrifices of such a life could only be contemplated if outweighed by the conviction that it was the will of God. When she entered to test her vocation there were often times of loneliness, even moments of panic, and when she made her decision and sealed it with vows, along with the joy there came pain, a resignation and a sense not unlike that of bereavement. One Sister recalled the night she entered the convent about this time. As she walked along Briar Road and looked up at the new moon above the trees, she thought: 'I will never be out to see you again.' She and her mother parted in the parlour, and she was led to her cell. As the door closed behind her she said to herself, 'Well, you've done it. You'll just have to put up with it. You'll never smile a day again.' (Nearly sixty years on she has in fact smiled many days, and she was smiling even as she told the story.)

During the war years, vocations to the Congregation had dried up almost entirely in Scotland, prompting Council to look again to Ireland for recruits. As early as 1942 they had sought permission of the archbishop of Dublin to open a vocations house in his diocese, but had been turned down. Subsequent enquiries in the rest of the country were also unsuccessful. The Irish bishops were being swamped with similar requests, especially from Orders in America, and they were anxious to prevent a hæmorrhage of vocations from their own Church.[11]

Council had finally succeeded in securing the permission of Bishop Mac-Neely of Raphoe, in the far north-west, and as soon as the war ended they began searching for a suitable house in Donegal. In March 1946 Mother Bernardine and her vicaress had travelled to Ireland, with a testimonial from Archbishop Campbell, to meet Bishop MacNeely and inspect two properties that were up for sale. Their journey brought home to them just how isolated west Donegal is, and how less than ideal it would be as a national centre for recruiting.[12]

In the end they chose the less remote of the two properties, a house with eight acres of open fields in the townland of Falcarragh, standing on the rim of the ocean and once home to coastguards. To the west it faced towards the point of Bloody Foreland and the isles of Inishbofin and Inishdooey, and beyond them Tory Island and the astonishing Atlantic sunset; behind it to the east the wild green hinterland of Donegal was bounded on the horizon by the dark masses of Muckish and far-off Errigal.

Bishop MacNeely readily gave his permission for its purchase,[13] but it was a further eighteen months before the house was made habitable for a community, and a community chosen. Mother M. Paul and her three companions moved in on 18 November 1947, and a fortnight later the convent was formally opened and blessed (Plate 20). The Sisters at once turned their attention to recruitment, mainly by placing notices in the Irish newspapers, but they found that even this bland approach was received warily by some diocesan administrators, who insisted on vetting their advertisements before they went to press.[14] Within three months their efforts bore fruit with the reception of their first postulant.[15]

In autumn 1949 the Merrylee community received a visit from Mgr Owen McCoy, Prefect Apostolic of Oyo in Nigeria (Plate 21). A White Father, he had been working on the Nigerian mission since 1943 under the authority of the archbishop of Lagos, and had that year been given charge of Oyo on its being made an independent prefecture. His first act on being appointed was to travel to Britain in search of a female religious Congregation willing to send workers to his part of the country.

Just as the mid-nineteenth century had seen the first flush of missionary activity in West Africa and the Church's first footholds there, so the mid-twentieth century was witnessing the second phase, that of consolidation, and once again the Church's leaders were urging religious Congregations to answer the new call for workers in the field. Mgr McCoy's tour of Britain and his visit to Merrylee were in fact a striking echo, in their context and purpose, of Fr Forbes' journey through northern France to Tourcoing a century before.

His appeal to the Sisters met with a warm response, and they must have made a good impression on him, for in October the abbess received a letter inviting her to establish a foundation in Oyo. She put the proposal to Council, who voted to accept it if volunteers could be found.[16]

At first it seemed that there might be none, though not for want of goodwill. This was an utterly new venture for a Congregation reared on familiar, long-established tasks. To the older Sisters it seemed work for young limbs; to the younger, one that demanded the wisdom of experience. One Sister not yet finally professed volunteered on the advice of the novice mistress, more to show support than through a sense of fitness, and was somewhat nonplussed to find herself chosen when the appointments were made.[17] One of the others selected was only a year ahead of her, another a year younger, and the fourth not much older. Council had clearly decided to go for youth, but in doing so they were taking a huge risk. Theirs was not in essence a missionary Congregation (except in the broader sense of the word): it had no tradition or real concept of the implications of work in the foreign missions. As its founders had thought to replicate Tourcoing in Glasgow, so now its Council imagined that they would be establishing a new Merrylee in Nigeria. As with the founders, experience would show how mistaken they were.

Srs Angela, Patricia, Immaculata and Fidelis boarded the Liverpool train at Central Station, each with two white habits in her case and £5 in her purse.[18] In the English port, an official of the Elder Dempster Line insisted on taking them to buy large tropical helmets, a purchase that accounted for £12 of their £20 before they even left Britain. A tug took them out to their ship, the *David Livingstone*.

She was a rusty tub of a vessel, making her second-last voyage before being broken up. Often her engines would fail, and even on full steam she was dilatory. She was a cargo ship not designed for passengers. She had no deck, but the captain found four chairs and set them in the gangway for the Sisters, where any passing sailor had to step over them. They took their meals with the crew – huge dinners that they could do no justice to. Between their horror of the ants that crawled over the rations, their seasickness, and their nausea at the awful smell of the cargo (it seemed to be a combination of fish and onions), they had little appetite. For three weeks the days passed thus, enlivened only by the endlessly repeated playing of the half-dozen gramophone records that the ship possessed – 'I wandered today by the mill, Maggie' . . . 'Silver threads among the gold'. They hoped to break the monotony by going ashore wherever they docked, but the first stop at Bathurst (now Banjul) involved being lowered overboard in a basket and their nerve failed. They did manage to get ashore at Freetown and even ventured a short walk, but always kept the ship in sight, fearful and apprehensive of this unknown thing: 'Africa'.

The captain was as helpful as his circumstances allowed, but he did not like carrying sick passengers, and in any case by the time they docked at Takoradi in the Gold Coast his engine was in urgent need of repair. He therefore arranged for the Sisters to make the last stage of their journey by mail boat. The new vessel had ample decks and cabins with toilets, and she was fast. They made Lagos in two days, arriving on 17 September. But her speed had brought them too early: vainly they scanned the pier for a monsignor's purple. No-one remotely like a missionary was to be seen. Fortunately the ship's purser knew the two convents in Lagos and contacted them; both offered to put the newcomers up.

In the midst of the noisy humid city, they found the Holy Child convent a grateful haven, quiet save the croaking of frogs, and still but for the lizards that scuttled along the walls and crept behind the Stations of the Cross. They spent the day resting. At 6 p.m. the tropical night fell suddenly.

After a few days with no news, Fr John Byrne WF came down from Oyo. He took them to look round a Catholic school in the city and the following day drove them to Ibadan for an overnight stay with the nuns there. All this (they found out) was to waste time, because their convent at Osogbo was still not ready. Finally he took them north on dusty roads to Ife and on towards Osogbo, the four of them squeezed into the back of the car lent to him by the local king.

They were met on the outskirts of Osogbo by Mgr McCoy and a troupe of boy scouts and swept into town by a thronging crowd, unaware that the welcome and the bunting were for them. Then the rain began to fall, suddenly and so heavily that they could barely see through it, pounding on the tin roofs and the heads of the children who ran out to dance in it. It seemed to release everyone's emotions. It was the beginning of the rainy season for which the town had long been waiting, and the new arrivals were at once christened 'the Sisters who brought the rain'.

They were taken to the priests' house, a mud building with a veranda on which they were left standing, staring and smiling at the drenched crowd that stared and smiled back at them. They could not be invited inside because the priests had given away their chairs and tables to help furnish the convent. From there they walked to the church, where evening Benediction was to be celebrated by the many priests who had gathered from all over the diocese to welcome them. Its pan roof had holes in it, through which came the rain. Inside, all was noise and excitement and devotion.

By now it was night. They were led under a great moon into the bush, on narrow trampled paths through elephant-grass higher than a man and tangled fronds that tripped them, until they reached the clearing where their convent stood. It was a fine-looking building with slatted shutters (Plate 22), but once inside they found it a mere shell. Not a wall nor a door was painted. In the middle of the otherwise bare main room stood a safe waiting to be set into the wall. The house's one light was a borrowed kerosene lamp with a cracked globe. Mgr McCoy had been impatient to get his Sisters with all speed, but he had not the money to house them.

They set to work painting with raffia brushes, but ended with more paint on themselves than the house. The kerosene they put to good use, not only to fuel the lamp but to stand the few items of furniture in, as a defence against the columns of ants that marched irresistibly across floors and ceilings, up walls, and in and out of windows. On 4 November they held their first Mass in the temporary chapel. In choosing the feast of St Francis they were following a tradition of the Congregation. In a sense, indeed, they were making a statement that Nigeria was its second beginning, for the date exactly repeated that of the first Mass celebrated in the original convent in Charlotte Street 101 years before.

A fortnight later Sr Angela made her permanent profession in the presence of the monsignor. (Ever since, she has claimed that among all the Sisters in the Congregation she is the 'real McCoy'). The ceremony must have brought home to him just how young and inexperienced his new team were (Plate 23). Sr Immaculata had still a year to go before her final vows. If ever there were 'innocents abroad' it was they.

Sr Angela was appointed headmistress of the school and Sr Patricia administrator. At first there were few girls, for most parents believed that daughters were not worth educating, but those who did attend were amenable and very keen to learn. The main difficulty, apart from the lack of resources, was their age. Having begun their primary education late – at the age of nine at the earliest, and sometimes as old as seventeen – they were in their mid-teens or even their twenties before they finished. Some did not know their age, in fact, and when asked would answer, 'How old do you want me to be?' Little girls were sharing the dormitory with women, sleeping on planks laid across trestles, the younger ones mothered by the older, for all were frightened at night, being used to sleeping in family groups. They even got it into their heads that one of them was a witch, and would not sleep until she was moved to a separate room.

Since most of the pupils were of the Yoruba tribe, and girls of whatever tribe could get by in English as their second language, lessons were conducted in English by the Sisters and in Yoruba by three Nigerian lay teachers. The different groups lived together without acrimony. The only dissent was over *gari*, a favourite food that the pupils brought from home and fought over at night. One of its effects was to give them sores, and it was in fact partly thanks to the nutritious school meals which improved their skin that the parents were gradually won over to the idea of education for girls.

For Srs Immaculata and Fidelis who looked after the boarders, the main concern was to keep them occupied in the evenings and at weekends. At first they had no concept of 'play' and would just stand about during recreation time. The Sisters kept them busy with tasks – washing their beds for mites, cutting the high grass with cutlasses, and cleaning dormitories and classrooms with bundles of reeds. In later years, the girls told them how useful this work had proved for their own housekeeping as wives.

Whether cleaning, clearing, painting, plastering or laboriously smoothing the rough mahogany table with a broken pane of glass, Osogbo was in fact a DIY school. And for the larger tasks there was always Brother Nicodemus. For years he personally undertook or supervised all of their building works and major repairs. The girls grew used to seeing him about the compound: short, sandy-haired, in his White Fathers' *gondora* and tropical helmet, a tool bag in one hand and working with the fingers of the other the black and white rosary that hung about his neck. An unassuming man of great faith and a ready smile, ever a pipe in his mouth but smoke rising from it never, and his answer to every question, 'eventually!'

When the community had been two years in Osogbo, Mgr McCoy wrote to Glasgow asking for a suitably qualified Sister to take charge of the women's training college that he was planning to open in the town. The abbess sent Sr M. Michael Scanlon, BComm, and St Clare's received its first thirty students in January 1953. Because of the monsignor's optimism and admirable impatience to make things happen, it too started without a stick of furniture.[19]

It was about this time that Catherine Olagunju entered the convent as its first Nigerian postulant. She was a devout girl, already engaged to a local man, but so determined was she to try her vocation that she cancelled the engagement and had the bride-price repaid. Her arrival posed a question for which there was no precedent: where should she spend her periods of trial and formation? Council decided that her postulancy should be spent in Osogbo, but that since she was the only candidate her novitiate must take place in Glasgow.[20] She moved into the convent, receiving personal tuition from Sr Angela – for she had had no schooling – and herself looking after the young pupils boarding there. The news of her reception was greeted with delight by the Congregation in Scotland, as being a milestone on the road of its new mission in Africa. There have been numerous further milestones in the half-century since that first reception, in a mission that has enjoyed a wonderful growth and vitality.[21]

In January 1954 a second convent was opened at Ilesa and Sr Patricia, one of the pioneers at Osogbo, was appointed Reverend Mother. In 1955 Mgr McCoy paid a second visit to Scotland, during which he twice called at Merrylee to give a progress report on the mission and discuss its future with Council. He was warm in his praise but also stressed the utterly different world that was Africa, which only those who had experienced it personally could begin to grasp, and the particular difficulties this placed upon a community so young and inexperienced. As a result, Council decided to send the Congregation's vicaress Sr Philippa Gilhooley (Plate 32) to see the situation for herself.

She arrived in Nigeria on 1 July.[22] Her coming was eagerly awaited in Osogbo, where the staff and pupils had made everything tidy, bright and welcoming. She was sure to be impressed. Then, with two days to go, the boarders disappeared. One of the lay teachers had maliciously told them that it was holiday time, and they had all gone home. Fortunately, the following day was Sunday. The Sisters toured the parishes, and announcements were made at all the Masses that the pupils who had run away must return at once, and that they must pay a fine for absconding (to prevent a recurrence). Before the end of the day they were back, shame-faced and holding out the money; some had walked miles. When Sr Philippa arrived, they were all at their desks and she none the wiser.[23]

That year education was made free and compulsory in Nigeria. The following year Council accepted Mgr McCoy's proposal to open a grammar school in Oyo, a sparsely populated district of savannah in the heart of Yoruba country some eighty miles from Osogbo. On receiving permission from the ministry of education, the monsignor at once set about building a single-storey school, dormitory and convent. St Bernardine's, named after Mother Abbess, was a beautiful modern building and the talk of the town when it opened in February 1956. But the convent, with its striking green roof, was still a shell. Srs Michael, Immaculata and Raphael had to use part of the girls' dormitory for sleeping, eating and bathing (for which they set up a zinc bath in the dining area), while Brother Nicodemus and his team raced to make their house habitable.[24] They were learning that things took time in Nigeria: that attitudes were different and things were done differently.

They were learning too that in many ways their own needs were different. This was most obvious with the habit, which remained essentially unchanged (except in colour) from that designed for Tourcoing. Less than convenient even on the streets of Glasgow, it was hopelessly impracticable for the hothouse climate and do-it-yourself lifestyle of West Africa. The Sisters appealed to be permitted minor adaptations – a single top veil, shorter sleeves narrowed at the cuff, and a cord of lighter weight – and these Council agreed to, though not without reservations.[25] They were small enough changes, but this was the first time that reality on the ground had caused the leadership to look again at that which was assumed to be unchangeable, and it set a precedent.

The needs of their young Nigerian recruits were also different. The decision to send the first postulants to Glasgow for their novitiate had proved disastrous, as might have been anticipated. For all their hosts' attempts to welcome them, homesickness and culture shock had almost guaranteed that they would not stay the course. In 1957 Mgr McCoy appealed to the abbess to open a novitiate in Nigeria itself and give the community there responsibility for training their African novices in Africa. His request made obvious sense, but it was also part of a broader strategy on his part. Hitherto it had been the practice for Nigerian Sisters to form independent diocesan Congregations once numbers were sufficient, but in this case he hoped that they would remain Franciscan Sisters and eventually form a Nigerian Province of the Congregation.[26] Council agreed with his reasoning and accepted his request, but it would take seven years for the novitiate to materialise, a long time to wait in a fast-developing mission.

For seventy unbroken years the Sisters in Glasgow had been making their twice-weekly visits to Duke Street prison, and they had witnessed many changes there. The old archway entrance was unaltered, and the seventeen plaques inside the west wall still marked the graves of those hanged within

its precincts, including that of the child-killer Susan Newell. The grim grey
buildings still stood, too, but they were almost empty. The female wing,
built for two hundred, now housed only forty-five. The male wing was
completely deserted apart from ten men 'on loan' from Barlinnie to undertake heavy manual and maintenance work. The women still passed their
time making clothes and linens, cleaning and working in the laundry,
dressed in the same brown clothes and checked overalls, but now with the
luxury of a best dress of green. With a staff of forty to look after them and
scores of empty rooms, the place was wholly uneconomic and had long
since been marked for closure.[27]

In June 1955 the remaining female prisoners were transferred to Gateside, the women's prison in Greenock. Up until the very last week, the Sisters
kept up their visitation. Now the work was passed to their colleagues in the
Greenock convent, who continued the tradition into the late 1970s, when
Gateside itself ceased taking women.[28]

Falcarragh had been opened in 1947 as a base for recruiting Irish
postulants, but in the ten years since their arrival the community had been
gradually drawn into local education. The process had started when local
parents asked them to open a pre-school nursery, for which there was no
provision in the area. In the words of one who was involved, 'things just
grew from there, as they do'.[29]

Bishop MacNeely's priority was to introduce secondary schooling in the
locality, since at this time the nearest provision for boys was in Letterkenny
and for girls even further afield. He was aware of proposals at county level
for a mixed secondary school under lay leadership, a development he was
anxious to forestall since the local people wished for single-sex education
run by religious. He was confident that if separate boys' and girls' schools
could be opened in time the proposals would come to nothing.[30] By early
1957 he was already on the way to setting up a boys' school and engaged in
tentative discussions with Mother M. Crysostom Garland at Falcarragh
regarding a school for girls. He asked her to seek the views of Council in
Glasgow, and to explain that since the district lay within the *Gaeltacht* the
staff would need to be 'competent' in Irish in order for the school to be
recognised and eligible for government grants.

Following discussion in Council the new abbess, Mother Philippa, wrote
to him expressing interest but seeking clarification as to the Gaelic
qualification required. She had in mind for the headship Sr Michael
Scanlon, principal at St Bernardine's secondary in Oyo, who though not a
native Irish speaker held a degree from University College Dublin and
had some 'book' knowledge of the language. The bishop's reply was
encouraging. He suggested that one religious as head with a lay assistant
teacher able to teach through the medium of Irish would suffice in the

meantime to get the school running and have it recognised. He confirmed that Sr Michael had the necessary paper qualification and pressed Mother Philippa to appoint her. He clearly wanted the school opened at all costs and as soon as possible, and did not consider her actual fluency in Irish or her ability to promote the language a matter of first importance, so long as her qualification met the criteria for recognition and funding. She could acquire mastery of the spoken language once she arrived.[31] In his haste to pre-empt the mixed school, he was willing to cut corners.

Clochar Proinsias opened in September, in a room in the convent and with a roll of eighteen. But Sr Michael's appointment had caused resentment locally. Her assistant, Miss Houston, was a native speaker from Donegal with considerably more teaching experience than the new head. Within two months the priests of the district requested that Sr Michael stand down in favour of the older woman[32] and Council ceded to the request, on the understanding that this would be a temporary arrangement pending a suitable Irish-speaking Sister becoming available. In fact, Miss Houston was to remain the head for nine years.[33]

The school quickly prospered. In autumn 1958 the first phase of a building programme was completed with government funding for the *Gaeltacht*, adding three classrooms to house a student roll that now stood at over thirty.[34] Within the next four years it would double again.[35]

Every year since 1847 the Sisters had been caring for the sick–poor wherever they had set up convents, in the centuries-old tradition of Tourcoing, Comines and the *Sœurs Grises*. Now in the postwar British welfare state, the Congregation saw the need for some its members to gain formal training and qualifications in nursing, to make their long-established work more effective. Attempts to have them trained in Glasgow had been frustrated by regulations that forbad the wearing of the habit by anyone working in the city's hospitals, and in 1954 Council had decided to send two Sisters as an experiment to train at the Fulham hospital in London.[36] These and the others who had followed them lived in community with the Misericorde Sisters in Hammersmith.

Though the arrangement was working well, it did not offer a long-term solution and by 1957 Council were actively seeking a property of their own in west London. It would serve a triple purpose – as a home for the trainee nurses, as a stopping-off place on the Congregation's now frequent journeys to and from Nigeria, and as a short-break holiday house in the capital. Archbishop Godfrey of Westminster gave his permission and promised to provide a chaplain. Finding a property at an affordable price proved less easy, but by summer 1958 a house had been secured in Ealing, and Sr M. Margaret Kelly was appointed Reverend Mother. She moved in with her three companions on 2 July.[37]

Elmwood was now under the leadership of Sr Gabriel Palmer and still admired for the rounded education it provided and its flourishing extra-curricular activities. Its Scottish country dance teams had been sweeping all before them since the mid-1950s under the tutelage of Miss Coen, who returned as Mrs Cawley in 1957 to lead them to further success; one team even appeared on children's TV. Following a pioneering visit in Marian Year school trips to Lourdes had become a regular event, over a hundred girls accompanying Sr Gabriel in 1958.[38] The seniors' Third Order branch remained strong, and several societies abandoned during the war had been revived – the FPs' Association in 1953, the literature and debating society in 1955, and the dramatic society two years later. The 'L & D' was now under the guidance of Miss Josephine Angus, with its original founder from the 1920s, Miss Eunice Rea, elected honorary president. It ran an imaginative annual programme, including mock trials (Chaucer, Everyman and Burns were three notable defendants, the last charged with lowering the name of Scotland but acquitted), as well as a 'tall story night', Christmas dinner, Burns Supper, a debate against Charlotte Street and a shield presented to the year's best speaker.[39]

The school roll remained high at over 700. The boarders were still under the diligent, kindly care of Sr Martha Rooney, a much-loved Lay Sister who entirely lived up to her religious name and seemed to have been there for ever. But the numbers had continued to dwindle, until by 1956 there were only five left. The decision was taken to close the boarding department and lease it to the Lanarkshire EA to provide extra classroom space.[40] In June 1958 Miss Rea left the school after thirty-three years in the English department and moved to a cottage in the Cotswolds, where sadly she lived to enjoy only seventeen months of retirement.

The late 1950s witnessed both progress and setback in the Nigerian mission. In April 1958 a tornado struck the town of Osogbo, causing fires that destroyed the convent and badly damaged the school and training college. In St Bernardine's Oyo, where Mother John had succeeded Sr Michael as head, the roll had risen to 108 and was still rising. Families of all faiths sent their daughters to it from far afield, attracted by its high standards of learning, morals and behaviour and its all-round excellence. With its uniform of green skirt and cream blouse, white socks and sandals (and Panama hat on Sundays), its Latin motto, British GCE syllabus, its tennis courts and Scottish country dancing, it was like a Charlotte Street or an Elmwood in the Nigerian grassland. At the same time, the indigenous culture was promoted, and from 1959 girls were prepared for the new West African school certificate.[41]

Two years previously, Mgr McCoy had asked the Congregation to con-sider building a church at Oyo. His request had been timely, since Council was at that time debating how best to use the £4,000 gifted by the Former Pupils' Association in the centenary year, money that was still lying unspent. There being now no prospect of the original plan of a memorial hall at Merrylee being realised, they voted to donate the money to Oyo.[42] There was eloquent symbolism in the decision: it spoke of new beginnings and of hope, continuity and a single mission across continents. Building work began in 1959 under the supervision of Brother Nicodemus and was completed in time for the new chapel to be blessed on the feast of the Immaculate Conception in 1961.[43]

The Forest of Dean is a lovely, sparse landscape of hills and woods, extending for some hundred square miles between the valleys of the Severn and Wye on England's border with Wales. From the ancient forest that gives it its name, men have felled timber, mined for coal and burned charcoal since time immemorial. It is thinly populated, with a rim of villages about its high wooded crown and one or two towns of more substance – Lydney at its southern end, and Cinderford close to its north-east edge.

Though it lies within the RC Diocese of Clifton, there were in fact hardly any Catholics there until recent years, and not a single priest until 1931. In 1936 the Salesians had established several Mass centres, including one at Cinderford which served a congregation of ten. Despite the paucity of numbers and funds, a permanent church, Our Lady of Victories, was opened in the town on the eve of the war.[44]

In November 1956 Mother Philippa was passing close to Cinderford on her way home from the Marillac Sanatorium, where one of the Sisters was convalescing, and decided to call on the parish priest, Fr Morrison, who was her cousin. He talked to her about his far-flung parish and the fact that there was not one Catholic school in the whole of the Forest.[45] He asked if she would consider opening a private school in Cinderford, adding that Gloucestershire county council would probably be building a Catholic primary school there in the near future, and that if this was indeed the case the Sisters would be strong candidates to take charge of it.

Encouraged by her response, he approached his bishop Joseph Rudderham, who wrote to her in the new year granting his permission.[46] Council discussed the proposal and gave it unanimous support. The bishop then sent her further details. She could expect a roll of about 180 children aged 5–15, he wrote, most of them non-Catholic. A property was presently on the market which had previously been a private school and would suit their needs. But he warned that Fr Morrison might have been 'somewhat too optimistic' regarding the county primary school. There was a proposal before the LEA for a small school, certainly, but it was wholly uncertain whether it would actually be built, since there were higher priorities in areas of the county where the Catholic population was greater.[47] In April 1957 Mother Philippa visited Cinderford to look at properties and confirm arrangements with the diocese.

Three years elapsed before a suitable purchase could be concluded, permissions secured and the house-cum-school made ready for occupation. On 1 August 1960 a community of four arrived with forty tea chests of belongings. Two days later the furniture was delivered, and they moved in. They found the school wing still unfinished, lacking plaster and even floorboards, unpainted, empty of desks, and the tradesmen on a fortnight's holiday. If it was to be ready for the children's arrival, they would have to paint and plaster it themselves. This they did, in time for its official opening and blessing on 12 August.[48]

That day the headmistress, Sr Gertrude Shields, admitted eighteen pupils (Plate 24), but as word spread the roll grew steadily, and within two years the community were forced to look for larger premises. Several plans were considered for a new school building and for buying adjacent property, which were eventually approved by Council.[49] The hoped-for new primary school, which would have reduced the pressure on space or even perhaps rendered the private school redundant, showed no signs of being built, and indeed never has been built: St Anthony's remains to this day the only Catholic school in the Forest of Dean.

This was a time of great optimism for the Congregation. Vocations were flourishing. No less than twenty-one new Sisters entered in the three years from 1959 to 1962.[50] Most were seniors from Charlotte Street and Elm–wood, and their example kindled an interest in the religious life among many of the younger pupils. In 1961, Council decided to establish a special sodality, the Vocation Guild, to keep that interest alive among those who had expressed a desire to join but were too young to enter. It was set up initially in Charlotte Street and held its first meeting that autumn. In October the organisers hosted a day retreat, for which invitations were sent to Catholic schools throughout the west of Scotland. One hundred girls attended and the success of the venture prompted similar guilds to be formed at Elmwood and the Greenock and Merrylee convent schools.[51] There seemed every prospect that vocations would continue to flourish.

Financially, also, the Congregation was stronger than it had ever been. Through prudent housekeeping income was keeping pace with expenditure, so that in 1962, even after a major outlay, its balance stood at close to £130,000.[52] In what was a substantial capital enterprise, all spelled good management, security and success.

Nor had the Sisters ever been more highly regarded in society. Their long and outstanding service in the parish schools was recognised; their small private schools, though not part of the educational mainstream, were exemplars of their kind; and above all, Charlotte Street and Elmwood were admired even beyond the Catholic community as models of secondary education in the west of Scotland.

It was a time, in short, when the long growth of more than a century seemed to be coming to full fruition, to a full harvest at home and the promise of things to come abroad. The Congregation was comfortable. And with this, a certain comfortable attitude had perhaps crept in – a staidness even – far removed from the pioneer spirit of the early days. Writing at the time of the 150th anniversary in 1997, the Superior General Sr Martina Morgan looked back on this era and described it thus:

> With that steady growth came stability, security, success . . . even financial prosperity . . . We were as a Congregation well established, fully committed, and able to face the future with serenity . . . We were at the peak . . . The chaos and frenetic activity of the early days were gone, and in their place was a well ordered pattern of life that – inevitably – had become institutionalised. It's a well established fact that the more secure and stable an organisation becomes, the more the founding vision tends to fade.[53]

Institutionalisation may take a grip in any organisation, but it is perhaps particularly endemic in monastic religious Orders, since they are closed systems with their own 'separate framework of meaning from the outside world'.[54] They form and enshrine their own customs – of lifestyle, timetable, practice, structures of authority, etc. – which often over time become elevated into principles. The Franciscan Sisters were no exception. Thus when one of them at this time questioned the hazardous practice of lowering the veil at communion and asked why it was done since it seemed more a distraction than an aid to devotion, she was told 'because we have always done it'.[55]

All of the Congregation's Constitutions and customs had a valid original spiritual purpose, but if taken to excess and deified, that purpose tended to get lost. Thus the weekly Chapter of Faults was intended as an exercise in humility, but if it required a novice who broke a dish while washing up to publicly kneel and kiss the refectory floor, was it achieving its purpose? And when in the name of obedience a young Sister was ordered to water the garden flowers during a downpour, had obedience not become an end in itself, and could such blind external obedience possibly aid the growth of a mature inner obedience?

Such caricatures of the real intention of the Rule were not everyday events, of course.[56] In the great majority of cases the Constitutions were applied properly. But they were still applied legalistically, and this too could cause distress, for though they were intended to be paths to the perfection of the human person, they sometimes appeared to have little compassion for that person's human needs. One of the Sisters at this time had a widowed mother living some miles away who was diagnosed as having cancer. The Constitution allowed her a special dispensation to visit once a week, but this was with a timescale so tight that it gave mother and daughter only twenty minutes together, and even then it demanded that they take their lunch in separate rooms. Only in the final weeks, when she knew that her mother was dying, did the Sister take her cup of tea to the bedside, consciously choosing to break the rules to do so. Surely there should not have been such rules, that compassion required them to be broken? Shortly after, when her mother's death was imminent, the Sister sought permission to be excused from a school trip abroad, but was refused: she was told it was 'her duty' to go. While she was away, her mother died.

Perhaps, also, some of the Congregation's founding vision had become obscured.[57] There was now less obvious opportunity for the Sisters to pursue their original purpose of caring for the poorest in society. They were continuing to teach in some parish schools, and to make their prison visits unnoticed and unsung, and in Charlotte Street and Elmwood they were serving the largely working-class communities of Glasgow and Lanarkshire. But those communities had changed and were continuing to change. The postwar years had seen the much more visible emergence of a well-educated Catholic laity actively and effectively involved in society and in their Church.[58] Though poverty was still everywhere to be seen, it could not be compared with the penury that had met the Congregation's founders. The 1960s was a decade of massive rebuilding in and around Glasgow, with the clearance of old homes and factories from the centre where the Sisters had first set up schools, and the rising of new communities on the perimeter. It was a time of transition as a new society began to emerge, bringing its own new poverties, which required new responses. But to date the Sisters were still doing – and very well – the things they had always done.

The institutionalisation and fading of the original vision noted in almost all religious Orders has been called by one commentator 'sclerosis',[59] and if the term is harsh it is perhaps a fair description of some extreme cases. It could certainly not be applied to the Franciscan Sisters of the Immaculate Conception, even at their most institutionalised. The vision, if a little faded, was never lost. The arteries never hardened. But the blood was no longer coursing in them quite as it had in the Congregation's youth.

Yet even at this time there were small signs from within that people were willing to look at the vision anew. The new realities of the foreign mission were already in small ways making the old certainties less certain. At home, some of the Sisters were beginning to question the old ways. Were all the customs fitting? Why, if they were 'with and for the people', did they have to rise at five in the morning when the world was sleeping and close their doors at seven in the evening when it was just waking up? What about the new spiritually poor? Why the perimeter wall at Merrylee, and why within it the comfort and security? They did not yet know it, but their comfortable, secure house was about to be assailed and shaken by the gusting wind of change.

ENDNOTES TO CHAPTER SIX

1 Mother John to Mother Bernardine Simpson, abbess, 20.9.1944; Mother Bernardine Simpson to B. Caulfield & McGowan, Solicitors, 13.11.1944, both 044.11, AF.

2 Purchased in September 1945 for £2,500 – Council Meeting Minutes, 1.9.1945 and 29.9.1945, 034.10, 2, AF; and B. Caulfield & McGowan, Solicitors, to abbess, 11.9.1945, 044.11, AF.

3 The Education (Scotland) Act – 26 Geo 5, and 1 Edw 8 ch 42 – had legislated for the change as long ago as 1936, but the date on which it was due to become effective, 1 September 1939, was just two days before Britain's declaration of war. Shelved for the duration of hostilities, it was reintroduced in the Education Act of 1945, to be implemented from August 1947.

4 *Our Lady & St Francis Magazine*, 1948 issue.

5 The annual subscription was 2/6. The first year's programme included a dance at the Grosvenor Hotel, a Christmas party and visit to the pantomime, a motor run, whist drives and a Mass for deceased pupils – *OLSF Magazine*, 1949 and 1951 issues. Scottish country dancing, keep fit and drama were added at a later date.

6 OLSF Log, 18.8.1944, D ED 7 160.2, ML.

7 OLSF Log, 18.7.1947; and *OLSF Magazine*, 1948 issue.

8 The primary department finally closed in 1954.

9 Details from *OLSF Magazine*, 1946, 1948 and 1949 issues. The Third Order branch was formed in January 1946; in 1949 they took part in the national Third Order rally at Carfin Grotto.

10 This and the following paragraphs based on Srs Angela McFaul, Francis Campbell and Felicitas Bradley interviews.

11 Bishop Henry Graham, assistant bishop of Glasgow, to Diocesan Authority, Archdiocese of Dublin, on behalf of abbess, March 1942, 071.01, AF. Re the reason for refusal, Sr Dolores Cochrane interview.

12 Council Meeting Minutes, 5.3.1946 and 18.3.1946, 034.10, no. 2, AF.

13 Bishop William MacNeely to abbess, 28.5.1946, 071.01, AF.

14 E.g., R. Connor, Bishop's House Dublin, to abbess, 16.5.1951, 071.01, AF.

15 Council Meeting Minutes, 18.1.1948. Anne McMahon was accepted as a postulant on 18 January, arrived on 29 February and received the novice's habit on 30 October.

16 Council Meeting Minutes, 28.10.1949; and Intermediate Reports, Merrylee, 1953, 030.1, AF.

17 Sr Angela McFaul interview.

18 Account of the voyage, arrival and early days based on Sr Angela McFaul and Sr Immaculata Leonard interviews.

19 Council Meeting Minutes, 19.10.1952; and *Journey So Far* (2000), p. 40 (see note 21 *infra*).

20 Council Meeting Minutes, 9.11.1952.

21 It would be quite impossible to do them any kind of justice within the scope of the present book, whose subsequent chapters can only attempt to touch on some of them. For a more detailed account, compiled largely by those involved, the reader is referred to *The Journey So Far: Fifty Years of the Franciscan Sisters in Nigeria* (Ibadan, 2000).

22 Council Meeting Minutes, supplementary 1955–68, July 1955, filed with Log Books, AF.

23 Sr Immaculata Leonard interview. Sr Philippa later wrote an account of her visit in *OLSF Magazine*, 1956 issue.

24 Sr Raphael Swan interview.

25 Council Meeting Minutes, 15.1.1957.

26 Council Meeting Minutes, 9.7.1957; Sr Dolores Cochrane interview; *Journey So Far*, p. 91.

27 Details from House J. 'Behind Prison Gates', *Evening News*, 11 and 13.6.1955.

28 Council Meeting Minutes, supplementary 1955–68, Jun 1955. Gateside ceased taking women when the new Cornton Vale women's prison was opened. It lay empty for some time, before being refurbished as a men's prison.

29 Sr Dolores Cochrane interview.

30 The present account based largely on Bishop MacNeely to abbess, 28.3.1957, 071.01, AF.

31 *Ibid.*, and Bishop MacNeely to abbess, 13.4.1957, 071.01, AF.

32 Council Meeting Minutes, 29.11.1957.

33 Miss Houston was finally replaced by Sr Patricia Coyle in September 1966 – Council Meeting Minutes, supplementary 1955–68, 26.3.1966–7.4.1966. The takeover was amicable and she continued to teach at the school as an assistant, and after her retirement several times visited her friends there – Sr Dolores Cochrane interview.

34 Council Meeting Minutes, 24.6.1958; Falcarragh Triennial Reports, 1959, 030.1, AF; Reports to Chapter, Merrylee, 1962, 030.1, AF. The cost of the first phase was £7,000, of which £5,000 was covered by *Gaeltacht* funding.

35 Falcarragh Triennial Reports, 1962, 030.1, AF, when the roll had risen to 65.

36 Council Meeting Minutes, 24.10.1954.

37 Council Meeting Minutes, supplementary 1955–68, October and November 1957; Archbishop Godfrey to abbess, 8.11.1957, 071.01, AF; Council Meeting Minutes, 12.3.1958, 16.6.1958 and 12.7.1958.

38 Sr Gabriel was a great traveller, a 'pilgrim' in the Franciscan tradition. She also took parties of pupils to Rome and Oberammergau.

39 Details from *The Elmwood Magazine*, 1955, 1956, 1957 and 1959 issues. Sr Gabriel had been appointed headmistress in 1950. A Burns' Supper guest one year was the school chaplain, Fr (later Cardinal) Thomas Winning, who arrived complete with bonnet and toasted the lassies.

40 044.12, AF. Re Sr Martha: *Obituary Book*, no. 210. Sr Martha also cared for the school chaplains and undertook laundry, cooking and care of the sick in the convent. A legend at Elmwood, she died in April 1993 aged 99 and in the 72nd year of her profession.

41 St Bernardine's Triennial Reports, 1959, 030.1, AF, and Sr Raphael Swan interview. The first nine pupils were presented in 1961.

42 Council Meeting Minutes, 9.7.1957.

43 St Bernardine's Triennial Reports, 1962, 030.1, AF.

44 Based on Bishop Rudderham, speech at the school, 15.5.1965, and the school's *40th Anniversary Celebration Magazine*, 21.5.2000.

45 Council Meeting Minutes, 27.11.1956.

46 Bishop Rudderham to Mother General, 20.2.1957, 071.01, AF.

47 Bishop Rudderham to Mother General, 8.3.1957, 071.01, AF.

48 Council Meeting Minutes, supplementary 1955–68, August 1960; and *40th Anniversary Celebration Magazine*.

49 Council Meeting Minutes, 30.8.1962, 3.11.1962 and 15.9.1963; and Triennial Reports, Merrylee, 1962.

50 Triennial Reports, Merrylee, 1962; and Council Meeting Minutes, 13.12.1959 – 5.9.1960. In one ten-month period in 1960 eight postulants were received.

51 Council Meeting Minutes, supplementary 1955–68, October 1961, September 1967 and May 1968.

52 Triennial Reports, Merrylee, 1956, 1959, 1962. In round figures the balance stood at £131,000 in 1956, and at £128,000 in 1962. Annual turnover was c. £28,000.

53 Mother Martina Morgan 'Where do we go from here?', in *The Franciscan Sisters of the Immaculate Conception, Celebrating 150 years in Glasgow, 1847–1997*, 1997, p.184.

54 Schneiders, Sr S.M., 1986, especially p. 27ff.

55 Sr Loyola Kelly interview. The practice was discontinued following a vote at the 1962 General Chapter.

56 *Ibid.*

57 It is perhaps significant that its two most recent initiatives had been in private education. One was the new building planned for Merrylee private school, the other the purchase of two adjacent properties in Circus Drive, Dennistoun for a daughter house and private school. The transaction for the second was completed between July 1961 and April 1962 – Council Meeting Minutes, 15.2.1962 – 30.9.1962, 1.5.1961, 7.4.1962, 6.5.1962 and 10.8.1962; Triennial Reports, Merrylee, 1962. The Dennistoun private school opened in 1964 (cf. p. 172 *infra*).

58 Cf. Ross A., 1978J, p. 50f.

59 Schneiders Sr S.M., *op. cit.*, p. 33.

PART THREE

Wind

Be praised, my Lord, through Brother Wind,
Through air and cloud, clear skies and all weathers,
By which you give sustenance to your creatures.

St Francis, *Canticle of the Creatures*

CHAPTER SEVEN

The Wind of Change (1960–1968)

On 1 October 1960 Nigeria gained her independence and became a federal state. The change was to have profound consequences for the Congregation. In the short term, the inter-tribal clashes that followed independence would lead to civil war, in which the Sisters would give aid to the wounded and the dying. Later, in assuming responsibility for education and medical care, the state would take over the projects begun by the Congregation, totally changing them, and in some cases replacing the Sisters altogether.

Mother Philippa travelled to the country in the very first days of the new régime and stayed two months, inspecting all of the Congregation's houses and activities, including the weekly visitations to Ilesa prison that had begun earlier that year.[1] On her return journey she stopped off at Rome to discuss possible emendments to the Constitutions. Even at this early date she and her Council were aware of the call for change. She had herself proposed abolishing the distinction between Lay and Choir Sisters as early as 1956, and had been supported in principle.[2] She now learned that Rome intended to abolish it in all religious Orders as anachronistic and unjustifiable. On her return to Glasgow she sent a letter to the Sacred Congregation for Religious with details of the proposed changes and a petition regarding Lay Sisters. In July she received a Rescript from Rome granting her permission to abolish the term.[3]

The changes were relatively minor, but their significance may be gauged by the fact that since the rewriting of the Constitutions by Elizabeth Hayes in 1864–6 there had only been one other emendment until now, that made in 1933–4 in response to Pius XI's Constitution on the Rule of the Third Order Regular.[4] The Sisters' resistance to attempts by Rome at that time to impose other Constitutions on them had showed just how precious, indeed sacrosanct, their own were to them, and how scrupulously guarded in the smallest detail.[5] The fact that they were now taking the initiative for change, albeit on a small scale, showed a radical new willingness to embrace reform. Like the first crack in an ice-floe, it was the presage of far greater movement to come.

Following a visit to Merrylee in April 1961, Bishop Ward voiced some doubts concerning the Sisters' involvement in Nigeria.[6] 'While congratulating you on the work being done in the Foreign Missions,' he wrote, 'I feel I must say that it would be a pity to let that work expand to the detriment of the work in the schools in and around Glasgow for which the Community was established here.' He was not the first Glasgow bishop to try to rein in their commitment elsewhere – Archbishop Eyre had done so seventy years before – nor would he be the last.[7]

He was assuming that, in order to remain true to their origins, their apostolate should never change. Ironically, it was an assumption utterly at variance with those origins, in which the Congregation's founders had responded, like Francis, to the new needs of the times. As such, it was a plea that could not be heeded. In any case, the work in Nigeria could not be reined in. It already had its own momentum.

Even while his report was being written, the Sisters in Osogbo were branching out into medical care. The project had been started by Mrs Virginia Swann, an American nurse on a two-year placement in Nigeria, who had set up a temporary outpatient clinic for expectant mothers. She later opened a permanent clinic with the help of a Polish doctor also on a work placement. When Sr Emmanuel Gallagher joined them, conditions were still primitive. The examination table comprised two benches pulled together, and there were no facilities for admissions or operations.

Late in 1961, shortly before Mrs Swann and Dr Sabilo ended their placements, Sr Emmanuel took charge of the clinic and began admitting patients into what now became the labour ward. The four beds did not begin to meet local needs, and when Mother Philippa visited again that summer and arrived unannounced she found Sr Emmanuel in tears at not being able to help more women. The abbess at once pressed into her hand enough money to buy another ten beds.[8]

This was the beginning of the Catholic maternity hospital in Osogbo, later renamed Our Lady of Fatima Catholic Mission General Hospital.[9] A second clinic was opened at Ipe the following year, and two Spanish doctors were recruited to serve the town of Osogbo and the surrounding area, again on a two-year leave of absence arranged between the Nigerian government and their employers at home.

A similar arrangement existed for seconding teachers, several of whom were appointed to the Sisters' schools. Maurice O'Donnell was the first of them, teaching in Oyo where he lived with his wife and young family. The influence of such people was of great help to the work of the Sisters. In a society where men often had several wives they acted as an example of Christian family living, and to Nigerians whose only experience of white lay people was in 'the big house' their modest lifestyle did not go unnoticed: people could hardly believe it when the foreign teachers actually sat among them in church, and even went to confession like any other sinners.

The mission's sole postulant, Catherine Olagunju, had completed her teacher training and moved to Glasgow in 1960 to undertake her novitiate. The hopes of her mentors in Osogbo and of the whole Congregation lay upon her. But, as with hindsight they might have realised, the climate, culture shock and homesickness proved too much for her. She persevered for eighteen months and then went home. She returned to her family after ten years away and tried to rebuild her life. In time she found a fulfilling post in teaching, married and began a family of her own.

In October 1962 the Second Vatican Council was convened by John XXIII. In time it was to change everything for the Sisters, and its first effect was felt within the year. When Mother Philippa visited Rome in April 1963 to discuss the proposed emendments to the Constitutions with the Sacred Congregation for Religious,[10] she learned that they already had preparations in hand for far more radical changes for institutions like hers.

Though the foundation that Adélaide and Veronica had started could trace its ancestry right back to the thirteenth century, its immediate model had been the monastery of Tourcoing, and its structure reflected this. Its Constitutions were in essence monastic. From the beginning, this had caused a strain between the demands of the horarium and the public apostolate, but with the subsequent foundation of daughter houses, first in Scotland and later in England, Ireland and Africa, the monastic structure itself had become unworkable and a type of hybrid or compromise structure had evolved.

Thus, according to the true monastic model, all the new foundations should have been independent, but in fact all had remained under the direct control of Glasgow. The incongruity was most evident in Nigeria, with its utterly different circumstances and needs. Incredibly, the sisters there had to seek the permission of Mother Abbess in Scotland, even in small matters such as travelling more than one hundred miles, staying away from the convent overnight or learning to drive a car. Again, according to the monastic model, ultimate authority lay with the Chapter of all fully professed Sisters, but with houses in Nigeria such a gathering was now quite impracticable, so that the real decision-making remained in the hands of the communities 'at home', with only a token voice from Africa. Between Chapters, executive power lay with Council, but since this body was composed entirely of members of the mother house this merely consolidated central control. The system 'worked', but increasingly it failed to reflect or represent the broader membership. It was also uncanonical: valid for Scotland, doubtful in the case of Falcarragh and Cinderford which came under different hierarchies, and certainly invalid for Nigeria.

Now Rome was insisting on change. There were two logical alternatives.

The first, to retain the monastic structure and grant independence to all of the non-Scottish houses, was in reality not an option, since Nigeria was clearly not ready to go it alone and would not survive the attempt. The second was to abandon the monastic structure and become a Congregation with central control and representation for every community.

In theory the choice lay with the Sisters; indeed only they, meeting together in Chapter, had the authority to take the decision. But the Sacred Congregation for Religious effectively decided the outcome when it issued 'instructions' for their becoming a Pontifical Congregation that autumn (1963). The document, which arrived in October, decreed that the abbess was to change her title to 'Mother General'; every house was to have its own local Superior with real powers; the Council members were to be drawn from different houses; and there was to be radical change to the composition of the Chapter, reflecting the new demography, although this remained unspecified. The changes were to be operative from 17 November and would require a wholesale rewriting of the Constitutions as soon as possible.[11] They could not be ratified, of course, until the General Chapter met in summer 1968, but by then they would have been operating *de facto* for four-and-a-half years, making their rejection most unlikely.

Meantime new initiatives continued at home and in Africa. In April 1964 a major extension to Charlotte Street school was officially opened by Archbishop Scanlon on the site of the eye infirmary, formerly No. 76, damaged in the war and since demolished. For the Sisters it was a happy return to the venue of the original convent opened by Veronica in 1849.

St Anthony's Cinderford was growing by the year. With the nearest Catholic primary school fifteen miles away in Gloucester, parents were willing to pay for their children's education, as Bishop Rudderham had predicted, and the roll had now reached three figures. The Sisters had purchased the detached house next door to allow for expansion, and had an extension built to accommodate a further seventy-five children. Because of the limited land available, the two-storey building was constructed on piers to create space for a covered playground beneath.[12] It was opened by the bishop, who in his speech contrasted the animosity that had existed towards Catholics before the war with the friendly acceptance that the Church now enjoyed, exemplified by the number of non-Catholic parents who chose the school for their children. The change of heart, he added, was in no small measure due to the quiet Christian example given by the Sisters.[13]

In the same year, the community in Circus Drive, Dennistoun opened the private school that had been planned when the property was first purchased in 1961. The first intake of five- to six-year-olds enrolled at the beginning of the school session in September.

In Nigeria the impact of the recent education laws was now beginning to be felt. Already in 1963 the Sisters had been forced to close St Clare's teacher training centre in Osogbo in the face of the government's new requirements for upgrading, which were beyond their means. Now in summer 1964 the state took over all mission primary schools. The Congregation lost St Francis' Osogbo and St Theresa's Ilesa immediately, and knew that it was only a matter of time before their small secondary modern schools in the two towns would be phased out also. They still had charge of St Bernardine's, but for how long?

Mother Philippa paid a third visit to the country that autumn. The long-promised novitiate had recently been opened at Otan and she was anxious to see it for herself.[14] She also wished to inspect the school next door, where the Sisters were teaching boys. If she was expecting an African Dennistoun she had a rude awakening. As she entered the classroom the pupils were all seated, but they at once stood up, to their full six feet of height, thundering out a well-rehearsed 'Good afternoon, Mudda!' in cheerful bass voices.

Philippa took their young teacher aside. 'Sister, these are not boys, they are *men*!' she said with an anxious glance. Soon afterwards, she replaced the teacher with an older Sister.[15] The incident was another lesson for 'central office' in distant Glasgow.

Mother Philippa also saw for herself that in Nigeria every teaching Sister was always much more than a teacher. She might also be cook, sacristan, choir mistress, liturgist, infirmarian, supervisor of boarders. Often she was all of them.

In 1965 Sr Emmanuel had a small operating theatre built at the hospital in Osogbo. When it was completed, she approached some of the British and Irish tradesmen who were in charge of services in the town and persuaded them to give up their evenings to install light, heat and water. Her chief organiser and go-between was Con Murphy, a Corkman large of body and heart, who like herself was hard to say 'no' to.[16]

That autumn she returned to Scotland on leave, spending much of her time hunting for bargains to equip the clinic and theatre. In an army stores she picked up beds for almost nothing. In the house at Saltcoats she discovered a wheelchair with no owner. She also found electric urns that would serve admirably as sterilisers, and several filing cabinets that seemed surplus to requirements. She bought bedding and other items from the Barras. She never admitted to having the asking prices, and stall keepers of all faiths and none reduced them without fail when they knew where the goods were bound for. It reached the stage where none of the other Sisters would be seen shopping with her.

She arrived back in Lagos on 11 January 1966. That same day, the minister of finance signed a document giving her permission to bring her accumulated possessions into the country. It must have been one of his last official acts, for that night both he and the president were assassinated. It was the first coup, the beginning of the civil war.

The coup was the work of members of the Ibo tribe, whose heartland was in eastern Nigeria. In its aftermath, as the Biafran War developed, thousands of Ibos living in the north of the country were driven from their homes. The able-bodied made their way overland on foot to the east, but the old and the wounded could only escape by taking the train south and hoping to reach safety somehow from there. Most of the train drivers were themselves Ibos and would stop if they saw a fellow tribesman lying by the track. In this way they arrived at Osogbo, where the Sisters found several hundred of them at the station. Since their convent and hospital were some distance away, they tended them where they lay, on the platform. Most had taken wounds on their arms warding off machetes, trying to escape decapitation. The Sisters managed to save some of them and have them moved to the town's general hospital, but for others tetanus had already taken a fatal hold.

In January 1966 four Nigerian postulants were preparing to be received as novices, and it was necessary for Mother Philippa and Bishop McCoy to consider their future. Both preferred that the postulants should remain members of the Franciscan Congregation rather than join a diocesan community, but they recognised that since this was not the normal practice in Nigeria the matter would have to be brought to Rome.[17] At the end of May the four were received in a historic ceremony at St Benedict's Cathedral in Osogbo, the former prefecture church that had first welcomed the Sisters from Scotland in 1950.

That summer, Con Murphy's contract ended and he returned to Ireland. As a parting gesture he donated his Peugeot station wagon to the hospital, enabling Sr Emmanuel and her colleagues to travel for the first time without needing to hire taxis. Change was imminent in the field of medicine, as in the Sisters' other main apostolate education. Visiting the Osogbo convent in August, Bishop McCoy exhorted the community 'to work with optimism in spite of difficulties cropping up at the present time', and to be ready to adapt to changing circumstances.[18] His plea was timely and only too prophetic.

For several years Council had been seriously considering closing the private school in Greenock. It was losing money and its boarding roll had declined to a mere five. They had intended closing it in 1963 and only agreed to a reprieve in response to a show of support by the parents, following which a parents' association had been formed in the hope of raising the school's fortunes.[19] But in November 1966 Council decided it could bear the loss no longer and that the school would close the following June. When the news broke, the parents held an emergency meeting which voted unanimously to fight to save the school. In their letter to Mother Philippa, they pointed to its healthy roll of over fifty, the sacrifices willingly made by parents from as far afield as Dunoon and Kilmacolm, and the certainty that if it closed many pupils would be forced to enrol in non-Catholic schools. The government was planning to destroy parental choice, they added, and with equal foresight warned that if the trend of closing convent schools continued, the place of religious in education might eventually disappear altogether in Scotland.[20] Their case was received sympathetically, but the decision for closure stood.

The threat to parental choice applied with even greater force to moves being made by the Lanarkshire EA at this time, for their plans to set up co-educational comprehensive education throughout the county naturally involved the abolition of single-sex schools. The Elmwood staff learned of the EA's intentions through a 'leak' by a friend on the council and at once began to mobilise opposition.

When the new policy was finally made public in October, interested parties were given just four weeks to make written submissions concerning it.[21] Letters flooded in from Elmwood parents and alumnae spanning sixty years, all of them vehemently opposed to closure. A public meeting was organised at which a deputation was appointed to meet representatives of the EA, and when the two sides met in February the authority was left in no doubt as to the strength of the parents' feelings.[22] As a result, the director of education drew up an alternative plan, involving the retention of Elmwood and costing little more than the original. This was considered by the Executive in March but rejected, no particular reason being given. The members agreed that Elmwood should be retained until the plan was implemented, which for financial reasons they expected would not be for some years.[23]

Such a 'concession' did nothing to mollify the Catholic community, but it did give it time to mount a more effective campaign. Representations at the highest level began at once. Local MP James Hamilton raised the issue with Bruce Millen, the Scottish Secretary, on a number of occasions that spring, and the two men had a lengthy meeting in July, which however brought no positive result. Millen stated that he considered Lanarkshire's plan reasonable, and that though he had sympathy with the parents he was not willing to intervene.[24] It was a rebuff to their hopes, but only the beginning of their fight.

The Second Vatican Council had come to a close in December 1965. Its conclusions were contained in sixteen documents issued between 1964 and 1966, of which a complete annotated English translation with commentaries was published in 1966.[25] The world already knew their general thrust, and observers in the English-speaking world were now able to study the documents in detail and reflect upon their implications. The key texts, most far-reaching in their effect, were the Council's core statement *Lumen Gentium* ('The Dogmatic Constitution on the Church'), and *Gaudium et Spes* ('The Pastoral Constitution on the Church in the Modern World').

One of the main issues addressed in these documents was the effect upon the Church of what might be called a dualist view of the created world. This was not a view prominent in the teaching of Christ, nor in the primitive Church, but had emerged around the fourth century and had dominated its thinking at certain times thereafter.

It seems to have arisen from a coincidence of philosophical and political circumstances. On the one hand, as theologians reflected upon their faith and attempted to give it a cogent philosophical foundation, they inevitably overlaid the original Gospel message with the prevalent thinking of the day, and in particular with the teachings of the neo-Platonists. Under their influence, they tended to overemphasise the contrast between spirit and matter, sacred and profane, the things of God and the things of 'the world'. At the same time, when the Church under the Emperor Constantine moved from being a persecuted minority of committed people to a state religion to which the whole community belonged, a distinction began to be drawn between the deeply committed few in every generation and the wider membership. Following Christ's words 'If you would be perfect give up all that you possess . . . and follow me', deep commitment came to be associated especially with a rejection of the world, with eremitism and cenobitism, and with vows in imitation of His poverty, chastity and obedience. The religious and secular lives became separated, the first seen as a way to perfection for a spiritual élite, the second a lesser way for the faithful at large.

This dualism, which still coloured the Church's thinking in the mid-twentieth century, the documents sought to redress. The very chapter titles of *Lumen Gentium* indicated this. Chapter 2, entitled 'The People of God', stressed the oneness of the entire Christian body, while chapter 5, 'The Call of the Whole Church to Holiness', issued a reminder that holiness is not the preserve of an élite but of all, and that the religious life is complementary to the lay state, not superior *per se*.

There is indeed a real duality between the spiritual and the material, the lasting and the temporal, the heavenly and earthly Jerusalem, and this the documents recognised. But they rejected any notion of holding the latter in contempt, rather seeing good in both. As *Gaudium et Spes* affirmed, Christians are 'citizens of two cities' and must embrace both and discharge their duties to both.[26] The Church cannot and must not separate itself from 'the world' or the rest of humankind; on the contrary, it 'goes forward together with humanity and experiences the same earthly lot which the world does'.[27] To be a Christian is to work for the spiritual and material welfare of all in this world, not merely to attend to one's own preparation for the next.

In thus calling for a new 'communion', the Council documents sent out a particular challenge to the religious Orders. As *Lumen Gentium* put it, 'let no-one think that by their consecration religious have become strangers to their fellow men or useless citizens of this earthly city'.[28] The words were at once a powerful affirmation of their worth within the Church and society, and a challenge to any thoughts of isolationism.

The particular meaning of renewal for religious was spelled out in detail in the decree *Perfectae Caritatis*. This document urged all Orders and Congregations to seek renewal through a return to their origins, firstly to the scriptures as the ultimate source of the faith, and secondly to the 'original inspiration' of their own founders. At the same time, while looking back, they should look also to the present and future, adapting and redefining their role 'as the tenor of the times dictates'.[29] By doing so they would rediscover their 'authentic character', and having done so they must courageously jettison anything not in keeping with it.

In such practical matters as 'enclosure' and 'the habit' that might hitherto have seemed unchangeable, the decree demanded an open and flexible approach. It called also for a new vision of the religious vows. Thus it affirmed poverty not just for its own sake but as 'a witness' in today's acquisitive society, pointing out the valuable example of those 'poor in both fact and spirit' and the practical support and solidarity that chosen poverty can offer to those poor by force of circumstance. It urged that obedience, too, should be seen with a new insight. Often it was merely external, passive and concerned with the letter of the law, whereas it should be 'active and responsible', a thinking, internalised obedience compatible with spiritual and emotional maturity.[30] Implicit was a whole new concept of authority within religious communities.

A crucial theme of the document, indeed, concerned internalisation. It insisted that if true renewal was to be achieved it must involve not merely external change – that would be the easy part – but 'a renewal of spirit' without which no changes would have life.

Many people felt that *Lumen Gentium* had in effect downgraded the religious life. *Perfectae Caritatis* had made a point of affirming its 'surpassing value', certainly, and its 'necessary role in the circumstances of the present age'.[31] Yet since it called for radical change it was perhaps inevitable that it too would cause anxiety and tension among religious.[32] It was a painful time for them. Yet it could also be a time of creativity. Many gladly welcomed the wind of change that the Council had let into their cloisters when it 'threw open the windows' of the Church. They greeted it as the breath of the Holy Spirit entering and were convinced that the pain and uncertainty were right for them and salutory for their Orders. As they saw it, the religious life should not be, as so often in the past, 'a privilege filled with advantages', but rather 'a charism rich in risks'.[33]

For our Franciscan Sisters it was doubly a time of uncertainty. They shared the general anxieties of all religious, but in addition, as a Congregation with an active public apostolate, they were caught up in the changes taking place in society and in the Catholic community they served. Industrial Scotland was witnessing the demise of old communities and the birth of new, rapid changes in employment, and a general rise in aspirations. The Catholic community itself was changing, becoming generally better educated and more discriminating, yet a less distinct and homogeneous group than in the past and uncertain as to the direction that its Church was taking.

In particular, as a teaching Congregation the Sisters were confronted with the new developments in education and a new questioning among the young. It was the era of the Beatles, long hair and new morals; a time of teacher shortage, a rash of new schools replacing old, and the change to comprehensive education with its radical effects upon curricula and teaching methods. It was a time, in fact, when the very bases of pedagogy were being called into question by the new realities of the classroom. As one commentator has described the situation at this time: 'It became evident that the model of the school as a sheltered environment quietly discharging its function unaffected by the moral and spiritual ferment of the outside world no longer applied, and that the position of the teacher as a dominant authority in the purveying of knowledge and formation of attitudes was under deadly threat.'[34]

The new ethos was felt most in the huge new comprehensives. Because the Sisters were teaching in the primary schools, Charlotte Street and Elmwood, and their own private schools, the impact of the changes was less severe and immediate, but they were not untouched by them. The problems they posed for them as educators – challenges to authority and to the sheltered life – were precisely those already being posed for them as religious by the Vatican Council. For the teaching Sisters it was doubly a time of ferment. As they boarded the bus in the morning they left behind the uncertainties of the convent only to face new questions in the school.

Most, it must be said, were ready to meet the challenge. Indeed, we might add, the message of *Perfectae Caritatis* and of Vatican II had particular appeal and resonance for them as Franciscans. So much of what the Council documents spoke of – an incarnational God to be loved above all *and in all*; fraternal encounter and solidarity with the whole of humankind; the call of all to holiness; the imperative to social action; *aggiornamento*; risk taking; the concept of the religious as servant – was also at the heart of the Franciscan message. It has been persuasively argued, indeed, that the Council pointed the Church into the path of Francis.[35]

Within the Franciscan family there was, however, a particular problem regarding renewal for the Third Order Regular. The First Order, the Friars Minor, followed a Rule composed by Francis himself. The Second, the Poor Clares, used the Rule drawn up by St Clare in collaboration with him. But not only was the Rule of the Third Order compiled by an 'outsider', Pope Nicholas IV, six decades after Francis' death, it suffered changes over the succeeding centuries, notably the emendments of Leo X in 1521 and Pius XI in 1927,[36] and now bore little resemblance to any work of the founder.

When members of the Order began looking into their origins as Vatican II had instructed, it became clear just how far the Rule had strayed. Some even claimed that it had almost nothing specifically Franciscan about it other than its opening sentence and occasional pious references to 'the Seraphic Father'. As a result, they concluded, most Third Order Congregations were now 'Franciscan in name only'. Only by composing a wholly new Rule based on a close study of Francis' life and writings would they be able to rediscover their authentic charism.[37]

Many of the Congregations took up the challenge. Those from France and Belgium began collaboration on a new Rule in 1965. The Dutch institutes followed two years later, as did the Germans. They worked independently and in time produced provisional documents: the so-called 'Dutch Rule', 'French Project' and 'German Rule'.[38] From the mid-1960s the spirit of self-searching grew on an international scale and affected everyone, Glasgow included. It was becoming clear that renewal had far greater implications than at first imagined: it was going to involve a whole radical rediscovery.

In summer 1966 Rome published its *Norms* for implementing the decree *Perfectae Caritatis*. Every religious institute was instructed to call a Special General Chapter within two, or at most three, years, at which the necessary changes to its Constitutions were to be introduced 'on an experimental basis'. These would then be tried out, emended where need be, and finally approved at the following General Chapter (with a permitted extension of one further Chapter if required).[39] Since the Sisters held their General Chapter every six years and the next was due in 1968, this gave them at most fourteen years to complete the process of renewal, with everything to be concluded by the Chapter of 1980.

The *Norms* instructed that the whole Congregation was to take a real share in the enterprise, and that in preparing for the Chapter there must be 'an extensive and completely free consultation of the members'. Rome knew that the initial Chapter would set the tone for the whole process and was determined that it should be as open, collaborative and democratic as possible, with real discussion of the issues. For most Congregations this would be a novel experience. It promised new 'power' to the members and would demand a special openness, if not a whole change of heart, from Superiors. Some would respond willingly, but for others it would seem a threat to their authority.

To dispel these very natural fears, the Superiors were asked to reflect upon 'the theology of the head and members': to recognise that each member is unique and needed; that all are interdependent; that close collaboration between head and members creates a healthy body, and far from destroying the authority of the head actually strengthens it; and that an ethos of dialogue, listening and trust brings out the best in all, whereas an authoritarian, blaming culture only promotes a spiritual paralysis incompatible with genuine renewal.[40]

The Sisters had already begun to emend some of their most inappropriate customs. In summer 1965, Council voted to abolish the practices of kissing the floor at the Chapter of Faults and of kneeling before the Superior.[41] The following spring Mother Philippa called at Rome on her way to Nigeria and there sought advice regarding further changes, particularly concerning annual leave, the Office and the habit. Regarding the first, she was given permission to grant one week's holiday per year, and after consultation with Archbishop Scanlon this was granted as a right to all Sisters five years professed.[42] Regarding the second, on Rome's recommendation she made a start at replacing the Latin Little Office with the standard Office in English, introducing the hours of Lauds, Vespers and Compline that year.[43] The changes were warmly welcomed.

Far more controversial were the changes to the habit. The decision to abandon the ceremonial cloak was widely supported, but the modernisation of the habit itself split the community, meeting strong resistance from some but welcomed by others as sensible and overdue. Mother Philippa explained that the decision was Rome's and therefore not up for debate, though the precise form of change was open to discussion. This did not ease the real distress it caused, though. Especially regretted was the loss of the Franciscan cord: its three knots represented the three religious vows that the Sisters had taken at the time of their profession, and it symbolised all that they had given their lives to. Many were in tears at its loss.

It was regrettable that the ruling appeared to some as a heartless diktat, since renewal was intended to bring a more caring ethos to religious communities. One further change of practice introduced by Council at this time was certainly made in this spirit. In January 1968 Sr Kevin Salmon died. Her funeral took place at Dalbeth cemetery, and for the first time several of the Sisters were permitted to attend.[44] It was a small change, but one of great significance. At last it was recognised that members of a religious community are also friends, and that having been friends in this life they should be allowed as friends to commit the dead into the next.

Mother Philippa began the preparations for the General Chapter early to ensure that everyone would be well informed and ready. In October 1967 she requested that all of the convents begin weekly meetings to study the Constitutions in the light of *Perfectae Caritatis* and *Lumen Gentium*. The following month she circulated Rome's directives for revising Constitutions. In January she issued ballot papers for the election of a commission to summarise the issues and prepare the agenda. Finally, in March she invited the study groups to submit their proposals for changes to the Constitutions.[45]

This was new territory for them, as it was for religious communities struggling with similar tasks around the world. Everyone was calling for some kind of 'road map' to guide them, and when a comprehensive handbook by Elio Gambari was issued from the Vatican it was seized upon. The Italian edition ran to four reprints within six months, and an English version was rushed out within the year.[46] This latter became the Sisters' *vade mecum*, and it proved invaluable.

In March everyone was sent a questionnaire inviting her to support or reject the proposed constitutional change from monastery to Congregation.[47] Rome's instructions for the composition of future Chapters were also distributed. Hitherto all professed Sisters had taken part, but in future they were to be streamlined, with a smaller number of *ex officio* members and elected delegates.[48] The forthcoming Chapter would be the last under the old system.

Mother Philippa knew that the proposed change to a Congregation, and the new composition of Chapters that would go with it, were causing alarm, particularly among some of the older Sisters, and she did all that she could to allay their fears. They had always thought of themselves as an Order, and the very name 'Congregation' dismayed them. And the loss of voting rights at Chapter made some feel that vital decisions affecting their future were being taken out of their hands.[49]

In May Mother Philippa travelled to Rome to take advice on the issues being raised at Chapter, returning in early June in time to issue the results of the questionnaire.[50] For all their anxiety, the Sisters knew in their hearts that they had already moved beyond the scope of monastic government, but some still held out for what they had always known. The final result was desperately close. Thirty-eight voted for a centralised structure against nineteen for a monastic, exactly the two-thirds majority required.[51]

The change could now be ratified at Chapter. Unlike previous gatherings, which had been peremptory affairs lasting two days and comprising little more than elections and house reports plus 'any other business', this and future Chapters would be far more protracted. There would be position papers, extended debates, sub-committees, voting, conclusions and summaries – the whole cumbersome democratic process, in fact. The meetings would certainly extend beyond the school holidays and would need to continue thereafter at weekends.[52]

The Sisters had all read the advice in Fr Gambari's handbook urging them to accept change willingly. He had written of roots and leaves: of returning to their roots to strengthen them, and of letting dead leaves fall in order to enrich themselves with new buds.[53] But as they waited anxiously for a Chapter that was sure to be a watershed, many must have felt that the wind of change was tearing away the leaves and scattering them, and some perhaps feared that it was threatening to uproot the tree itself.

ENDNOTES TO CHAPTER SEVEN

1 Council Meeting Minutes, supplementary 1955–68, filed with Log Books, Oct.–Nov. 1960; and *The Franciscan Sisters of the Immaculate Conception – celebrating 150 years in Glasgow 1847–1997*, 1997, p. 97. Ilesa has one of the largest prisons in Nigeria.

2 Chapter notes, Register of Elections, 11.7.1956, 028.2, AF. She had made the proposal on the grounds that all applicants now had a secondary education and could therefore be trained for professional work. Though Chapter supported her, no date was specified for implementing the change.

3 Council Meeting Minutes, supplementary, Feb. 1961. Her letter was endorsed by Archbishop Campbell. Re Rome's *Rescript* abolishing the distinction, Chapter notes, Register of Elections, 8.8.1962, 028.2, AF.

4 Pius XI's Constitution *Rerum Conditio* had been issued on 4.10.1927; see also p. 58 *supra*.

5 Re the revision, Council Meeting Minutes, 21.1.1934 and Sept. 1934, 034.10 no. 2, AF. Rome afterwards asked the Congregation to accept the Constitutions of the Maltese Sisters. The Council's minute of 28.11.1937 records the response – 'The Councillors have read these Constitutions and are not prepared to accept them. Our own Constitutions are very dear to us as we have been following them since 1866.'

6 Bishop James Ward, Report, 25.6.1961, of his visitation of 29.4.1961, 071.03, AF.

7 Cf. p. 191f. *infra* re Archbishop Scanlon.

8 Sr Emmanuel Gallagher interview.

9 The new name was adopted in 1967 to mark the 50th anniversary of the visions at Fatima, and (in the word 'General') in recognition of its broadened role.

10 Council Meeting Minutes, supplementary, 22–24.4.1963.

11 Council Meeting Minutes, 1.11.1963, 034.10 no. 2, AF.

12 The original estimate for the extension was £15,000 and the final cost over

£19,000 – Knight, Frank and Rutley to abbess, 20.1.1963 and 11.12.1964, 046.1, AF.

13 Account of the opening and summary of the bishop's speech in *Dean Forest Mercury*, 7.5.1965.

14 Council Meeting Minutes, June 1966. The novitiate, named 'Mount Alvernia', opened on 9.5.1964, staffed by Srs Bernard and Immaculata.

15 Sr M. Baptist, 'Teaching Memories', in *Journey So Far*, 2000, p. 188ff.

16 This and the following paragraphs based on Sr Emmanuel Gallagher interview.

17 Council Meeting Minutes, 9.1.1966. Mgr McCoy had been consecrated bishop in April 1963, when Oyo was raised from a prefecture to a diocese.

18 Bishop Owen McCoy WF, Report of his visitation to St Francis' Convent Osogbo, 14.8.1966, 071.03, AF.

19 J. Campbell of Black, Cameron and Campbell, solicitors, to abbess, 7.2.1962; and Dr Robert and Mrs Margaret Lamb, parents, to same, 3.10.1963; both 043.1, AF.

20 Dr Robert Lamb to Superior General, 11.2.1967, with 67 signatures from the parents' meeting of 10 Feb.; and Dr Robert Lamb and John Farmer to same, April 1967; both 043.1, AF.

21 Minutes of meetings of the Lanarkshire EA Schools and Schemes Executive, 6.10.1966 (submission of plan by the director of education), and 26.10.1966 (approval of plan). Public submissions were to be received by 22 November. The present account also based on Miss Susan McCormick interview.

22 *Ibid.*, 24.1.1967 and 16.2.1967.

23 *Ibid.*, 10.3.1967 (director of education presents alternative plan, Executive decides in favour of original), and 6.4.1967 (Executive confirms decision); also Schools and Schemes Sub-committee Minute, 10.3.1967.

24 Bruce Millen to James Hamilton MP, 27.7.1967, 044.11, AF, following their meeting of the previous day.

25 Abbott W.M. (gen. ed.) and Gallagher J. (transl. ed.), 1966. The original documents were issued in Latin.

26 *Gaudium et Spes*, para 43.

27 *Ibid.*, para 40.

28 *Lumen Gentium*, chapter 6.

29 *Perfectae Caritatis*, (The Decree on the Appropriate Renewal of the Religious Life), especially paras 81–2.

30 *Perfectae Caritatis*, paras 13 (Poverty) and 14 (Obedience).

31 *Ibid.*, para 1.

32 The anxiety and tension among religious was of course only a part of the more widespread anxiety that the Council was bringing to the Church. Cf. Gambari E., 1966 (Engl. transl. 1967), p. 28: 'The Council set the Church, its institutions and its members in a state of dynamism . . . of anxious searching . . . in unremitting tension'.

33 *Theology of the Religious life and the Second Vatican Council*, n.d., p. 1.

34 Fitzpatrick T.A., 1986, p. 118.

35 Galli M., 1972, *passim*.

36 For a detailed account of the history of the Rule from the thirteenth century to the twentieth and the changes made to it, see Pazzelli R., 1989 (Eng. transl., Mullaney A., 1993), *passim*.

37 *Updating Franciscan Communities*, n.d., p. 101ff. The authors especially recommended that the new Rule be based upon Francis' *Letter to all the Faithful*.

38 Pazzelli R., *op. cit.*, p. 183.

39 *Norms for Executing the Decree of the Second Vatican Council 'Perfectae Caritatis'*, Rome, 6.8.1966. Changes were specifically required in such matters as the habit, enclosure appropriate to the apostolate, replacement of the Little Office of Our Lady by the standard Divine Office, and Formation as a lifelong process rather than merely a function of the novitiate.

40 Örsly L., SJ, *Government in Religious Life: The Council's Teaching*, Rome 1966. This particularly balanced, insightful and sympathetic work was widely used by the Congregation.

41 Council Meeting Minutes, 12.9.1965. The practice of kneeling before the Superior was now only to apply when seeking permissions, receiving corrections or asking her blessing.

42 Council Meeting Minutes, supplementary, 22.4.1966; Council Meeting Minutes, 15.7.1966 and 22.4.1967; Mother Philippa to Archbishop Scanlon, 21.3.1966, 071.01, AF.

43 Mgr. S. Kilpatrick, Archdiocesan Chancellor, to Superior General, 29.7.1966, relaying the archbishop's permission; Council Meeting Minutes, 11.6.1967 and 23.9.1967.

44 Council Meeting Minutes, supplementary, 20.1.1968.

45 Sr Philippa to Rev. Mothers and Sisters of Convents, 9.3.1968, 030.33, AF.

46 Gambari E., Rome 1966; Engl. transl. as *Renewal in Religious Life – General Principles, Constitution, Formation*, Boston 1967. The author was one of the members of the Sacred Congregation for Religious who attended the Second Vatican Council, and was later Consultor at the post-Conciliar Commission for Religious.

47 Mother Philippa to Rev. Mother and Sisters at Merrylee, 14.3.1968, 030.33, AF.

48 Mother Philippa to Rev. Mothers and Sisters of Convents, 25.3.1968, 030.33, AF. She had requested that the change be postponed to the following Chapter because of the difficulty of arranging a vote in Nigeria, but Rome had insisted that it apply immediately.

49 Sr Dolores Cochrane interview.

50 Mother Philippa to Rev. Mothers and Sisters of Convents, 12.6.1968, 030.33, AF. She was in Rome from 29 May to 5 June. She had been forced to go there in person because of a postal strike.

51 Mother Philippa to Rev. Mothers and Sisters of Convents, 12.6.1968.

52 *Ibid*. The reader may gain some idea of the radical change in the whole concept of a Chapter from the fact that in the Congregation's archives the minutes of all the Chapters from 1854–1965 (admittedly incomplete) are contained in two box files, whereas those for the thirty years 1968–98 run to fourteen!

53 Gambari E., *op. cit.*, especially p. 143.

CHAPTER EIGHT

Blowing in the Wind (1968–1980)

The Chapter convened on 12 August, and its first session was devoted to elections. Sr Gabriel Palmer was elected Superior General in succession to Mother Philippa, and Sr Felicitas Bradley Assistant General. They were excellent choices for the task in hand. Mother Philippa had achieved much for the Congregation during her term of office and had overseen many fruitful developments, but in regard to radical internal change she had probably taken it as far as she could. She was of the older generation, but she had managed to introduce some changes and lead it, as it were, to the threshold of greater change. Now was a good time for new leadership. Srs Gabriel and Felicitas, though deeply loyal to the traditions, had the will and the energy to embrace change and see it through.

The remaining sessions were devoted to discussion of the key Vatican documents and deciding the Congregation's priorities for renewal in the light of them. Eight priority areas were identified: Franciscan spirituality, prayer, poverty, chastity, obedience, common life, apostolic life and the religious life. The particular choice, involving a return to their Franciscan origins, a new look at the Evangelical Counsels, and a reconsideration of the apostolate and the meaning of community, closely followed the documents' imperatives.

A commission was appointed for each priority area[1] to gather the views of the whole membership, collate and consider their responses, and publish a statement of recommendations by Easter 1969. These were to form the agenda for the Chapter when it reconvened the following autumn, when new Constitutions covering the eight areas would be hammered out and agreed, ready for testing experimentally as the *Norms* required. In addition, Council were asked to appoint a team of six to design a new sample habit for consideration at the 1969 session.

The commissions began their work in November.[2] Democratic discussion of this kind was a new experience for most of the members, and at first their deliberations were tentative and not always comfortable, but every group produced its questionnaire form for issue by the end of the year.

The responses revealed a wide range of opinion. Some saw little need for change, while others welcomed it. Those who did so took their suggestions directly from the Vatican documents. Those who mentioned 'spirituality', for example, called for a deeper study of the Gospels and the Franciscan literature, and more flexibility in community life; those who referred to 'obedience' proposed greater personal responsibility in a climate of dialogue and trust; and those who mentioned 'the apostolate' called for an identification with the poor and an openness to current needs.[3]

When the commissions presented their written statements to Council[4] a consistent message emerged. Key words and phrases recurred throughout them – 'creative'; 'continuous and honest dialogue'; 'the spirit of love rather than the letter of the law'; 'interiority'; 'maturity'; 'humility'; and 'service'. They showed that the Sisters had thoroughly understood the issues raised by the Vatican Council, and that many had embraced its imperatives with conviction and were now impatient to put them to the test.

Like every hospital in Nigeria, the Fatima General in Osogbo had to charge its patients in order to exist. But unlike most, it never demanded a deposit before admitting them – a practice that caused many deaths among the poor – nor indeed insisted on any fee from those unable to pay. Such fees as the staff did gather went some way to covering the running of the hospital, but were never enough to pay for any extensions. For this Sr Emmanuel had to turn to the charities. In 1967 she had added a kitchen and laundry with funding from the German charity *Miserior*, and had also built a male ward towards which she received £1,500 from the infant Scottish Catholic International Aid Fund (SCIAF).[5] The ward was a major undertaking which left her accounts badly in the red, but in September 1968 Council voted to give her £5,000 from the generalate funds, enabling her to clear all her debts and even consider more building.

That autumn she paid another visit to Scotland. She had ambitious plans for the hospital to show to Council – a new female ward, outpatients' department, pharmacy, consulting rooms, X-ray facility and a lab. It was a daunting list but Council accepted it in principle and promised to support it with cash. An appeal was launched and money began coming in at once. Items were also donated from Merrylee and the other convents, and Charlotte Street gifted her their Christmas decorations. When she left she had sixty-four cases of luggage.[6]

That same year Bishop McCoy set up a department of pastoral care for women in his diocese and appointed Sr Juliana McAuley as its first adviser. Her remit was to establish and oversee local 'women's councils', which in turn would encourage the formation of activity groups in their neighbourhoods. She began in Osogbo, Oyo and Ilesa where the Congregation had convents which could be used as bases. The councils set up women's groups covering a range of activities including sewing, knitting, trading skills and adult literacy.[7] Their common purpose was self-improvement and 'empowerment', and their popularity spread.

Three of the four Nigerian girls received into the novitiate in 1966 had persevered in their vocation and were due to make their first vows in the autumn. It had been agreed between Mother Philippa and Bishop McCoy that they would be professed as members of the Franciscan Congregation rather than for the diocese, but Mother Gabriel, who had not herself been involved in the arrangement, was anxious to receive confirmation that it was acceptable to Rome. At her request, Bishop McCoy contacted the Sacred Congregation for Religious for a definitive ruling on the matter. Rome's response was that the Sisters should be given a thorough explanation of the issues and then make the decision themselves. All three chose to remain with the Congregation. They took their vows in October, the first fruits of the Nigerian novitiate and a vindication of Council's decision to train its African Sisters in Africa.[8]

In April 1969 the decision was taken to give more authority to the local Superiors in Nigeria. It was sensible and overdue. No longer would they have to apply to Merrylee every time a Sister wished to travel more than a hundred miles, visit home or hold a driving licence. The following year they were granted further discretion to admit novices, decide obediences and embark on new apostolates. It was a recognition that the mission was mature enough to be trusted and that those on the ground knew their own needs best.[9]

Sr Emmanuel had her sixty-four crates of equipment still unopened, and it seemed likely that she might have to wait years for the buildings to put them in. Then in May Council learned that a developer was interested in buying the convent in Gunnersbury Avenue that was used by the nursing Sisters training at Hammersmith hospital, and was willing to pay £33,000 for it. Council agreed to the sale, and the deal was signed that August. Mother Gabriel decided that since the money was in a sense 'medical' it should be used for medical purposes. She therefore donated the entire sum to Osogbo, along with a further £10,000 realised from the appeal.[10] It was enough to cover almost everything.

In order to bypass Nigerian import regulations, Sr Emmanuel transferred the money into the Italian account of Ponti and Co., the firm contracted to undertake the building programme. Ponti was to prove a generous friend to the Congregation over the years. Once the work began, his men often gave their labour free at the weekends to do other jobs not included in the contract. In this way the hospital was painted and given a tarmac drive, and a veranda was built round the maternity ward. Nor was this the only help Sister received. Oxfam paid for a blood bank, and Fr Kingston WF funded equipment for the theatre and X-ray room, as well as collecting vestments and altar linens for the hospital chapel from well-wishers in USA. In the space of a year the far-off dream had become a reality.

Chapter reconvened at the beginning of October in the hope of concluding its business by the end of the month. Some of the topics, such as the new habit, were dealt with and voted upon with little debate, but others proved more intractable. It soon became clear that they would not be resolved overnight and there was a real danger that the meetings would become entirely bogged down. Mother Gabriel proposed that rather than rush matters they should set up new commissions where necessary and call a further Chapter in 1970 to conclude the outstanding issues. This might seem cumbersome, but it was crucial to get the new Constitutions exactly right.[11]

The members accepted her proposal. At the plenary session they sanctioned Council to prepare revised Constitutions covering the topics already resolved, and to appoint new commissions on the two major issues still outstanding: 'formation' and 'government'.[12] Regarding the first, further work was necessary in the light of new documents recently published by Rome instructing that formation should be interpreted far more broadly than before, to cover not merely the training of novices but every Sister's lifelong spiritual journey.[13] The second was also considered vital, since upon its outcome would depend the Congregation's decision-making and the direction it would take in future years.

As the Sisters dispersed it now dawned on them that this had been the last meeting in which the whole Congregation would take part, for next year's and all future Chapters would be made up of *ex officio* members and elected delegates only. Perhaps more than anything else, this realisation brought it home to them that things would never be the same again.[14] The new terms they were now to use – 'Mother General' for 'Mother Abbess', 'Assistant General' for 'Mother Vicaress' and 'Sister Superior' for 'Reverend Mother' – were also signs of irrevocable change. They sounded strange and somehow less homely than the old terms.

One decision taken during the Chapter marked a new direction in the Congregation's teaching apostolate. Vatican II had called on the religious Orders to embrace a new vision of poverty 'as witness', and with it a preferential option for the poor, and it was in this spirit that the commission on poverty had drawn up its statement for the Chapter. One of its recommendations was that the Sisters should no longer teach in fee-paying schools except where no other Catholic education was available.[15]

It proved a controversial issue that met with a mixed response when debated in Chapter. Most of those who actually worked in the Congregation's private schools defended them stoutly. They pointed to the great loyalty and sacrifices of the parents, and to the fact that they brought young lives and energies into the convents; they provided work for the novices, for dedicated lay staff often past retirement age, and for the Sisters themselves, most of whom were untrained as teachers and would not find posts in the state schools were their own to be closed. And since they had always been the Congregation's means of funding its work among the poor, it could be argued that they actually abetted its renewed commitment to poverty.[16] The vote was carried, nonetheless, spelling the beginning of the end of a tradition.

The following year, another longstanding school tradition was ended. The Sisters had been in charge of St Mary's Abercromby Street girls' and infants' since 1870. Since 1913 they had been sharing the building in Forbes Street with the boys' school, using separate classrooms and playgrounds. Calton was almost their spiritual home – the place of Veronica's first posting and Adélaide's death, and of the care of thousands in the industrial and parish schools and the houses of the poor. But by 1970 some of its old streets were now mere tracings on waste ground and its still-standing tenements were decaying like beached hulks. The population of the once huge parish was in decline. On grounds of efficiency, the education authority decided to amalgamate the two schools under a single staff. The headship was given to the long-serving Br Casimir, whose Marist Order had been running the boys' school for decades. Sr M. Francis Campbell moved to nearby St Dennis', and the Congregation's hundred years of service to the parish came to an end.

The commissions on formation and government produced their statements in spring 1970. Chapter convened in September. The new stream-lined body of elected delegates and *ex officio* members succeeded in reaching decisions quite quickly on all of the outstanding issues, on the basis of which they left it to Council to write up the interim Constitutions. The task was completed by Easter 1971, after which the summer was spent producing copies for the whole Congregation. These were finally issued in October with a covering letter from Mother Gabriel instructing that they were to be followed until the Chapter of 1974, when they would be reconsidered.[17] The process had taken three years, and they were already halfway into the experimental period.

It was one of the recommendations of *Perfectae Caritatis* that religious institutes with a similar mission should form confederations for mutual support and joint activity.[18] The intention was to increase their effectiveness, combat isolationism and broaden horizons. In response to this call, the Association of Franciscan Sisters of England and Wales was established in April 1970.[19] By coincidence, the Chapter members meeting in Merrylee that September were discussing the same question and voted to approach the other Franciscan women's Congregations in Scotland with a view to

forming some kind of federation. It was while contacting these that Mother
Gabriel learned of the new association already in existence south of the
border.[20]

She made herself known to them and was invited down for their
November meeting, at which a Constitution was drawn up and office bearers
were elected, she herself being voted onto the three-person committee. It was
the association's hope to form links with similar Franciscan associations
around the world.[21] The old self-sufficiency was giving way to a new spirit of
collaboration, a recognition of the worldwide Franciscan family and a will to
build on all that united its members.

The parents and friends of Elmwood had been keeping up the fight to save
the school for four years now. The campaign had been led at the grassroots
level by Charles Downie, and in official circles by James Dempsey MP,
himself a parent and a member of the parent–teacher association, and
Lanarkshire education committee member Mrs Charlotte Toal. Some
20,000 signatures had been presented to St Andrew's House.[22]

Key to the EA's plan was the building of a new mixed Catholic comprehensive school in Bellshill. It had wide support, between the many
believers in co-education, the local Bellshill lobby, and even some people in
Catholic education envious of Elmwood's popularity. Bishop Thomson of
Motherwell was generally consulted on major decisions regarding
Lanarkshire's Catholic schools, but his view was especially important in
this case given the strength of feeling on both sides. In spring 1971 he made
it known that on balance he too preferred the Bellshill option.[23] His support
proved vital when the EA put the issue to the vote in May.

The following day, the *Hamilton Advertiser* carried the banner headline
'New RC School for Bellshill Means Elmwood Closure', and it was thus
that headmistress Sr Benedicta Collins and her staff first learned that the
decision had been taken.

When several days later the official confirmation arrived, she penned a
circular letter to the parents inviting them to a meeting on 23 June, at which
she and others called for the fight to continue. At the same time Mother
Gabriel contacted the Scottish Secretary of the Conservative government of
the day, urging him to put the plan on hold at least until he had met
representatives of the PTA; she hoped that he might be only too willing to
frustrate the plans of a Labour authority. If so, his reply brought her little joy.
Under the current government, he explained, introducing comprehensive
education was no longer obligatory for EAs as it had been under Labour but
was now a matter of local choice. The decision was Lanarkshire's, therefore.
He had studied their plans, and saw no grounds to intervene.[24]

Though many religious Orders had responded prudently to the Vatican Council and embraced renewal without great damage, others had been left in turmoil. This was particularly the case among the women's teaching Orders in USA. Their disenchantment sprang in part from their work conditions in the Catholic schools, where their salaries were often derisory. (All Catholic schools in USA were private and fee-paying, but for the parents' sakes fees were usually kept to a minimum; and it was the fees that paid the teachers' salaries.) But more generally, many American Orders had responded to Vatican II far more precipitately than those in Britain – discarding the habit entirely, for example – and in the trauma and confusion large numbers of Sisters had abandoned their vocation. In many places the schools suddenly found themselves without teachers.

One such was St Joseph's in Renovo, Pennsylvania, where the Immaculate Heart of Mary Sisters taught up until 1971. Knowing that they were pulling out that summer, the parish priest, Fr Orlando, spent the spring desperately trying to replace them, writing to every Congregation in the directory. Having scoured America without success, he turned his attention to Europe. By chance his bishop's father was Scottish and had been taught by the Franciscan Sisters in Greenock. It was he who suggested that Fr Orlando should write to Merrylee.

On 24 June Mother Gabriel informed Archbishop Scanlon of the request and the fact that the Congregation was seriously considering it.[25] Four days later Council voted to support it if three volunteers could be found. Speed was of the essence if they were to set up house in Renovo and be ready for the beginning of term. Six sisters volunteered, of whom Council chose Srs Gertrude Shields, Gerard O'Donnell and Angela McFaul. On 1 July single flight tickets were bought for them, along with a return for Mother Gabriel. The archbishop had in the meantime written to Mother Gabriel requesting her to meet his assistant, Bishop Ward, before taking any decision regarding America.[26] But his letter did not arrive until the 3rd, by which time there was no going back. On 8 July the four flew to Kennedy Airport, and on the 9th they drove up to Renovo (Plate 26).

It was a tiny town among the hills, no more than three blocks in length, the kind of place one came upon suddenly and left equally abruptly. Half of its inhabitants had never made the winding twenty-five mile journey down into Lock Haven, the nearest town large enough to be marked on the map. It was an inward-looking community, a backwater of deprivation which councils bypassed and to which clergy were sent as a last resort. Most of its children received free school meals, and the signs of long neglect were everywhere.

The Sisters had been told none of this when the arrangements were being made. Now they understood why their predecessors had pulled out. But after the first shock they realised that it was, after all, the very place they should be working in, and that providence had brought them there.[27]

The school had been spring-cleaned to greet them and shone with new paint. Sr Gertrude was appointed principal, and she and the other two shared the six grades between them, assisted by two non-Catholic lay teachers.[28] They were given a limousine for their use. It was a monster even by American standards, and although two of them held international driving licences it was weeks before they dared take it on the road.

If the decision to send Sisters to America had upset Archbishop Scanlon, the particular choices infuriated him. Sr Gertrude had been earmarked as the new head of St Patrick's primary school in Anderston, and her going made it doubtful whether the Congregation could provide a suitable candidate for the post. When the archdiocese heard about it, Bishop Ward sent a sharp rebuke to Merrylee. Why had Mother Gabriel not mentioned Sr Gertrude when she spoke to him? Why had they learned about it only by phone after the party had already arrived in America? She must be airmailed immediately and told to contact the archbishop at once. The Sister who passed the message on warned her of his anger. 'His whole tone took my breath away,' she wrote.[29]

Mother Gabriel wrote personally to Archbishop Scanlon from Renovo. She understood the problem regarding St Patrick's, she assured him, and would put another candidate forward for the headship there. She respected his view that since the Congregation had been founded to serve Glasgow it should make the city its priority, but pointed out that this was no longer the Glasgow of 1847. As a gesture of co-operation she was willing to keep the Dennistoun private school open meantime, 'according to his wish', despite the fact that Council had just voted to close it[30]. The archbishop left it to his assistant to reply. The letter was cool and angry and left her in little doubt that had His Grace been consulted he would not have sanctioned the move to America.[31]

To compound the problem, Sr Angela had been released from her post as head of St Lawrence's Greenock to go to Renovo, and it seemed likely that she too might not be replaced by a religious. The secretary of the Paisley diocese, though more courteous in his reply, was equally concerned for the outcome. He would do all he could, he assured Mother Gabriel, to have her alternative candidate appointed, but Renfrewshire's rules were restrictive regarding promoted posts. It would be 'nothing short of tragedy,' he added, if St Lawrence's passed out of the hands of the Sisters, since he felt that only the religious Orders really guaranteed the Catholic ethos of a school.[32]

In the event Mother Gabriel's candidate, the infant mistress Sr M. Baptist, was not appointed, the post going to the assistant head, Miss Gallagher.

With St Patrick's also lost, the Congregation's long reigns at the two schools ended, after 97 and 115 years.[33]

Mother Gabriel left Renovo after four weeks, just as the leaves were turning. It was an enchanted place in the fall, ablaze with gold, red and russet. It styled itself 'the town of the flaming foliage' and held its own annual festival of that name, with bazaars and a grand parade in which the school took part.[34] As soon as it was over and on local advice the Sisters bought boots. Winter was not far away, and the snowploughs were out from November. The little town settled to its months of isolation, with grey days when the street lamps came on early, and dark snow-gusting nights. But the newcomers were warmed by the neighbourliness, the invitations to visit and the many Christmas gifts. Their December entry in the school log book recorded: 'We are beginning to feel we belong here.'

The youngest of the Renovo community, Sr Gerard O'Donnell, had taken her final vows only four months before leaving Scotland. Her profession had made history, for it was the first ever permitted to take place in a Sister's own home parish.[35] The initiative was a part of the ongoing process that had begun in the mid-1960s of making community life freer and more human. In the same spirit, the practice of the Superior reading all incoming and outgoing mail had already been discontinued, and the arrangements for holidays were about to be further relaxed, giving the Sisters an entitlement to three weeks in the summer, three days at Christmas, one full day per month at home, and a free half-day per week to be spent at their discretion.[36]

The following year, the rather demeaning process of having to request petty cash for every outing was replaced by a 'float' system in which spending money was made available without question and accounts squared at the end of the month. The regulations for Silence were also further relaxed in 1973. A start had been made five years before, when the hour for beginning the Great Silence had been put back from 9.00 p.m. to 10.30. Now the daytime silence was made less rigorous, initially by being restricted to the cloister, chapel and oratory, and later by being made a desideratum rather than a strict rule, with the community required to observe 'a sense of silence' rather than silence as such.[37]

Most significant of all, the government of the convents was made more democratic by giving all professed Sisters the opportunity to arrange and chair meetings by rotation, and by holding occasional open discussion meetings without the Superior being present.[38] Such freedoms could not have been imagined ten years before.

In the spirit of Vatican II, the Congregation also began exploring new forms of mission to meet the new needs of the Church and the 'new poverties' of the times.[39] The first in which it became involved was the care of alcoholics. The Sanctuary Association had been founded in Glasgow in 1969 by Sr Rosaria McGeady and a number of lay volunteer assistants, as a result of their experience helping at the city's Wayside Club and model lodging houses. In October 1971 the association opened Sanctuary House in Pollokshields as a residential therapeutic and care home open to all denominations. By 1974 it had extended its outreach to drug addicts, discharged prisoners and destitute men. With a large associate membership of supporters and an action group of young fundraisers, it was able to begin negotiations for a second house in Paisley.[40]

Fr Desmond Maguire had seen for himself the special needs of mentally handicapped young people when he accompanied a group to Lourdes with their leader, Jean Vannier. On his return he set up meetings of parents to discuss what help the Glasgow archdiocese might give to their children. Their view was that though the Church supported them with prayer, it had never offered practical aid. There was a real need, they felt, for specialist provision for young people with serious learning difficulties.[41]

In 1973 Fr Maguire opened four clubs in the city. The one serving the south side was based at St Helen's Langside, barely a mile from Merrylee where Sr Gertrude Shields was now headmistress of the private school. As membership of the club grew and St Helen's became too cramped, Sr Gertrude asked permission for the school premises to be made available to them. The convent itself was already being used for a range of parish activities (in the spirit of the 1969 Chapter), and Mother Gabriel willingly agreed to her request. This was the beginning of what was to be one of the Congregation's most successful new apostolates, and an example of highly fruitful collaboration between it and the state.

Such collaboration was already blossoming in other fields of care. The Congregation had two Sisters employed in NHS hospitals, as well as three trained nursery nurses, one of whom was working in a corporation nursery in Pollokshaws. Council were also considering enrolling Sisters to train for the social work diploma with a view to their finding employment as guidance counsellors in the city.[42] The concept of Sisters gaining nationally recognised qualifications in order to work in the state sector, which had begun in the field of education in 1918 and in nursing in the 1960s, was now broadening as state provision itself broadened. It would increasingly be the pattern for the future.

The new apostolates were offering opportunities for the Sisters to realise their own potential as never before. One for whom Vatican II had opened up a whole new vocation was Sr Agnes Delaney. As a Lay Sister she had spent nearly thirty years virtually enclosed in Merrylee, her work confined to domestic tasks. Liberated by the Vatican decree abolishing the class of

Lay Sister, she had been admitted to study sociology at university and on qualifying had requested to join a parish to undertake social care work.

She was appointed to St Patrick's Kilsyth in 1971, where she discovered a host of untapped talents and where her outgoing nature, verve, zest for life and ability to communicate made her an instant success. She started numerous groups, from altar girls to alcoholics. She was joined a year later by Sr Gertrude, and together they so impressed Fr Dennis O'Connell and his curate, Fr Keith Patrick O'Brien, that in 1973 the parish priest invited them to open a convent in a cottage he had purchased beside the church.[43]

Council discussed the proposal, which would be a radical new departure for the Congregation. In the past, parish work had always been undertaken over and above the Sisters' main apostolate, but at Kilsyth it was to *be* their main apostolate, their full-time work, and the convent would be opened for this specific purpose.[44] It was unanimously agreed to go ahead.[45] After a year spent on renovation, St Andrew's convent opened in August 1974. The first house ever set up for an apostolate other than teaching, it too would set a pattern for the future. In time the community grew to five, with Sr Agnes appointed Superior.[46]

The Congregation was taking on these new tasks at a time of contraction. It had not been decimated in the fallout from Vatican II, as some had, but there had been losses. Between the 1968 and 1974 Chapters, four Sisters were granted temporary exclaustration, of whom only two returned, and another was dispensed from her vows.[47] An abnormally high proportion of novices, confused by the mixed messages they were receiving from progressive and traditionalist mentors, were not proceeding to profession, and new vocations, which had been abundant ten years before, were beginning to dry up. Recruiting was now openly talked of as 'a problem', and for the first time ever Sisters had been appointed to promote vocations in the schools and parishes. In 1971–2 there was only one novice in the whole Congregation outside Nigeria.[48]

There were also signs of tension in the convents. They were now being used by the public, often by society's most broken members. But some of the Sisters, schooled in the tradition of the monastery, had not yet learned that people's needs do not run by the clock. If a Sister was desperately trying to talk an addict out of self-damage, she could not suddenly fall silent at 10.30 p.m., yet some saw her talking during the hours of the Silence as disobedience. There was pain and guilt on both sides.[49] The Congregation was suffering the travail of new birth.

This was also a time of change and difficulty for the Sisters in Nigeria, where the government was stepping up its policy of 'Nigerianisation', with every justification but often with disastrous results. The signs had been clear since 1969 when Sr Callista McGarry, the headteacher of St Bernardine's, died and the Sisters had discovered that they no longer enjoyed control over appointments to their school. The ministry of education had 'permitted' them to bring Sr Michael back as temporary head, but only until it could make its own appointment. Their chosen candidate, Miss Cowley, had proved less than satisfactory and had been dismissed after a few months at the request of the local bishop and replaced by a Nigerian woman who proved little better.[50]

Finally, in 1973, the government assumed full responsibility for all secondary schools. The St Bernardine's campus was taken over almost in its entirety: the convent and chapel as well as the school. The community was forced to move out that August when their home was allocated to the new principal. The following year the school was made co-educational and put in the charge of a non-Catholic layman. All that the Sisters had built was gone.[51]

Rome's policy regarding its African missions was also for 'Africanisation', and it was in accordance with this that Bishop McCoy resigned in February 1972 after twenty-three years at the helm, handing the diocese over to his assistant, Bishop Adelakun.

This milestone for the Church was matched by one similar for the Congregation, for just months before Srs Monica Ilesanmi and Cecilia Okoro had taken their final vows in Glasgow, the first Nigerian Sisters to be fully professed. The event was judged at the time to be the highlight in the Congregation's Nigerian journey to date.[52] Looking back today we can see it as the first buds of a remarkable flowering.

The Merrylee, Bothwell and Dennistoun private schools were all running at a loss, despite the fees being raised twice in as many years, and the losses could no longer be ignored.[53] At Merrylee a parents' fundraising committee was formed in the summer of 1973, but the school still failed to pay its way. By the end of the year Council were seriously discussing the closure of all three schools – which had in any case been agreed as a matter of principle at the 1969 Chapter – and even questioning the future of the Merrylee convent itself, which they were subsidising from the generalate fund.[54] The palmy days of the early 1960s were long gone, and economies would have to be found somewhere. In February 1974 they voted to close the Bothwell convent school and also to sell the Saltcoats house, which, following the relaxation of rules on holidays, was now surplus to their needs.[55]

Lanarkshire EA were still holding firm to their plan to close Elmwood and had now named the date, summer 1977, when the girls would transfer to Cardinal Newman school in Bellshill. One of the most disheartening tasks in education is to oversee the last years of a school due for closure, as numbers dwindle, morale wanes and money is channelled elsewhere. Sr Benedicta Collins had been head since 1970, and it was the advice of James Dempsey when he met Mother Gabriel early in 1974 that it would be painful and dispiriting for her to remain at the helm to the bitter end. Council shared his opinion. They were aware that Elmwood was already suffering staffing difficulties; perhaps also they reflected that Sr Benedicta had been to the fore and vocal in the fight to save the school, and that it is a perilous activity to challenge the wishes of one's employers, even in the 'civilised' world of education. After much discussion of the matter, they unanimously agreed that she should withdraw from the headship.[56]

Mother Gabriel wrote to her informing her of the decision and asking her to tender her resignation.[57] It might have been more sensitive to inform her in person, and indeed the two did meet the following week. The decision was discussed, as was the possibility of a headship in Nigeria, but the reason behind it was not mentioned.[58] Sr Benedicta was of the 'old school', in which Sisters expected to be moved on the word of the abbess, and she did not question the decision. As she herself put it, she interpreted Mother Gabriel's letter as 'a command not a request'. Her own letter of resignation to the director of education merely stated that she was acting on the instructions of her superiors. Nor would she be drawn by the curiosity of the local press, but maintained a dignified and discreet silence throughout.[59]

The depute head, Miss Greta Aitken, was close to retirement age. A convert to Catholicism while at university, she had spent most of her teaching days at Elmwood, first as a brilliant leader of the English department and latterly as Sister's able lieutenant. She agreed to end her career seeing out the school she loved. Sr Benedicta herself was moved to the Glasgow EA, where with humility and courage she accepted a post as principal teacher of guidance at St Augustine's secondary in the giant Milton housing scheme. Typically, she put her back into her new work and enjoyed it, finding most of the children loveable and appreciating the dedication of her colleagues. But it was not Elmwood; nor could there ever be another Elmwood.

In spring 1974 Council drew up a draft revision of the Constitutions to present to the General Chapter that summer.[60] Based on feedback from the trial of the experimental Constitutions issued three years previously, it proposed surprisingly few changes, a sign that the Chapters of 1968–9 and 1970 had done their work well. The Chapter itself confirmed this impression, accepting nearly all of the proposals with only minor emendments. The members recognised that more work was needed on the apostolate, as well as on the complex issues of government and formation, which were still far from resolved. All convents were asked to form small study groups to discuss these topics over the coming months. The groups would then feed their findings into a series of one-day mini-Chapter meetings in spring–summer 1975, when individual sections of the new Constitutions would be written up and ratified.[61]

This was an entirely new style of Chapter, and it worked well. By the end of summer 1975, every issue had been agreed and a final version of the Constitutions drawn up. The greatest changes were in the section on 'the apostolate'. Though education remained the Sisters' main work, the new rubric specified that the term should be understood in its broadest sense, and that they must be prepared to 'adapt to meet the needs of the times' to take on 'any work', especially for the poor and underprivileged. In doing so they must be ready to co-operate with other religious and with the laity, and even 'as far as possible' with local authority social work departments. They were to avail themselves of secular training courses and acquire up-to-date techniques. Only those 'spiritually and psychologically suited and pro-fessionally trained' should be sent abroad, and they should constantly strive to deepen their understanding of those they served by acquainting them-selves with their language, culture and customs. This last instruction was prompted by the experience of more than one Sister who had been sent to Africa young, wide-eyed and unprepared, by a Congregation itself without a specialist missionary pedigree.[62]

At the end of the summer term the Dennistoun private school was finally closed. The decision was taken by Chapter with regret and only after much debate and prayer. The fact that the members voted to convert the building from a private school into a home for women in distress said everything about their changing vision of the apostolate.[63]

Charlotte Street had perhaps never been stronger, nor its reputation higher, than in the early 1970s. Sr Felicitas Bradley (Plates 25 and 32) had been appointed to the headship while still in her thirties and had now been in charge for eighteen years. She was in the great tradition of Charlotte Street heads, highly respected and perhaps even a little feared by the education authority, and had raised standards to their highest level ever. In 1972 the pupils had taken eight of the top fifty places in the Glasgow University bursary examination. But it was probably when in public that they were seen at their best, a winning mix of impeccable behaviour and bonhomie, whether at the annual prize-giving at the city halls (Plate 27), the monthly exodus to St Alphonsus' for 'first Friday' confessions, or when the entire school took the chartered Clyde steamer for the day to Millport.

But in August 1974 they returned to a school that had been made com-prehensive overnight. This involved amalgamation with the girls' classes of St Mary's junior secondary, the non-selective school of the inner east end. St Mary's had endured numerous problems in its latter years[64] and built itself an unenviable name. The last of the city's junior secondary schools, it was an anachronism as far as possible ignored by the authorities. A hardy minority of its staff laboured to retain standards, but the children, most of them good girls at heart, learned little in it but wildness.

Thus, suddenly, perhaps the best Catholic school for girls in Glasgow was joined to one of the worst, with resentment on both sides and everyone housed together in the motley cramped Charlotte Street buildings, hastily extended for the purpose. There was a real danger that the work of generations would go under. Sister judged that the public parts of the school, the stairs and corridors, would be the key to the outcome. For the whole first week the entire staff occupied the staircases like a file of police, corralling the girls into line. By the Friday they could barely stand, but they had won. Discipline remained to the fore that autumn, and just before the October break a retreat was organised for the whole school. The break was the watershed. After it there were still occasional flashpoints, but Charlotte Street remained Charlotte Street. Gradually the new girls forgot their resentment and accepted the order and the uniforms, with the cost of which the school assisted many of them.[65] The staff for their part sought to make them welcome, and to adapt their curricula and methods to the new needs.

The pro-life organisation 'The Innocents' had been founded in Merryland Street, the home of the Franciscan Minoresses who ran St Francis' maternity home, and within two years it had opened several branches in Glasgow as well as others in Greenock, Kilmarnock and Clydebank. It was in 1973, when she was still working for Sanctuary, that Sr Rosaria McGeady had her first contact with the organisation. One day the cook arrived and gave the staff news of her daughter's pregnancy. The girl was unmarried and her mother was pressing her to seek an abortion. Rosaria introduced the daughter to The Innocents, who persuaded her to defy her mother and keep the baby.

In autumn 1975 the senate of priests of the Motherwell diocese asked Bishop Thomson to take an initiative not simply to oppose abortion but to offer practical help to pregnant women in need. In response he appointed Fr Hugh Kelly to chair a committee of professional lay people to set up and run a diocesan pro-life service. Fr Kelly affiliated this body to The Innocents, who already had practical experience in the work.[66]

The following spring, the bishop contacted Mother Gabriel to enquire whether she could spare two Sisters to staff a new Innocents' house that Fr Kelly was planning to open. Remembering her experience of three years before, Sr Rosaria volunteered.[67] The house in question was the former St Patrick's presbytery in Coatbridge, and when she and Sr Maria Goretti moved in that autumn the building had no furniture, carpets or heating. They appealed for donations and received so much furniture that they had to make several bonfires of the surplus. They also recruited volunteer counsellors and organised training sessions for them led by doctors, nurses and lawyers. They themselves were on call twenty-four hours a day, relieved from time to time by the volunteers. Fr Kelly offered his services as chaplain, a post he has held ever since.

The Sisters had room enough to offer residential accommodation to six girls waiting to have babies. Some had been put out of their houses by their parents; others had concealed their pregnancies; several had been abandoned by the baby's father. Whoever they were they were taken in, irrespective of their religion and without judgment, and given caring support until they and their babies could move on. The work was unfunded and depended entirely on donations.

Fr Desmond Maguire's experience in organising his four youth clubs for the mentally handicapped had brought home to him just how great the need was. He estimated that there were up to three hundred young people in the Glasgow archdiocese who could benefit from such support, many of whom had never been contacted. Early in 1976 Bishop Renfrew circulated the city's religious communities on his behalf, appealing for Sisters able to give a few hours a week to visit potential club members at home and encourage them to join the clubs.[68] Mother Gabriel notified the Congregation's two Glasgow convents and invited volunteers, setting an example by volunteering herself. From among the names received, she chose Srs Gertrude Shields and Bernadette Gill.

With the growing demand the number of clubs increased, but it was becoming clear that parents as well as the young people needed support. Speaking one day to a mother who had left her autistic son in Dumfries for a short 'parents' respite' holiday, it struck the bishop how helpful it would be if such breaks could be provided nearer home. He began making enquiries. Among his contacts was Sr Agnes of the Sisters of St Joseph of Cluny, headmistress of her Order's Regina Mundi School in Mitre Road, Jordanhill and already a supporter of the clubs. Above the school was a flat which she thought might answer his needs. Sr Gertrude was put in charge of it and had it renovated and fitted to accommodate two young people every second weekend. The carers who stayed with them were themselves teenagers, carefully chosen and trusted, and they proved a wonderful asset. Energetic, fun-loving and unsentimental, they brought their often noisy charges to Mitre House on Friday evenings and back home on Sunday nights on crowded buses without the least self-consciousness.

In February 1977 Bishop Renfrew enquired as to the possibility of the Congregation moving into Possilpark to undertake parish and social work in one of Glasgow's areas of greatest deprivation. Council agreed to release three Sisters for the task as soon as premises could be found. In the footsteps of Adélaide, Veronica and many since their time, they were again choosing the 'poorest of Glasgow's poor'. In his letter of thanks Archbishop Winning declared himself delighted and grateful, and certain that they would 'do tremendous work for God' among the most needy.[69] At the time Council thought that the work would be only temporary, but in fact the Sisters have remained in Possilpark ever since, fully justifying the archbishop's faith, and their commitment has grown over the years until today it is their main house in Scotland and their centre for the Congregation worldwide.

Mother Gabriel had remained on the executive of the British Association of Franciscan Sisters of the Third Order Regular. Since 1973 the Association had been arranging refresher courses at the newly opened Franciscan Study Centre in Canterbury, and these courses had brought its members into contact with members of the men's Congregations studying there. When representatives of the latter, including the Friars Minor, Conventuals, Capuchins and Third Order, met in March 1973 to prepare for the 750th anniversary of the first Franciscans' arrival in Britain, they invited a member of the Sisters' association onto the organising committee.[70] All those involved recognised that this collaboration of male and female, and of the various branches of Franciscanism so long divided, was a historic milestone. 'Please God,' the minute recorded, 'we are at the beginning of something great.'[71]

These developments in Britain were part of a worldwide drawing together of the long-separated Franciscan family at this time. Within it, the Congregations of the Third Order Regular were themselves drawing together and discerning their common purpose. By returning to their roots in obedience to the Vatican Council, they were rediscovering the distinct and unifying charism that Francis had planned for them as an Order of Penance within his wider movement.

Superiors of the men's Third Order Congregations had been holding international congresses since 1950 on matters of common interest. The most recent had taken place in Madrid in 1974 on the theme 'The Rule of the Third Order', and in view of its crucial importance they invited the women's Congregations to participate for the first time. Before adjourning, the delegates appointed a commission, with male and female equally represented, to draw up a provisional Statement of Franciscan Penitential Life that they hoped would form the basis of a new Rule acceptable to all.[72]

With their consciousness of the global Franciscan family heightened by the experience of Madrid, the women's Congregations established an international commission of Franciscan Sisters in 1976. The new body sponsored its first conference that autumn for the purpose of finding common ground among the various Rules being developed in different parts of the world. It was attended by eighty delegates from nineteen countries, including Srs Felicitas, Dolores and Annunciata representing the Franciscan Sisters of the Immaculate Conception.[73]

In the same spirit, the Congregation in Scotland was now seeking every opportunity for collaboration with others: with fellow Franciscans at the annual Franciscan Day and wherever possible between-times; with other religious, notably in a programme of 'spiritual evenings' first established in 1977; and increasingly with the laity through its new apostolates.[74]

In January 1978 seven Sisters moved from Merrylee to the Dennistoun convent, and two months later three more transferred to Possilpark when the new house opened there. Merrylee was emptying, and there were rumours that its very future was in doubt. Not only had it become a financial drain, the justification of owning such a property had been questioned at the 1974 Chapter as being contrary to the Franciscan spirit of poverty.[75] It was also well known that the archdiocese was anxious to acquire it for use as a seminary.

In summer 1978 Mother Gabriel personally visited all the Scottish convents to discuss the issue, and invited the Sisters to submit their views to her before the next Council meeting. Their replies revealed a sharply divided Congregation. Feelings were strongest among those opposed to closure, who very naturally wanted to hold onto something that had been their life for so long. 'A disaster', 'the last straw', 'fatal to the continuance of our Order', 'many hearts are being broken' were typical comments. Those who supported the sale of Merrylee did so on practical grounds as 'the only realistic step' or, as one expressed it, because as Franciscans their commitment should be to Christ and the needs of the Church, not to buildings.[76]

Council met on 14 September. The replies were read, and after much prayer and long debate the vote was taken. It came out 4:1 for closure. Mother Gabriel communicated the result to every Sister by individual letter. 'Let us all,' she urged, 'now that the decision has been taken, accept it in good faith and help to make it work.'[77] But feelings were running too high for that. Her predecessor, Mother Philippa, was so upset that she took the matter personally to Bishop Renfrew. The wound would never really heal until some had passed on.

In January 1979 the older Sisters were given the opportunity to move to the community of their choice. On 18 April the convent was handed over to the archdiocese, from whom the Congregation had purchased a new, smaller home in Park Circus.

Their lawyers had recommended accepting £500,000 for Merrylee, a figure far below its true value, but Council had reduced the asking price to £300,000 since the buyer was the Church. At the same time they agreed to pay £200,000 for the Park Circus property, leaving themselves with a derisory profit of £100,000 and a new home that bore no comparison to the old.

Financially it was a disastrous transaction, brought about perhaps by misunderstanding on both sides. The archdiocese may have believed that finance was not a priority issue for the Congregation. And Council, none of whose members was trained in Canon Law, could not have been aware of the Church's rules on a religious Congregation's stewardship of its material patrimony. Nor perhaps did they foresee that as vocations dried up and the community grew too old to be salary-earning, financial prudence would become a life-and-death issue for them. For a Congregation whose wealth until recently had been such as to breed a certain carelessness, the sale was a financial body blow from which it would never fully recover.[78]

January 1977 was the coldest on record at Renovo, with night temperatures often falling to −32°C. The hill town was virtually cut off for weeks, and the river remained frozen until March. That summer three of the Sisters moved to Altoona to open a new house there and take charge of the local Mount Carmel School. Altoona was a railroad town, with picture postcards of the distant Alleghenies and giant locomotives hauling incredibly long trains on the famed Horseshoe Curve close by. It had seen better days, but some of the old railroad repair shops remained open, remnants of its former importance. The parish had been run by Franciscans of the Third Order for more than a hundred years.

Sr Martina Morgan took over a school that had been allowed to slide into decline and was dubbed 'the zoo' by local residents. She at once set about instilling some firm Scottish order by policing the classrooms and corridors, to such effect that before the year was out 'the zoo' was forgotten and the locals had coined a new name for the school – 'Scotland Yard'. The parents loved her for it.[79]

The reputation of St Joseph's Renovo had also been growing steadily. Academic standards had risen, the parents had voted to introduce uniforms, and there were plans to add a 7th and an 8th grade to the exsiting six. But finance continued to set a ceiling on progress. The hopes that America's Catholic schools had harboured in the early 1970s for generous state subsidies had been dashed by the Supreme Court,[80] leaving them entirely dependent on fees and private fundraising. Most of them, especially in communities like Renovo, had continued to keep their fees low in order to remain within the reach of working-class families, but this set limits on their resources and the calibre of teacher they could attract. As parental aspirations rose, they could only maintain their popularity by raising standards; yet this was only possible by raising their fees beyond the reach of those they sought to serve.

Renovo endured another ferocious winter in 1979 when snow frustrated the best efforts of the ploughs and sealed the town off completely. Rumours abounded that spring that the fees at St Joseph's were to be raised, as a result of which a number of children transferred to the local public school and only ten new pupils enrolled in August. The principal gave an assurance that the fees would remain at $50 per annum, and the parents rallied to raise funds. But the parish could not sustain the losses indefinitely. In November Sister Gabriel announced that she would be withdrawing the Sisters at the end of the academic year.

In January 1980 one of them, Sr Ninian McLaughlin, transferred to the Altoona convent in order to take up the principalship of St Mary's in nearby Holidaysburg. When the rest followed in June they left St Joseph's in impeccable order for their successors. It was their wish to depart quietly, but the PTA put on a surprise farewell party for them to which the town turned out in gratitude and affection.

Commissions were appointed in autumn 1979 to seek the views of the Congregation one last time on the issues which had been the subject of trial for the past dozen years and, based on these, to draw up final draft Constitutions for the 1980 Chapter. In this they were assisted by Fr Raffaele Pazzelli, one of the Church's foremost experts in the field, whose presence before and during the Chapter was to prove crucial to its success.[81]

The seven *ex officio* members and fourteen elected delegates convened at Falcarragh on 1 July. It was the first time ever that a Chapter had been held outside Glasgow, and the significance of the venue was recognised by all. The Sisters no longer had a mother house, as under the old monastic régime. Falcarragh symbolised decentralisation, their growing international apostolate and their commitment to the future.

The members spent the first week in retreat before the Chapter proper opened on 8 July. They all understood that this was the last chance to produce the new permanent Constitutions required by Rome. Mother Gabriel controlled the agenda firmly, addressing each article in turn, allowing only relevant discussion and pressing on to a vote. Through her skill, the good preparatory work of the commissions and Fr Pazzelli's expertise, the 'whittling down' process went surprisingly swiftly and consensus was achieved on every issue within four working days.[82]

She then halted the agenda for elections. Her lieutenant for the past twelve years, Sr Felicitas Bradley, was appointed to succeed her and now took the chair. The final three days were devoted to drawing the articles into a single document, approving it and tidying up minor matters. A committee of three was appointed to write up the approved version for presentation to the Sacred Congregation for Religious. It was expected that Rome's response would arrive early in 1981, giving time for any required emendments before final approval at a reconvened plenary session in April.[83] Their business now concluded, Chapter adjourned.

Mother Gabriel's work was done. She had led the Congregation through the stormiest years in its history. Under her predecessors the Sisters' lives had seemed changeless, but in her time they had been buffeted by change upon change. They had been called upon to face whatever new came their way; to jettison the old and embrace the unfamiliar; to renew more strongly their original option for the poor, now not merely for the poor but with them; to give up their securities and certainties, and for their lovely mother house substitute small temporary homes and an uncertain future. To cope with these external changes, they had been required to make an inner change of heart: to empty themselves, let go, trust from year to year, even from day to day. All these things had been asked of them, some of them in the late autumn of their lives. And all, of course, were exactly and entirely in the spirit of St Francis.

Their retiring leader understood this. She also knew that they were now setting out upon uncharted waters. As she entrusted the helm to her successor, her parting words recalled the recent storms and looked forward to the voyage ahead, with the same serenity and faith in providence that she was counting on from them: 'Sisters . . . you have heard of the events of the past years; these are now with God. Let us go forward in trust, accepting His love and care each day. The future is in His hands. Could there be better?'

ENDNOTES TO CHAPTER EIGHT

1 Special General Chapter, 1968, 'Appointment of Commissions', 030.33, AF.
2 Mother Gabriel to Fr Bernard Ransing CSC, 6.11.1969. 030.33, AF. The appointments were delayed until November partly because Sr Felicitas Bradley, who was to play an important part in organising the programme, could not be released from her post as headmistress of Charlotte Street until that month. Each commission was made up of 5–9 members, including at least one with experience as a local Superior.
3 Responses to commission questionnaires, spring 1969, 030.31, AF. Specific examples of openness to current needs included working in the new housing schemes and use of the convent buildings by the laity.
4 Findings of the commissions, April 1969, 030.33, AF.
5 Michael Foylan, secretary of the Episcopal Conference, to Mother Gabriel, 16.2.1968, 071.01, AF. SCIAF was still at this time under the direct control of the Bishops' Conference in regard to decisions on funding.
6 Sr Emmanuel Gallagher interview. She also persuaded the ship's captain to waive the charge for her cargo.
7 House Reports to Chapter, 1968, Ilesa, Oyo, Osogbo, 030.33, AF.
8 *Journey So Far*, Ibadan 2000, p. 95. Despite the success of Otan it was closed on 3 March 1969 and the novitiate transferred to Oyo, a town where there

were already facilities for training teachers and nurses. It was felt that as more young Nigerian Sisters came through it would be useful to have them together in one location.

9 Council Meeting Minutes, 27.4.1969 and 10.12.1970, 034.10, no. 2, AF.

10 Council Meeting Minutes, 4.5.1969, 1.6.1969 and 24.8.1969; and Sr Emmanuel Gallagher interview, upon which the following two paragraphs are also based.

11 Of the five habits presented, that with scapular effect was favoured on the first ballot – Secret Vote on Habit, 030.31, AF. Mother Gabriel made her proposal for new commissions and reconvening of the Chapter on the recommendation of Fr Joseph Magee OFM, Superior of the friary at South Ascot, whose advice she had sought – Fr Joseph Magee to Mother Gabriel, 14.10.1969; and Mother Gabriel to Fr Magee, 21.10.1969, both 030.33, AF.

12 Mother Gabriel to Fr Bernard Ransing CSC, Sacred Congregation for Religious, 6.11.1969, 030.33, AF. She visited Rome from 21–28 November and discussed both the matters concluded and the outstanding issues with him. The two Commissions were appointed immediately upon her return – Council Meeting Minutes, 30.11.1969.

13 Chapter notes, Register of Elections, October 1969, 028.2, AF.

14 Sr Dolores Cochrane interview.

15 Findings of the Commissions, Poverty Commission Statement, 1969, 030.33, AF.

16 Sr Angela McFaul interview.

17 Council Meeting Minutes, 7.3.1971; and 'Capitular Acts of the Second Session of the Special General Chapter to Serve as our Constitutions until the Chapter of 1974', Sept.–Oct. 1970, issued with covering letter October 1971, 030.43, AF.

18 *Perfectae Caritatis*, §§ 22 and 23.

19 The Association was based on an American model, the *Federation of Franciscan Sisters of USA*, formed in 1966 – cf. Federation of Franciscan Sisters of USA, *Statutes*, n.d., copy 072.01, AF. The initiative for the English–Welsh Association had come from Sr Michael Alexander, Superior of the Franciscan Abbey of St Mary in Mill Hill, London, who was herself American. Re its foundation – Association of Franciscan Female Congregations, report of exploratory meeting, 18.3.1970, 072.01, AF. The meeting was attended by Cardinal Heenan, himself a Franciscan tertiary and an advocate of confederation. Those present resisted the concept of a Federation on the American model, fearing that it could be restrictive of the autonomy of their Congregations, and voted instead for a more loose Association.

20 Mother Gabriel to Sr Michael Alexander, 12.10.1970, 072.01, AF. Some of the other Franciscan Congregations in Scotland knew of the English–Welsh association because they themselves were English-based.

21 Association minute of meeting of 25.11.1970, 072.01, AF. In its first year the association began the publication of a newsletter, organised an annual retreat and Franciscan Day, and published its Statutes.

22 Except where otherwise stated the present account is based on Sr Benedicta Collins and Miss Susan McCormick interviews, and Sr Benedicta letter to the author, 16.9.2003, which includes detailed information supplied by Mrs Dempsey, the MP's widow.

23 Sr Benedicta Collins interview. James Dempsey told her personally that when he and others asked Bishop Thomson 'straight' which option he favoured, this was the reply they received.

24 Mother Gabriel to Edward Taylor MP, 24.6.1971; and Taylor to Mother Gabriel, 26.7.1971; both 044.11, AF. As well as being Secretary of State for Scotland, Taylor was MP for Cathcart, whose constituency included Merrylee.

25 Mother Gabriel to Mgr Samuel Kilpatrick, Archdiocesan Chancellor, 24.6.1971, 071.01, AF.

26 Mgr Kilpatrick (on behalf of Archbishop Scanlon) to Mother Gabriel, 2.7.1971, 071.01, AF.

27 Sr Angela McFaul interview.

28 The present account based largely on Sr Gertrude Shields and Sr Kevin Breen interviews.

29 Sr Stanislaus airmail to Mother Gabriel, 18.7.1971, 071.01, AF.

30 Mother Gabriel to Archbishop Scanlon, Renovo, 27.7.1971, 071.01, AF. Re Dennistoun – Mother Gabriel to Mgr Kilpatrick, 1.4.1971; and response, 5.4.1971; both 071.01, AF.

31 Bishop Ward to Mother Gabriel, 3.8.1971, 071.01, AF.

32 Fr James Watters to Mother Gabriel, n.d., 071.01, AF. It was a rule of Renfrewshire EA that no promoted teacher could be considered for another promoted position unless the teacher had been in post for at least three years.

33 Sr Baptist Henry continued to teach in St Lawrence's until 1974, at which date the school moved into a new building in Ingleston Street.

34 St Joseph's Renovo Log, 1971, AF.

35 Council Meeting Minutes, 7.3.1971.

36 Council Meeting Minutes, 28.9.1968, 30.11.1968 and 28.2.1972. Council also discussed the possibility of funding a visit to Assisi for all Sisters professed twenty-five years or more.

37 Re petty cash, Merrylee Chapter Minutes, 4.3.1973, 2.10.1973 and 30.11.1973; re the Great Silence, Council Meeting Minutes, 16.12.1968; re daytime silence, Merrylee Chapter Meetings, 2.2.1973, 30.11.1973 and 3.2.1974; all 040.13, AF.

38 Merrylee Chapter Meetings, 1972 to May 1973. The 'monastic' term 'Chapter Meeting' still used at this time shows that despite the changes the thinking still hearkened back to the traditional. It was not changed to 'Community Meeting' until 1976.

39 Cf. *Perfectae Caritatis*, § 20.

40 Sanctuary Association *Newsletter* no. 2, May 1975; *Sanctuary* magazine no. 4, 1975; Press Release, n.d. but late autumn 1975; Sr Rosaria McGeady interview.

41 This and much of the following paragraph based on Sr Gertrude Shields interview. Jean Vannier is renowned for his work with the mentally handicapped, and is founder of *L'Arche*.

42 Merrylee Report to 1974 Chapter, 030.33, AF; and Council Meeting Minutes, 7.2.1971.

43 Re Sr Agnes, *Obituary Book*, entry 219; re the parish initiative, Merrylee Chapter Minutes, 18.9.1972 and 3.11.1972, 040.13, AF, and Merrylee Report to 1974 Chapter, 030.33, AF.

44 Generalate Report, 1980 Chapter, 030.41, AF, which stresses the radical nature of the new-style apostolate.

45 The parish of Kilsyth forms a far-western spur of St Andrew's and Edinburgh diocese jutting into Glasgow territory. It was therefore necessary to gain the permission of both Ordinaries. Cardinal Gray gladly gave it his blessing, having heard from the parish priest of the 'splendid work' that the Sisters were doing – Cardinal Gray to Mother Gabriel, 4.9.1973, and Mother Gabriel to Cardinal Gray, 16.9.1973, 071.01, AF. Archbishop Scanlon contacted Mother Gabriel through his Assistant Bishop Ward, informing her that he was prepared to sanction it despite the problems of staffing 'another new convent', provided that she could give a guarantee that the Congregation's work in Glasgow would not suffer – Bishop Ward to Mother Gabriel, 6.9.1973, 071.01, AF.

46 Sr M. Agnes Delany, Superior Kilsyth, to Cardinal Gray, 21.8.1979, DE 170/165, SCA.

47 Generalate Report to 1974 Chapter, 030.33, AF.

48 Re novices – Sr Loyola Kelly interview; re vocations – Council Meeting Minutes, 30.11.1968, 24.9.1970 and 18.10.1970. With the fall in vocations, the Congregation turned again to Ireland. The original purpose of Falcarragh had been somewhat neglected as the community had spent its energies on an ever-expanding school. But in 1973 the local education authority amalgamated the school with its local boys' counterpart and placed a priest in charge of the combined school. The Sisters continued to run the school hostel for girls from the islands. The change gave them the chance to devote more time to promoting a vocations drive. From January 1973 the Congregation was also represented at meetings of UNISON, the newly formed Dublin-based national body for vocations.

49 Sr Loyola Kelly interview.

50 *Journey So Far*, p. 77. Sr Callista died on 10.11.1969. Also, Council Meeting Minutes, 10.9.1972; and 1974 Chapter Document, Report from the Missions, 030.33, AF.

51 *Journey So Far*, p. 63.

52 1974 Chapter Document, Report from the Missions. The date of their profession was 4 October. Sr Monica left the Congregation in 1983, and Sr Cecilia later transferred to a diocesan community.

53 Mother Gabriel circular letter to the parents of Merrylee and Bothwell schools, 9.2.1971, 044.11, AF.

54 Council Meeting Minutes, 9.12.1973; and Merrylee Report to 1974 Chapter.

55 Council Meeting Minutes, 3.2.1974. Prior to the relaxation of the rules, the only two permitted venues for the annual summer holiday were Merrylee and Saltcoats. After the changing of the rules, Saltcoats ceased to be used and was given to Charlotte Street school as an outdoor centre but was latterly put to little use.

56 Re James Dempsey's advice – Sr Benedicta Collins letter to the author, 16.9.2003, including information given to Sr Benedicta by Mr Dempsey's widow. Re the Council decision, Council Meeting Minutes, 3.3.1974.

57 Mother Gabriel to Sr Benedicta, 5.3.1974, 044.11, AF.

58 Sr Benedicta remained unaware of the reason and the advice given by James Dempsey for thirty years, only finding out about them after contacting Mrs Dempsey in 2003 while making enquiries on my behalf.

59 Sr Benedicta to Mother Gabriel, 18.3.1974; and same to Dr John McEwan, Director of Education Lanarkshire EA, 18.3.1974; both 044.11, AF. And *Hamilton Advertiser*, 31.5.1974.

60 'Draft Proposals for Revision of Capitular Acts (1971) Drawn up for 1974 Special General Chapter . . . to Serve as Constitutions until the Chapter of 1980', 030.43, AF.

61 1974 Chapter Document, 030.33, AF.

62 Chapter Meetings Minutes, 8.2.1975, 15–16.3.1975, 7.5.1975 and 15.6.1975, 030.33, AF.

63 Mother Gabriel to Archbishop Winning, 17.3.1975, 071.01, AF; and General Report to 1980 Chapter, 030.41, AF. In fact, at the request of the archbishop, the building was handed over for local parish use. The house at nearby 2 Broompark Circus was sold to the Marist Brothers.

64 Among the problems it suffered were a change of catchment, split site, high staff turnover, a wholesale removal and a hutted annexe.

65 Sr Felicitas Bradley interview.

66 The proposal had been put to the senate of priests by Mgr Philip Flanagan, who had been appointed parish priest of Sacred Heart Bellshill in 1967, the year of the Abortion Act. His parish was responsible for the largest maternity hospital in the county. Fr Kelly was chosen to head the work because he was at the time Mgr Flanagan's curate at Sacred Heart.

67 The present account based on Sr Rosaria McGeady interview, *The Innocents' Story* (Glasgow, n.d.), and *The Society of the Innocents, Lanarkshire, Silver Jubilee 1977–2002* (Hamilton, 2002). Sr Rosaria had resigned from the presidency of Sanctuary in 1975 because of her commitments on the Congregation's Council and as secretary to Mother Gabriel.

68 Bishop Renfrew to Mother Gabriel, circular letter, 3.2.1976, 071. 01, AF. The bishop had been appointed the archdiocese's Vicar Episcopal for Religious in 1974. The rest of the present account is based on Sr Gertrude Shields interview.

69 Mother Gabriel to Archbishop Winning, 23.2.1977, and Archbishop Winning to Mother Gabriel, 28.2.1977, 071.01, AF.

70 Association of the Franciscan Sisters of the Third Order Regular of England and Wales, AGM minutes, 27.5.1972; Committee Meeting minutes, 12.7.1972; and Association Meeting minutes, 2.3.1973; all 072.01, AF.

71 Minute of the 750th Anniversary Organising Committee, 2.12.1973, enclosed with Association Meeting minutes, 072.01, AF.

72 For an account of the background, the Congresses of 1950, 1955 and 1961 and the 1974 Congress itself, see Secondo G., TOR, *Analecta*, xiv, 1978, especially pp. 149ff. Rome had actually sought to unify all of the women's TOR groups as early as 1910, but the move had been vigorously resisted and abandoned – cf. Circular letter Archbishop Maguire 14.2.1910, and ditto D. Gabriel de Carolis, Assisi, 27.10.1910, RO8/38, AGA. The Scottish Congregation had voted unanimously against it.

73 On her return Sr Dolores gave a full report to the British Association and used material from the conference as the basis of a series of study meetings in Merrylee between spring 1977 and early 1978 – Association Meeting minutes, 29.1.1977, 072.01, AF; and Merrylee Community (previously 'Chapter') Meeting minutes, Oct. and Dec. 1977 and Feb. 1978, 040.13, AF.

74 The 'spiritual evenings' were at first held annually. Their themes were, significantly, 'The type of Religious Community than can hope to survive' (1977), and 'The Gospel without compromise in Religious Communities' (1978). Re links with the Lay Council – Circular letter Sr Mary Kilday, FMSJ, Merrylee, to Superiors of Communities, 27.9.1977, copy 071.01, AF.

75 General Report to 1980 Chapter, 030.41, AF. The original Merrylee House building had already been turned over for use as a diocesan ecumenical centre, following the 1974 Chapter.

76 Individual letters of response, Sept. 1978, 040.14, AF.

77 Sister Gabriel to all Sisters of the Congregation, 19.9.1978, 040.13, AF; and Sr Felicitas Bradley interview.

78 The archdiocese maintained that it had been granted permission by Rome to accept Merrylee as a gift, and that the greatly reduced purchase price was thus quite justified morally and in Canon Law.

79 Sr Kevin Breen interview. Re Renovo and Holidaysburg, St Joseph's Renovo Log, 1979–80, AF.

80 Government Acts 194 and 195 (1972) had provided grants for textbooks, equipment and ancillary services, but after objections that they were unconstitutional they were repealed following a ruling of the Supreme Court.

81 Re the consultation process – Preparation for the General Chapter of 1980, Questionnaires, 040.31, AF. Re Fr Pazzelli's importance – Sr Dolores Cochrane interview. Fr Pazzelli was Consultant to the BFI during its 'Rule' project (1979–82), Director of the TOR International Historical Commission, Definitor General of TOR (1977–89), and author of two seminal works on the Franciscan Third Order and Women's Congregations (see Bibliography).

82 Minutes of Chapter, 7.7.1980 (preliminary session), and 8–11.7.1980; 030.43, AF.

83 General Statutes, final 1980 draft; and Paper: 'The Implementation of the Decisions of the General Chapter', July 1980; both 030.43, AF. Three copies were sent to the Sacred Congregation in October. Sr M. Francis Campbell was elected Assistant General at the time of Sr Felicitas' election. It was necessary to leave one matter for the reconvened Chapter in April 1981: during the discussions it had become clear that formation (ongoing and lifelong) was the key to the renewal of the Congregation and the spiritual growth of every member. At Fr Pazzelli's suggestion, a special commission was appointed to study the literature on the issue, canvass the membership and produce a draft section for insertion into the Constitutions in April 1981. This was permissible, since the April 1981 meeting would in fact be the final plenary session of the 1980 Chapter. At the same time, in the cause of formation, Sr Dolores Cochrane was commissioned to research and write a biography of the foundresses/history of the Congregation.

PART FOUR

Water

Be praised, my Lord, through Sister Water,
Who is most useful and humble,
Precious and chaste.

St Francis, *Canticle of the Creatures*

CHAPTER NINE

Return to the Well Spring (1980–1998)

The election of Sr Felicitas to the office of Superior General meant her giving up the headship of Charlotte Street. Upon her retirement her years of outstanding service to education were recognised by the award of an OBE and the Papal Cross 'Pro Ecclesia et Pontifice'. The Congregation now faced the tricky question of finding a successor. When she had been appointed, it had been merely a matter of the abbess putting her name forward to the education authority, who had accepted it virtually automatically. This was no longer the case, as Strathclyde EA now insisted on open competition for all its posts.

The Church authorities fully supported this policy, and the Sisters themselves were not opposed to it. In the early 1970s they had in fact reached an agreement with the hierarchy that they should make way for lay applicants for headships where possible. They had agreed to this not out of duress but by conviction, having always seen it as their task to produce good lay teachers who would in time take over their mantle. They had already relinquished the headships of four schools – St Mary's Calton in 1970 (after 104 years), St Lawrence's Greenock and St Patrick's Anderston in 1971 after 97 and 115 years respectively, and now in this year of the Chapter, 1980, the Sacred Heart in Bridgeton after 106 years.

These had been parish schools. But Our Lady and St Francis' was their own school and their creation, and giving up the headship would be a far greater wrench. Whatever their views in general, they would have preferred to keep it if they could. But in fact that summer they had no-one available with the necessary qualifications and Scottish experience for such a crucial, prestigious and demanding post.[1] A lay appointment was therefore inevitable, and they could only hope it would be one that would be in keeping with all that they had built.

They were delighted when the EA appointed Mrs Alice Felletti, since she was already assistant headteacher and her qualities were well known. An honours graduate in languages and a very able teacher and leader, she was not Franciscan-educated but could be expected to maintain the school's ethos while at the same time bringing to it a fresh experience and vision. Her predecessor was a hard act to follow, to be sure, but (in the words of a close associate) she 'coped wonderfully well'. Looking back today, Sr Felicitas herself believes that the appointment could not have been better.[2]

The 1980 Chapter had highlighted a worrying decline in new recruits in Scotland and Ireland and the need for specialist vocations directors in each country. The appointments were made in September: Sr Patricia Coyle for Ireland and Sr Francis Campbell for Scotland.[3]

Council were conscious of the need for care when recruiting and of the danger of unsuitable vocations. They knew that the religious life can sometimes attract the wrong kind of person, women temperamentally unsuited to community life or who join for the wrong reasons. They knew of past cases in their own Congregation of girls entering by 'their mother's vocation', and even of simple-minded girls being placed in the convent by their families in order to be looked after. Once a girl was accepted it was hard to refuse her proceeding to profession and all too tempting to 'let her through' from a misplaced sense of charity and a reluctance to dash her young hopes. But the effect could be disastrous for the girl and damaging for the Congregation, whether she stayed or left, with the prospect of protracted and acrimonious dispute and perhaps the heavy financial burden of providing for her if she was later laicised.

It was partly for this reason that in 1975 Council raised the age of application to eighteen and also made changes in the process of formation. Previously formation had consisted of a six-month postulancy followed by two years of novitiate and three of temporary profession, the new Sister spending the whole period in the novice house and not joining the community until after her final vows. The process gave her no experience of 'real' community life or of the Congregation's public work upon which to base her final decision. Under the new dispensation, the period of postulancy was to be flexible and her progress and suitability carefully monitored. It was followed by a novitiate lasting two years, the first a 'spiritual year', the second spent gaining practical experience in one of the convent communities. Subsequent temporary profession was to last five years, again spent in community and involving two separate vows. The whole process was to be flexible and tailored to individual needs. It promised to offer a far more relevant formation and a realistic opportunity to test one's vocation before making a permanent commitment.[4]

Gradually, also, the leadership were becoming aware that a Sister's need for support was lifelong. In the past, 'problems' had been thought of as weaknesses and a matter to be solved privately. As a consequence, much had been left hidden or swept under the carpet, and the result had sometimes been pain and guilt. Now it was coming to be recognised that more could and should be done to offer support when problems inevitably arose, both by providing individual ongoing formation and, more generally, by simply listening and talking.

The work of Mitre House had made a deep impression upon the Glasgow social work department, who in autumn 1980 approached Fr Maguire with a view to his opening a second, larger home. Having no suitable property for the project he persuaded the housing department to release a block of four council flats in Househillwood on the south-west edge of the city, which were at the time empty and undergoing refurbishment (Plate 28). Knowing Sr Gertrude's previous work he invited her to run the new home. She was already happily employed in teaching and, reluctant to agree yet unwilling to disappoint him, referred the decision to her new Superior General. To her horror Mother Felicitas agreed for her.

While 'Assisi House' was being made ready, Sr Gertrude learned all she could about her new kind of work by visiting the city's three schools for the profoundly handicapped and the adult centres run by the charity Enable.[5] She received the keys in June 1981 and welcomed the first residents in August. The four flats had been knocked into one. The two on the ground floor provided bedroom, bathroom and dining facilities for nine residents; upstairs, one flat provided round-the-clock living space for herself and Sr Helena, and the other an office and daytime accommodation for the volunteer helpers.

The volunteers were crucial, for without them the house could not possibly have run full-time. The Sisters were able to offer weekday residence in addition to the weekend breaks, which as well as giving parents a respite prepared some of the young people for long-term residential care. The staff were able to offer them experiences that would otherwise have been denied to them: football and swimming, visits to the sports centre, the fire station, a local farm, and concerts at Bellarmine secondary school. The Sisters knew the importance of fun and stimulation to these young minds, and always made a point of finding out their personal interests, despite the huge difficulties of communication.

Because Househillwood was designated an area of multiple deprivation, the project benefited from Scottish Office funding. The same source also part-funded a third house acquired by Fr Maguire for the Congregation in Tollcross in 1983 and run by Sr Bernard McAtamney.[6] It was on the same pattern as the Househillwood property, a block of four flats knocked into one, with the ground floor adapted to accommodate nine young people who (it was assumed) could not possibly cope with stairs. It was only after one of them raided the Sisters' first-floor flat that the staff realised that some of them had more ability than supposed. It was a turning point. Thereafter, every opportunity was sought to 'push' them in small ways to realise their potential and develop latent skills.

When shortly afterwards a parks department cottage in Eastbank Street in Shettleston became vacant, the city council agreed to lease it to the Sisters. A ramp was installed and the premises refurbished to accommodate three of the Tollcross residents judged capable of coping with greater independence. The house still had to be permanently manned, but the night staff were able to sleep in rather than remaining on full duty. The new project proved a remarkable success. Through patient care, support and stimulation, young people who might otherwise have remained confined to the high-dependency Lennox Castle hospital were now living relatively independent lives and coping well.

One boy, 'Andy', epitomised the success of all. He had come to Assisi House unable to speak, communicating only by moving his contorted limbs and face. At first he often trashed his room in frustration and rage. But in time he was able to move to Eskbank Street, and eventually he enrolled in Wheatley College. When Sr Bernard visited him there he pointed to his jacket and let her understand that she should look in the pocket. There she found his student card, his great pride. He grinned as he motioned her to take a seat, insisting on going up to the canteen hatch to order lunch for the two of them.

After the army took control in Nigeria in 1975, the Congregation's Fatima hospital had been integrated into the state health service.[7] In 1980 the military stood down and an elected government took power. Sr Emmanuel and her staff were now able to provide free treatment for the first time, paid for by the state, and for a while the people benefited. But by 1983 the government funds had run out and the system fell into decline. It was a time of frustration for the Sisters, who were bound by the state but could get no effective support from it. When equipment broke down they would send it to the appropriate authority only for it to be returned weeks later labelled 'out of order'. They did what they could to keep up standards from their own slender means, beautifying the grounds with flowers and decorating every ward in a different style.

Sr Emmanuel had rescued her first abandoned baby in 1963 but it was around 1980 that such rescue became a regular part of her work (Plate 29). One cause may have been the new importance given to girls' education, for most of the mothers abandoning their babies were schoolgirls unwilling to give up their studies. Whenever the police had babies handed in to them they would bring them to the Sisters, who gave them care, medical attention and love. Emmanuel insisted that every baby was cuddled and given regular human contact, and it was well known that her staff would be forgiven anything except 'lack of love'. She received generous donations from firms such as Ostermilk and even from the British High Commission. As the work became well known, local childless women would come in the hope of adopting. When the babies reached a year and were old enough to take solid food she let them go, if a relative or a suitable local person could be found for them.

Two whom she kept were Taju and Ayo (Plate 30). They were two of triplets whose mother had died in childbirth, at the same time as the third baby. No-one came forward to take them and at first they lived in the hospital. When they reached school age they were enrolled free of charge with the Sisters at St Clare's, and went to live with one of the teachers. They continued under the care of the Congregation into their teen years. At the age of seventeen they were both involved in a road accident while travelling by bus to Lagos, and tragically Ayo was killed. Taju survived, though who knows the effect upon him of losing a second triplet. He continued his education nonetheless, and is today studying for a degree at a German university.[8]

In 1982 the local *oba* (king) called Sr Emmanuel to his palace to confer on her the title of chieftain in recognition of her work, and naming her 'mother of all the children who did not die'. She arrived not in her habit but in a lilac Yoruba costume bought for her by the *oba* to match the dresses of his four wives, and with beads upon her neck and wrists. The ceremony was witnessed by a great gathering of hospital staff and students, along with the bishop, priests and representatives of all the Christian churches. After it they all processed to the hospital for a reception. According to tradition, the staff had bought and killed a cow for the meal. At Emmanuel's request they all wore their own national costumes, and each group performed a national dance. The Filipinos weaved slow involved patterns while balancing glasses of wine on their palms, and a little Indian girl handed out flowers as she danced and sang among the crowd. Finally there were presentations of gifts for the new chieftain, 108 in all, which took them well into the night.

The Sisters had built St Bernardine's into one of the most prestigious girls' schools in Nigeria (Plate 31), but after the state takeover the first two lay heads appointed to succeed them had proved quite unequal to the task. The education authority knew that unless it took action standards would plummet. It made a number of male staff appointments in the hope of eventually promoting one of them to the headship, but deaths and transfers thwarted its plans. By the time Tony Adeleke took office in 1983 the school's reputation was in freefall. Its religious ethos had all but evaporated and the chapel with its excellent acoustics was being put to a great variety of uses, few of them liturgical. An experienced and conscientious educator and a committed Catholic, he at once set about reversing the decline. His first initiative was to have the chapel rededicated and made fit for the regular celebration of Mass. His hope was to have it returned to the Sisters, along with the land they had lost when the school was taken over.[9]

Since its separation from the convent the school had become an easy target for intruders. When the new head alerted the authorities to the damage being done to the property, they asked him to search for the original plans that had been drawn up when it was first leased to the Congregation. This gave him the opportunity that he had been waiting for: to reclaim the chapel and part of the land for the Sisters and to separate them from the school by a high fence.

Securing their Nigerian property was in fact the Congregation's priority at this time. Until now all of their houses, schools and hospitals had been held on lease from the mission. But the new novitiate now under construction at Oyo was sited on land gifted to them by Bishop Adelakun, and it pointed to the way forward. With their experience at St Bernardine's fresh in the memory, and the prospect of the state tightening its control over education and medicine, the future seemed to lie with private property, since only this offered protection against sudden loss.[10]

The year 1985 marked another milestone for the Nigerian Region when the first indigenous communities were established. The new convent of St Mary opened in Oyo in May, with Sr M. Augustina Fabule Superior, and in August a house was founded in Ilesa under the leadership of Sr M. Josephine Obi. Step by step the Congregation in Africa was coming of age.

The International Association of Franciscan Sisters had followed up their first Assisi conference with a second in 1979 – with Mother Gabriel again in attendance – at which the delegates decided to explore the possibility of compiling a Rule in collaboration with the Franciscan men's Orders. The following year, when all the groups met again at Grottaferrata, a firm decision was taken to press ahead in the belief that a single Rule could be produced for the entire Third Order Regular, male and female, in which 'every Congregation would be able to recognise itself'.[11]

The hallmarks of Franciscanism – humility, poverty and penance – are present in all the Franciscan Orders. But within them the First Order, of Friars Minor, especially emphasises humility or 'minority'; the Second, the Poor Clares, lays particular stress upon poverty; and the Third, as its original title the 'Order of Penitents' suggests, has as its special charism *metanoia* or penance/conversion. It was upon this blueprint that the lineaments of the new Rule of the Third Order Regular were drawn up. A first draft was completed and distributed for discussion in late 1981, following which a second version was presented to the General Assembly held in Rome in March 1982. There the delegates, representing almost two hundred Congregations from five continents, unanimously affirmed the revised text and authorised its publication, subject to ratification by the Vatican. Papal approval was confirmed the following year, and the *Rule and Life* was at once published and translated into the major languages, the English version appearing in 1984.[12]

Its whole tenor was quite different from the Rule of 1927 that it replaced. Throughout, it echoed and re-echoed the radical call of the founder to 'follow the example of the Lord who emptied himself' in humility, poverty, penance and service: 'to have nothing except food and clothing . . . rejoicing to live among the outcast and despised . . . truly poor in spirit . . . living in this world as pilgrims and strangers . . . wishing to live this evangelical conversion in a spirit of prayer, poverty and humility . . . called to heal the wounded, bind up those who are bruised and reclaim the erring . . . never wanting to be in charge of others, but on the contrary to be servants and subject to every human creature for the Lord's sake'. If ever a document set out to return an Order to the original pure well spring of its foundation, without dilution or concession, it was this.

When the Motherwell diocese opened its new offices, Bishop Thomson's house in Bothwell was no longer required for administration work. Finding it now too large for his own needs he generously donated it to The Innocents and himself moved out.[13] The fine stone villa stood in secluded grounds in a quiet part of town, with ample space for meeting rooms, an oratory and a flatlet for the Sisters. Not everyone in the respectable neighbourhood welcomed their arrival, however. Some objected to the presence of unmarried mothers in their midst, or to the prospect of noise and ambulances, and petitions of complaint were sent to the council and the Church. But other neighbours gave them a Christian welcome. One in particular, James McNally, who ran a small decorating business, painted the house free of charge and continued to help them for many years.

At a time when there was still a stigma attached to unmarried motherhood, some of the women came from as far afield as England and Ireland. One, from a 'good' Donegal Catholic family, had been put out on the doorstep with her suitcase when her parents heard she was expecting. She and her mother were later reconciled, but her father never spoke to her till the day he died. In the Bothwell house, she and others like her found a warm welcome and no judgment. They were shown compassion, whatever decision they took, and even those who finally chose abortion often returned later, sometimes for trauma counselling, knowing that they were not being judged.

Many, like 'Margaret' from Glasgow, first made contact in order to have a pregnancy test. She already had a daughter at the toddler stage. After testing positive, she disappeared for seven months and nothing was heard from her until one evening when she phoned to say that she had decided to keep the baby, which was now due any day. Sr Rosaria urged her to come up to Bothwell, but again heard nothing further. Then on Easter Monday she appeared at the door, her two-year-old in one hand and the baby in the other, wrapped in her working overall and with the umbilical cord around his neck. She had travelled from Glasgow on the train, and her baby had been born in the station toilet with his sister waiting outside the cubicle door. From there she had struggled up the hill with the two of them. Little Thomas was already turning blue. Rosaria bathed him, wrapped him in a shawl and set him by the fire, where Fr Kelly's dog Barney curled up beside him. Fr Kelly always claimed later that it was Barney's body heat that saved him.[14]

It was a blow when ill health forced Mrs Alice Felletti to resign the headship of Charlotte Street in October 1984 after only four years in post, but her successor, Mrs Anna Keegan, proved an admirable replacement. The new head had begun her career in primary teaching but had transferred to the secondary sector after raising her family and had there gained wide experience in challenging posts in Baillieston, Cranhill and Castlemilk before being appointed assistant headteacher at Holyrood. Educated at Charlotte Street from the age of five, she was steeped in the tradition, as were her staff, a third of whom had spent their entire careers there.

Thus blessed with excellent headteachers, a committed staff and a succession of first-class chaplains, the school had retained its standards under lay leadership. It was particularly known for its extra-curricular activities and work for charity. Its choir and instrumentalists still performed regularly in public, whether at concerts or Burns festivals, or just carol singing at Central Station. The Charlotte Street area had a bad name, not least for prostitution, but whether walking through it for evening events or slipping out to buy their lunch at the Geezapiece Sandwich Bar, the girls never encountered trouble. The people had a solicitude for them.[15]

Though its days as a senior secondary were long gone, family pride in the school remained high. Despite the many cases of hardship everyone still wore uniform. The fact that several of the staff chose it for their own children in preference to more affluent schools closer to home sent out the message that Charlotte Street remained a match for any. Other families made a similar choice: no less than a third of all the pupils at this time attended as a result of placing-requests, travelling from outside the official catchment area at their own expense.[16] They preferred this school in the heart of the inner city, with its antiquated and cramped classrooms, to anything they could get on the outskirts.

The HMI report of 1987 confirmed what the parents already knew. The inspectors noted the undersized classrooms, the spartan facilities for PE, the cramped library, and the fact that some departments were still housed in the old St Alphonsus' primary school, but praised the 'resilience and enterprise' of staff and pupils in coping with these shortcomings. They lauded the management of the school, its timetable and guidance system, and its powerful sense of living tradition and community. They were impressed by the pupils' 'striking commitment' and 'sense of personal identity and security', the obvious mutual respect between them and the staff, the strong moral values, and the evident esteem in which the school was held by the local community. With its present roll predicted to rise, they concluded that it was 'well equipped to build further on its substantial achievements'.[17]

Yet all this counted for little when the school received word just months later that the EA were planning to amalgamate it with St Mungo's Boys'. Their arguments for doing so were based partly on quality of provision, since amalgamation would bring the girls into the new, purpose-built St Mungo's building; partly on economics, since maintaining two schools running below capacity was seen as a waste of resources; and partly on opposition to single-sex schooling, which some councillors and officials considered violated the comprehensive principle.[18]

A campaign was at once launched to save the school, and this very quickly revealed the huge body of support that it enjoyed. The parents, FPs and other friends could hardly have been more effective – articulate, and tireless in attending meetings, making representations and raising funds. The lawyer and former provost Peter McCann was like a terrier for the cause. As someone who had suffered polio in his childhood, he remembered his own happy days in the primary school on the eve of war when the senior girls used to hurl him round the playground in his wheelchair, and he was now ever ready to offer his time and legal skills free. He was one of many.

The staff and parents prepared submissions to Strathclyde council arguing the school's case. They identified discrepancies in the EA's calculations regarding capacity and cost, reminded them of the excellent HMI report, and demonstrated how well the school's roll and examination results had held up since becoming comprehensive. They claimed that its single-sex status was no argument for closure, but was on the contrary a positive argument for its retention in the name of parental choice. They spoke of its growing role of service to people of the East End, and how much it meant to that community. This was perhaps best expressed in a letter appended to the parents' submission. The writer's mother had been a pupil in the 1900s and had been determined to send her seven daughters to the school she loved, whatever the sacrifice, making up their blazers from remnants, and hand-knitting all their jumpers and socks. Now her own three daughters were there: she would not have thought of sending them anywhere else, for she knew what the school had given to her family, and what they in turn had given to the city.[19]

The pupils also played their part in the campaign. One sixth-year student penned a cogently argued, hard-hitting article for the press, in which she denounced the irresponsibility of Strathclyde council and praised the school's unique contribution to the inner city. Its closure, she wrote, would mean 'the loss of part of the East End's heritage'.[20]

The one weakness in its case was that its use of space had fallen marginally below the 80 per cent capacity required to ensure its survival, and this proved decisive when the education committee met to decide the issue. They voted for amalgamation as from August 1989. The combined school would retain the name 'St Mungo's', and 'Our Lady and St Francis' would disappear.[21]

The news was greeted with dismay and some bitterness. The courtesies were maintained, but there were those who – rightly or wrongly – could not bring themselves to speak to the authorities or the archbishop.

Spring 1989 saw the appointment of the new staff. The choice of the boys' school head, Tom Burnett, as headteacher was straightforward, since his opposite number, Anna Keegan, let it be known that she would not be applying but would be seeking early retirement. A number of her staff elected not to accept posts in the amalgamated school, preferring not to teach mixed classes, but others were appointed to key positions, one as assistant head and several as departmental principals, ensuring that something at least of their old school would be absorbed into the new.

Both staffs had a strong will to make amalgamation work, once the decision was taken. Fusing the two traditions happily and harmoniously promised to be a delicate task, nonetheless, for Mr Burnett and his senior colleagues. It was due in no small measure to their diplomacy, consideration and respect for sensitivities that the new St Mungo's thrived and in time built its own excellent traditions.

Inevitably though, closure after 140 years brought a huge loss. It would have been impossible to retain everything of Charlotte Street in the new environment, no matter how good. For generations of girls it had been a family, a nursery of lifelong friendships; a prayerful world, where they had learned to pray; for some it had been a haven; for all a caring community where the whole person was valued and led to reach her fullest potential intellectually and spiritually, and from where, as a result, girls had gone on to make a quite disproportionate contribution to society and the Church. In this case, these were not mere glib phrases.

Its location and cramped buildings had been a constant restriction, certainly, but its buoyant spirit had turned even this necessity into a virtue so that, in the words of the booklet published to mark its closure, many distinguished visitors left marvelling that such a school could be found in such a place.[22]

All this had not appeared out of nothing; rather it had been built over decades on the vision, skill and industry of the Sisters and their well-chosen staffs, and on the loyalty and pride of working-class families. Not least it had been built on the girls themselves. They had always shone out, as one Glasgow journalist memorably put it at the time, like 'jewels in the glour'. Ultimately it was they who were the school's best argument, and who remain its best legacy.

In the mid-1980s there seemed to be a bright future for the Congregation in USA. In 1982 they had opened a house in Bedford, some thirty-five miles from Altoona. By 1987, when they opened a fourth convent in Johnston, there were fourteen Sisters working in Pennsylvania. Their life was thought of as 'comfortable' by the rest of the Congregation. Comparatively, they enjoyed something of the American standard of living – they normally ate out on Sundays, for example – and their private, fee-paying schools were pleasant to teach in, with few of the problems of poverty and unruliness found in industrial Scotland.

But 1987 proved to be the high point of their fortunes. Their weakness had always been a lack of local vocations. They had in fact only ever recruited one American woman, Sr Elizabeth Ann McGuire, who had been drawn to the Congregation while teaching at their school in Holidaysburg. Several others had tried their vocation as postulants but had not stayed. With many American Congregations urgently seeking members, it was never likely that American women would join what they still thought of as 'the Scottish Sisters'.[23] And with their own Congregation beginning to feel the decline in vocations at home yet still trying to develop new work in Scotland and Ireland as well as support growth in Africa, no more could now be spared for USA.

The Sisters were forced to pull out of Johnston after only one year, and in 1990 they also gave up the house and school in Bedford. Sr Kevin Breen, who had been headmistress there for seven years, moved to Altoona to take charge of Our Lady of Mount Carmel School. In her time it was merged with three other local schools to create a single all-through institution, Altoona Central Catholic, serving the twelve parishes in the area, to which she was appointed principal. It was a key local appointment and an accolade for the Congregation, but generally the 1990s were a time of retraction of its presence and work in America, and the beginning of a seemingly unstoppable decline.

In spring 1989 Bishop Ndingi invited the Sisters to establish a mission in his diocese of Nakuru in the interior of Kenya. The proposal had great appeal. It would be a totally new venture, 'starting afresh' yet again in the tradition of Adélaide and Veronica and the spirit of St Francis. Also, it seemed a good time. They were fully stretched by their present work, certainly. But Nigeria was now a Region: stable, apparently viable, and with a steady influx of vocations. The Kenyan Church was young and full of youthful promise, and the diminutive Bishop Ndingi a spiritual dynamo.

In April Sr Loyola Kelly wrote to him on Council's behalf, accepting his invitation.[24] Early that autumn she and Sr Rosaria McGeady flew to Nairobi, from where they were taken to visit six possible projects. All were up country. The most far-flung was a girls' school at Kasok, six thousand feet up in the Tugen Hills, where qualified teachers were urgently needed.

It had first opened in 1984 in Kipsaraman, the nearest real town, with lessons held under a tree and the boarders sleeping on shop floors. Academic standards were high, but the Kenyan president, Daniel Moi, had been appalled by the primitive conditions and had personally ordered the school to be moved up to Kasok, fifteen minutes' drive away, where construction had begun in 1987 on four classrooms and a dormitory. The work, largely financed from the proceeds of two huge *harambees*, had been completed sixteen months before the two Sisters arrived.[25]

To reach Kasok, they were driven for miles on an ever-rising road, leaving far behind the lush growth of the valleys. Suddenly they were climbing steeply, the road running up the sharp edge of a mountain *arête* and the land falling away dizzily on either hand. They looked down upon lakes far below and beyond them a vast plain. The air was full of the sound of crickets. Around them stood broken, sharp-edged peaks. Yet when they reached the top they hardly knew they were on the summit of a mountain. They were in the midst of trees and the sloping, terraced fields of scattered farms, with the school set among them. Hundreds of people had gathered to greet them and share a community meal, and to beg them to make this place their choice. It was certainly the most arduous of the projects – far from friends, without water or electricity, and on a road like they had never seen. Their hearts warmed to it at once.

The school roll was 200, the staff were unqualified, and there were vacancies in most subjects. The headmaster, Mr Wilson Chelagat, proposed that the Congregation provide teachers for English, religious education and the sciences.[26] Terms were agreed for the first two Sisters to take up the English posts at the start of the 1990 autumn term, with other subject specialists to follow as soon as they could be released.

Srs Martina Morgan and Placida McCann were withdrawn from the USA and arrived in Kenya in August, only to discover that their convent was still unfinished. They stayed in Kipsaraman while it was hastily put together, watching the teams of donkeys carrying stone up the mountain. The work was completed within a month, and when they moved in they found everything brand new and in order, right down to the shower fittings (only there was no water) and the light bulbs (but with no electricity).[27]

Later that autumn Srs Maximilian Bremner and Clement O'Connell arrived to teach maths and biology. They took to their new life at once and made a deep impression on all around them. Sr Clement lit up the convent with her infectious humour, while young Sr Maximilian loved the work and the place – she used to address her letters 'Paradise' – and was greatly loved by the children.

On 8 May 1991 the two of them borrowed the convent car to chauffeur two visiting Sisters down to Nairobi airport. They were due back that evening but did not arrive. Sr Placida waited up, but finally went to bed. She was not unduly worried, for delays were common enough in rural Kenya. At midnight she heard a knock at the door and went to open it. Three priests and three female religious were on the step. They sat her down and broke the news. Clement and Maximilian had been returning on the Marigat road when they had apparently swerved to avoid a stray animal – there could be no other explanation since there was no-one else on the road. Their car had gone out of control and somersaulted twice. Clement had been killed instantly; Maximilian had been rushed to the Marigat dispensary but had died without regaining consciousness.

Their bodies were taken to Nairobi where Bishop Ndingi concelebrated their funeral Mass before a packed congregation at the Holy Family Basilica. During the service he read out a personal message of condolence from Daniel Moi. Though they had only been among his people for a few brief months, the president wrote, their work had earned them 'a tremendous popularity and respect in the school, the mission and the neighbourhood'.[28]

For the fledgling community, far from home, it was a hard bereavement. It was now that they really needed and appreciated the great solidarity that exists among the religious Orders in Kenya. They felt support all around them, and their loss served to strengthen bonds already strong. Later that summer, Srs Anne Mary Wilson and Assumpta Hegarty arrived from Scotland to take their dead colleagues' places.

In September 1989 the Congregation opened a second convent in Dublin to serve both as Regional house and house of studies. Sr Imelda Costello moved from Donegal to take charge of the community, Sr Dolores Cochrane replacing her as Superior at Falcarragh.

Since the amalgamation of the boys' and girls' schools under a male head, the Sisters' main work in Falcarragh had been supervision of the hostel for the island girls who attended as boarders. There had long been talk of the island children having their own secondary school on Aranmore, and by now there were persistent rumours that this was about to go ahead.[29] Since its opening would signal the end of the hostel, Sr Dolores arranged to meet the director of education in April 1990 to learn the latest official position. He assured her that there was no possibility of a secondary school on Aranmore in the immediate future. She was in Dublin for the summer vacation when she read in the press that it was to open in September.

Mother Felicitas travelled to Ireland early in the autumn to discuss a closure date for the hostel with the Regional Superior and the Falcarragh community. It was agreed to keep it open for one more academic year for the sake of the senior pupils, who were to see out their education on the mainland. Bishop Hegarty was informed of the decision in December, and the parents in new year 1991. The last girls left in June.[30]

The following month an auction was held of the moveable furnishings, and shortly afterwards two of the community transferred to Dublin. The two remaining Sisters now devoted their time to parish visiting,[31] but it was work that could have been done anywhere. The task for which the convent had been founded was finished, and very obviously its days were numbered. The Sisters were now only there as caretakers until it could be sold.

Too large and too remote for most private house-buyers, it remained on the market for some time. When it was finally purchased, the Sisters took great pleasure from the sale. A local couple whose son Seamus (Plate 33) suffered from cerebral palsy were at the time trying to set up a resource centre for disabled young people in the area. With grants from the health board and Udaras na Gaeltachta, and monies collected from fundraising and donations, they were able to buy the convent, which was ideal for their needs. The sale was concluded in 1992 and the centre opened the following year.[32] The invaluable support that it offered through a programme of arts and crafts, music, swimming and basic education was exactly how the Sisters would have wished their old convent to be used.

In her years at Mitre House Sr Gertrude had built up an excellent relationship with the Glasgow social work department, whose director, Fred Edwards, proved a valuable friend. When in 1991 the department asked the Congregation to consider changing the respite home in House-hillwood into a residential home for young adults with profound needs, she supported the proposal. Council agreed to it, and the archdiocese gave its approval on condition that the city provided alternative premises to continue the respite home.

It was arranged that Sr Gertrude and several of the existing staff would remain at Houshillwood to give a sense of security to the residents, all of whom were 'old hands' from its days as a respite home. The new work was totally different from anything they had done before and called for quite new skills. The entire care of the residents fell to them twenty-four hours a day and for every aspect of their lives (Plate 34). For the young people also, life away from home was a new and anxious experience, and though the house and staff were familiar to them, some found it hard to accept. One used to carry her family photo album everywhere, never letting it out of her grasp for months, until one day she put it down and Sr Gertrude knew that she had accepted her new home. To help them settle each was allocated a volunteer befriender, and to stimulate them and help them towards greater independence each was given a goal plan – to learn to dress, for example – as well as a particular house-task to be personally 'in charge of'.[33]

When Sr Veronica McGrath entered the Congregation in 1975, she had come with a secretarial certificate and seven years' office experience.[34] When, two years later, Archbishop Winning asked Mother Gabriel if she had anyone qualified and available to take committee minutes once a month in the diocesan offices, she was the obvious candidate. Within weeks, the general secretary left and Veronica, who had only been professed the previous week, found herself in a full-time post in Park Circus. She held the position until 1984, when she was sent to the convent in Holidaysburg.

On her return from America in 1990 she was appointed to run the Missio[35] office in Drumchapel. Two years later, Missio moved into a former warehouse behind the cathedral and the new curial office in Clyde Street, where Sr Veronica often had occasion to meet the diocesan staff, some of whom she had known from her Park Circus days. Shortly afterwards she received a personal invitation from the archbishop to join the Chancery Office. So highly did he value her that he created the post of Vice Chancellor for her, the first woman ever to hold such a senior position. He enjoyed her straight-talking approach, and when she warned him that she had no intention of being the 'token woman' at headquarters, he countered that he saw her rather as 'the human face of the Chancery'. Such a presence was valuable, in fact, at a time when many of the clergy still thought of the Chancery as a place they visited if they were to be moved or reprimanded. Sr Veronica is still at Clyde Street, involved in its taxing and complex tasks, and though much has changed in the past decade she still sees 'oiling the wheels' as an important part of her contribution. Her work is unique in the Congregation, yet in its own way is genuinely Franciscan.

In 1991 Mother Felicitas visited Nigeria and saw for herself the progress and the problems there. It was clear that under the existing régime the European Sisters could be told to leave the country at any time. Furthermore, difficulties remained in regard to the purchase of property, which could only be held by trustees. Both problems, she saw, might be solved by the creation of a Nigerian Province.

It was almost thirty years since the Constitution had been changed to give authority to the Council in principle to erect Provinces 'in distant countries' when the time was appropriate,[36] and since the late 1960s Council had indeed been granting ever greater autonomy to the Nigerian mission, with this eventual aim in mind. They had first explored the possibility in practice immediately after the 1974 Chapter, but had been advised at the time that numbers did not yet justify it.[37] Six years later they had moved some way by granting the mission the status of a Region.

Believing that further delay could now be fatal, Mother Felicitas took the opportunity of her visit to take action on her own authority, conferring provincial status upon the Region and appointing a Provincial Superior and Council. The change could only become official when ratified by Chapter, of course, and the first opportunity for this was the Chapter of July 1992.

At that meeting she stood down as Superior General and was succeeded by Sr Martina Morgan (Plate 35). The new Superior introduced the item, for which the outcome was inevitable since the Province was already a *fait accompli*. The meeting then formally elected Mother Felicitas' appointments to office. A Scottish Sister, Raphael Swan (Plate 39), was elected Provincial, with a Nigerian, Sr Josephine Obi, her assistant. Both Nigerians and Scots were voted onto the Provincial Council. Strictly speaking, the appointments were provisional, pending the Vatican's permission for the creation of a Province, which was required in Canon Law[38] and which the Congregation now had to seek retrospectively. Rome approved, but pointed out that the change would require a revision of the relevant parts of the Constitutions. To undertake the work, Council appointed five commissions, the most important of them a commission on government, to be chaired by the new Superior General.[39]

Since the appointment of Sr Celestine McKenna to the headship of St Anthony's Cinderford, standards at the school had continued to rise. The numbers passing the examination to the high school in Gloucester were consistently high, and further property had been acquired and renovated in order to provide a nursery for the first time.[40] But the recession that hit the Forest of Dean in the late 1980s and early 1990s took its toll upon the school, which relied almost entirely on pupils' fees for its income. In the financial year 1992–3 it recorded a loss of £17,000, and it was clear that action would need to be taken if it was to survive. The school board set up a working group charged with the task of restoring it to solvency. They tackled the problem on several fronts – persuading the staff to accept a wage freeze, fundraising, and recruiting new pupils – and so successful were they that within three years the school was recording an annual profit of close to £30,000.[41]

The working group's energy and enterprise reflected the loyalty and effective support that the parents had always shown towards the school. School–parent partnership was in fact one of its most notable strengths, and one of the things that most impressed government inspectors who visited. The HMIs also praised the excellence of the teaching staff and the highly stimulating and happy learning environment, in which the children were treated as individuals and responded with exemplary behaviour and courtesy.[42]

At a time when the Sisters were shedding their fee-paying schools in Britain, St Anthony's remained the odd one out, meeting an evident demand from the scattered Catholics of the Forest. It remains so yet, a place of obvious excellence and happiness to anyone who visits, still under the leadership of Sr Celestine, who has been living now for sixteen years as a 'community' of one in Cinderford.

In the eight years since the founding of the Congregation's first indigenous Nigerian communities in 1985, a further five had now been opened.[43] African Sisters had also taken up important posts within their dioceses. Sr Henrietta Eziashi had been appointed to organise the Catholic 'youth corpers', young graduates who volunteered to leave their state of origin to serve the Church and the people. Sr Margaret Mary Oniwinde had been appointed director of religious education for the diocese of Oyo and was responsible for training catechists and prayer leaders for the outstations. Sr Mary Anne Monye was in charge of the Regional Pastoral Institute (Plate 36), overseeing its publications and organising workshops and seminars for priests and religious. Sr Clementina Yemisi Obeme was running the justice and peace department of Oyo diocese, where she had set up numerous initiatives to empower the downtrodden – subsistence farmers, prisoners and the unemployed.[44]

Some of the Congregation's most important work for prisoners was in the hands of Sr Gerard O'Donnell, the principal of its school in Ilesa.[45] The town housed one of the largest prisons in the country and the Sisters had been visiting its inmates since 1960. Many were wretched victims of an appallingly harsh and corrupt system. Sr Gerard regularly met men awaiting execution, often for quite petty crimes. One had done nothing more than steal six fluorescent light bulbs to sell in order to feed his family. Bringing some small solace to these abandoned ones was her after-school apostolate. Often she brought them food cooked by the pupils at her school and also assisted them financially, with money gifted by her own home parish of St Thomas' Riddrie.

By 1993 the Sisters were looking to extend their work in Kenya, and Sr Bernard McAtamney was sent out to investigate a proposed new project there. The town of Ndanai is in the Kericho valley, seven hours' drive from Kasok. The land is low-lying and fertile, but malarial, and in the rainy season it is often completely cut off. The project involved setting up a dispensary and mobile clinic. The decision was taken to go ahead, but it was two years before Sr Bernard moved in with Srs Françoise Simpson and Anne Mary Wilson.

The venture was beset with problems from the outset. For two years they had no suitable house, and the bishop appeared unable to help them. They finally got hold of a run-down old dormitory building, which they stripped and cleaned to make it habitable. They set up their dispensary in a store room attached to the local church. The mobile 'clinic' came from St Patrick's Dumbarton, where one of the parishioners who dealt in Land Rovers discovered a superannuated RAF ambulance available for £300 and with the help of workmates rebuilt it and filled it with medicines gathered by the parish.[46]

The Sisters were vulnerable in their primitive convent, suffering nine break-ins in eighteen months. During one of them, the intruders locked them in, and when they finally managed to climb out the neighbours refused to help them and the police hinted that they had invented the incident. They felt like intruders themselves.

One December night in 1996 one of them answered the door and found herself confronted by a masked man who struck her on the leg with a stone. They stayed up all that night and the next morning drove to Kasok. Sr Françoise decided to return to Scotland, but Bernard and Anne Mary elected to give Ndanai one last try. After months of waiting they received permission to take over a house three miles out of the town, which they renovated with a grant from Missio and where they laid the foundations for a permanent clinic.

But word must have got out that the dispensary money was kept in the house. One night a gang of four men slipped into the grounds, overpowered and bound the watchman and knocked on the convent door. When Sr Bernard opened it they pushed her aside. Believing that they intended harm to her young colleague she flew at them with her fists. One knocked her unconscious and another slashed her across the head with a cutlass. When she came round Anne Mary was bending anxiously over her. The men had gone, but not before beating and terrifying her. The two women waited no longer but drove at rally speed to the hospital in Kaplong, from where the next day the flying doctors airlifted them to Nairobi. Within a few days Sr Loyola Kelly arrived in the capital to be with them, but they had already decided to go home. The convent was closed almost before it opened, and the Ndanai mission was abandoned.[47] The closure put in question the Congregation's very future in Kenya. With the two Sisters at Kasok now their only foothold there, Council seriously considered withdrawing from the country altogether.[48]

On 13 April 1997 the cathedral in Clyde Street was packed to the door, with as many again in the street outside, as Cardinal Winning concelebrated a special Mass for former pupils of Charlotte Street, to mark the 150th anniversary of the arrival of the Franciscan Sisters in Glasgow. Alumnae had flown in from Europe, America and Australia to be there. On 15 June, the nearest Sunday to the actual arrival date, the official anniversary Mass was celebrated in St Mary's Calton, the parish founded by Fr Forbes where Veronica first worked and Adélaide died and with which the Congregation had so many ties. A final Mass was held in St Bride's Bothwell on 6 September for all associated with Elmwood school. Further celebrations were held (Plates 41 and 42) and other initiatives were announced during the year, notably the sponsoring of several Scottish priests to visit the Kenya mission, and the publication of a handsome illustrated commemorative volume which was avidly snapped up by FPs and friends and sold out in no time.[49]

In June, Sr Anthony Coyle retired as head of St Patrick's primary school in Greenock after twenty-seven years in post. St Patrick's had replaced the old St Mary's school in 1968, and her retirement brought to an end 119 years of leadership of the schools by the Franciscan Sisters. It was a gauge of their outstanding calibre that only six Sisters had held the headship during that time,[50] and Sr Anthony had been as successful as any. The school served a close-knit working-class community well known for its warmth and generosity, and she and her staff had worked closely with the parish to create a caring and spiritual ethos.[51] The report of the last government inspection before her retirement was eloquent in its praise of her. The school was 'outstanding', the HMIs wrote, and was highly valued by pupils, parents and the local community. Her own leadership and her undiminished commitment and enthusiasm 'had earned her the respect and admiration of staff and parents alike'.[52] She loved the people, and they loved her. Upon her retirement she was awarded the MBE for her service to them.

She was the last of the Congregation's parish school heads in Scotland, and her retirement marked the end not just of an era but of an apostolate. She remains in St Mary's parish with Sr Thérèse Clary, retaining links with a community that remembers the Franciscan Sisters with deep gratitude and affection.[53]

The commissions appointed at the 1992 Chapter had now completed their work and had reached some radical conclusions. In particular, it had become clear that the Congregation's authority structure was still in essence hierarchical and that it would require wholesale revision of the Con-stitutions to bring about the 'collegiality' that the Church now demanded.[54]

In summer 1997, with a General Chapter only a year away, questionnaires were issued which revealed that almost everyone wanted change towards a more consultative, participatory régime. To this end the sections of the Constitutions covering government were rewritten with the help of a Canon lawyer, Fr Morrissey OMI, and circulated to every Sister for comment.[55]

Three further drafts followed between the autumn and spring 1998, each the fruit of similar consultation. The whole process was itself in fact an attempt at collegiality.

In its final form, the text represented a complete upending of the traditional concept of government. The flow of initiative and decision-making 'from General to Provincial to Local' was reversed, putting the local communities at the heart of the process. In its style and vocabulary, also, the whole thrust of the document was for participation, consultation, delegation and local initiative.[56]

The Chapter convened on 10 July with seven *ex officio* members and nineteen elected delegates, six of them representing Nigeria. It began with a weekend reflection on the theme of 'vision', which was deliberately chosen to set the tone for what (it was hoped) would be a visionary and forward-looking gathering. The Chapter proper began on the Monday, when Mother Martina presented a report in which she spoke of the present position of the Congregation and of her hopes for its future.[57]

There were now ninety-nine Sisters in the Congregation, she reminded her audience, almost exactly divided between UK–Ireland and Nigeria.[58] But these raw figures hid a stark imbalance: since the last General Chapter Nigeria had seen thirty-two new entrants, compared with three in the rest of the Congregation, and twelve final professions (with five more due that autumn), as against only two elsewhere. The Congregation's average age of just under fifty sounded healthy, but it masked the youth of Nigeria (average thirty-seven years) and the ageing at home (average sixty).

She welcomed this divergence, and the new diversity of community life-styles and apostolates, as an enrichment. It was the single Franciscan vision that united them all, she argued, and that unity did not require uniformity. Nigeria indeed challenged them to see themselves as an international Con-gregation. The priority was to bridge the gap between Africa and Europe, and in this she saw the role of Kenya as crucial. Far from abandoning their mission there, as some were proposing, they should expand it and open a novitiate for native Sisters. The Nigerian Province should then be developed into an African Province to include Kenya, with its own Sisters taking 'ownership' as soon as the time was right.

She also identified formation and finance as immediate priorities for the Chapter. The first, long recognised as important, was now the more so given the changing face of the Congregation at home and the relative inexperience of the leadership in Nigeria. As to the second, with their financial state far less healthy than formerly, there was an urgent need to rationalise their remaining resources and make prudent investments. If these issues were addressed, she believed the Congregation could face the future with confidence.

The members then moved on to the main agenda item, consideration of the new Constitutions, which took the whole of the week and over-shadowed all other issues.

On 22 July the debate was interrupted for elections. Everyone under-stood their importance. Although the Congregation had abandoned the old authority model of 'Mother Abbess', it had never really succeeded in replacing it, and this had led to some confusion and a loss of cohesion and morale. The drift could not continue. Leadership was now 'a survival issue', they were warned. The report on government had pointed the way forward, and choosing leaders able and willing to implement it would be critical for their very future.[59]

With Mother Martina standing down for health reasons, Sr Loyola Kelly (Plates 39 and 40) was elected Superior General, with Sr Bernard McAtamney assistant. The new Superior at once struck a blow for collegiality by requesting that she be known as 'Sister' rather than 'Mother', a small but highly symbolic change and a marker as to the kind of leadership she intended to give.[60]

The members now returned to vote on the issues discussed the previous week. The preparatory work of Fr Morrissey and the commissions, and the guidance offered in Mother Martina's report, made the task relatively straightforward. All of the recommendations were supported. The members readily approved the final draft report on government *in toto*. They also accepted the priority of a coherent formation programme and authorised the appointment of a group to examine the question. They endorsed the retention and development of the Kenya mission, with the opening of a novitiate and its inclusion within an expanded African Province. Finally, they accepted the urgent need to address the Congregation's financial position, and to make 'prudent and principled investments'.[61]

The debate on the Constitutions had taken the members into fundamental questions about the very nature of the Congregation, and it was here that Fr Morrissey's presence proved vital. As we saw in earlier chapters, the Sisters had always felt a tension between the dictates of community life and the demands of the public apostolate. Time and again from the earliest days they had sought to reconcile the two, by adjusting the horarium or adapting their public work. To the extent that they had achieved a *modus vivendi* they could perhaps claim to have been successful, but only at great cost to their health and peace of mind. The problem had been all the more painful in that it had never really been articulated, with the result that Sisters had often attributed the imbalance to some personal shortcoming rather than something inherent in the system. It had even driven a few to seek their vocations elsewhere, while the whole Congregation had for years suffered a vague but stubborn disquiet and even guilt over the matter.

When Fr Morrissey now articulated the problem and identified it as one widespread among active religious Orders, his words brought everyone – in the words of the new Superior General –'a tremendous sense of relief'.[62] They did not solve the difficulty, of course, but they clarified it. The only real solution, he advised, would be to spell out in the Constitutions which aspect of their life should take precedence. This the members did, revising the relevant paragraph of the text to define the Congregation as first and foremost 'an apostolic institute'.[63] At a stroke the uncertainty was ended and the way ahead made clear.

Chapter left a number of questions unanswered, nonetheless. With an ageing membership at home, how could the diminishing number of wage earners support the growing number of elderly Sisters? How could the new small convents maintain genuine community life? What future was there for the Congregation in the USA which, with the single American-born Sister working and residing in Virginia, was now reduced to a two-person presence in Altoona? As to Kenya, although they had voted to retain and develop the mission, only time would tell if this could be successfully achieved.[64]

The final version of the Constitutions approved by Chapter was an inspiring text, encapsulating all of the Sisters' study, reflection, praxis and developing insight over the previous thirty years. It was to the Congregation what the 1982–4 Rule was to the Third Order Regular, and indeed it echoed that document throughout. It committed the Sisters unambiguously to the Franciscan penitential tradition, 'living out their public profession of chastity, poverty and obedience in community, ever striving to a fuller expression of their baptismal call to conversion'. In the spirit of St Francis, who 'constantly encouraged his friars to begin again', it called for this 'conversion and renewal' to be continuous throughout the life of each member and of the Congregation itself. It asked of all an unqualified commitment to service, poverty of spirit and 'a charism rich in risks'.

The Chapter had been the most democratic, the most collegial ever. Before the delegates dispersed they were invited to evaluate it, the first time that such an exercise had been undertaken. They were unanimous in their praise.[65] 'The best Chapter ever'; 'memorably different from anything we have ever experienced before'; 'open and honest'; 'a sense of peace, joy and hope pervaded' were typical comments. Many made a point of praising Fr Morrissey for his 'inspirational' contribution, which had 'given them new hope'. Altogether they were delighted with both the process and the progress made: both seemed evidence of a real rejuvenation. 'If ever we had a dream for the Congregation,' one delegate wrote, 'I think it at the brink of being realised.'

The past eighteen years had been a time of both ebb and flow, when the tide had gone out on many of their long-cherished enterprises, but when other apostolates had grown and promising new work had begun. They departed full of optimism, with many problems certainly lying ahead, but as 'a community of committed women who are not afraid of the unknown, or even if afraid go forward in faith'.[66]

ENDNOTES TO CHAPTER NINE

1   Sr Felicitas Bradley interview. The Congregation's one candidate who would otherwise have been ideally qualified and experienced was Sr Patricia Coyle, but unfortunately nearly all of her senior experience was in the Irish education system at Falcarragh.

2   Mrs Anna Keegan and Sr Felicitas Bradley interviews.

3   The work took Sr Francis all over the country. She made most of her contacts through visits to the Catholic secondary schools in which she ran a Franciscan Vocations stall during their Caring Church Weeks for senior pupils. Thereafter she kept in touch with them by correspondence and through a monthly vocations Mass and annual retreat – Sr M. Francis Campbell interview.

4   To accommodate the new programme, the novitiate was moved to Bothwell in autumn 1982, where the convent's old coaching stables were rescued from decay and converted to house up to six novices.

5   The present account based on Sr Gertrude Shields interview. Enable was at the time known as The Scottish Society for the Mentally Handicapped.

6   Fr Desmond Maguire to Mother Felicitas, n.d., but 1983, 049.18, AF. The house was in Easterhill Street. Because of delays by the housing department, it was not opened until early 1984. The rest of the present account based on Sr Bernard McAtamney interview.

7   Account based on Sr Emmanuel Gallagher interview.

8   Sr Raphael Swan interview.

9   Tony Adeleke article 'Chapel of St Bernardine's – How Recovered', in *Journey So Far*, Ibadan 2000, p. 167ff.

10 The novitiate was planned and built by Brother Wolfgang WF and was completed in autumn 1984. The first novices moved in on 21 November, and the formal opening took place the following Easter – *Journey So Far*, p. 100ff.

11 This and the following paragraph from Pazzelli R., 1989, (Engl. transl. 1993), p. 185ff.

12 *The Rule and Life of the Brothers and Sisters of the Third Order Regular of St Francis*, decreed by Pope John Paul II 8.12.1982 (confirmation of approval received March 1983); English translation Doyle E. OFM (Lens, 1984).

13 1980 Chapter, House Reports, Innocents House, 030.41, AF; this and the two following paragraphs based on this source, and on *The Innocents Story*, 2002; Fr Hugh Kelly, Society of the Innocents of Lanarkshire, Silver Jubilee Statement, 2002; and Sr Rosaria McGeady interview.

14 In 1985 a second Innocents House was opened in the diocese when Sr Maria Goretti moved into a cottage in East Kilbride at the request of the parish priest, Fr Rodgers. She divided her time between the pro-life cause and general pastoral work in the parish.

15 Mrs Anna Keegan interview. Mrs Keegan once met two prostitutes at the front gate during an evening event. They spoke of the pupils with affection and pride. 'We would never be here during the day,' they assured her. The school put on several full musicals at this time – *Oliver* in 1984, *Cinderella* in 1987 and *The Wizard of Oz* in 1988.

16 In 1987, 33 per cent of S1 and 34 per cent of S2 pupils were placing-requests.

17 Report of HMI inspection, Jan. to Feb. 1987, SED.

18 The present account based on Mrs Anna Keegan and Sr Felicitas Bradley interviews, unless otherwise stated. Regarding accommodation and capacity, the rolls of both schools had declined from their peak in the early 1970s, but OLSF far less than St Mungo's: its roll now stood at 84 per cent of the 1973–4 figure, while that of St Mungo's had fallen to just 35 per cent. Amalgamation had been mooted in Sr Felicitas' day, and had even been agreed by the archdiocese, but had been successfully resisted.

19 Letter from Mrs Claire Parker in *A School Worth Saving*, submission to Strathclyde Regional Council (parents' submission), 1988, Appendix 5.

20 Mairi Darroch, 'Why my School Should be Saved', *The Glaswegian*, no. 13, May/June 1988.

21 The decision was the harder to take in that Notre Dame, the city's only other Catholic Girls' school, was saved on the 80 per cent criterion.

22 *Our Lady and St Francis Yesterday and Today 1849–1989* (Glasgow 1989).

23 Present account from Sr Kevin Breen interview.

24 Bishop Ndingi to Sr Loyola Kelly, 13.6.1989, 056.1, AF, thanking her for her letter of acceptance of 24.4.1989. The Congregation first heard of the needs in Kenya almost by chance, when Sr Loyola Kelly was visiting her sister in Nairobi and met Bishop Ndingi when he was a guest at dinner.

25 Wilson Chelagat, headmaster, 'A History 1984–90', in *Kasok Girls' School Magazine*, issue 1, 1994. A *harambee* is a community gathering for the purpose of fundraising by donations. The proceeds amounted to 1.4 million Kenyan shillings (c. £14,000 sterling).

26 Maurice Lwanga, Vicar General, Nukuru diocese, to Sr Loyola Kelly, 10.11.1989, 056.1, AF.

27 Sr Placida McCann, *Brief History of Our Congregation in Kenya*, 2.2.2003, and interview. Sr Martina was withdrawn from Altoona, and Sr Placida from Bedford, where the house was closed to enable Kasok to open.

28 Message of Condolences from HE The President, 11.5.1991; and report of the funeral in *Sunday Nation* (Nairobi), 12.5.1991.

29 Account based on Sr Dolores Cochrane interview.

30 Falcarragh Log, November 1990, January and June 1991, AF. The last pupils' Mass was celebrated on 12.6.1991.

31 Falcarragh Log, 6.7.1991 and 4.10.1991. The auction realised a profit of over £5,000.

32 Seamus Patrick McIntyre, 'Falcarragh, a New Era', in *The Franciscan Sisters of the Immaculate Conception, Celebrating 150 Years in Glasgow: 1847–1997* (Glasgow, 1997), pp. 141f.

33 *Ibid.*

34 The present account (apart from the words of praise for her) based on Sr Veronica McGrath interview.

35 Missio Scotland (Pontifical Mission Societies) is the official organ of the Catholic Church in Scotland for promoting missions. An umbrella organisation, it was established in 1923.

36 Chapter notes, 8.8.1962, Register of Elections, 028.2, AF.

37 Fr Urban Judge OFM to Sr Gertrude Shields, 30.11.1974, 030.33, AF, in which he had advised that the threshold number would be about 75.

38 *Ibid.*, explaining that though authority for creating Provinces lay with the Congregation's General Chapter, the permission of the Sacred Congregation for Religious was necessary for the creation of the *first* Province. The requisite permission was confirmed in December 1993 – letter Cardinal Eduardo Martinez Somalo, Prefect Congregation Institutes of Consecrated Life, Rome, to Mother Martina Morgan, 2.12.1993, AF not filed.

39 The other commissions were on Apostolate for the Mission, Contemplation for the Mission, Vows for the Mission and Evangelisation for the Mission, the last composed of Sisters in Nigeria and Kenya.

40 Sr Celestine was appointed in 1980. At the time of writing (2004) she is still in post. It first became possible for pupils to graduate to St Peter's RC high school in 1981. The premises in Belle Vue Road were officially opened by Bishop Mervyn Alexander in May 1982: cf. St Anthony's school *40th Anniversary Celebration Magazine*, 21.5.2000.

41 St Anthony's school, financial statements: 1992–3, income £132,000 (including £120,000 in fees), expenditure £149,000 (fees £680 per term main school, £530 Nursery); 1995–6, income £231,000 (including £188,000 in fees), expenditure £202,000; 046.1, AF. (Figures to nearest £1,000).

42 Report by HMI G. Sleightholme, DfEE, 18.6.1998. The most recent OFSTED inspection report, DfES ref. No. 916/6049, May 2004, is equally positive, praising among other things the strong staff–pupil community and the very effective personal development and excellent behaviour of the pupils, and attributing much of the school's success to 'the clear vision and inspiring leadership' of the headteacher.

43 Strictly speaking, only three were wholly indigenous, those at Ede (1988), Oyo (1989) and Igbo–Ora (1993); the houses at Inisa (1989) and Badagry (1990) were partly indigenous.

44 *Journey So Far*, pp.149ff., 153 and 156ff.; *The Franciscan Sisters . . . 1847–1997*, (Glasgow 1997), p. 81ff. Sr Clementina's initiatives included a Catholic Lawyers' Association, credit savings schemes, human rights awareness forums, relief services, and groups for making and selling cream and soap.

45 Sr M. Gerard O'Donnell, 'Behind the Wall: A Prison Apostolate', in *The Franciscan Sisters . . . 1847–1997*, p. 97ff.

46 The parish effort followed a talk there by Mother Martina. The vehicle was bought and rebuilt by Danny Pless – *Lennox Herald*, 20.10.1996, and *Land Rover* magazine, 1996. St Patrick's Dumbarton was Sr Anne Mary Wilson's home parish.

47 Sr Bernard McAtamney interview.

48 Cf., 1998 General Chapter, Community Reports, Kenya Report, 030.72, AF.

49 The concelebrated Mass for Charlotte Street FPs was brought forward from June to April in order not to clash with examinations. In all, six people were sponsored to visit Kenya. The commemorative volume, *The Franciscan Sisters of the Immaculate Conception, Celebrating 150 Years in Glasgow: 1847–1997*, Glasgow 1997, was put together by Sr Loyola Kelly and Bart Condon. The early history sections were largely the work of the Congregation's archivist, Sr Dolores Cochrane. Bart Condon's longtime friendship and help to the Congregation were recognised when he was made its first associate member (Plate 42).

50 The first five headmistresses were M. Angela Farnon (1878–98), M. Placida Laffan (1898–1920), Genevieve Currid (1920–27), Teresa O'Connor (1927–50) and Sebastian McEleney (1950–70).

51 Sr Anthony Coyle interview. The school had changed its name when it moved into a new building in St Patrick's parish in 1968. It served both parishes until 1975 when the St Mary's pupils moved into the former St Mary's secondary (originally a higher grade school) building in Patrick Street.

52 St Patrick's school Greenock, HMI Report, 1.11.1993.

53 At the time of writing (2004) there is also a second house in St Joseph's parish in another part of the town, with one Scottish and three Nigerian Sisters. In addition, Sr Helena Logue resides at the Diocesan Centre Greenock where she cares for Bishop Emeritus Stephen McGill.

54 This and the following paragraph based on Mother Martina Morgan, circular letter to each individual member of the Congregation, 24.9.1997, 030.72, AF. The commissions had met between 1993 and 1995 and their findings had been discussed at a general Convention of the Congregation in October 1995.

55 As well as being a Canon lawyer, Fr Morrissey was a member of the Sacred Congregation for Religious and thus ideally qualified to advise. He had been co-opted onto the Commission on Government the previous year.

56 1998 Chapter, report of the commission on government, 030.72, AF.

57 1998 General Chapter, Minutes, no box number, AF.

58 Superior General's Report to the 1998 General Chapter, no box number, AF. There were 46 professed Sisters in UK–Ireland (including those in USA and Kenya), as against the 41 professed and 5 novices in Nigeria.

59 1998 General Chapter, Report of the Working Group on Leadership, 030.72, AF.

60 She had in fact first proposed the change at the 1992 Chapter, but on that occasion her motion had been defeated.

61 Chapter Minutes, *loc. cit.* The question of the habit was also debated. A questionnaire issued the previous autumn had indicated clear majority support

for retaining the habit largely as it was. The one main doubt had concerned the colour, some believing that (now that its original purpose no longer obtained) black was too forbidding – Questionnaire on the Habit, Returns to Date, 11.11.1997, 030.72, AF. Chapter voted to retain the simple habit with veil and ring, but allowed black, blue or brown as alternative colours and made the veil discretionary on certain special occasions. Their decision still applies at the time of writing.

62 Srs Dolores Cochrane and Loyola Kelly interviews. In a sense, the tension had existed from the days of Adélaide and Veronica, whose visions for their new community were very different and might have proved incompatible had Adélaide lived (cf. p. 27 *supra*). Put crudely, Adélaide represented the monastic and Veronica the active emphasis.

63 Draft Constitutions and Statutes approved by the 1998 General Chapter, para. C2, no box number, AF.

64 Observations of the committee appointed to review the 1998 Chapter, 030.72, AF. Re the small convents in Britain–Ireland (there were now two single-person houses and five with three Sisters or fewer), Chapter suggested the possibility of some kind of 'association'. Re USA, concerning which Chapter believed that it should either be reinforced with fresh blood from Scotland or abandoned, see also 1998 Chapter, Community Reports, Altoona, 030.72, AF, and Sr Kevin Breen interview.

65 The questionnaire invited an evaluation of 'context' and 'content' on a 1–7 scale of satisfaction. 'Context' scored an average 6.88 and 'content' 6.80. Within these, the report of the Superior General scored 6.93, while the daily timetable and the contribution of Fr Morrissey were both given 7s – 1998 General Chapter, Evaluation Questionnaire returns, no box number, AF.

66 From 1998 General Chapter, Report of the Working Group on 'Religious Life in the Community', 030.72, AF.

CHAPTER TEN

Putting out into the Deep (1998–2004)

The year before the 1998 Chapter, Mother Martina and her Council had taken the decision to sell Park Circus, the Congregation's main house in Scotland. It was vacated in 1998 and sold to the Church for the use of SCIAF. It fell to the new Superior General and Council to find an alternative home for the Sisters, and consideration of the problem opened up a wider question – how best to use the Congregation's remaining property. In deciding this they had to take into account both present and future needs. The Chapter had instructed that there be economies and 'rationalisation'. Some of the older properties were now becoming too costly to maintain, and the Sisters were growing older and fewer in number by the year.

Their one remaining large residence was The Lindens in Bothwell. It was full of beauty and memories of their history, and was the last place they would have wished to give up. But it was hopeless for an ageing community: its mezzanine and upper floors were reached by a spiral stair so difficult for the frail or poor-sighted that at least one Sister was reduced to climbing it on her hands and knees. Their architects advised that it would be impossible to install a lift; nor could they recommend any of the Congregation's other houses as suitable for the elderly. Council concluded that the only solution would be to build from new, and that to do so it would be necessary to make further sales.

The properties they selected for sale were the Glenlea convent in Greenock,[1] the twin houses in Dennistoun, and The Lindens itself. The first two were sold off in 1999, and preparations were made for the sale of the last whenever the new house was completed.

The site chosen was in the large grounds of St Teresa's in Possilpark. It was suitable for several reasons. Sisters had been living and working in the parish for twenty years. The area was one of Glasgow's most deprived neighbourhoods, and to locate their main house there would be a visible witness of solidarity with the people. The parish had shrunk through rehousing and was now down to a single priest, part of whose huge presbytery was already being used by the Congregation for administration work and receiving visitors. By building their main convent nearby, everyone would benefit. When Council proposed the move, the Sisters supported it almost unanimously.[2]

The building work began in January 2000 and was completed in November (Plate 43). The sale of The Lindens was so timed that the Sisters were able to move straight from Bothwell to their new home. As they did so, they no doubt remembered the call that John Paul II had made that year to the Church for the new millennium, to 'put out into the deep in faith'. It must have crossed their minds that their step-by-step journey from Merrylee to Possilpark reflected their spiritual journey as a Congregation in the post-Vatican II era.

They now had a 'hub' for the older Sisters in the city, and a ring of small satellites from Greenock in the west to Edinburgh in the east, from Kilsyth in the north to Motherwell in the south, where those still active pursued a wide variety of lone apostolates. In Motherwell, Srs Rosaria and Maria Goretti were still working for The Innocents, as they had been for twenty-five years. In Crosshill the house originally purchased to be the Congregation's postulancy was now a house of prayer run by Sr Felicitas, who also gave endless hours to home visits with an energy remarkable for one of her age. Living with her was Sr Pauline Dempsey, a teacher in a special school by day and heavily involved in parish work and hospital chaplaincy in her spare hours.

Chaplaincy was in fact an apostolate of growing importance. At Bishopbriggs, Laura Venditozzi, the Congregation's youngest Sister and last Charlotte Street vocation, worked as a chaplain at the Marie Curie cancer hospital. In Greenock, Sr Anthony Coyle, the retired headmistress of St Patrick's PS, was chaplain in the town hospital, while Granton-based Sr Anne Marie McLaughlin was employed as diocesan school chaplaincy adviser at the Gillis Centre, Edinburgh.[3]

The Congregation's houses in Granton (Edinburgh) and Garthamlock (Glasgow) served severely deprived parishes. The latter had been in existence since 1989 when the Sisters had moved into the former presbytery to offer pastoral support to the people of St Mungo's parish after its amalgamation with St Dominic's Craigend. Sr Francesca Wilson had been there from the beginning and was now one of a community of three.

Francesca was also the Congregation's representative on the umbrella organisation 'Francis of Glasgow', set up by Fr Noel O'Dwyer OFM to promote greater collaboration between the city's Franciscan communities.[4] Its members were at this time seeking a joint project to weld them together and she was able to propose one that caught their imagination. She had just returned from a visit to the Open Heart House in Dublin and had been deeply impressed by it. It had been established as a care centre in 1997 by six religious communities in an attempt to do something for the huge drugs and HIV problem in the city. It had itself been inspired by the amazing success of the Living Centre in Boston, USA, and like its American model offered care and mutual peer support in a safe drug- and alcohol-free environment of remarkable peace and tolerance. Based in a former school donated by the Archbishop of Dublin, it now had a membership of some 300, all of them HIV-positive.[5]

Sr Francesca suggested that the group might set up something similar in Glasgow, and when they agreed, the germ of an organisation was born to which they gave the name 'Anam Cara' (soul friend). On further investigation they realised that there was a need not only among HIV sufferers but also among victims of all blood-borne viruses, whose diseases were very often linked to drug-taking. A rehabilitation centre for drug users, Phoenix House, already existed in the city, but there was no organisation to support them in their subsequent re-entry into society. When Sr Loyola approached Phoenix House in September 2001 and told them of Anam Cara, its staff welcomed the new organisation as an ideal follow-up to their own work.[6]

From this developed the weekly group meetings held in the Possilpark convent. The project was led by Sr Francesca and run by a committee composed (on the Boston model) of a majority of HIV sufferers. There was in fact a remarkably similar spirit between the Franciscan Anam Cara and the non-religious Living Centre project. Both sought to restore dignity; both were built around the community meal; both required their members to sign a code of rights and responsibilities composed by the members themselves; and both stressed mutual support, working not *for* people but *with* them in the conviction that 'together we can achieve'.

The Congregation gave a high priority to the project, and committed considerable resources to it. Eventually they hoped to part-finance a permanent home for it, to provide the space needed to meet demand as well as the independent address required for council funding. Meantime its presence in the convent benefited the Sisters, opening their eyes and helping to change their views. Gradually they lost their nervousness; they no longer saw drug addicts as a threat. One elderly Sister, who was so traditional that the community questioned how she would ever get round to dying since she had never tried it before, and who at first kept at a distance, could latterly often be seen chatting with one of the men, urging him to persevere with words of support: 'You stick at it, son!'

If having addicts in their midst was an enriching experience, so was the experience of living with their own old and dying Sisters, and so also was the experience of living in dwindling communities. As one Sister put it, 'The smaller we became, the more we talked to one another.'[7] On the other hand, the smaller the group the less 'safety in numbers' and the greater the influence of individuals, whether for good or ill. This was not a new problem, of course. It had existed from the earliest days, as we have seen. The Congregation had

31. St Bernardine's Secondary School, Oyo. *Photo: AF*

32. Mother Philippa and Sr M. Martha, golden jubilarians, with Srs Dolores and Felicitas. *Photo: AF*

33. Seamus McIntyre and Sr Bernard. *Photo: AF*

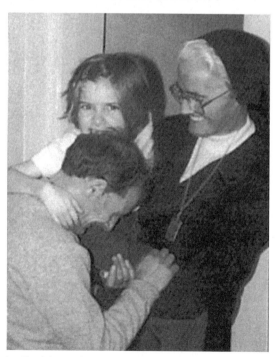

34. Sr Gertrude Shields with residents, Assisi House. *Photo: AF*

35. General Chapter 1992, elected leadership: Mother Martina Morgan, the incoming Superior General, is the tall Sister in centre. *Photo: AF*

36. Sr Anne Monye at the Pastoral Institute, Ede. *Photo: AF*

37. Mass concelebrated by three bishops, Oyo. *Photo: AF*

38. Sisters celebrating St Francis' feast day, Osogbo, 1996. *Photo: AF*

39. Nigerian Sisters with Provincial Sr Raphael Swan and Superior General Sr Loyola Kelly. *Photo: AF*

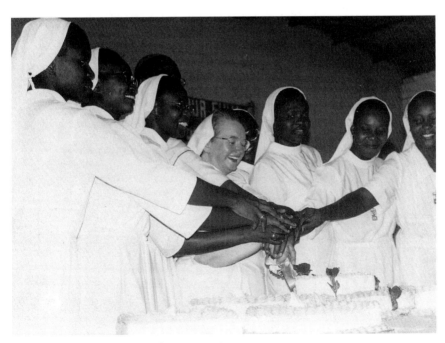

40. Nigerian novices cut the cake. *Photo: AF*

41. The 150th anniversary celebrations, 1997. *Photo: AF*

42. Bart Condon, the Congregation's first
Associate Member, 1997. *Photo: AF*

43. The new convent at Possilpark under construction, June 2000.
Photo: AF

44. Children's group, Motobo, with Srs Rita and Placida and Ciorsdaidh
Watts. *Photo: Moira Watts*

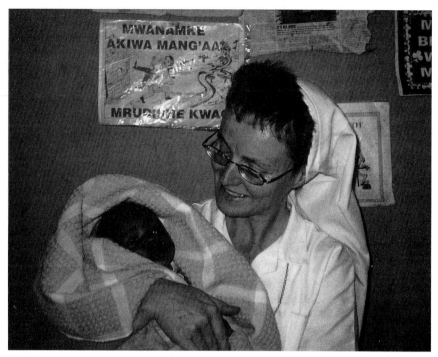

45. Sr Placida with one of the AIDS orphans, Motobo. *Photo: Ciorsdaidh Watts*

46. At the opening of the Novitiate, Molo, Kenya, 2004. *Photo: AF*

been the seed from which seven others had grown; yet despite this, and indeed partly because of it, it had always remained surprisingly small itself.

Dwindling numbers – not to mention age – were now also severely limiting the work that the Sisters could take on, and this was prompting them to look at new ways of working. They were beginning to recognise that they must harness the energies and talents of the laity, create wider groups for action in which they themselves might play the parts of facilitator, co-ordinator and leaven. In Possilpark, Sr Angela McFaul set up and developed Friends of Francis, a lay support group which met regularly to explore Franciscan spirituality and consider new models of lay–religious collaboration. Their discussions opened up exciting new possibilities for commitment and even associate membership on the part of the laity that might well set a pattern for the future.

In October 1998 the Nigerian Province held its first ever Provincial Assembly, at which appointments were made to the Provincial leadership. Sr Antonia Adeniji was appointed to succeed Sr Raphael Swan as Superior, and three of the other four chosen for the Council were also Africans, selected from a list of candidates drawn up by the Nigerian communities.[8] Assistant Superior Sr Gerard O'Donnell was now the sole European in the leadership group.

After half a century of growth there were now eleven houses in the Province, as well as the novitiate in Aawe. Most were devoted to the longstanding apostolates of education and medicine, for these remained the country's prime need. The Sisters' work as educators, particularly, had been of profound importance to the fledgling nation before and after Independence, and they were remembered with gratitude by their protégées not only as builders of character but as nation builders.[9]

The training of the younger Nigerian Sisters, and the courses they were now following in business administration, management, media/communications, agriculture and computing, showed on the one hand the recent broadening of their work and on the other the pressing need to equip them for their growing role in running their own affairs. For things were moving fast – almost too fast – in this direction, and there were growing pains. After her appointment as the first ever Nigerian Provincial Superior in 1998, Sr Antonia Adeniji made it clear that she did not wish to be considered for a second three-year term. Another Provincial Assembly was therefore held in 2001, at which Sr Josephine Obi was appointed as her successor. Shortly afterwards Sr Antonia left the Congregation to pursue medical studies in the USA.[10] In the same year, Assistant Superior Sr Gerard O'Donnell returned to Scotland, leaving the Provincial Council in solely Nigerian hands.

Like the others, Sr Gerard had been a steadying influence and a great help to the Nigerian councillors. The European Sisters had always commanded the respect of their Nigerian colleagues, both as their former educators and because they were 'outsiders' untouched by tribal rivalries. Crucially also, and for similar reasons, they had enjoyed far more respect and co-operation than had the native Sisters from the local priests and bishops, many of whom they had taught as little boys!

When in 2002 the last of the Europeans, Sr Emmanuel Gallagher, came home after four decades, the entire Province was now African for the first time.

These were milestones, eagerly welcomed at the time, but they brought their own difficulties. For the youthful Provincial leaders it was a headlong learning experience, with occasional mistakes inevitable. For the leadership in Scotland it was a time for giving the Province its head, accepting error and 'leaving room for the Holy Spirit'. For both it reduced the contact between them, and with it their mutual awareness.[11] Sr Loyola and her Council sought to ease the problem by bringing a number of Nigerian Sisters to the Scottish, Irish and American houses, sometimes to study and where possible to take posts of responsibility.[12] They hoped that by doing so, both parties might come to a better understanding of each other's needs and circumstances. It was partly with the same end in mind that Chapter had made the development of the Kenya mission a joint project between Nigeria and Europe.

In 1995, Kasok girls' school had finally been fitted with a solar power system that worked, and by 1999 plans were in hand for bringing piped water to the site.[13] But in other respects the school was in decline. Out of town and away from the eyes of the inspectors, the staff were neglecting their duties and defying the headteacher. The following year, Sr Assumpta Hegarty was appointed to take charge, and with the support of an excellent school board she set about restoring the school's good name.[14]

In autumn 2000 the Congregation's presence in Kenya was strengthened by the arrival of Srs Rita Maris Onah and Agnes Awolola from Nigeria and Sr Briege Clarke from Ireland. Before starting their apostolate all three enrolled in a course of basic Kiswahili at the college in Molo. The following spring Rita and Briege joined Sr Placida McCann in a new house she was opening in Motobo in the diocese of Kericho, in the heart of Kenya's tea-growing country.

Motobo is a shanty town that lies across the river from Kericho, and although they were now accustomed to Kenya the Sisters were shocked by what they saw when they arrived. The convent was up on the hill, over-looking a warren of one-roomed homes of corrugated iron and boards. The town's one shop resembled a hen house. The labyrinth of streets were raised catwalks of trampled rubbish above the running sewers on either side. Goats nosed among the detritus of the market. The one building of substance was the tall Catholic church, striking in its exterior but bare and unfinished within for lack of funds.

While Sr Placida took a post at Kericho high school, Rita and Briege began work in the parish. In a country where 700 people die of AIDS every day Motobo was decimated by the disease, and the Sisters encountered its effects almost at once. From their first meeting with three young widows, they conceived the idea of a centre for HIV victims. So vital was their work seen to be that Sr Placida was withdrawn from the school to lead the project. Within two years the Live With Hope Centre built up a membership of over thirty adults, to whom it offered meals, counselling, medical advice and companionship. Whenever one died there were always several others waiting to take his or her place, and with numbers restricted by lack of space a campaign was launched in Scotland to raise funds towards the £20,000 needed for a permanent centre.[15] A special group was also set up for children, some of them AIDS orphans and every one HIV-positive from birth (Plates 44 and 45).

Since the 1998 Chapter the Congregation had been committed to opening a novitiate in Kenya. It already had a number of young women interested in the religious life, and for them an introductory programme was established in 2001. The following year, Nigerian Sr Pauline Famoriyo was appointed Formator and joined the four postulants already in temporary residence in Kasok. When Council started making enquiries for a site for a permanent novitiate the obvious location was Molo, where the Sisters already had contacts.

It is a lovely corner of the country, an hour's run from Motobo, 8,000 feet up in the Highlands but set in a gentle valley dotted with small farms, where deciduous trees flourish alongside evergreens and the blue-leafed eucalyptus, and where the cooling breeze is never far away. It is a beautiful, peaceful place for young Sisters.

The one concern was security, since the area is isolated and has a reputation for robberies and armed attacks. But the site itself promised safety, since the Franciscan Brothers and two other Orders already had numerous houses there, grouped close together on what was virtually a single campus, known locally as 'Vatican City', with good telephone links and armed watchmen. The new novitiate would be equipped with steel doors and other security features. It was to be a substantial and well-appointed building, large enough for future needs and a long-term investment. Construction work began in spring 2003 and was completed within twelve months (Plate 46).

By autumn 2003, when preparations for the 2004 Chapter began in earnest, the Nigerian and European poles of the Congregation had never been further apart.[16] Their numerical equilibrium of 1998 had now swung to an African majority of 2:1, while the age gap had widened, with the average for Europe now 64.9 years as against 33.7 for Nigeria.[17] As well as the huge cultural and ecclesial differences between them, there was now a real generation gap.

It applied not only to the ages of the Sisters but to the two parts of the Congregation itself. There is a well recognised life-graph of religious Congregations, which might best be described as a skewed parabola or wave (fig. below), in which early growth and vigour are followed by a period of mature consolidation, and then by often rapid decline as the founding vision becomes increasingly out of harmony with a changing world.[18]

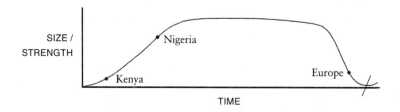

The European Sisters were now with a few exceptions middle-aged or elderly. But in addition, the European Congregation itself was of 150-plus years' standing and at the 'elderly' end of the life-graph. It displayed the characteristics of its age: maturity, fidelity, prudence, and sometimes a palpable serenity and sanctity, but also feelings of powerlessness and anxiety for the future. In Nigeria, not only were the Sisters young, the Congregation itself was at the 'adolescent' stage of the life-graph, with both the strengths and weaknesses of adolescence. It had great vigour, hope and often a deep spirituality, but also a tendency to see only the short term, a reluctance to listen to the parents, and a youthful growth that was almost too fast for the body's resources. (Kenya was the third piece in the puzzle, still an 'infant', everyone's pride and joy, and where the only worry for those looking after it was exhaustion.)

In the face of such different needs and circumstances, maintaining unity was bound to be a delicate matter. The problem had been growing since the 1990s and had become increasingly manifest with the creation of the Province.[19] It had been the threat of division that had prompted Mother Martina in 1998 to urge that the unifying force of the Franciscan charism must override local differences,[20] but her words had not really been heeded. In spring 2000 every Sister had received her printed copy of the new Constitutions and had pledged herself to them in a Service of Commitment. Their visionary call to radical poverty, humility, service, chastity and obedience should have put an end not to authentic difference but to the causes of division. But unless they are embraced with conviction Constitutions remain a dead letter, and more than one local Superior when questioned about the 1998 document had replied, 'We really haven't had time to digest it yet.' The withdrawal of the last Scottish Sisters from Nigeria in 2001–2 had seen the two poles move further apart.

No-one wished for the breakup of the Congregation,[21] but the centrifugal forces could not be allowed to go unchecked. The Superior General believed that if their causes were not addressed thoroughly and honestly at the 2004 Chapter, they could become irreversible. As she saw it, the key issue for the Chapter was unity.[22] On it depended the Congregation's very existence.

But for the Sisters in Britain–Ireland there was an even more fundamental preliminary question. On the life-graph, Nigeria and Kenya were rising upon the wave: their future was assured. But Europe was close to its trough, where – experience shows – Congregations face a choice. They may do nothing, in which case they will eventually die a natural death; they may choose to disband, satisfied that their work is done; or they may 'refound', radically changing their original founding purpose (and usually also their structure). In recent years many long-established Congregations have faced the choice, and perhaps only one in five has found the will and the energy to 'begin again'. For the Franciscan Sisters, these options had been spelled out by Mother Martina as a matter of urgency in 1997,[23] and six years on making a choice had become even more urgent.

It was for this reason that her successor convened two meetings of the Scottish and Irish Sisters at Possilpark in September 2003, where she confronted them with the present reality and the stark alternative – refound or go out of business. She stressed the painful and exhausting changes that would be involved in refounding, and then put the question bluntly, 'Do we want it?'

Unanimously they replied that they did. She then asked for volunteers to prepare the ground for it in advance of the Chapter. Fifteen Sisters volunteered to join a study group to explore the implications; others stepped forward to form a preparation committee for the Chapter. The rest offered to make up a prayer support group. After an initial meeting, the study group agreed to divide in two, one half to explore the founding charism of the Congregation, the other to look at models of community. Both were to report their findings to Council in March 2004, whereafter a sub-group would prepare a document on refounding for presentation to the Chapter.

In the past, the Superior General had always presented her report on the first day of the Chapter, but Sr Loyola decided to issue hers several months before the event, to serve as a guide to the group preparing the agenda and set the tone for the Chapter itself.[24] Such preparatory work was crucial if she and her colleagues were to create the right conditions for what might be a make-or-break gathering.

Her report was circulated in April. As she explained in her covering letter, to gloss over unpalatable truths would have been easy but also insulting and unhelpful to those about to meet and take crucial decisions for the future.[25] The result was a report impressively frank, comprehensive, targeted and insightful, which placed the Congregation in the context of its original founding vision, offered a searching analysis of its present strengths and weaknesses, and identified immediate issues to be addressed.

Nothing was missed: the teething troubles of the African Province and the need to reappraise its working; its urgent need for leadership training and local support; questions of loyalty to the vows; the danger of splitting from within; and the key question – whether the Sisters' stated desire to be one Congregation was strong enough to make it happen. Her report faced the particular problems of the European Congregation – its loss of the 'evangelical daring' of the founders, its 'overwhelming sense of end time', its fears for the future, and the need for financial safeguards to ensure that it would never be left abandoned. In arguing its need to 'start afresh from Christ', she used the title of a recent Vatican document,[26] and emphasised the point with a memorable image of her own: that of the hunter who could tame wild animals with his magic flute but was at last devoured by a lion who, because of deafness, could not hear it. If their flute, for long so magically effective, had now lost its usefulness, and if people had grown deaf to it, it was time to break it and throw it away.

But, she reminded them, rising above the Congregation's weaknesses was its essential abiding strength. It had been a 'great force for good' and an inspiration to others for 157 years, and was still so today. Its problems were great, but not insurmountable. Overriding all, and incumbent upon all, was the question of building mutual trust. On this depended their unity; indeed, she believed that it offered the solution to all their problems. Building *trust* and a 'spirituality of communion' was their key task in the forthcoming Chapter.

On 15 May a pre-Chapter conference was held at Possilpark, with Archbishop Conti one of the two speakers. Its purpose was to set the tone for the Chapter itself, for which reason it was recorded on video for the communities abroad and those Sisters in Scotland unable to attend. Its theme was the Congregation's achievements over the years, the single-minded purpose of generations of Sisters in the face of many obstacles, and the rich spiritual patrimony inherited by the present generation to guard, build upon and hand on in turn. As a follow-up every Sister was requested to compose a personal statement of her vision for the future.

The Chapter convened at Scotus College on 12 July. Among the messages of greeting from well-wishers was one from Bishop Adelakun of Oyo, thanking the Congregation for its 'great contribution' to his country and stating that it was now time for the Nigerian Sisters to 'give something back' to an institution in which African and European each needed the other.[27] Given the concerns regarding possible schism hanging over the Chapter, his letter could not have been more timely.

Sr Loyola had asked for a fortnight of honest discussion, and she got it. From the opening debate on finance, at which searching questions were asked regarding stewardship and communication, the tone was set for an openness that was sustained through every agenda item that followed. In this the delegates benefited enormously from the presence of the facilitators, Fr Aidan McGrath OFM and Br Joseph O'Toole OFM, who proved generous but unflinching guides adept at drawing the best from everyone present. And since (for the first time at a General Chapter) the business was conducted mainly through small groups, all found the courage and the opportunity to have their say.[28]

At the heart of the agenda was the debate on 'vision'. It was nearing its conclusion and the delegates getting close to consensus when a gust of wind blew open the door and overturned a candle, setting alight the flipchart already covered with key words. When the blaze was put out, just three words remained in the one unburned corner of the paper – 'unity . . . dialogue . . . trust'. It was as if they and only they had been somehow 'saved' and were to stand as a summary not only of the debate but of the Chapter itself, its priorities, and the spirit in which its business was conducted.

In such a climate much that was fruitful emerged, more even than the organisers had dared hope. The European delegates, for example, felt able to speak openly for the first time of their deep anxieties for their own future as their numbers declined. This was completely unexpected news for the Nigerian Sisters. They were astonished. 'How can you say you are declining,' they asked, 'while we are here for you and with you?' It was a watershed moment in the Chapter, and in years to come will probably be seen as a turning point in the Congregation's history. A family problem to be solved had drawn the family together. It was as if the balance of giving and receiving had swung; as if – to take up again the metaphor of 'the generations' – the Congregation in Nigeria, which on becoming a Province had passed from childhood dependence to a sometimes painful adolescent independence, had now taken a decisive step towards a new, adult interdependence.

This new responsibility and strength was reflected in the elections held on the penultimate day, when Nigerians Srs Cecilia Ojetunde, mistress of postulants at the new Kenyan novitiate in Kasok, and Immaculata Owhetemu, a staff nurse at the Beaumont hospital in Dublin about to qualify with a BSc degree in nursing studies, were both voted on to the General Council, the first ever to be so honoured.[29] Sr Loyola Kelly was elected to a second term as Superior General, with Sr Kevin Breen of Altoona, USA her assistant. The remaining position on the Council went to the Congregation's treasurer, Sr Louise McGlone.

The result gave the Congregation an immediate problem, since moving Srs Kevin and Cecilia to Glasgow was sure to put in jeopardy the future of the Altoona and Kasok communities. But it was a powerful affirmation of the coming of age of the African Province, and of the Congregation's genuine internationality: it was the most important 'statement' in half a century.

The Chapter set the Congregation an ambitious range of tasks to accomplish, with firm deadlines for their completion: to put internationality into practice, improve communication, pursue a team approach to leadership, experiment with new types of community, establish Regions and Regional government, review existing apostolates, and make a start on associate membership.[30] It was pushing forward change with a will.

There was a distinct end-of-term feeling to the last day, with the delegates exhausted but satisfied. They were joined for the concluding Mass and lunch by as many of the Congregation as could reach Bearsden. When all were gathered, the elation, sense of achievement and love were tangible. In his homily the chief concelebrant, Archbishop Conti, expressed gratitude for the Congregation's record of service over the years. 'It is impossible to give a measure of it,' he concluded, in words that echoed those of his predecessor Bishop Murdoch 150 years before. The greeting of peace was the signal for hugs by young and old for anyone within reach, and the final hymn put a strain upon the barrel-vaulted ceiling of the lovely college chapel. Several of the Sisters were in tears.

The same spirit continued through lunch, the refectory noisy with laughter and song. And in the knots of conversation, and in the parting words as the Sisters dispersed afterwards, one could catch their sense of anticipation, their impatience to begin a 'new term', their readiness to embark upon the course mapped out for them. As they went their various ways from a Chapter whose watchwords had been Faith and Love, their overriding mood was Hope. Theirs was 'a vision eager for its fulfilment',[31] and they could hardly wait.

ENDNOTES TO CHAPTER TEN

1 The adjacent boarding house and private school, Belltrees, had been sold to the Diocese of Paisley in 1983. At the time of writing (2004) the residence of the retired Bishop McGill, who is cared for there by Sr Helena Logue.

2 Sr Loyola Kelly interview. The site's future was under no threat since the church was a listed building and would remain even if further depopulation were ever to force the closure of the parish itself.

3 Sr Gerard O'Donnell was also working as a hospital chaplain in Dublin. Sr Anne Marie McLaughlin is the same Sr Ninian McLaughlin referred to on p. 204 *supra*. One of the changes made by the Congregation in the post-Vatican II era was to permit Sisters to revert from their religious to their baptismal names if they so desired; this Sr Ninian did.

4 Fr O'Dwyer is a priest of Blessed John Duns Scotus parish. The other communities involved were his own OFM, the Franciscan Missionaries of Mary, the Franciscan Sisters Minoress, the Franciscan Missionary Sisters of Africa, the Secular Franciscan Order and the Anglican Franciscans in Barrowfield.

5 As part of their investigation, Srs Francesca and Loyola also visited the Boston Living Centre.

6 Sr Francesca Wilson interview.

7 Sr Veronica McGrath interview.

8 Sr Raphael Swan had been taken seriously ill in the run-up to the 1998 Chapter, and after being brought back to Scotland for treatment was forbidden by her doctor to return to Nigeria. Her term of office was in any case now completed, and she herself was anxious for a Nigerian sister to be appointed to the office of Provincial Superior.

9 Memories of Mrs Lucia Emiola Afolabi and Mrs Victoria Adeleke, in *Journey So Far* (Ibadan 2000), pp. 163 and 166.

10 Srs Loyola Kelly and Dolores Cochrane interviews; the individual consultation forms reveal a high majority preference for Sr Josephine. Sr Antonia, who had previously trained as a nurse and had always wished to qualify as a doctor, went to the USA and has since begun her studies in medicine.

11 Sr Dolores Cochrane interview.

12 To date, three Nigerian sisters have taken a Franciscan Formation course at the Franciscan International Study Centre in Canterbury; two have studied Canon Law and one Education & Management in the USA; two Nursing in Dublin; one Accountancy, one Social Care and one Computing in Scotland. An example of one who has been given a post of responsibility is Sr Augustina Fabule, already with considerable leadership experience in Nigeria, who is currently Assistant Superior in the Possilpark house.

13 A solar heating system had originally been installed in 1991, but it was defective. In 1995 Francis Hillman of BP in Nairobi had visited the site and overhauled it free of charge. Drilling the bore hole for piped water commenced in March 2002 and pumping began in June 2003. The convent has no piped water to date – Sr Placida McCann interview.

14 Sr Placida McCann *A Brief History of Our Congregation in Kenya*, February

2003, and interview. The inspiration on the school board was the new chairperson Ms Ruth Kiptui. She herself had risen from poverty, and she brought several eminent Kenyan women speakers to the school to show the girls what they could achieve with determination and hard work. Sadly, she was killed in a road accident in 2002. In recognition of her outstanding work the school was renamed after her, though she was not herself a Catholic, at the suggestion of Sr Assumpta and with the agreement of the Kenyan president.

15 *Ibid.*; and 'Scots Franciscan Sisters Extend Mission in Kenya', *Flourish*, September 2002. The Novitiate opened on 25.4.2004.

16 I use the term European to cover Scotland, Ireland and the single community at Cinderford. The small community in the USA felt themselves to be *hors de guerre* in matters of the Congregation's 'politics' – Sr Kevin Breen interview.

17 Superior General's Report to the 2004 Chapter (made available to the author), based on figures from the beginning of the year. There had been one final profession in Europe, as against sixteen in Nigeria; seven Scottish and Irish Sisters had died.

18 The present historial account has attempted in its structure to reflect this typical dynamic, though using a different metaphor – cf. p. 3 *supra*.

19 The problem was in no way unique to the Congregation, of course, nor to Nigeria. Several Orders and Congregations, who had similarly withdrawn their European Sisters from their African Provinces, were by this date starting to send some back because of similar experiences.

20 Superior General's Report to the 1998 Chapter, unfiled, AF.

21 Superior General's Report to the 2004 Chapter – 'We as a Council have not heard any Sister in the UK or Africa express the desire that we become two separate Congregations. On the contrary, there is a strong expression throughout the Congregation of the desire to be one.'

22 Sr Loyola Kelly interview.

23 Mother Martina Morgan, 'Where Do We Go from Here?', in *Franciscan Sisters of the Immaculate Conception, Celebrating 150 Years in Glasgow, 1847–1997*, 1997, p. 185.

24 Sr Loyola Kelly interview.

25 Sr Loyola Kelly letter to all Sisters, accompanying her report to the 2004 Chapter, March 2004, made available to the author.

26 *Consecrated Life in the Third Millennium, Starting Afresh from Christ*, English transl., 2002.

27 Bishop J.B. Adelakun, Goodwill Message to the General Chapter, 11.7.2004.

28 Except where otherwise specified, the present account of the Chapter is based on Sr Loyola Kelly interview and the author's own observations as an invited guest for part of the proceedings.

29 Sr Immaculata was already qualified in general nursing and midwifery in Nigeria before taking up employment at the Beaumont Hospital. While in Dublin she took the opportunity to take her BSc in nursing studies, qualifying in summer 2004.

30 Chapter Mandate, 2004, unfiled, AF. It also called for a renewed spirit of prayer, and a commitment to safeguard and protect the welfare of every Sister.

31 *Habakuk*, 2.3.

EPILOGUE

What is Theirs to Do

I have done what was mine to do; may Christ teach you what is yours.

The dying St Francis to his Brothers,
Bonaventure, *Major Life*, xiv.3.

As I write, the General Chapter of 2004 is still fresh in the memory. It has spelled out for the Congregation its path over the coming six years. At the end of that period another General Chapter will be held, no doubt at least as crucial as those of the recent past. By then the imbalance between Europe–America and Africa will be even more acute: it is likely that there will be at least seventy fully professed Sisters in Nigeria, Kenya will have its first fully professed Sisters, and the number of European Sisters under the age of eighty will have fallen to two dozen at the very most.

We can expect to see in 2010 the implementation of new initiatives to reflect the new reality. Looking further ahead, future General Chapters are likely to herald even greater changes. Sooner or later one will be held in Africa for the first time; and eventually, when the time is right, an African Sister will be elected Superior General.

While the Congregation wrestles with such problems of 'maintenance' it must at the same time continue to develop its understanding of 'mission'. It must forge a vision for the future. It will be a radically new vision, yet one firmly rooted in the past, drawing on the spiritual patrimony that it has inherited, based on the foundation laid by Veronica and built upon by each generation since. Tomorrow's Sisters, like yesterday's, will be driven by the same reckless love for Christ, the same spirit of prayer, and the same compassion without judgment that drove their Congregation's founders. They will continue to befriend the most derelict and to choose the hardest and most thankless places to bring God's love. They will bring it 'not with a gale or an earthquake or a great fire, but with a gentle breeze'.[1] And 'as they walk through the bitter valley they will make it a place of springs', as they have always tried to do.[2]

In undertaking new work in new places, they will also be following their predecessors, for they too were often pioneers, ahead of the society around them in responding to the latest need. When society later caught up, and their very success in certain enterprises rendered them redundant, this, they understood, was a fulfilment rather than any sort of failure.[3] So Sisters in the future, as in the past, will look 'for no lasting city'[4] but will move into new tasks, break the ground and if need be move on, often leaving others to reap what they have sown. Somehow, in the people and places that they touch their spirit will live on.

Such a readiness is typically Franciscan. Francis began his movement as a response to a crisis of the times and a crisis within the Church, not so unlike today's situation. He discerned new needs and a new means of responding to them. Veronica's founding vision was also of a new need and a new method – to serve the new poor of the industrial city, and to do so not by bringing them to the Sisters as at Tourcoing but by sending the Sisters out among them. Like Francis she set her followers the challenge of reading the signs of the times. They never forgot her vision, and in the last thirty years have reclaimed it in its fulness.

Such a readiness is exactly what the Church asks of its consecrated religious today. The most recent Vatican document, *Consecrated Life in the Third Millennium*, calls upon them 'to surprise the world with new forms of effective evangelical love which respond to the needs of our time'. It looks to them to confront the world with 'an alternative way of living', to offer 'a spiritual therapy for the evils of our time' by the 'contagion' of their example.[5] In particular, it argues that their three vows of poverty, chastity and obedience represent a powerful alternative to the 'triple concupiscence' of greed, the craving for pleasure and the idolatry of power that marks society today.[6]

The Congregation will continue to answer this call in its own distinctive way. Its Franciscan message appears especially apt for a society troubled by restlessness and a search for meaning not unlike that which troubled the twelfth- to thirteenth-century world of St Francis. Its non-possessive respect for creation and its gentleness challenge society's destructiveness and aggression.[7] Its particular poverty presents an antidote to materialism, its humility an alternative to the cult of celebrity, its solidarity with the marginalised a riposte to the growing gap between rich and poor.

In response to ruthless competitiveness, it offers a Franciscan tenderness, the more so in that it is a female Congregation, with what the same Vatican document calls 'the particular richness of the "feminine genius"' of the women's Orders.[8] This facet of its charism will grow in relevance as the feminine grows in significance in society and the Church.

It will offer these things wherever it is working. In Africa it will probably continue meantime in apostolates that are clearly needed and successful, in education, medicine, welfare, human rights, empowerment, and work among the victims of injustice and the AIDS pandemic. In Britain, Ireland and the USA it will continue to develop new radical apostolates, as the Rule of the Third Order Regular and its own most recent Constitutions demand, among the marginalised and the alienated. In particular, it may seek contact with a young adult generation largely alienated from organised religion; a generation that appears different in kind from any previous one, often lacking permanent commitment whether to religion, politics, marriage or career, looking for immediate gratification, commonly using drugs as a matter of course, affluent yet overwhelmed by debt.

The methods that it will adopt in such circumstances will certainly need to be different from those of the past. So, too, will the kind of commitment that it can expect from future generations. Lifelong religious vocations, flowering meantime in Africa, are likely to be few and far between in Britain and Ireland. In their stead the Congregation will experiment – it has indeed already started experimenting – with alternative, less binding forms of commitment. It may be ready to accept members who take annually renewable vows, for instance. It may welcome back former members who have discontinued their vocations, gratefully using their experience for temporary help in particular tasks rather than viewing their leaving as a failure not to be spoken of. It will certainly develop an associate membership of 'cojourners', lay men and women wishing to give of themselves in whatever form, degree or duration they feel able. Afterwards, such people would remain, as it were, pollen carriers of the Franciscan way of life, bearing it with them to germinate and flower in unexpected places.

To many observers, the current 'vocations crisis' in the religious Orders appears in essence a 'crisis of significance': people are not joining because they do not see the life and work as meaningful.[9] If so, it is to be hoped that new apostolates and new 'vocations' may blossom together, the one nurturing the other, and that some women (and men) may be drawn to assist the Congregation – and perhaps from there to become a part of it, whether temporary or permanent – through seeing its work as being powerfully relevant to today's world.

For now, its future in Britain, Ireland and America remains shrouded in some uncertainty. Its general direction is clear enough, but its particular path remains open and may be surprising. The communities there look forward, armed with a vision, trust and little else: exactly as Veronica did when she founded the Congregation all those years ago. With their Sisters in Africa, they remain ready and committed to doing whatever is theirs to do, completing the as yet unfinished verses of their Canticle of Love.

ENDNOTES TO THE EPILOGUE

2 *1 Kings*, 19:11–12.

2 *Psalms*, 83:7.

3 Cf. Mother Martina Morgan's vision for the future in *The Franciscan Sisters of the Immaculate Conception – Celebrating 150 Years in Glasgow 1847–1997*, 1997, p. 183.

4 *Hebrews*, 13:14.

5 *Consecrated Life in the Third Millennium, Starting Afresh from Christ*, Congregation for Institutes of Consecrated Life and Societies of Apostolic Life, Rome 2002, English transl. London 2002, pp. 48 and 21.

6 *Ibid.*, p. 54.

7 Cf. Pazzelli R., 1982, English transl. 1989, p. 49; Short W.J., 1999, chap 8.

8 *Op. cit.*, p. 11.

9 Cf. e.g., Chittester J., 2002 J, p. 21.

APPENDIX ONE

Superiors of the Congregation

M. Adélaide Vaast	(acting, 1847–9)
M. Veronica Cordier	(acting, 1849–54)
	1854–6 Prioress
M. Angela McSwiney	1856–60
M. Vincent Dolan	1860–3
M. Aloysius Mackintosh	1863–6
M. Angela McSwiney	1866–9
M. Gonzaga Sim	1869–84 Abbess
M. of the Cross Black	1884–96
M. Athanasius MacLean	1896–1908
M. Lucy Maguire	1908–20
M. Wallburga Broe	1920–6
M. Camilla Hamilton	1926–37 (died in office)
M. Anthony MacNeil	(acting 1937–8)
	1938–43 (died in office)
M. Bernardine Simpson	1944–56
M. Philippa Gilhooley	1956–68
M. Gabriel Palmer	1968–80 Superior General
M. Felicitas Bradley	1980–92
M. Martina Morgan	1992–8
M. Loyola Kelly	1998–present

APPENDIX TWO

Communities of the Congregation

Scotland

Glasgow – Charlotte Street	1847–1930
Inverness	1854–1935
Lanark	1855
Aberdeen	1855–1901
Glasgow – Abercromby Street	1861–1930
Innellan	1872–4
Greenock – Bank House	1873–1913
Bothwell – Elmwood	1878–1950
Edinburgh	1880–93
Glasgow – Crosshill	1894–1910
Girvan	1898–1905
Bishopbriggs (Kenmure)	1898–1953
Saltcoats	1904–14, 1920–2

(thereafter only as holiday house to 1974)

Greenock – Glenlea	1913–99
Glasgow – Merrylee	1923–79
Bothwell – The Lindens	1950–2000
Dennistoun	1962–99
Kilsyth	1974–present
Coatbridge	1976–9
Glasgow – Possilpark (from Lambhill)	1978–2000
Glasgow – Lambhill	1978–present
Glasgow – Park Circus	1979–98
Motherwell	1979–present
Glasgow – Househillwood	1981–94
Glasgow – Dixon Avenue	1982–present
Glasgow – Tollcross	1984–97
East Kilbride	1986–99
Glasgow – Garthamlock	1989–present
Glasgow – St Teresa's Possilpark	1997–present

Prestwick	1998–present
Edinburgh – Granton	1999–present
Greenock – Newark St	2000–present
Glasgow – Bishopbriggs	2000–present
Glasgow – Garrowhill	2000–present
Glasgow – Saracen Street	2000–present
Greenock – Rowan St	2000–present

England

Bayswater	1858–9
	(whereafter became a separate Congregation)
Ealing	1958–70
Cinderford	1960–present

Ireland

Falcarragh	1947–92
Dublin – Riverside Park	1983 present
Dublin – Glasnevin	1989–present

Nigeria

Osogbo	1950–present
Ilesa	1954–present
Oyo – St Bernardine's	1956–73
Otan	1964–9 (as novitiate)
	1964–92 (as community)
Aawe	1984–present
Oyo – St Mary's	1985–present
Ede	1988–present
Oyo – San Damiano	1989–present
Inisa	1990–present
	(from 1997 as postulate)
Badagry	1990–present
Igbo–Ora	1993–present
Ojo Alaba	1998–present
Iloti	1999–present
Ibadan	1999–present
Ogwashi–Uku	2003–present

United States of America

Renovo	1971–80
Altoona	1977–present
Bedford	1982–90
Johnston	1987–8

Kenya

Kasok	1990–present
Ndanai	1995–7
Motobo	2001–present
Molo	2004–present

In addition, the following independent communities were founded with and used the Rule and Constitutions of the Congregation:

Jamaica

East Queen Street/Duke Street	1857–79 (1940)
Mount Alvernia	1859–79 (1940)
	(whereafter they were absorbed into the Allegany Franciscan Congregation)

France

Sèvres	1866–70 (disbanded)

('Present' refers to the situation at the time of writing, autumn 2004)

APPENDIX THREE

Headmistresses of Our Lady & St Francis and Elmwood Secondary Schools

OUR LADY & ST FRANCIS

M. Jerome Gordon	1894–1918
M. Clare Paterson	1918–21 (died in post)
M. Jerome Gordon	1921
M. Bernardine Simpson	1922–39
M. Philippa Gilhooley	1939–56
M. Felicitas Bradley	1956–80
Mrs Alice Felletti	1981–5
Mrs Anna Keegan	1985–9

ELMWOOD

M. Anthony MacNeil	1904–32
M. Philippa Gilhooley	1932–9
M. John Slattery	1939–50
M. Gabriel Palmer	1950–68
(Miss Margaret Aitken, acting)	1968–70
M. Benedicta Collins	1970–4
Miss Margaret Aitken	1974–7

APPENDIX FOUR

Parish Schools run by the Congregation

Glasgow – St Andrew's	1851–1932
Glasgow – St John's	1851–1932
Glasgow – St Joseph's	1851–60
Glasgow – St Alphonsus'	1852–4, 1860–1939
	(at first in St Andrew's)
Inverness – St Mary's	1854–1935
Aberdeen – St Joseph's	1856–1901
Glasgow – St Patrick's	1856–1971
Glasgow – St Mary's	1866–1970
Glasgow – St Vincent's	1867–1878
Glasgow – St Peter's	1868–1870s (exact date unknown)
Glasgow – St Mungo's	1872–9, 1939–85
Greenock – St Lawrence's	1874–1971
Glasgow – Sacred Heart	1874–1980
Glasgow – St Francis'	1875–8
Greenock – St Mary's	1878–1968 (St Patrick's, 1968–97)
Glasgow – Our Lady & St Margaret's	
	1880–1929
Edinburgh – St John's	1880–93
Hamilton – St Mary's	1896–1932
Uddingston – St John the Baptist	
	1900–33
Glasgow – St Martin's	1904–15 (when joins St Patrick's)
Bothwell – St Bride's	1910–65
Gourock – St Ninian's	1916–19
Viewpark – St Columba's	1939–46

APPENDIX FIVE

Education and Hospitals run by the Congregation in Nigeria

EDUCATION

Osogbo – St Francis' Primary	1951–64
Osogbo – St Francis' Secondary	1952–66
Osogbo – St Clare's Teacher Training College	1953–63
Ilesa – St Theresa's Primary	1954–64
Secondary	1958–70
Oyo – St Bernardine's Secondary Grammar	1956–70
Osogbo – St Clare's Nursery and Primary	1964–present
Ilesa – Nursery and Primary	1970–present
Abiodun–Atiba – St Francis' Nursery and Primary	1979–present
St Francis' Continuing Education Centre	1986–present
Inisa – Owen McCoy Nursery and Primary	1990–present
Igangan – Nursery and Primary	1993–present
Lanlate – St Felix's Nursery and Primary	1993–present
Ilesa – St Anthony's College	1995–present
Oyo – St Francis' College	1996–present
Ojo, Alaba – M. of Perpet. Help Nursery and Primary	
	1998–present

HOSPITALS AND CLINICS

Osogbo – Our Lady of Fatima [H]	1962–present
Otan – St Nicholas' [C]	1964–92
(after which continued as diocesan)	
Badagry – Sacred Heart [C]	1990–present

APPENDIX SIX

A Note on the Later History of Tourcoing

In the lifetime of Mother Veronica, *c.*1900, in the face of government hostility to religious institutions, the monastery removed across the Belgian border to Néchin.

Shortly after her death, during World War I, the Sisters were able to return to Tourcoing, but they also kept open the house at Néchin.

At the end of World War II a convent was opened in Lille to serve as the mother house. Tourcoing and Néchin were kept open, the latter as a house for aged Sisters.[1]

In 1959, with declining numbers, the Congregation was absorbed into the Augustines of the Precious Blood, whose mother house was in Arras, the Sisters taking their new vows on 22 August of that year.[2]

By 1970 only seven Sisters remained at Tourcoing, six of them former Franciscans. With the mother house now Arras, the convent at Lille was used for the old and infirm Sisters.[3]

In the 1990s the convent of Notre Dame des Anges Tourcoing was vacated by the Congregation, and lay empty for several years. In 2001, the town council began renovation and conversion of the premises for community use. The new facility opened in 2003.

ENDNOTES TO APPENDIX SIX

1 Sr M. Gabrielle, Prieure, to Mother M. Bernardine Simpson, 9.3.1947, 012.1, AF. The establishment of the mother house at Lille must have been recent, for the prioress was still using Néchin-headed notepaper.
2 Sr M. Suzanne, Secretary, *pp* Prieure Générale, to Mother Philippa Gilhooley, 24.1.1961, 012.1, AF.
3 Sr M. Joseph to Mother Gabriel Palmer, 15.7.1970, 012.1, AF.

Bibliography of Sources referred to in the Text

PRIMARY SOURCES – *Manuscript*

Scottish Catholic Archives (SCA)
>   Diocese of St Andrews and Edinburgh Papers (DE)
>   Diocese of Motherwell Papers (DM)
>   Oban Letters (OL)
>   Scottish Mission Papers (SM)

Archives of the Franciscan Sisters of the Immaculate Conception, Possilpark (AF)

011   Transcripts from the Tourcoing Archives
        Annals of the Congregation
012.2   Reports of Inspections of Industrial School Abercromby
        Street, 1888–96
        Rule for Parlour Boarders
014.1   Documents and holdings mainly concerning Jamaica
025.1   Dispensations and Transfers
026.2   Obituary Register
028.2   Register of Elections
030.1 & 030.33   House Reports to Chapter, 1880–1974
030.31 Questionnaires and Reports of Commissions for 1968–9 Chapter
030.33 Correspondence concerning 1968–9 and 1974 Chapters
        Questionnaires and Reports of Commissions for 1974 Chapter
030.41 Reports of Commissions for 1980 Chapter, Chapter Minutes
030.43 Capitular Acts of 1968–9 Chapter
        1980 Chapter Minutes, Statutes and follow-up papers
030.72 Reports of Commissions, House Reports and Chapter Minutes,
        1998
031.2 & 031.30   Manuscript Rule and Constitutions, 1853–1866
034.10 Council Meeting Minutes, 1854–1974
        Ditto supplementary, 1955–68, wrongly filed no code
040.12 Correspondence and Statements, mainly financial
040.13 Merrylee Community Meetings, 1972–8, and miscellaneous

040.14 Merrylee Correspondence and miscellaneous

041.10 Documents concerning Charlotte Street

041.11 Correspondence and Statements mainly concerning Charlotte Street

043.1 Correspondence mainly concerning Greenock

044.11 Correspondence, Minutes, etc. concerning Elmwood

044.12 Documents concerning Bothwell

046.1 Documents concerning St Anthony's School Cinderford

049.18 Misc. Correspondence

056.1 Documents concerning the Kenya Mission

071.01 Correspondence and statements, 1870–1977

071.03 Reports of Canonican visitations, 1896–1966

072.01 Minutes of Association of Franciscan Sisters of the Third Order Regular of Britain, 1970–9

086 Misc. Correspondence

UNCLASSIFIED

Falcarragh Log Book, 1980–92

History of the Convent of the Immaculate Conception Glasgow, 1961

Live With Hope Centre, St Mary's Parish Motobo, 2003

McCann, Sr Placida, Motobo: The Pilot Project, 2003

McCann, Sr Placida, Brief History of Our Congregation in Kenya, 2003

McKenna, Sr Celestine, St Anthony's Convent School Cinderford: A Short History, 2003

Record Book of St Joseph's Convent Renovo, Pennsylvania, 1971–80

St Bride's School Bothwell Log Book, 1910–65

Archives of the Archdiocese of Glasgow (AGA)

ED 1/1–1/7 Diocesan Education Board Minutes, 1869–1946

ED 7–8 Education Papers: Reports of Religious Inspections, 1875–1934

FR 1/1–1/6 Diocesan Finance Board Minutes, 1869–1921

GC 2–45 General Correspondence, 1870–1913

RO 8/2–8/53 Franciscan File (mainly correspondence)

Mercy International Centre Archives, Dublin (MIA)

　　300–2.5　Statement of Bishop Alexander Smith, c. 1850

Mitchell Library (ML)

CO2 5.6 no. 38 3　St Lawrence's Girls' School Greenock Log Book
CO2 5/6/9/32　St Mary's Girls' School Greenock Log Book
D ED7 160.1 & 160.2　Charlotte Street (later OLSF) Log Books, 1894–1947
D ED7 161 2/2　Our Lady and St Margaret's Girls' School Glagow Log Book
D ED7 190/3　St Alphonsus' Girls' School Glasgow Log Book
D ED7 192.2　St Andrew's School Glasgow Log Book
D ED7 222 2.2　St John's School Glasgow Log Book

St Mary's PS Hamilton

St Mary's Log Book 1872–date

Archives of the Sisters of Notre Dame de Namur, British Province, Liverpool (NDA)

Correspondence Canon James Cameron and Archbishop Eyre with Sr Mary of St Philip Lescher, 1893

In Private Possession (Mrs Anna Keegan)

Report of HMI Inspection, Our Lady and St Francis School, 1987
'A School Worth Saving', Parents' Submission to Strathclyde EA, 1987
'A School Worth Saving', Staff Submission to Strathclyde EA, 1987

Copies supplied by Hannah McCarthy

Letters Miss Mary Margaret Brewster to Mrs Kyle, 13.10.1849 and 29.12.1849

Written Communication

Letter Sr Benedicta Collins to the author, 16.9.2003
Letters Sr Loyola Kelly to the author, 23.6.2003 and 11.8.2003

PRIMARY SOURCES – *Published*

Printed Rules and Constitutions (chronological)

Rule, 1223, confirmed by Honorius, in Armstrong R.J. and Brady I. eds., 1982.

Rule and Constitutions Written by our Dear Departed Father, The Rt. Revd. Dr. Smith, Glasgow 1855.

Pius XI, *Rerum Conditio*, Constitution on the *Rule of the Third Order Regular*, Rome 1927.

John Paul II, *The Rule and Life of the Brothers and Sisters of the Third Order Regular of St Francis*, Rome 1982; English transl. Doyle E., Lens 1984.

Other Printed Documents of the Congregation

The Elmwood Magazine, 1927–39, 1947–61, 1975

Kasok Girls' School Magazine, Issue 1, 1994

Our Lady and St Francis School Magazine, 1946–56

Various Published Sources

Abbott W. M. gen. ed., *The Documents of Vatican II*, English transl., 1966, London 1972 ed.

Anon, *Catholicism in Glasgow Thirty Years Ago*, Glasgow n.d. but 1863.

Anon, *Memories of the Life and Works of Mother Mary Ignatius of Jesus*, n.d., n.p.

Argyll Commission, *Second Report – Elementary Schools*, Edinburgh 1867.

Armstrong R. J. and Brady I. eds., *Francis and Clare: The Complete Works*, New York 1982.

Buchanan R., *The Schoolmaster in the Wynds*, Glasgow and Edinburgh 1850.

Catholic Church in Greenock, The, Greenock 1880.

Chadwick E. ed., *The Sanitary Condition of the Labouring Population of Great Britain*, 1842 (ed. M. W. Flinn, Edinburgh 1965).

Consecrated Life in the Third Millenium, Starting Afresh from Christ, Congregation for Institutes of Consecrated Life and Societies of Apostolic Life, 2000, English transl., London 2002.

Cowan R., *Vital Statistics of Glasgow*, Glasgow and Edinburgh 1838.

de la Salle, J. B., *Conduit des Écoles Chrétiennes*, 1724.

Franciscan Link, internal newsletter of the Franciscan Sisters of the Immaculate Conception, Glasgow 2002–04 issues.

Habig M. ed., *St Francis of Assisi, Writings and Early Biographies –
English Omnibus of the Sources*, 1972, Chicago 1983 ed.

*Innocents Story, The, c.*2000.

John Paul II, *Vita Consecrata*, post-Synodal Apostolic Exhortation on the
Consecrated Life and its Mission in the Church and in the World, 1996,
English transl. London 1996.

Kelly H. P., *Society of the Innocents Lanarkshire*, Motherwell 2002.

*Local Reports on the Sanitary Conditions of the Labouring Population of
Scotland in consequence of an inquiry directed to be made by the Poor
Law Commissioners*, CMD, London 1842.

Logan W., *An Exposure from Personal Observation of Female Prostitution
in London, Leeds and Rochdale, and especially in the city of Glasgow*,
Glasgow 1843.

Logan W., *The Moral Statistics of Glasgow*, Glasgow 1849.

Mary Ignatius of Jesus, Sr (Elizabeth Hayes), *Diary* (ed. M. F. Shaw),
Rome 1994.

New Statistical Account of Scotland, vol. 6, Lanarkshire, 1841.

*Norms for Executing the Decree of the Second Vatican Council 'Perfectae
Caritatis'*, Rome 1966.

Pagan J., *Sketch of the History of Glasgow*, Glasgow 1847.

Report on the State of the Irish Poor in Great Britain, British
Parliamentary Papers, (40), xxxiv, Appendix G of *First Report for
Inquiring into the Condition of the Poorer Classes in Ireland*, London
1836.

Scottish Catholic Directory, 1846–79.

Smith J., *The Grievances of the Working Classes; and the Pauperism and
Crime of Glasgow; with their Causes, Extent and Remedies*, Glasgow
1846.

'Third Order Regular of St Francis in Scotland, compiled from its annals',
Scottish Catholic Monthly, May–July 1894.

Contemporary Newspapers

Catholic Opinion (Kingston, Jamaica)
Dean Forest Mercury
Flourish
Glasgow Evening News
Glasgow Herald

The Glaswegian
Greenock Telegraph
Hamilton Advertiser
Sunday Nation
    (Nairobi, Kenya)

PRIMARY SOURCES – *Interviews*

Sr Angela McFaul
Sr Anthony Coyle
Sr Benedicta Collins
Sr Bernard McAtamney
Sr Dolores Cochrane
Sr Emmanuel Gallagher
Sr Felicitas Bradley
Sr Francesca Wilson
Sr Francis Campbell
Sr Gertrude Shields
Sr Immaculata Leonard
Sr Kevin Breen
Sr Loyola Kelly
Sr Placida McCann
Sr Raphael Swan
Sr Rosaria McGeady
Sr Veronica McGrath
Mrs Anna Keegan
Miss Susan McCormick
Miss Ciorsdaidh Watts

SECONDARY SOURCES – *Books*

Anon, *Love Counts Nothing Hard*, Lincoln, Massachussetts, n.d. but 1994.
Anon, *The Sisters of Mercy in Glasgow 1849–1976*, Glasgow 1976.
Bodo M., *The Way of St Francis*, 1984, Glasgow 1985 ed.
Bone T. R. ed., *Studies in the History of Scottish Education 1872–1939*, London 1967.
Bone T. R., *School Inspection in Scotland 1840–1966*, London 1968.
Boyd W. ed., *Evacuation in Scotland*, London 1944.
Checkland O., *Philanthropy in Victorian Scotland*, Edinburgh 1980.
Chesterton G. K., *St Francis of Assisi*, London 1923.
Cruickshank M., *A History of the Training of Teachers in Scotland*, London 1970.

de Breffny B., *Unless the Seed Die: The Life of Elizabeth Hayes*, Rome 1980.

Delany F. X., *History of the Catholic Church in Jamaica*, New York 1930.

Devine T. M. ed., *Irish Immigrants and Scottish Society in the Nineteenth and Twentieth Centuries*, Edinburgh 1991.

Devine T. M. ed., *St Mary's Hamilton: A Social History 1846–1996*, Edinburgh 1995.

Devine T. M. and McMillan J.F. eds., *Celebrating Columba – Irish-Scottish Connections 597–1997*, Edinburgh 1999.

Donnelly B., *Hill of Doves*, Glasgow 1997.

Dunlop F. M., *St Mary's Greenock: The Story of a Community*, Greenock 2001.

Fiand B., *Refocusing the Vision: Religious Life into the Future*, New York 2001.

Fitzpatrick T. A., *Catholic Secondary Education in South-West Scotland before 1972*, Aberdeen 1986.

Fraser W. Hamish and Maver I. eds., *Glasgow*, vol. 2, Manchester and New York 1996.

Gambari E., *Renewal in Religious Life: General Principles, Constitutions, Formation*, Rome 1967 (Italian), English transl. Boston 1967.

Gillies D., *A Pioneer of Catholic Teacher-Training in Scotland*, Quidenham 1978.

Go Rebuild My Church: A Comprehensive Course on the Franciscan Mission Charism, Bonn 1994 ed.

Handley J., *The Irish in Scotland*, Tralee 1943.

House A., *Francis of Assisi*, London 2000.

Journey So Far, The: Fifty Years of the Franciscan Sisters in Nigeria, Ibadan 2000.

Julian H., *Living the Gospel: The Spirituality of St Francis and St Clare*, Oxford 2001.

Kenneth, Br, *History of St Mary's Boys' School, Calton, Glasgow, 1863–1963*, Glasgow 1963.

King M. I., *Mother Catherine McAuley: A Woman for All Seasons*, Glasgow n.d.

Levitt I. and Smout C., *The State of the Scottish Working Class in 1843*, Edinburgh 1979.

'M.A., Sr' (McEvoy) *A Short Life of Mother Mary Elizabeth Lockhart and a Brief History of her Franciscan Sisters*, Hinckley 1959).

Markus T. A. ed., *Order and Space in Society: Architectural Form and its Context in the Scottish Enlightenment*, Edinburgh 1982.

Maver I., *Glasgow*, Edinburgh 2000.

Mitchell M. J., *The Irish in the West of Scotland 1797–1848*, Edinburgh 1998.

Mitchell M. J., 'The Catholic Irish in the West of Scotland: "A Separate and Despised Community"?', in Devine T.M. and McMillan J.F. eds., 1999.

Murray N., *The Scottish Handloom Weavers 1790–1850*, Edinburgh 1978.

Neal F., *Black '47 – Britain and the Famine Irish*, Basingstoke and London 1998.

Örsy L., *Government in Religious Life: The Council's Teaching*, Rome 1966.

Osborne F. J., *History of the Catholic Church in Jamaica*, Chicago 1988.

Pazzelli R., *St Francis and the Third Order: The Franciscan and Pre-Franciscan Penitential Movement*, 1982 (Italian), English transl. Chicago 1989.

Pazzelli R., *The Franciscan Sisters: Outlines of History and Spirituality*, 1989 (Italian), English transl. Steubenville 1993.

Ramon, Br, *Franciscan Spirituality*, London 1994.

Robson M., *St Francis of Assisi, The Legend and the Life*, London 1997.

Rodrigues V. I., *Reflection on a Heritage*, Allegany NY 1976.

Schneiders S. M., *New Wineskins: Re-Imagining Religious Life Today*, New York 1986.

Scotland J., *The History of Scottish Education*, 2 vols., London 1969.

Short W. J., *The Franciscans*, Wilmington 1989.

Short W. J., *Poverty and Joy: The Franciscan Tradition*, London 1999.

'Sister of Notre Dame, A', *Sr Mary of St Philip (Frances Mary Lescher, 1825–1904)*, London 1922.

Smout T. C., *A Century of the Scottish People 1830–1950*, 1986, Glasgow 1987 ed.

Wade N. A., *Post-Primary Education in the Primary Schools of Scotland 1872–1936*, London 1939.

SECONDARY SOURCES – *Pamphlets*

Calogeras A. et al., *Doing Peace: A History of the Early Franciscan Years*,
   Chicago 1985.
Canning B., *Adventure in Faith: St Ninian's Gourock 1880–1980*,
   Glasgow 1980.
Catholic Church in Greenock, The, publ. by *Greenock Telegraph*, 1880.
Cause of Rejoicing, A: One Hundred Years in Greenock 1874–1974,
   Greenock 1974.
Franciscan Centenary, Kingston, Jamaica 1957.
'Franciscan Sister, A', *The Franciscan Nuns in Scotland 1847–1930*,
   Glasgow 1930.
*Institute of the Missionary Franciscan Sisters of the Immaculate
   Conception, The*, Rome 1939.
Missionary Franciscan Sisters of the Immaculate Conception 1873–1973,
   n.p. 1973.
O'Hagan F., *Change, Challenge and Achievement: A Study of the
   Development of Catholic Education in Glasgow in the Nineteenth and
   Twentieth Centuries*, Glasgow n.d.
Our Lady and St Francis Charlotte Street Yesterday and Today 1849–1989,
   Glasgow 1989.
St Mary's Hamilton 150th Year Commemorative Brochure 1846–1996,
   Hamilton 1996.
St Patrick's Primary School Greenock Centenary 1878–1978, Glasgow
   1978.
The Society of The Innocents Lanarkshire Silver Jubilee 1977–2002,
   Hamilton 2002.

SECONDARY SOURCES – *Journal Articles*

Aspinwall B., 'Some aspects of Scotland and the Catholic revival in the
   early nineteenth century', *Innes Review*, xxvi, 1, Spring 1975.
Aspinwall B., 'The formation of the Catholic community in the West of
   Scotland: some preliminary outlines', *Innes Review*, xxxiii, 1982.
Aspinwall B., 'A Glasgow pastoral plan 1850–1860: social and spiritual
   renewal', *Innes Review*, xxxv, 1984.
Aspinwall B., 'Children of the Dead End; the formation of the modern
   Archdiocese of Glasgow, 1815–1914', *Innes Review*, xliii, 2, Autumn
   1992.

Aspinwall B., 'Catholic teachers for Scotland: the Liverpool connection', *Innes Review*, xlv, 1, Spring 1994.

Bruce S., 'Out of the ghetto: the ironies of acceptance', *Innes Review*, xliii, 2, Autumn 1992.

Chittester J., 'The fall of the temple – a call to formation', *UISG publication no. 118*, reproduced in *ROC News*, 2002.

Darragh J., 'The Catholic population of Scotland 1878–1977', *Innes Review*, xxix, 1978.

Darragh J., 'The Apostolic Visitations of Scotland, 1912 and 1917', *Innes Review*, xlii, 1, Spring 1990.

Dilworth M., 'Religious Orders in Scotland, 1878–1978', *Innes Review*, xxix, 1978.

Gourlay T., 'Catholic schooling in Scotland since 1918', *Innes Review*, xli, 1, Spring 1990.

Handley J., 'French influence on Scottish Catholic education in the nineteenth century', *Innes Review*, i, 1950.

Hillis P., 'Education and evangelisation – Presbyterian missions in mid-nineteenth century Glasgow', *Scot. Hist. Review*, lxvi, 1, April 1987.

Johnson C., 'Scottish secular clergy, 1830–1878: the Northern and Eastern Districts', *Innes Review*, xl, 1, Spring 1989.

Johnson C., 'Scottish secular clergy, 1830–1878: the Western District', *Innes Review*, xl, 2, Autumn 1989.

Kehoe S.K., 'Nursing the mission: the Franciscan Sisters of the Immaculate Conception and the Sisters of Mercy in Glasgow, 1847–1866', *Innes Review*, lvi, 1, Spring 2005.

McCaffrey J. F., 'Irish immigrants and radical movements in the West of Scotland in the early nineteenth century', *Innes Review*, xxxix, 1, Spring 1988.

McRoberts D., 'The restoration of the Scottish Catholic hierarchy in 1878', *Innes Review*, xxix, 1978.

Martin J. R., 'Poor Law in olden times', paper 16, *Old Glasgow Club Transactions*, vol. ii, 1908–1912.

Muirhead I. A., 'Catholic Emancipation: Scottish reactions in 1829', *Innes Review*, xxiv, 1, Spring 1973.

Muirhead I. A., 'Catholic Emancipation in Scotland: the debate and the aftermath', *Innes Review*, xxiv, 2, Autumn 1973.

Ross A., 'The development of the Scottish Catholic community 1878–1978', *Innes Review*, xxix, 1978.

Secondo L., 'The mission of the Third Order Regular of St Francis in the modern world', *Analecta Tertii Ordinis Regularis Sancti Francisci*, xiv, 1978.

Treble J. H., 'The development of Roman Catholic education in Scotland 1878–1978', *Innes Review*, xxix, 1978.

Treble J. H., 'The working of the 1918 Education Act in Glasgow archdiocese', *Innes Review*, xxxi, 1, Spring 1980.

SECONDARY SOURCES – *Theses*

Kehoe S. K., 'Special Daughters of Rome: Glasgow and its Roman Catholic Sisters, 1847–1913', PhD thesis, Glasgow University 2004.

O'Hagan F. G., 'The contribution of the Religious Orders to education in Glasgow during the period 1847–1918', PhD thesis, Glasgow University 2002.

Index

St Margaret's convent, Edinburgh
  (Ursulines) 80
St Mary's Franciscan Abbey, Mill Hill
  206
St Mary's J. S. School, Glasgow 129,
  142, 198
St Mary's parish, Pollokshaws 24
St Mungo Street 116
St Mungo's Academy 91, 221, 222
St Mungo's parish, Garthamlock,
  Glasgow 241
St Nicholas' clinic, Otan 263
St Patrick's parish, Dumbarton 230, 238
St Patrick's, Kilsyth, community at 195,
  208, 258
St Paul's parish, Shettleston, Glasgow 24
St Peter's RC High School, Gloucester
  237
St Rollox chemical works 12
St Sulpice 19
St Teresa's parish, Possilpark, Glasgow
  240, 258
St Thomas' Island 57, 64
St Thomas' parish, Riddrie, Glasgow 229
St Vincent's Asylum, Dublin 99
Salesians, the 159
Saltcoats, house at 102, 111, 149, 196,
  208, 258
Saltmarket 16
Sanctuary Association/House 194, 199,
  209
Saracen Street, Glasgow, community at
  259
Scanlon, Archbishop James 172, 180,
  182, 191, 192, 208
Schools (parish)
  accommodation 107–8
  class sizes 108
  fees 46
  free schooling 85
  funding 36, 106
  inspection of 36, 65–6, 88, 109–10,
    139, 231
  night schools 46, 110
  raising of leaving age to 14 106
    to 15 144, 163
  recruiting staff 65, 88
  standards and attendance 108–10
  transferred to EAs 113
  valuation of 114
  post-elementary classes 129

  'Advanced Division Centres' 129
  J. S. and S. S. schools 129–30
  mixed-sex schools 130
  arrangements *re* headships 130, 140
  effects of raising leaving age 144
  effects of educational and social
    change 178
Schools owned/run by the Congregation
  and associated parishes
  Crosshill private school 85
  Mary of Perpetual Help N. & P., Ojo
    Alaba 263
  Our Lady & St Margaret's, Glasgow
    63, 93, 106, 108, 109, 262
  Sacred Heart, Glasgow 63, 64, 93,
    106, 124, 213, 262
  St Alphonsus', Glasgow 35, 44, 100,
    108, 109, 120, 130–1, 221, 262
    parish/church 24, 135, 146, 198
  St Andrew's, Glasgow 35–6, 44, 46,
    82, 108, 130, 145, 262
    church (cathedral) 17, 18, 27, 33,
      37, 145, 230–1
  St Anthony's, Cinderford 160, 172,
    228–9
  St Anthony's College, Ilesa 263
  St Bernardine's, Oyo 155, 158, 196,
    217–18, 262, 263
  St Bride's, Bothwell 100, 132, 133–4,
    262
    church 231
  St Clare's Training College, Osogbo
    263
  St Columba's, Viewpark 140, 262
  St Dennis' private school, Glasgow
    189
  St Felix's N. & P. S., Lanlate 263
  St Francis' P.S., Abiodun-Atiba 263
  St Francis', Glasgow 262
  St Francis' P.S., Osogbo 263
  St Francis' S.S., Osogbo 263
  St Francis' College, Oyo 263
  St Francis' Continuing Education
    Centre 263
  St John's, Edinburgh 80, 86–7, 262
    parish/church (St Mary's) 80
  St John's, Glasgow 35–6, 46, 82,
    100, 107–8, 109, 120, 262
    parish 24
  St John the Baptist, Uddingston 95,
    130, 134, 140, 262